communicating**identity**
CRITICAL APPROACHES

revised edition

edited by
jason **zingsheim**
dustin bradley **goltz**

cognella
San Diego, CA

Bassim Hamadeh, CEO and Publisher
Christopher Foster, General Vice President
Michael Simpson, Vice President of Acquisitions
Jessica Knott, Managing Editor
Kevin Fahey, Cognella Marketing Manager
Jess Busch, Senior Graphic Designer
Jamie Giganti, Project Editor
Brian Fahey, Licensing Associate

First published in the United States of America in 2013 by Cognella, Inc.

Printed in the United States of America

ISBN: 978-1-62131-397-7 (pbk)

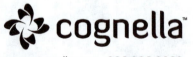

www.cognella.com 800.200.3908

CONTENTS

Part IV Performing Identity

235

Part I
Introducing Identity

Introducing Theory
Models, Maps, and Metaphors

By Jason Zingsheim and Dustin Bradley Goltz

"Identity is complicated. Everybody thinks they've got one" (Gauntlett, 2007, p. 1).

I dentity *is* complicated. Everyone thinks they have at least one identity and some of us think we have a few, while still others have more than they can count. If you'd like to pick up a few extra identities, new ones can be adopted online in chat rooms, in Second Life, and in an increasing number of video games. These can last for only a short time, can extend for years, or can be swapped out at a moment's notice with the change of a profile or avatar. Despite the relative ease of obtaining identities, it is not uncommon to hear about people losing their identities. Your identity can be stolen without you even knowing that it is gone. Other folks, keenly aware that they are without an identity, head out in search of "finding themselves." At other points, you may claim a friend "became someone else" or "lost his identity" when he started dating so-and-so. On one hand, in this society, we talk as if there is a stable, singular self—that I am always the same person. "Oh, that was just an act, that wasn't the real me." "I know who I am." On the other hand, in this society, we talk as if identity—or rather identities—were interchangeable, multiple, and fluid. "People

change." "I'm a new woman." Identity is indeed complicated.

How we navigate and negotiate our identities is the focus of this book. In the readings gathered here, we invite you to explore the ways we communicate our selves to the world around us and how communication works to (re)create our identities. Throughout the anthology, there are readings from people both inside and outside departments of Communication. Regardless of their disciplinary "home," each of these authors is concerned with the relationships between communication and identity. They each explore how we use communication and symbols to make sense of identity, and how the concept of identity makes sense of us. For the most part, these readings approach identity from an affirmative poststructuralist position (more on that later). Essentially, this means identity is viewed as fragmented, mutable, and multiple instead of whole, unchanging, and singular. Rather than one "real" me, there are multiple "me's," all of which are real even though they may conflict with one another. As Walt Whitman writes, "Do I contradict myself? Very well then I contradict myself, (I am large, I contain multitudes)" (1942, p. 75, s. 51). Our identities are multitudes, and we have the means to contradict ourselves. As a result, who we are is uncertain, always temporary, and rife with ambiguity. We invite you to see this multiplicity and ambiguity as positive and full of hope. Change is not only possible but also inevitable, which means we can always recreate ourselves and our world in ways that are more just for more people, more of the time.

To explore the multitudes that we refer to as our identity, we have organized this book into four units. The first section, "Theorizing Identity," provides a poststructuralist introduction to identity through a number of different conceptual frameworks that highlight the performative, relational, and intersectional dimensions of identity. The second unit, "Organizing Identity," looks to institutional contexts to examine how systems of power and hierarchal structures within organizations work to shape, mold, constrain, and produce disciplined identities. This section also explores how broader social discourses, like nationality or race, work to organize our identities—allowing certain identities while denying the possibilities of others. "Representing Identity" is the third unit, where we turn to popular culture and writing practices as sites of identity representation, production, and negotiation. The final section, "Performing Identity," shifts attention to the spatial, temporal, and embodied dimensions of identity work, theorizing performative dimensions of identity that resist and rearticulate identity discourses. Despite how we have divided up the readings into these four sections, most of the chapters would be appropriate in multiple sections. As you read each chapter, regardless of the unit, we encourage you to think about what the selection reveals about how identity is theorized, organized, represented, and performed.

Moving forward in this chapter, we lay out a biographical sketch of this thing we call identity. Think of it as a brief synopsis of how academics have studied and talked about identity over the last few centuries. Then we turn to a series of maps, metaphors, and models for thinking about

identity today. Each one offers a useful set of terms and ideas to help us think about how we navigate identity on a daily basis. The following section provides a brief glossary of key terms that surface throughout the readings and will help to frame your class discussions. Finally, as with each of the subsequent unit introductions, we end with a brief overview of the readings to come and provide some questions for you to ponder and discuss as you read each selection.

A HISTORY OF THE SELF

There are many ways to trace the history of identity, or what we might call the story of the self. For our current purposes, we begin with a view of the self as transcendental and follow its mutations into a social self, a symbolic self, a dramaturgical self, and finally a discursive self. For the most part, the remainder of this anthology will explore the dimensions of the discursive self, but it is helpful to know some of the major plot points and twists that led us to this point in the story.

The Enlightenment position of a transcendental self was deeply influenced by the work of French philosopher René Descartes (1596–1650) and is powerfully illustrated in his assertion, "I think, therefore I am." From this rationalist perspective, there was a split between the mind and the body, and identity—who one is—was located firmly in the mind, far removed from the intricacies of everyday life and the experiencing body. In other words, "this transcendental self was disembodied, separated, and distinguished from the very corporeal body upon which it otherwise philosophically mused and cast judgment" (Holstein & Gubrium, 2000, p. 18). This view of identity was challenged by Scotsman David Hume (1711–1776) and empiricists who believed that any grounds for knowing must be based on a growing body of experiences with the external world, which are made available only through the embodied senses. In other words, rather than the self being located in the mind or defined by thought, the self was created through observable experiences with the world around us. It was Immanuel Kant (1724–1804) from Germany who provided a middle road, combining the insights—while critiquing the limitations—of both rationalist and empiricist perspectives. For Kant, "the key was to think about the concepts that are needed by a human subject in order for that subject to have experience of an objective world" (Ashe et al., 1999, p. 91). In other words, knowledge is not derived within an independent mind, or solely through experience with the external world, but through the interplay between the two. As a knowing subject, our experiences with the external world conform to categories and constructs in the mind that pre-existed the experience. Kant's notion of the self as a stable, independent, and transcendental subject can still be seen today when folks talk about a "real" self or a "true" self that is not influenced by one's context.

The Kantian transcendental self was challenged and recast by American pragmatists as a social self. American philosopher William James (1824–1910) relied upon the role of everyday experience to establish his idea of the empirical self, which can generally be divided into three categories: the material me, the social me, and the spiritual me. These different "me's" are not static entities, but shift based on the various contexts one finds oneself in. Rather than transcending the everyday life, the social self "emerges, grows, and is altered within our daily affairs" (Holstein & Gubrium, 2000, p. 24). Going further towards sociality, George Herbert Mead (1863–1931) of the University of Chicago introduced the interacting self, which is based in language and communicative action. Like the empirical self, the interacting self is flexible rather than fixed; however, for Mead this flexibility is rooted in

language systems rather than one's ability to simply adapt to different social contexts. Mead's ideas, as developed by Herbert Blumer (1900–1987), who was also at the University of Chicago, led to symbolic interactionism. In terms of the self, symbolic interactionism proposes that "individuals respond to the meanings they construct as they interact with one another" (p. 32). Canadian-born Erving Goffman (1922–1982) elaborated on this line of thinking with his contribution of the dramaturgical self, arguing our identity is realized through the performance of socially approved roles (1959). His writing included the use of theater and performance metaphors to affect a shift from an independent or interacting self to one that was also contextually influenced. From Goffman's perspective, the self was not only social, but this social interaction occurred within (and was influenced by) larger social performances and contexts. Consequently, the self, or more accurately selves, are constructed within and in response to the situations and circumstances of everyday life. The role you play as a student is different from the role your instructor embodies, though these both occur within the same larger context of higher education. Additionally, when you move out of this social context and into other performances of self, you will adopt additional roles (perhaps partner, child, roommate, co-worker, best friend, etc).

Contemporary thought on identity is largely influenced by postmodernism and poststructuralism. In light of rapid advances in technology, media, and globalization this perspective sees the self as being multiplied, fragmented, and constantly shifting. In response to these circumstances, there are generally two schools of thought. For skeptical postmodern theorists such as Jean Baudrillard (1929–2007), this leads to a self that is merely one image in a sea of endless floating images. We are copies of copies of copies who have forgotten that we are copies, and there is no original. This perspective leaves little room for change or for any kind of control over one's self.

Instead, as mentioned earlier, more and more scholarship on identity and communication falls under the affirmative poststructuralist school of thought. Michel Foucault (1926–1984) illustrates this line of thinking about poststructuralist identity as still existing, though in fragmented, multiple, and radically contextual incarnations. Affirmative poststructuralists acknowledge that identities are constructed through discourses of power, and within these discourses there is always already the possibility for resistance and agency. By discourses of power, we mean those social systems of meanings that work to serve the interests of some over the interests of others. In our society, discourse—or social systems of meanings—around gender tend to be patriarchal and favor those regarded as male and masculine often at the expense of those who are feminine and/or female. These widespread discourses are constantly shifting in order to maintain a powerful position, and this movement creates possibilities for resistance and the renegotiation of meanings, such as when *Bitch* magazine reclaims a derogatory term as empowering. As Tracy (2000) explains, "The self is both constituting and constituted, motivated by self-agency yet produced and created by historical and discursive forces" (p. 114). From this position, contemporary theories of identity acknowledge the fragmented nature of the self without abandoning the self, its material conditions, or the desire for coherence (even if the coherence is temporary and partially illusory) (McKerrow, 1993). In other words, it is possible to embrace the instability of identities along with their "made-up yet necessary character" (Gamson, 2006, p. 249).

Before we move further, it is important to clarify the difference between subjectivity and identity. **Subjectivities** are the socially understood categories "that shape our relation to ourselves" (Rabinow

& Rose, 2003, p. xx). These are subject positions that are recognized as intelligible, that are offered as possible given the existing systems of meaning. Subjectivities refer to the ways we are positioned and located in social discourses like gender, race, and sexuality. Alternately, **identity** denotes our relation to ourselves. Identity is where our sense of self is continually (re)constructed among, over, and through various (and variously shifting) subjectivities. Identity refers to the whole self that is raced, gendered, sexualized, etc., all at the same time. Subjectivity refers to the individual components of race, or gender, or sexuality, etc. that are part of one's entire identity. While our immediate focus in this anthology is at the level of identity, we cannot separate poststructuralist identity from the various subjectivities that work to construct and position real, live individuals.

MODELS, MAPS, & METAPHORS

In this section, we summarize four theoretical frameworks for identity: the matrix of domination and intersectionality; crystallized identity; relational and coalitional subjectivity; and mutational identity. Each of these frameworks is consistent with the poststructuralist approach, though their authors may not always invoke the term. As theories, each of these models, maps, and metaphors help us to see identity in a new way. They are not mutually exclusive, and no one theory will always be the most useful for understanding identity in every context. Think of each of these as a tool for explaining how identity works and how we can make sense out of our selves. Each tool comes with its own set of concepts and vocabulary for talking about identity. Depending on the context, one tool may be more useful for you than others.

The Matrix of Domination and Intersectionality

In her book, *Black Feminist Thought: Knowledge, Consciousness, and the Politics of Empowerment,* Patricia Hill Collins (1990) explores the relationship between knowledge and experience. She advocates for viewing knowledge as arising out of experience. What we know, individually and socially, is based on what we have experienced. This means that all knowledge is partial, just as our experiences of this world are partial. The goal then is to understand as many different partial perspectives as possible since each approach brings a new, though incomplete, understanding. She works to locate Black women's experiences at the center of analysis, rather than straight white men's experiences (as most Western research has done over the centuries). Centering the experiences of Black women leads to a "both/and conceptual lens of the simultaneity of race, class, and gender oppression" (p. 221). In other words, when it comes to oppression we cannot separate gender oppression from racial oppression and/or class oppression. We must enter such discussions with a both/and approach because all of these structures of oppression are interrelated. At the time (Collins's book was published twenty years ago), this thinking of oppressions as interlocking instead of additive was a radical shift. Rather than adding up the number of oppressed subjectivities (racially marginalized + woman + bisexual = 3xs oppressed), Collins calls on us to explore how the experiences of such an identity are more than the sum of its parts. You cannot simply add bisexual oppression onto the oppression of women added to the oppression of Latinos. The experience of being a bisexual Latina is wholly unique because of the ways these practices of gendered, racial, and sexual oppression work in conjunction and contradiction with one another within a single system of oppression. Based on the tradition of Black feminist thought, these oppressions are all part and parcel of a single, overarching **matrix of domination**. We are all located within this system of oppression. Based on our location, we receive *both* unearned privileges *and* disadvantages. This both/and lens illuminates how "all groups possess varying amounts of penalty and privilege in one historically created system" (p. 225). Based on the context, an individual can find her/himself in the role of oppressor, oppressed, or both simultaneously. Particularly important to note is that our locations place us in relation to others. It is often (though not always) easy to see your own oppression, but it is often very difficult to understand how your location in the matrix works to perpetuate and maintain the oppression of someone else (p. 229).

How we experience the matrix of domination depends on our locations along multiple axes of identity like race, class, gender, sexuality, etc. The matrix also functions on multiple social levels, specifically the personal, the cultural group/community, and institutional levels. These levels are not mutually exclusive; they often overlap or blur into one another. How a person experiences the world as an individual is related to her affiliations with particular cultural groups and how social institutions, like the media or education, represent and position those groups (and her) in this life. Collins reminds us that while domination can be experienced at each of these levels, so too can we resist domination at each of these levels. She explains, "Empowerment involves rejecting the dimensions of knowledge, whether personal, cultural, or institutional, that perpetuate objectification and dehumanization" (1990, p. 230). All experience and knowledge is partial, but certain forms of knowledge recognize and affirm the humanity of others. Through dialogue and empathy, Black feminist thought works to pursue, embrace, and develop those multiple forms of knowledge and experience that resist the subjugation of others.

The matrix of domination, as an interlocking model of oppression, is consistent with Kimberle Crenshaw's (1991) conceptualization of **intersectionality**. Crenshaw is a legal scholar who coined the term "intersectionality," providing a name for what many feminists of color had been writing about for years. Namely, that on the level of the personal, being a Black woman is not the same as simply being Black and being a woman, but is altogether a different and unique experience of being both. Crenshaw highlighted how African American women, by virtue of their racialized gender and gendered race, were located within the social structure in ways that made their experiences of "domestic violence, rape, and remedial reform qualitatively different from that of white women" (Crenshaw, 1991, p. 1245). Additionally, women of color often experience political intersectionality where, as members of multiple subordinated groups, they are positioned within competing political agendas (for an example, see Chapter Six by Brenda Allen). Speaking of ourselves as having intersectional identities helps to draw attention to the locations we occupy within the matrix of domination.

Crystallized Identity

The notion that there is a "real" me and a "fake" me is pervasive throughout our society—it can be seen in numerous self-help books and heard in countless break rooms. People often talk about how they put on a different face and "fake it" in order to get through a difficult situation (dealing with an unpleasant co-worker, boss, family member, etc.). By framing our actions in these situations as "not really me," we create a separation between what and who we think we "really" are and who we "have to be" for whatever reason. Organizational communication scholars Sarah J. Tracy and Angela Trethewey (2005) explain how this real-self↔fake-self dichotomy functions to serve the interests of

the workplace at the expense of the individual employees. This has detrimental effects on an individual's identity, not just in the workplace, but throughout one's life (since our identities are never "off the clock"). As people try to reconcile their "real self" with the "fake self" sometimes required by work, four different subject positions are possible: strategized self-subordination, perpetually deferred identities, "auto-dressage," or "good little copers."

In **strategic self-subordination**, employees willingly adopt identities preferred by the organization and work to assimilate their own needs and preferences into alignment with organizational goals. These employees give their best time and their best selves to the organization, often preferring to spend time at work instead of at home. Other employees adopt **perpetually deferred identities,** where they may go along with the organizational demands on themselves for now, but only because it is supposed to allow them to realize some goal in the future. Putting in more time for the company now is thought to lead to more economic freedom and power later. These future-selves are used to legitimate decisions and practices in the present, yet this pattern continues to repeat "where one's nonwork life concerns are continually placed 'on hold'—something to attend to in a future that never comes to fruition" (Tracy & Trethewey, 2005, p. 180). **Auto-dressage** is a term to describe how some individuals willingly engage in work behavior simply for its own sake. The word dressage is often used to describe the training of animals, specifically show horses, to perform stylized acts to be observed and judged in competition. This labor by the horses does not produce anything tangible—no fields are tilled, riders are not carried great distances or into battle (typically, the horses just circle the judges in the show ring). This is work for the sake of being looked at. By turning the phrase back onto the individual by adding "auto" to "dressage," Tracy and Trethewey extend the concept to highlight how employees work for the sake of looking at themselves. They exhibit control and discipline not because management is watching, and not because they are actually producing anything, but for their own sense of self.

So far, these three subject positions allow individuals to focus on feeling like most of their time is spent being the "real me" at work by shaping the "real me" to fit the demands of the organization. For others, aligning one's self with one's work may be so distasteful that they compartmentalize who they are at work separately from who they "really" are in the rest of their life. When a job is particularly stigmatized or emotionally demanding, such as sex workers or prison guards, employees may work to keep an emotional and psychological distance between themselves and their work. In this respect, they learn to cope with being "fake" at work in order to survive and become what Tracy and Trethewey (2005) term **"good little copers."** In each of these situations, the identities of individuals are subjugated for a significant portion of one's life to the power and control of the workplace.

To remedy this situation, Tracy and Trethewey (2005) suggest a move from a binary model of a "real-self" versus a "fake-self" to a multidimensional illustration of a **crystallized identity**. This metaphor for identity offers many benefits. First, it acknowledges the many social influences on identity. The workplace is indeed one of these influences, but so are other contexts, relations, and subjectivities. These multiple influences are framed as contributing to the beauty and complexity of identity (p. 186). Consequently, the diversity of identity—the different versions of "I"—is also accounted for, as the particular form of these crystallized selves vary depending on the multiple discourses through which they are constructed and constrained. Various social influences exert force on different facets of the crystal in different ways.

Finally, crystals allow for a sense of movement, as organic crystals do "grow, change, alter" over time (p. 186; Richardson, 2000, p. 934). However, this continual shifting of identity does not lead to multiple personalities, because crystals also "may feel solid, stable, and fixed" (Tracy & Trethewey, 2005, p. 186). So then, "by conceiving of identities as ongoing, emergent, and not entirely predictable crystals, people are forced to acknowledge a range of possible selves embodied in a range of contexts—even as they are constrained by discourses of power" (p. 189). While this theory was developed out of organizational and workplace contexts, it is not limited to those places. Thinking of ourselves as crystallized can inform how we navigate and negotiate identity throughout our lives. Individuals are empowered to embrace each performance of self as legitimate and authentic, though ultimately only one of many; one that is more or less preferred, but never not real.

Relational & Coalitional Subjectivities

Feminist and queer scholarship has advanced our understanding of identity, or the self, as relational. This body of work delves into the complex and often contradictory ways that who we are, and who we might become, is intricately enabled and constrained by our relational ties with others. Aimee Carrillo Rowe (2005) suggests "the meaning of self is never individual, but a shifting set of relations that we move in and out of, often without reflection" (p. 16). Rather than seeing identity as a result of our location, she argues that we mindfully focus on how the self comes into being as a result of our shifting belongings with/to others. Such a move redirects our attention to the **politics of relation**—the emotional ties, the longings to belong, the privileges and oppressions, and the spaces between bodies that connect us to one another—which emphasize how we are accountable to others.

This accountability creates the possibility of a **co-alitional subjectivity** where alliances are crafted across lines of differences. For example, Kimberlee Pérez and Dustin Bradley Goltz (2010) illustrate coalitional subjectivities in their performance of *Lines in the Sand,* where they explore the politics of their relations as a "brown-dyke-girl" and a "white-Jew-gay-guy." Their performances of self, both on the stage and in everyday life, display accountability to one another and to the other's histories across racial and gender lines of differences. More than simply a convenient political coalition for a specific goal, their work embodies the depth and struggles of coalitional subjectivity and demonstrates the political, resistant, and revolutionary power of viewing oneself as uniquely enabled by (and accountable to) the relational ties that bind us to another.

These ties also make each of us vulnerable, since these relations shift over time and can ultimately be severed. Judith Butler (1993, 1999, 2004a, 2004b, 2005) has written extensively on the relationships between subjects, subjectivities and discourse. One key idea that relates here is the notion of being **ecstatic**, which "means, literally, to be outside oneself... to be *beside oneself*" (2004b, p. 20). While we often think of ecstatic as a positive emotion, Butler writes about how this experience can also be caused by extreme emotions like rage or grief. When losing a loved one, we may feel beside ourselves. She suggests that this is because who we are is based on our relationships, including our ties to the now deceased. With their passing, we are forever changed, but in ways that we cannot anticipate in advance (Butler, 2004b). It is in these moments of loss, these unexpected experiences of being thrown beside ourselves, that we see the degree to which we are not our own. Our selves are intimately and intricately woven into those around us in ways we cannot fully control.

It is in light of this vulnerability, this emotion, and this accountability that Carrillo Rowe (2005; 2008) encourages us to pursue what she terms "differential belonging," building on Chela Sandoval's work on modes of consciousness. **Differential belonging** is mindful and intentional movement between four different modes of belonging, never staying in one mode long enough to become trapped by it or comfortable in it. The four modes includes *assimilationist* belonging where we focus on our similarities with the dominant, normative culture (and might say things like "we all want the same things"). On the other hand, in *revolutionary* modes of belonging, we focus on what makes us different and emphasize how those differences make us special, make us who we are as humans. *Supremacist* belonging extends this focus on our differences as we long for them to be acknowledged and valued by others because we believe these differences make us better in some ways. The fourth mode of belonging also acknowledges our differences, but wants to celebrate them with others who share them. This *separatist* mode of belonging creates a space where we can be with others who are like us, to cultivate and develop those differences while nurturing and restoring the soul. Each of these modes is useful and important in certain contexts, but remaining tethered to only one is problematic. Differential belonging requires us to move between these modes, learning the lessons from each one and growing from them, but constantly moving betwixt and between them. Carrillo Rowe explains that we can be politically productive in making our world a better place for more people if we are able to shift between modes of belonging that: nurture our differences, proclaim them to be better than others, affirm their importance in our sense of self, and embrace our similarities.

Mutational Identity Theory

Mutational identity works to integrate many of the key features of the preceding models through the metaphor of mutation. In this approach to identity, Jason Zingsheim (forthcoming) suggests mutants in popular culture offer a productive way to understand how identity works in today's world. Drawing upon how mutants have been represented in the X-Men films and the television series *Heroes*, he develops a four-part framework for analyzing and understanding how identity operates. Before detailing the framework, it is important to note that from this perspective, an individual is not a singular mutant. While children may daydream about becoming superheroes, this theory of identity suggests that it is more useful to think of each individual as being made up of multiple mutants—as being an entire team of mutants. In other words, our identity (team) is composed of many subjectivities (mutants)—but how many, or how powerful or important a particular subjectivity (mutant) is, will depend on the context.

Mutational identity is comprised of four key terms that guide our understanding of identity and provide a vocabulary to talk about identity in ways that make sense to us. As described earlier, Tracy and Trethewey (2005) have demonstrated how limiting the notion and language of a real self versus a fake self can be. In answering their call to develop more useful vocabularies for talking about our selves, Zingsheim (forthcoming) suggests we think of identity in terms of evolution, multiplicity, embodiment, and agency. **Evolution** draws our attention to the ways subjectivities (mutants) and identities (teams of mutants) are constantly shifting, or evolving. In the X-Men movies, each mutant at Professor Xavier's school is working to develop, refine, and improve his or her powers. Additionally, the teams of mutants are always being rearranged and reconfigured as mutants join and/or leave the group. Nightcrawler joins the X-Men team in the second movie and then disappears before the third as a group of younger mutants take on larger responsibilities. As another example, what it means to

be African American (or any specific race or ethnicity) changes over time. Meanwhile, what it means to be female is also, and has always been, shifting. These subjectivities are constantly evolving (though we cannot always tell or predict in which direction or at what speed) and as a consequence, the teams or identities that are made up of these subjectivities are also changing in complex ways. If your identity includes the raced subjectivity of Black and the gendered subjectivity of woman, then how you organize, represent, and perform your identity as a Black woman is affected by, and effects, how these subjectivities evolve over time.

Multiplicity draws our attention to how our identities are always made up of multiple subjectivities. We can think of this multiplicity as occurring on two levels. At the internal level, each subjectivity is itself already multiple as it continues to evolve. While this may be very literal with Multiple Man in the third X-Men movie, we can also clearly see multiplicity in Rogue as she adopts the powers and personality of other mutants when she touches them. There is not a single masculine subjectivity, but many different masculine subject positions, and each of them keeps changing. On the second (or external) level, each identity is made up of many different subjectivities. Not only does each subjectivity shift, but also which ones we call upon as part of our team/identity change with the context. Sometimes your age may play an important role in your identity, say at a 21st birthday, and at others it may not be an active subjectivity—perhaps right now. Similarly, other subject positions will be more or less important to your identity depending on the context. In this way, you have multiple teams of mutants (or multiple identities composed of different groupings of subjectivities) at your disposal.

As a key concept in mutational identity theory, **embodiment** forces us to account for the ways our identities are tied to our bodies. The body we inhabit allows certain subjectivities to be easily mapped onto us. In the third X-Men film, Beast comments on the differently enabled bodies of mutants when he tells Storm, "you don't shed on the furniture." His large blue, furry body makes his mutation visible, whereas Storm, with her African American female body, can pass as a regular human. We are accustomed to seeing someone and making immediate determinations about their race or sex. For those with white male bodies, they are positioned as white males, often without an awareness of how their body locates them in discourse. At the same time, our bodies also prevent us from occupying other subject positions (e.g., the white male body is rarely allowed to occupy the position of Black or female). On the flip side, while our bodies influence identities, our identities also exert power over our bodies. Your age and gender play a role in determining how you shape your body (through diet and exercise) and adorn your body (through clothing and jewelry choices).

The mutants in the X-Men films have differing levels of control over their powers. For example, Rogue cannot turn her power off even when she wants to, Iceman always chooses when to freeze things, and Storm sometimes does not realize she is affecting the weather. The same goes for our identities—sometimes we can control them and sometimes we cannot. The concept of **agency** draws our attention to the ways our control shifts. As mentioned above, in most cases, we cannot control our racial or gendered subjectivities. We lack the agency to determine how our white male bodies are understood and interpreted by others. Depending on the context, people may or may not be able to control their sexual subjectivities. In certain public places, often for reasons of safety, some gay men and lesbians may attempt to pass as straight. Their ability to control how other folks understand their bodies and identities will be based on a number of factors out of their control. Sometimes we have almost total control over certain subjectivities, such

as religious or political subjectivities. In most cases, a Protestant and/or a Democrat can make a conscious choice about whether or not to reveal these parts of her identity. On the other hand, a person whose identity includes a Hasidic Jewish subjectivity would likely not be able to control how that subject position is expressed, due to the clothing requirements of the faith. As Campbell explains it, agency is "perverse, that is, inherently protean, ambiguous, open to reversal" (2005, p. 2). As should be clear by this point, mutational identity is radically contextual. Where we are in time and space—our temporal and spatial contexts—will influence: how much agency any one of us has over our identities, the relationships between our identities and their embodiment, the multiple forms our identities and subjectivities can take, and the speed and direction with which our identities and subjectivities evolve.

KEYWORDS: A BRIEF GLOSSARY

Before previewing the remaining readings in this unit, we turn now to briefly identifying and describing some key words that will be useful for your discussions throughout the rest of this anthology. These terms are foundational to much work at the intersections of communication, critical theory, and cultural studies. When it comes to critical approaches to identity, you can think of **ideology** as an established set of ideas and beliefs about the world and how the world works. There are many ideologies, some of which are **dominant ideologies** that are widely accepted, typically support the status quo, and serve the interests of powerful groups in society. In the U.S., ideologies of capitalism, patriarchy, democracy, Christianity, heteronormativity, and whiteness, are all examples of dominant ideologies. There are also **resistant or subjugated ideologies** that are alternatives to the dominant ideologies but are rarely given the same kind of credibly by the majority in society. Resistant ideologies, such as Afrocentrism, feminism, libertarianism, and socialism, are established alternatives to dominant belief systems that seek to change the status quo (and may or may not be more socially just, depending on your perspective). We all ascribe to a number of different ideologies based on our life experiences.

These ideologies exist within social discourses. **Discourses** are systems or webs of social meanings. More than just beliefs, discourse includes the meanings and values we assign to practices and material objects through our language usage. Discourse helps us to make sense of our lives by providing established meanings to explain our world. However, there is constantly a struggle over these meanings, and dominant discourses work to stabilize meanings, while resistant discourses attempt to change meanings and values. Dominant discourses can appear normal or natural over time. Phrases like "it's always been done this way" or "that's just the way it is" often indicate an attempt to keep the dominant system in place. A closer look often reveals that there was a time when we did things differently (and it has not "always been done this way") or that "the way it is" is actually based on a number of choices and factors. Rather than highlighting how discursive meanings are socially constructed, and therefore open to shifting as society changes, dominant discourses work to maintain the status quo and serve the interests of those in power. Those meanings, practices, objects, or identities that "do not make sense" are often operating outside of, or in opposition to, dominant discourses. For example, transgendered and genderqueer individuals who may not easily fit into categories of man or woman "do not make sense" to folks who are heavily invested in the dominant discourse of rigid sex/gender binaries. "Although the word *discourse* has roughly the same meaning as the word *ideology*, and the two terms are often used interchangeably, the word *discourse* draws attention to the role of language as the vehicle of ideology" (Tyson, 2006, p. 285). You can think of ideology as primarily focused on systems of belief and discourse as larger systems of meaning for beliefs, practices, and material objects that are created and maintained through our use of language and symbols.

These descriptions of ideology and discourse are both related to the notion of power. Based on the work of French theorist Michel Foucault, **power** is both oppressive and productive. On one hand, power can be *power over*, where some folks have more power than others and can use that power to force or coerce others into doing what the powerful want. On the other hand (and at the same time), power can be *power to*, where there is the potential to act, to produce, or to resist the dominant. As a whole, then, we can see power circulating throughout society, flowing through the web of social relations, and being exercised at various points along that web in different ways. It is not a material possession that one can hoard away (like hiding money under your mattress or gold bars in a vault). Power is discursive—it operates through discourse as it is also used to productively create and recreate discourse.

There are three more terms that describe some of the different ways we can understand power operating through discourse and influencing our daily practices as they relate to identity. While each of these terms is connected to much larger bodies of work, we want to focus here on how they can help us to understand how our identities function within discourse.

Recall our earlier distinction between identity and subjectivities, where identity describes how we view our whole self and subjectivities are the many different socially recognized parts of that self. We can also describe subjectivities as various locations within discourse that we are called to (or allowed to) occupy. Discourses existed long before we were born, and they will continue to exist after we die. In order for our selves to make sense in this world, we have to fit somewhere within the social system of meanings. Subjectivities, or subject positions, are those locations. Louis Althusser was a French, Marxist philosopher who was concerned with how discourse hails us. In other words, how the social web of meanings calls us to come inhabit particular subject positions. Althusser's conceptualization of **interpellation** explains how we are called to occupy these locations by taking up dominant ideological values through our exposure to Ideological State Apparatuses (ISAs) such as the media, church, family, educational systems, etc. (as opposed to Repressive State Apparatuses [RSAs] of the police or military). We come to accept socially dominant meanings and values, to a greater or lesser extent, through the sheer bombardment of such values over the course of our lives. Particularly when it comes to identity, these dominant values are often implicit and pervasive. For example, from the moment you are born, you are hailed into a specific gendered subject position based on your biology. A male baby is delivered into this world and quickly wrapped in a blue blanket and ushered into the social system of meanings about what it means to be a good boy and eventually "a real man." As much feminist work has illustrated, throughout ISAs like the media, church, family, and educational systems, males are afforded a privileged position. So even if this boy leaves a particular school or religious institution, even if he is raised in a family committed to feminine equality, he will be faced with this persistent patriarchal value throughout the rest of society. Eventually, he may even discipline himself to maintain these values, which brings us to Foucault's work with the panopticon and surveillance.

Foucault used Jeremy Bentham's design of the panopticon to explain how **surveillance** functions in society. The panopticon was a prison design where the cells were placed in a circle around a central guard tower. The guards could see into each cell at all times, and the inmates never knew when they were being watched. As a result, they began to monitor their own behavior. On a social level, we never know when we are being watched, so we behave in ways that we believe are socially acceptable, just in case someone is watching us. Sitting home alone, with no plans to go out, a woman may still put on make-up, because you never know when you may be spotted. A man, also home alone, watching a sentimental movie, may fight back the tears because "real men" don't cry. In both cases, these individuals have learned to discipline themselves without knowing if anyone else is watching, because they are always watching themselves.

Whereas interpellation and surveillance describe how we come to hold dominant values through our location within discourse and then begin to discipline ourselves to maintain those values, our final term describes a much more active negotiation process between the dominant and subordinate classes. The Italian and neo-Marxist philosopher Antonio Gramsci developed the concept of hegemony. **Hegemony** describes how social groups work to maintain their power over other social groups through a constant struggle of manipulation and coercion, with the ruling class winning the consent of the subordinate classes (all the while trying to make the subordinate feel like they received something important out of the deal). Small concessions may be hard fought, so the marginalized classes feel as if something was accomplished, but the ruling class is allowed to maintain their privileged position and the larger picture of social relations does not change. Think of "casual Friday" as an example, where the employees are encouraged to express themselves, relax, and even rebel a little against the normative professional dress code. Still, no matter how casual Friday may be, the employees are still giving most of their time and energy to serve the interests of the company's upper management and owners. In addition, lower level employees work to uphold their own subordination by defending dominant interests from detractors among their own ranks.

THEORIZING IDENTITY: A PREVIEW

To conclude this opening chapter, we offer a brief summary of the three readings in this unit. This is admittedly an eclectic mix; however, we believe you will find it offers a useful introduction to some of the many ways we communicate our identities. We encourage you to keep the previous models, maps, and metaphors in mind as you read through these selections. How do the terms and concepts provided by the matrix of domination, crystallized identities, relational and coalitional subjectivities, and/or mutational identity offer a vocabulary that can help you to talk about the issues these authors raise in their writings? How might these perspectives be used to critique and extend the readings?

We begin with a chapter from Gloria Anzaldúa's book, *Borderlands/La Frontera: The New Mestiza*. In this excerpt, Anzaldúa writes about the intimate relationship between the language(s) we speak and our identities, ultimately claiming that we are our languages. The languages we use to communicate function to organize how we think of ourselves, provide resources for representing ourselves, and provide the scripts for performing ourselves. As a result, attempts to control, discipline, and erase certain languages have dramatic effects on the individuals who use those languages and who know themselves through those languages. She writes, "So, if you really want to hurt me, talk badly about my language" (p. 23, this volume). Languages have limitations, and as one example, Anzaldúa points out how language is overwhelmingly a masculine domain. There are many negative terms that are regularly applied to women without equivalent terms for men. Write down a list of negative terms for men and women in your home language and test this out for yourself. Even neutral terms often privilege the masculine, such as the word "we" in Spanish – "nosotros," which uses the masculine form. This subtly but consistently erases feminine individuals in language. We often do the same thing in English even without having masculine/feminine forms of words. How many times have you heard someone address a group as "Hey guys" or "How are you guys doing?" even when the group is made up of men and women or even all women? Languages are fluid and mutable. Like identities, they change over time and space. Anzaldúa first wrote this chapter in 1987, before many of the words we have today were in use. Yet then, and now, "the struggle of identities continues, the struggle of borders is our reality still" (p. 25, this volume). As you read through the chapter, consider:

- What new words/meanings have been added to the languages you speak during your lifetime (perhaps: staycation, twitter, truthiness, tweet, unfriend)?
- How do the words you have at your disposal influence the boundaries you have for imagining yourself and your life?
- How does the language you hear in discussions about the Mexican/U.S. border frame the identities of those involved? How else might we talk about the struggle of borders?

Devon Carbado complicates this discussion in his chapter by linking privilege and discrimination. While most folks are willing to say that discrimination is bad, few are willing to interrogate their own privileges—privileges that are necessary for discrimination to make any sense in the first place. Carbado demonstrates how we can better understand the connections between privileges and advantages we experience in daily life and the way those same privileges are denied to others. He explores the privileges and discrimination he experiences on a regular basis as a straight, black male. As you might have guessed, privilege and discrimination are intimately wrapped up in one another based on your location within the matrix of domination. Such systems are also what Carbado calls "bi-directional," which means they always work in two ways. Practices that privilege one person function to put another at a disadvantage, if only because they are denied the privilege. Additionally, the privileges that often accompany normative positions can be physical and material, but they are also psychological. It is an advantage to not have to think about it. We may question whether a specific experience is tied to systems of racism, but for those whose race is normative (whites), thinking about it at all is a choice. To not have to constantly be considering the racial implications of each interaction is an enormous mental advantage. Finally, Carbado articulates the tricky process of being an ally. Questioning our privileges and their relationships to discrimination is an important step, and we must continue to ask such questions even as we work together in anti-racist, anti-patriarchal, and anti-homophobic coalitions. How we stand with one another can easily function to recreate the very systems of discrimination we are working against. Carbado explores the way straight allies "out" themselves and, even though this can be well intentioned, how these practices can work to stigmatize sexual minorities. Like many readings in this book, Carbado provides no easy answers. How to best navigate identity will depend on the context we find ourselves in. And in order to understand those contexts, we need to understand how we are positioned to receive certain privileges by virtue of our identities and how those privileges sustain the discrimination of others. From there, we can start to figure out ways to resist such discrimination and

work to make the unearned advantages available to all.

- Carbado provides a few lists of specific daily experiences of privilege. What would your list look like?
- Which privileges do you share with him?
- What privileges do you experience that he does not mention?

We wrap up this section with Kate Bornstein's gender workbook and her Gender Aptitude Test. In this reading, Bornstein questions many of our taken-for-granted assumptions about identity discourses, specifically gender. She draws attention to the many ways that genders shift and change and how this can be both dramatic and mundane.

She also notes how talking about something like gender, a topic we often have very strong beliefs and feelings about, can make us uncomfortable—particularly when those beliefs and feelings are questioned or challenged. The same goes for this entire book. Many of the discussions you will likely have in class may make you uncomfortable; these are topics that affect each of us deeply but that we are not used to talking about with others. That is not a reason to sit quietly and wait for it to pass. Instead, we encourage you, with Bornstein, to treat yourself and your classmates with compassion and respect as you ask yourselves and each other difficult questions. As you work your way through this book, and the Gender Aptitude Test in this reading, answer each question honestly (keep in mind that there are no wrong answers) and think about the other answers that you do not choose. Do they make sense to you? Who might answer the question that way and why would that answer make perfect sense for them?

- What discourses, ideologies, and histories have led you to answer the way you do? Are you comfortable with your final Gender Aptitude score (and if not, how might you go about changing your Gender Aptitude)?

- Considering the previous readings in this section, how might your responses to the gender test be connected to your location in the matrix of domination?
- What privileges and/or discriminations are connected to your opinions about gender?
- How do languages and borders shape your responses? What if we began to think of gender as another border we cross (and that crosses us) in our daily experiences of life?

REFERENCES

Ashe, F., Finlayson, A., Lloyd, M., Mackenzie, I., Martin, J., & O'Neill, S. (Eds.). (1999). *Contemporary social and political theory*. Buckingham: Open University Press.

Butler, J. (1993). *Bodies that matter: On the discursive limits of "sex."* New York: Routledge.

Butler, J. (1999). *Gender trouble: Feminism and the subversion of identity* (10th anniversary ed.). New York: Routledge.

Butler, J. (2004a). *Precarious life: The powers of mourning and violence*. New York: Verso.

Butler, J. (2004b). *Undoing gender*. New York: Routledge.

Butler, J. (2005). *Giving an account of oneself*. New York: Fordham University Press.

Campbell, K. K. (2005). Agency: Promiscuous and protean. *Communication & Critical/Cultural Studies, 2*(1), 1–19.

Carrillo Rowe, A. (2005). Be longing: Toward a feminist politics of relation. *NWSA Journal, 17*(2), 15–46.

Carrillo Rowe, A. (2008). *Power lines: On the subject of feminist alliances*. Durham, NC: Duke University Press.

Collins, P. H. (1990). *Black feminist thought: Knowledge, consciousness, and the politics of empowerment*. New York: Routledge.

Crenshaw, K. (1991). Mapping the margins: Intersectionality, identity politics and violence against women of color. *Stanford Law Review, 43*(6), 1241–1299.

Gamson, J. (2006). Must identity movements self-destruct? A queer dilemma (1995). In D. Shneer & C. Aviv (Eds.), *American queer: Now and then* (pp. 249–264). Boulder, CO: Paradigm.

Gauntlett, D. (2007). *Creative explorations: New approaches to identities and audiences*. New York, NY: Routledge.

Goffman, E. (1959). *The presentation of self in everyday life*. Garden City, NY: Doubleday Anchor Books.

Holstein, J. A., & Gubrium, J. F. (2000). *The self we live by: Narrative identity in a postmodern world*. New York: Oxford University Press.

McKerrow, R. (1993). Critical rhetoric and the possibility of the subject. In I. Angus & L. Langsdorf (Eds.), *The critical turn: Rhetoric and philosophy in postmodern discourse* (pp. 51–65). Carbondale, IL: Southern Illinois University Press.

Pérez, K. & Goltz, D. B. (2010). Treading across *Lines in the Sand*: Performing bodies in coalitional subjectivity. *Text & Performance Quarterly, 30*, 247–268.

Rabinow, P., & Rose, N. (2003). Introduction. In P. Rabinow & N. Rose (Eds.), *The essential Foucault* (pp. vii–xxxv). New York: The New Press.

Tracy, S. J. (2000). Becoming a character for commerce: Emotion labor, self-subordination, and discursive construction of identity in a total institution. *Management Communication Quarterly, 14*(1), 90–128.

Tracy, S. J., & Trethewey, A. (2005). Fracturing the real-self ↔ fake-self dichotomy: Moving toward "crystallized" organizational discourses and identities. *Communication Theory, 15*(2), 168–195.

Tyson, L. (2006). *Critical theory today: A user-friendly guide* (2nd ed.). New York, NY: Routledge.

Whitman, W. (1942). Song of myself. In E. Holloway (Ed.), *Leaves of grass: The collected poems of Walt Whitman* (pp. 24–76). New York: Book League of America.

Zingsheim, J. (forthcoming). Developing mutational identity theory: Evolution, multiplicity, embodiment, and agency. *Cultural Studies ↔ Critical Methodologies, 10*(5).

ADDITIONAL SUGGESTED READINGS

Chávez, K. R. (2010). Border (in)securities: Normative and differential belonging in LGBTQ and immigrant rights discourse. *Communication and Critical/Cultural Studies, 7,* 136–155.

Collins, P. H. (1998a). *Fighting words: Black women and the search for justice*. Minneapolis: University of Minnesota Press.

Collins, P. H. (1998b). It's all in the family: Intersections of gender, race and nation. *Hypatia, 13,* 62–79.

Ehrenreich, B. (2001). *Nickel and dimed: On (not) getting by in America*. New York: Metropolitan Books.

Ehrenreich, B. (2005). *Bait and switch: The (futile) pursuit of the American dream*. New York: Metropolitan Books.

Flagg, B. (1993). Was blind, but now I see: White race consciousness and the requirement of discriminatory intent. *Michigan Law Review, 91,* 953–1018.

Malin, B. (2003). Gender, culture, power: Three theoretical views. In P. M. Backlund & M. R. Williams (Eds.), *Readings in gender communication* (pp. 65–75). Belmont, CA: Wadsworth.

McIntosh, P. (1995). White privilege and male privilege: A personal account of coming to see correspondences through work in Women's Studies. In M. L. Andersen & P. H. Collins (Eds.), *Race, Class, and Gender: An Anthology* (2nd ed., pp. 76–87). Belmont, CA: Wadsworth Publishing Company.

Prins, B. (2006). Narrative accounts of origins: A blind spot in the intersectional approach? *European Journal of Women's Studies, 13*(3), 277–290.

2 How to Tame a Wild Tongue

By Gloria Anzaldúa

"We're going to have to control your tongue," the dentist says, pulling out all the metal from my mouth. Silver bits plop and tinkle into the basin. My mouth is a motherlode.

The dentist is cleaning out my roots. I get a whiff of the stench when I gasp. "I can't cap that tooth yet, you're still draining," he says.

"We're going to have to do something about your tongue." I hear the anger rising in his voice. My tongue keeps pushing out the wads of cotton, pushing back the drills, the long thin needles. "I've never seen anything as strong or as stubborn," he says. And I think, how do you tame a wild tongue, train it to be quiet, how do you bridle and saddle it? How do you make it lie down?

> "Who is to say that robbing a people of
> its language is less violent than war?"
> —Ray Gwyn Smith[1]

I remember being caught speaking Spanish at recess—that was good for three licks on the knuckles with a sharp ruler. I remember being sent to the corner of the classroom for "talking back" to the Anglo teacher when all I was trying to do was tell her how to pronounce my name. "If you want to be American, speak 'American.' If you don't like it, go back to Mexico where you belong."

"I want you to speak English. *Pa'hallar buen trabajo tienes que saber hablar el inglés bien. Qué vale toda tu educatión si todavía hablas inglés con un* 'accent,'" my mother would say, mortified that I spoke English like a Mexican. At Pan American University, I, and all Chicano students were required to take two speech classes. Their purpose: to get rid of our accents.

Attacks on one's form of expression with the intent to censor are a violation of the First Amendment. *El Anglo con cara de inocente nos arrancó la lengua.* Wild tongues can't be tamed, they can only be cut out.

OVERCOMING THE TRADITION OF SILENCE

Ahogadas, escupimos el oscuro.
Peleando con nuestra propia sombra
el silencio nos sepulta.

En boca cerrada no entran moscas. "Flies don't enter a closed mouth" is a saying I kept hearing when I was a child. *Ser habladora* was to be a gossip and a liar, to talk too much. *Muchachitas bien criadas,* well-bred girls don't answer back. *Es una falta de respeto* to talk back to one's mother or father. I remember one of the sins I'd recite to the priest in the confession box the few times I went to confession: talking back to my mother, *hablar pa' 'trás, repelar. Hocicona, repelona, chismosa,* having a big mouth, questioning, carrying tales are all signs of being *mal criada.* In my culture they are all words that are derogatory if applied to women—I've never heard them applied to men.

The first time I heard two women, a Puerto Rican and a Cuban, say the word *"nosotras,"* I was shocked. I had not known the word existed. Chicanas use *nosotros* whether we're male or female. We are robbed of our female being by the masculine plural. Language is a male discourse.

> And our tongues have become dry
> the wilderness has dried out our tongues
> and we have forgotten speech.
> —Irena Klepfisz[2]

Even our own people, other Spanish speakers *nos quieren poner candados en la boca.* They would hold us back with their bag of *reglas de academia.*

OYÉ COMO LADRA: EL LENGUAJE DE LA FRONTERA

> *Quien tiene boca se equivoca.*
> —Mexican saying

"Pocho, cultural traitor, you're speaking the oppressor's language by speaking English, you're ruining the Spanish language," I have been accused by various Latinos and Latinas. Chicano Spanish is considered by the purist and by most Latinos deficient, a mutilation of Spanish.

But Chicano Spanish is a border tongue which developed naturally. Change, *evolución, enriquecimiento de palabras nuevas por invención o adopción* have created variants of Chicano Spanish, *un nuevo lenguaje. Un lenguaje que corresponde a un modo de vivir.* Chicano Spanish is not incorrect, it is a living language.

For a people who are neither Spanish nor live in a country in which Spanish is the first language; for a people who live in a country in which English is the reigning tongue but who are not Anglo; for a people who cannot entirely identify with either standard (formal, Castillian) Spanish nor standard English, what recourse is left to them but to create their own language? A language which they can connect their identity to, one capable of communicating the realities and values true to themselves—a language with terms that are neither *español ni inglés,* but both. We speak a patois, a forked tongue, a variation of two languages.

Chicano Spanish sprang out of the Chicanos' need to identify ourselves as a distinct people. We needed a language with which we could communicate with ourselves, a secret language. For some of us, language is a homeland closer than the Southwest—for many Chicanos today live in the Midwest and the East. And because we are a complex, heterogeneous people, we speak many languages. Some of the languages we speak are:

1. Standard English
2. Working class and slang English
3. Standard Spanish
4. Standard Mexican Spanish
5. North Mexican Spanish dialect
6. Chicano Spanish (Texas, New Mexico, Arizona and California have regional variations)
7. Tex-Mex
8. *Pachuco* (called *caló*)

My "home" tongues are the languages I speak with my sister and brothers, with my friends. They are the last five listed, with 6 and 7 being closest to my heart. From school, the media and job situations, I've picked up standard and working class English. From Mamagrande Locha and from reading Spanish and Mexican literature, I've picked up Standard Spanish and Standard Mexican Spanish. From *los recién llegados,* Mexican immigrants, and *braceros,* I learned the North Mexican dialect. With Mexicans I'll try to speak either Standard Mexican Spanish or the North Mexican dialect. From my parents and Chicanos living in the Valley, I picked up Chicano Texas Spanish, and I speak it with my mom, younger brother (who married a Mexican and who rarely mixes Spanish with English), aunts and older relatives.

With Chicanas from *Nuevo México* or *Arizona* I will speak Chicano Spanish a little, but often they don't understand what I'm saying. With most California Chicanas I speak entirely in English (unless I forget). When I first moved to San Francisco, I'd rattle off something in Spanish, unintentionally embarrassing them. Often it is only with another Chicana *tejana* that I can talk freely.

Words distorted by English are known as anglicisms or *pochismos.* The *pocho* is an anglicized Mexican or American of Mexican origin who speaks Spanish with an accent characteristic of North Americans and who distorts and reconstructs the language according to the influence of English.[3] Tex-Mex, or Spanglish, comes most naturally to me. I may switch back and forth from English to Spanish in the same sentence or in the same word. With my sister and my brother Nune and with Chicano *tejano* contemporaries I speak in Tex-Mex.

From kids and people my own age I picked up *Pachuco. Pachuco* (the language of the zoot suiters) is a language of rebellion, both against Standard Spanish and Standard English. It is a secret language. Adults of the culture and outsiders cannot understand it. It is made up of slang words from both English and Spanish. *Ruca* means girl or woman, *vato* means guy or dude, *chale* means no, *simón* means yes, *churo* is sure, talk is *periquiar, pigionear* means petting, *que gacho* means how nerdy, *ponte águila* means watch out, death is called *la pelona.* Through lack of practice and not having others who can speak it, I've lost most of the *Pachuco* tongue.

CHICANO SPANISH

Chicanos, after 250 years of Spanish/Anglo colonization have developed significant differences in the Spanish we speak. We collapse two adjacent vowels into a single syllable and sometimes shift the stress in certain words such as *maíz/maiz, cohete/cuete.* We leave out certain consonants when they appear between vowels; *lado/lao, mojado/mojao.* Chicanos from South Texas pronounced *f* as *j* as in *jue (fue).* Chicanos use "archaisms,"words that are no longer in the Spanish language, words that have been evolved out. We say *semos, truje, haiga, ansina,* and *naiden.* We retain the "archaic"*j,* as in *jalar,* that derives from an earlier *h,* (the French *halar* or the Germanic *halon* which was lost to standard Spanish in the 16th century), but which is still found in several regional dialects such as the one spoken in South Texas. (Due to geography, Chicanos from the Valley of South Texas were cut off linguistically from other Spanish speakers. We tend to use words that the Spaniards brought over from Medieval Spain. The majority of the Spanish colonizers in Mexico and the Southwest came from Extremadura—Hernán Cortés was one of them—and Andalucía. Andalucians pronounce *ll* like a *y,* and their *d's* tend to be absorbed by adjacent vowels: *tirado* becomes *tirao.* They brought *el lenguajepopular, dialectos y regionalismos.*[4])

Chicanos and other Spanish speakers also shift *ll* to *y* and *z* to *s.*[5] We leave out initial syllables, saying *tar* for *estar; toy* for *estoy, hora* for *ahora (cubanos* and *puertorriqueños* also leave out initial letters of some words.) We also leave out the final syllable such as *pa* for *para*. The intervocalic *y* the *ll* as in *tortilla, ella, botella,* gets replaced by *tortia* or *tortiya, ea, botea*. We add an additional syllable at the beginning of certain words: *atocar* for *tocar, agastar* for *gastar*. Sometimes we'll say *lavaste las vacijas,* other times *lavates* (substituting the *ates* verb endings for the *aste)*.

We use anglicisms, words borrowed from English: *bola* from ball, *carpeta* from carpet, *máchina de lavar* (instead of *lavadora)* from washing machine. Tex-Mex argot, created by adding a Spanish sound at the beginning or end of an English word such as *cookiar* for cook, *watchar* for watch, *parkiar* for park, and *rapiar* for rape, is the result of the pressures on Spanish speakers to adapt to English.

We don't use the word *vosotros/as* or its accompanying verb form. We don't say *claro* (to mean yes), *imagínate,* or *me emociona,* unless we picked up Spanish from Latinas, out of a book, or in a classroom. Other Spanish-speaking groups are going through the same, or similar, development in their Spanish.

LINGUISTIC TERRORISM

> *Deslenguadas. Somos los del español deficiente.* We are your linguistic nightmare, your linguistic aberration, your linguistic *mestizaje,* the subject of your *burla.* Because we speak with tongues of fire we are culturally crucified. Racially, culturally and linguistically *somos huérfanos—* we speak an orphan tongue.

Chicanas who grew up speaking Chicano Spanish have internalized the belief that we speak poor Spanish. It is illegitimate, a bastard language. And because we internalize how our language has been used against us by the dominant culture, we use our language differences against each other.

Chicana feminists often skirt around each other with suspicion and hesitation. For the longest time I couldn't figure it out. Then it dawned on me. To be close to another Chicana is like looking into the mirror. We are afraid of what we'll see there. *Pena.* Shame. Low estimation of self. In childhood we are told that our language is wrong. Repeated attacks on our native tongue diminish our sense of self. The attacks continue throughout our lives.

Chicanas feel uncomfortable talking in Spanish to Latinas, afraid of their censure. Their language was not outlawed in their countries. They had a whole lifetime of being immersed in their native tongue; generations, centuries in which Spanish was a first language, taught in school, heard on radio and TV, and read in the newspaper.

If a person, Chicana or Latina, has a low estimation of my native tongue, she also has a low estimation of me. Often with *mexicanas y latinas* we'll speak English as a neutral language. Even among Chicanas we tend to speak English at parties or conferences. Yet, at the same time, we're afraid the other will think we're *agringadas* because we don't speak Chicano Spanish. We oppress each other trying to out-Chicano each other, vying to be the "real" Chicanas, to speak like Chicanos. There is no one Chicano language just as there is no one Chicano experience. A monolingual Chicana whose first language is English or Spanish is just as much a Chicana as one who speaks several variants of Spanish. A Chicana from Michigan or Chicago or Detroit is just as much a Chicana as one from the Southwest. Chicano Spanish is as diverse linguistically as it is regionally.

By the end of this century, Spanish speakers will comprise the biggest minority group in the U.S., a country where students in high schools and colleges are encouraged to take French classes because French is considered more "cultured." But for a language to remain alive it must be used.[6] By the end of this century English, and not Spanish, will be the mother tongue of most Chicanos and Latinos.

So, if you want to really hurt me, talk badly about my language. Ethnic identity is twin skin to linguistic identity—I am my language. Until I can take pride in my language, I cannot take pride in myself. Until I can accept as legitimate Chicano Texas Spanish, Tex-Mex and all the other languages I speak, I cannot accept the legitimacy of myself. Until I am free to write bilingually and to switch codes without having always to translate, while I still have to speak English or Spanish when I would rather speak Spanglish, and as long as I have to accommodate the English speakers rather than having them accommodate me, my tongue will be illegitimate.

I will no longer be made to feel ashamed of existing. I will have my voice: Indian, Spanish, white. I will have my serpent's tongue—my woman's voice, my sexual voice, my poet's voice. I will overcome the tradition of silence.

My fingers
move sly against your palm
Like women everywhere, we speak in
code. ...

—Melanie Kaye/Kantrowitz[7]

"VISTAS," CORRIDOS, Y COMIDA: MY NATIVE TONGUE

In the 1960s, I read my first Chicano novel. It was *City of Night* by John Rechy, a gay Texan, son of a Scottish father and a Mexican mother. For days I walked around in stunned amazement that a Chicano could write and could get published. When I read *I Am Joaquín*[8] I was surprised to see a bilingual book by a Chicano in print. When I saw poetry written in Tex-Mex for the first time, a feeling of pure joy flashed through me. I felt like we

really existed as a people. In 1971, when I started teaching High School English to Chicano students, I tried to supplement the required texts with works by Chicanos, only to be reprimanded and forbidden to do so by the principal. He claimed that I was supposed to teach "American" and English literature. At the risk of being fired, I swore my students to secrecy and slipped in Chicano short stories, poems, a play. In graduate school, while working toward a Ph.D., I had to "argue" with one advisor after the other, semester after semester, before I was allowed to make Chicano literature an area of focus.

Even before I read books by Chicanos or Mexicans, it was the Mexican movies I saw at the drive-in—the Thursday night special of $1.00 a carload—that gave me a sense of belonging. *"Vámonos a las vistas,"* my mother would call out and we'd all—grandmother, brothers, sister and cousins—squeeze into the car. We'd wolf down cheese and bologna white bread sandwiches while watching Pedro Infante in melodramatic tear-jerkers like *Nosotros los pobres,* the first "real" Mexican movie (that was not an imitation of European movies). I remember seeing *Cuando los hijos se van* and surmising that all Mexican movies played up the love a mother has for her children and what ungrateful sons and daughters suffer when they are not devoted to their mothers. I remember the singing-type "westerns" of Jorge Negrete and Miguel Aceves Mejía. When watching Mexican movies, I felt a sense of homecoming as well as alienation. People who were to amount to something didn't go to Mexican movies, or *bailes* or tune their radios to *bolero, rancherita,* and *corrido* music.

The whole time I was growing up, there was *norteño* music sometimes called North Mexican border music, or Tex-Mex music, or Chicano music, or *cantina* (bar) music. I grew up listening to *conjuntos,* three- or four-piece bands made up of folk musicians playing guitar, *bajo sexto,* drums and button accordion, which Chicanos had borrowed from the German immigrants who had come to Central Texas and Mexico to farm and build breweries. In the Rio Grande Valley, Steve Jordan and Little Joe Hernández were popular, and Flaco Jiménez was the accordion king. The rhythms of Tex-Mex music are those of the polka, also adapted from the Germans, who in turn had borrowed the polka from the Czechs and Bohemians.

I remember the hot, sultry evenings when *corridos*—songs of love and death on the Texas-Mexican borderlands—reverberated out of cheap amplifiers from the local *cantinas* and wafted in through my bedroom window.

Corridos first became widely used along the South Texas/Mexican border during the early conflict between Chicanos and Anglos. The *corridos* are usually about Mexican heroes who do valiant deeds against the Anglo oppressors. Pancho Villa's song, *"La cucaracha,"* is the most famous one. *Corridos* of John F. Kennedy and his death are still very popular in the Valley. Older Chicanos remember Lydia Mendoza, one of the great border *corrido* singers who was called *la Gloria de Tejas*. Her *"El tango negro"* sung during the Great Depression, made her a singer of the people. The everpresent *corridos* narrated one hundred years of border history, bringing news of events as well as entertaining. These folk musicians and folk songs are our chief cultural mythmakers, and they made our hard lives seem bearable.

I grew up feeling ambivalent about our music. Country-western and rock-and-roll had more status. In the 50s and 60s, for the slightly educated and *agringado* Chicanos, there existed a sense of shame at being caught listening to our music. Yet I couldn't stop my feet from thumping to the music, could not stop humming the words, nor hide from myself the exhilaration I felt when I heard it.

There are more subtle ways that we internalize identification, especially in the forms of images and emotions. For me food and certain smells are tied to my identity, to my homeland. Woodsmoke curling up to an immense blue sky; woodsmoke perfuming my grandmother's clothes, her skin. The stench of cow manure and the yellow patches on the ground; the crack of a .22 rifle and the reek of cordite. Homemade white cheese sizzling in a pan, melting inside a folded *tortilla*. My sister Hilda's hot, spicy *menudo, chile Colorado* making it deep red, pieces of *panza* and hominy floating on top. My brother Carito barbecuing *fajitas* in the backyard. Even now and 3,000 miles away, I can see my mother spicing the ground beef, pork and venison with *chile*. My mouth salivates at the thought of the hot steaming *tamales* I would be eating if I were home.

Si le preguntas a mi mamá, "¿Qué eres?"

> "Identity is the essential core of who we are as individuals, the conscious experience of the self inside."
>
> —Kaufman[9]

Nosotros los Chicanos straddle the borderlands. On one side of us, we are constantly exposed to the Spanish of the Mexicans, on the other side we hear the Anglos' incessant clamoring so that we forget our language. Among ourselves we don't say *nosotros los americanos, o nosotros los españoles, o nosotros los hispanos*. We say *nosotros los mexicanos* (by *mexicanos* we do not mean citizens of Mexico; we do not mean a national identity, but a racial one). We distinguish between *mexicanos del otro lado* and *mexicanos de este lado*. Deep in our hearts we believe that being Mexican has nothing to do with which country one lives in. Being Mexican is a state of soul—not one of mind, not one of citizenship. Neither eagle nor serpent, but both. And like the ocean, neither animal respects borders.

Dime con quien andas y te diré quien eres.
(Tell me who your friends are and I'll tell
you who you are.)

—Mexican saying

*Si le preguntas a mi mamá, "¿Qué eres?" te dirá, "Soy
mexicana."* My brothers and sister say the same. I
sometimes will answer *"soy mexicana" and* at others
will say *"soy Chicana" o "soy tejana."* But I identified
as *"Raza"* before I ever identified as *"mexicana"* or
"Chicana."

As a culture, we call ourselves Spanish when
referring to ourselves as a linguistic group and
when copping out. It is then that we forget our
predominant Indian genes. We are 70 to 80%
Indian.[10] We call ourselves Hispanic[11] or Spanish-
American or Latin American or Latin when linking
ourselves to other Spanish-speaking peoples of the
Western hemisphere and when copping out. We
call ourselves Mexican-American[12] to signify we are
neither Mexican nor American, but more the noun
"American" than the adjective "Mexican" (and
when copping out).

Chicanos and other people of color suffer economically for not acculturating. This voluntary (yet forced)
alienation makes for psychological conflict, a kind
of dual identity—we don't identify with the Anglo-
American cultural values and we don't totally identify
with the Mexican cultural values. We are a synergy of
two cultures with various degrees of Mexicanness or
Angloness. I have so internalized the borderland conflict that sometimes I feel like one cancels out the other
and we are zero, nothing, no one. *A veces no soy nada ni
nadie. Pero hasta cuando no to soy, lo soy.*

When not copping out, when we know we are
more than nothing, we call ourselves Mexican, referring to race and ancestry; *mestizo* when affirming
both our Indian and Spanish (but we hardly ever
own our Black ancestry); Chicano when referring
to a politically aware people born and/or raised in
the U.S.; *Raza* when referring to Chicanos; *tejanos*
when we are Chicanos from Texas.

Chicanos did not know we were a people until
1965 when Cesar Chavez and the farmworkers
united and *I Am Joaquín* was published and *la Raza
Unida* party was formed in Texas. With that recognition, we became a distinct people. Something
momentous happened to the Chicano soul—we
became aware of our reality and acquired a name
and a language (Chicano Spanish) that reflected that
reality. Now that we had a name, some of the fragmented pieces began to fall together—who we were,
what we were, how we had evolved. We began to get
glimpses of what we might eventually become.

Yet the struggle of identities continues, the
struggle of borders is our reality still. One day the
inner struggle will cease and a true integration take
place. In the meantime, *tenemos que hacerla lucha.
¿Quién está protegiendo los ranchos de mi gente?
¿Quién está tratando de cerrar la fisura entre la india y
el blanco en nuestra sangre? El Chicano, sí, el Chicano
que anda como un ladrón en su propia casa.*

Los Chicanos, how patient we seem, how very
patient. There is the quiet of the Indian about us.[13]
We know how to survive. When other races have
given up their tongue, we've kept ours. We know
what it is to live under the hammer blow of the
dominant *norteamericano* culture. But more than we
count the blows, we count the days the weeks the
years the centuries the eons until the white laws and
commerce and customs will rot in the deserts they've
created, lie bleached. *Humildes* yet proud, *quietos*
yet wild, *nosotros los mexicanos-Chicanos* will walk
by the crumbling ashes as we go about our business.
Stubborn, persevering, impenetrable as stone, yet
possessing a malleability that renders us unbreakable,
we, the *mestizas* and *mestizos,* will remain.

NOTES

1. Ray Gwyn Smith, <u>Moorland is Cold Country</u>, unpublished book.

2. Irena Klepfisz, "*Di rayze aheym*/The Journey Home," in <u>The Tribe of Dina: A Jewish Women's Anthology</u>, Melanie Kaye/Kantrowitz and Irena Klepfisz, eds. (Montpelier, VT: Sinister Wisdom Books, 1986), 49.

3. R.C. Ortega, <u>Dialiectología Del Barrio</u>, trans. Hortencia S. Alwan (Los Angeles, CA: R.C. Ortega Publisher & Bookseller, 1977), 132.

4. Eduardo Hernandéz-Chávez, Andrew D. Cohen, and Anthony F. Beltramo, <u>El Lenguaje de los Chicanos: Regional and Social Characteristics of Language Used By Mexican Americans</u> (Arlington, VA: Center for Applied Linguistics, 1975), 39.

5. Hernandéz-Chávez, xvii.

6. Irena Klepfisz, "Secular Jewish Identity: Yidishkayt in America," in <u>The Tribe of Dina</u>, Kaye/Kantrowitz and Klepfisz, eds., 43.

7. Melanie Kaye/Kantrowitz, "Sign," in <u>We Speak In Code: Poems and Other Writings</u> (Pittsburgh, PA: Motheroot Publications, Inc., 1980), 85.

8. Rodolfo Gonzales, <u>I Am Joaquín/*Yo Soy Joaquín*</u> (New York, NY: Bantam Books, 1972). It was first published in 1967.

9. Kaufman, 68.

10. Chávez, 88–90.

11. "Hispanic" is derived from *Hispanis* (*España*, a name given to the Iberian Peninsula in ancient times when it was a part of the Roman Empire and is a term designated by the U.S. government to make it easier to handle us on paper.

12. The Treaty of Guadalupe Hidalgo created the Mexican-American in 1848.

13. Anglos, in order to alleviate their guilt for dispossessing the Chicano, stressed the Spanish part of us and perpetrated the myth of the Spanish Southwest. We have accepted the fiction that we are Hispanic, that is Spanish, in order to accommodate ourselves to the dominant culture and its abhorrence of Indians. Chávez, 88–91.

3

Privilege

By Devon W. Carbado

It may be ... that a damaging bias toward heterosocial or heterosexist assumptions inheres unavoidably in the very concept of gender. ... The ultimate definitional appeal in any gender-based analysis must necessarily be to the diacritical frontier between different genders. This gives heterosocial and heterosexual relationships a conceptual privilege of incalculable consequence.—Eve Kosofsky Sedgwick, *Epistemology of the Closet*

This essay is part of a larger intellectual project to encourage a shift in—or at least a broadening of—our conceptualization of discrimination. My aim is to expand our notion of what it means to be a perpetrator of discrimination. Typically, we define a perpetrator of discrimination as someone who acts intentionally to bring about some discriminatory result.[1] This is a narrow and politically palatable conception; it applies to very few of us. In this essay I suggest that those of us who unquestionably accept the racial, gender, and heterosexual privileges we have—those of us who fail to acknowledge our victimless status with

respect to racism, sexism, and homophobia—are also perpetrators of discrimination.[2]

Informing this privileged-centered understanding of discrimination is the notion that taking identity privileges for granted helps to legitimize problematic assumptions about identity and entitlement, assumptions that make it difficult for us to challenge the starting points of many of our most controversial conversations about equality. We simply assume, for example, that men should be able to fight for their country (the question is whether women should be entitled to this privilege); that heterosexuals should be able to get married (the question is whether the privilege should be extended to gays and lesbians); that white men should be able to compete for all the slots in a university's entering class (the question is whether people of color should be entitled to the privilege of "preferential treatment").

While a privileged-centered conception of discrimination usefully reveals the bi-directional effects of discrimination—namely, that discrimination allocates both burdens and benefits—the conception may prove entirely too much. After all, all of us enjoy some degree of privilege. Are all of us perpetrators of discrimination? The answer may

Devon W. Carbado, "Privilege," *Black Queer Studies: A Critical Anthology*, ed. E. Patrick Johnson and Mae G. Henderson, pp. 190-212. Copyright © 2005 by Duke University Press. Reprinted with permission.

depend on what we do with, and to, the privileges we have. Each of us makes personal and private choices with our privileges that entrench a variety of social practices, institutional arrangements, and laws that disadvantage other(ed) people.

For example, many of us get married and/or attend weddings, while lesbian and gay marriages are, in most parts of the United States (and the world), not legally recognized. Others of us have racially monolithic social encounters, live in de facto white only (or predominantly white) neighborhoods, or send our kids to white only (or predominantly white) schools. Still others of us have "straight only" associations—that is, our friends are all heterosexuals and our children's friends all have mommies and daddies. These choices are not just personal; they are political. And their cumulative effect is to entrench the very social practices—racism, sexism, classism, and homophobia—we profess to abhor.[3]

In other words, there is a link between identity privileges, and our negotiation of them, on the one hand, and discrimination, on the other.[4] Our identities are reflective and constitutive of systems of oppression. Racism requires white privilege. Sexism requires male privilege. Homophobia requires heterosexual privilege. The very intelligibility of our identities is their association, or lack thereof, with privilege. This creates an obligation on the part of those of us with privileged identities to expose and to challenge them.[5]

Significantly, this obligation exists not only as a matter of morality and responsibility. The obligation exists for a pragmatic reason as well. We cannot change the macro-effects of discrimination without ameliorating the power effects of our identities. Nor can our political commitments have traction unless we apply them to the seemingly "just personal" privileged aspects of our lives. Resistance to identity privileges may be futile, we cannot know for sure. However, to the extent that we do nothing, this much is clear: we perpetuate the systems

of discrimination out of which our identities are forged.

But precisely what constitutes an identity privilege? Further, how do we identify them? And, finally, what acts are necessary to deprivilege our identities and to disrupt their association with power. These questions drive this essay. I begin here with a discussion of male privileges and then engage the privileges of heterosexuality.

MALE PRIVILEGES

Ever since Simone de Beauvior articulated the idea that women are not born women but rather become women, feminists have been grappling with ways to strip the category "women" of its patriarchal trappings. The hope is to locate the pre-patriarchal woman—the woman whose personal identity has not been over-determined by her gender.

The search for the pre-patriarchal woman is not based on the notion that, in the absence of patriarchy, there is some true female essence. (Indeed, it might not even be meaningful to refer to a person whose identity has not been over-determined by female gender norms as a woman.) The point is that people who are body-coded female cannot experience their personhood outside of the social construction of their gender, and the social construction of gender is both agency-denying and subordinating.

Of course, gender for men is also socially constructed and agency denying. One must learn to be a man in this society because manhood is a socially produced category. Manhood is a performance.[6] A script.[7] It is accomplished and re-enacted in everyday social relationships. Yet, men have not been inclined to examine the sex/gender category we inhabit, reproduce, and legitimize. Nor have men developed a practice of exposing the contingency and false necessity of manhood.[8] There is little effort within male communities to locate, or even imagine, the pre-patriarchal man, the man whose personal identity has not been over-determined by his gender. We (men) sometimes discuss gender inequality, but rarely do we discuss gender privilege. The assumption is that our privileges as men are not politically contingent, but social givens—inevitable and unchangeable.

Part of the reason men, especially white heterosexual men, do not conceive of themselves as engendered, and part of the reason men do not recognize their privileges, relates to negative identity signification. A white heterosexual man lives on the white side of race, the male side of gender, and the straight side of sexual orientation. He is, in this sense, the norm. Mankind. The baseline. He is our reference. We are all defined with him in mind. We are the same as or different from him.

Those of us on the "other" side of race, gender, or sexual orientation have to contend with and respond to negative identity signification. That is, we simultaneously live with and contest our non-normativity. We are "different," and our identities have negative social meanings. For example, when I enter a department store, my "different" identity signifies not only that I am black and male but also that I am a potential criminal. My individual identity is lost in the social construction of black manhood. I can try to adopt race-negating strategies to challenge this dignity-destroying social meaning. I can work my identity (to attempt) to repudiate the stereotype.[9] I might, for example, dress "respectable" when I go shopping. There is, after all, something to the politics of dress, particularly in social contexts in which race matters—that is, in every American social context. I can appear less "black" in a social meaning sense via my sartorial practices.

Purchasing an item, especially something expensive, immediately on entering the store is another strategy I can employ to disabuse people of

my "blackness." This sort of signaling strategy will reveal to the department store's security personnel what might not otherwise be apparent because of my race and gender: that I am a shopper. If I am not in the mood to dress up and I do not want to spend any money, there is a third strategy I can employ: solicit the assistance of a white sales associate. This, too, must be done early in the shopping experience. A white salesperson would not be suspected of facilitating or contributing to black shoplifting and can be trusted to keep an eye on me. Finally, I might simply whistle Vivaldi as I move among the merchandise: only a good (safe, respectable) black man would know Vivaldi or whistle classical music.[10]

White people do not have to worry about employing these strategies. White people do not have to work their identities to respond to these racial concerns.[11] Nor should they have to—no one should. However, white people should recognize and grapple with the fact that they do not have to employ or think about employing these strategies. White people should recognize that they do not have to perform this work.[12] This is a necessary first step for white people to come to terms with white privilege. Barbara Flagg and Peggy Mcintosh[13]—two white women—make similar arguments. Their self-referential examination of whiteness is the analytical analogue to the examination of male identity and heterosexuality that this essay performs.

According to Barbara Flagg, "There is a profound cognitive dimension to the material and social privilege that attaches to whiteness in this society, in that the white person has an everyday option not to think of herself in racial terms at all." This, reasons Flagg, is indeed what defines whiteness: "To be white is not to think about it." Flagg refers to the propensity of whites not to think in racial terms as the "transparency phenomenon."[14]

Importantly, Flagg does not suggest that white people are unmindful of the racial identities of other whites or the racial "difference" of nonwhites: "Race is undeniably a powerful determinant of social status and so is always noticed, in a way that eye color, for example, may not be." Rather, her point is that because whiteness operates as the racial norm, whites are able "to relegate their own racial specificity to the realm of the subconscious."[15] As a result, racial distinctiveness is black, is Asian, is Latina/o, is Native American, but it is not white. To address transparency, Flagg suggests the "[reconceptualization of] white race consciousness … [to develop] a positive white racial identity, one neither founded on the implicit acceptance of white racial domination nor productive of distributive effects that systematically advantage whites."[16]

Peggy McIntosh's work provides a specific indication of some of the everyday "distributive effects" of white racial privilege. To illustrate the extent to which white privilege structures are implicated in day-to-day social encounters, McIntosh exposes the "unearned" advantages that she accrues on a daily basis because she is white. For example, precisely because she is white, McIntosh did not have to educate her children to be aware of systemic racism for their own daily physical protection.[17] Nor, observes McIntosh, does she have to worry about whether negative encounters with certain governmental entities (e.g., the IRS, the police) reflect racial harassment.[18]

McIntosh is careful to point out that the term "privilege" is something of a misnomer: "We usually think of privilege as being a favored state, whether earned, or conferred by birth or luck. … The word 'privilege' carries the connotation of being something everyone must want. Yet some of the conditions I have described here work to systematically over-empower certain groups." Accordingly, McIntosh distinguishes between "positive advantages that we can work to spread … and negative types of advantage that unless rejected will always reinforce our present hierarchies."[19]

Flagg's and McIntosh's interrogation of whiteness provides a methodology for men to interrogate gender. Their analysis suggests that men should challenge the social construction of gender employing *their* privileged gendered experiences as starting points. More particularly, men should detail and problematize the specific ways in which patriarchy materially advantages them. This experiential information should not displace or replace victim-centered or bottom-up accounts of sexism. That is, men's articulation of the ways in which they are the beneficiaries of patriarchy should not be a substitute for women's articulations of the ways in which they are the victims of patriarchy. Both narratives are valuable and illuminating. The telling of both helps to make clear that patriarchy is bi-directional. The patriarchal disempowerment of women is achieved through the empowerment of men.[20] The patriarchal construction of women as the second sex requires the construction of men as the first.[21] Patriarchy effectuates and maintains these relational differences.[22] It gives to men what it takes away from women.

The relational constitution of gender identities and experiences suggests that gender equality cannot be achieved unless gender privileges are relinquished. As Andrea Dworkin and Catherine Mackinnon put it: "Equality means someone loses power. … The mathematics are simple: taking power from the exploiters extends and multiplies the rights of those they have been exploiting."[23]

Broadly speaking, there are two categories of male privileges about which men should develop a consciousness. The first can be described as "an invisible package of unearned assets that [men] can count on cashing in each day."[24] The second category includes a series of disadvantages that men do not experience precisely because they are men. The following list presents examples from both.

1. I can walk in public, alone, without fear of being sexually violated.

2. Prospective employers will never ask me if I plan on having children.

3. I can be confident that my career path will never be tainted by accusations that I "slept my way to the top" (though it might be "tainted" by the perception that I am a beneficiary of affirmative action).

4. I don't have to worry about whether I am being paid less than my female colleagues (though I might worry about whether I'm being paid less than my white male colleagues).

5. When I get dressed in the morning, I do not worry about whether my clothing "invites" sexual harassment.

6. I can be moody, irritable, or brusque without it being attributed to my sex, to biological changes in my life, or to menstruating or experiencing "PMS" (though it might be attributable to my "preoccupation" with race).

7. My career opportunities are not dependent on the extent to which I am perceived to be "as good as a man" (though they may be dependent on the extent to which I am perceived to be "a good black"—i.e., racially assimilable).

8. I do not have to choose between having a family or having a career.

9. I do not have to worry about being called selfish for having a career instead of having a family.

10. It will almost always be the case that my supervisor will be a man (though rarely will my supervisor be black).

11. I can express outrage without being perceived as irrational, emotional, or too "sensitive" (except if I am expressing outrage about race).

12. I can fight for my country without controversy.

13. No one will qualify my intellectual or technical ability with the phrase "for a man" (though they may qualify my ability with the phrase "for a black man").

14. I can be outspoken without being called a "bitch" (though I might be referred to as uppity).

15. I do not have to concern myself with finding the line between being assertive and aggressive (except with respect to conversations about race).

16. I do not have to think about whether my race comes before my gender, about whether I am black first and a man second.

17. The politics of dress—to wear or not to wear make-up, high heels, or trousers, to straighten or not to straighten, to braid or not to braid my hair—affect me less than they do women.

18. More is known about "male" diseases and how medicine affects male bodies than about "female" diseases and female bodies (though diseases that disproportionately affect black people continue to be understudied).

19. I was not expected to change my name upon getting married.

20. I am rewarded for vigorously and aggressively pursuing my career.

21. I do not have to worry about opposite-sex strangers or close acquaintances committing gender violence against me (though I do have to worry about racial violence).

22. I am not less manly because I play sports (though I may be considered less black and less manly if I do not play sports).

23. My reputation does not diminish with each additional person with whom I have sexual relations.

24. There is no societal pressure for me to marry before the age of thirty.

25. I can dominate a conversation without being perceived as domineering (unless the discussion is about race).

26. I am praised for spending time with my children, cooking, cleaning, or doing other household chores.

27. I will rarely have to worry whether compliments from my boss contain a sexual subtext (though I will worry that they may contain a racial subtext).

28. I am not expected to have a small appetite.

29. The responsibility for birth control is not placed on men's shoulders and men are not accused of getting pregnant.

30. There is a presumption that a person of my gender can run the country (though there is uncertainty about whether a person of my race can run the country).

31. White men don't have to worry about whether their gender will interfere with their ability effectively to bargain for a house, car, etc.

32. If I kiss someone on a first date, I do not have to worry about whether I have provided that person with a defense to rape.

33. Men I know do not consistently address me by pet names such as "baby" or "sweetheart," nor do strangers employ such terms to refer to or greet me.

34. I do not have to worry about resisting chivalry—refusing to go through the door first, paying for myself, etc. in order to maintain my independence.

35. I do not have to think about the "female gaze" (though I do have to think about the racial gaze).

36. I do not have to worry about being heckled or harassed by strangers because of my gender (though I do have to worry about "drive by" racial harassment).

37. I do not have to worry about leaving particular events early such as a sporting event—to avoid a ridiculous wait at the bathroom.

38. I do not have to worry about varicose veins, spinal malalignment, or disk injury from wearing high heels.

39. To the extent that I dry-clean my clothes, I do not have to worry about the gender surcharge.

40. Every month is (White) Men's History Month.

This list does not reflect the male privileges of all men. It is both under and over inclusive. Class, race, and sexual orientation impact male identities, shaping the various dimensions of male privilege. For example, the list does not include as a privilege the fact that men are automatically perceived as authority figures. While this may be true of white men, it has not been my experience as a black man. Moreover, my list clearly reveals my class privilege. My relationship to patriarchy is thus not the same as that of a working-class black male. In constructing a list of male privilege, then, one has to be careful not to universalize manhood, not to present it as a "cohesive identity"[25] in ways that deny, obscure, or threaten the recognition of male multiplicity.

However, even taking male multiplicity into account, the preceding list of male advantages does not go far enough. The foregoing items do not directly address what one might call "male patriarchal agency"—the extent to which men make choices that entrench men's advantages and women's disadvantages. Some of the privileges I have identified are the products of the cumulative choices that men make every day in their personal and professional lives. The identification of privileges, then, is not enough. Resistance is also necessary, an issue I engage in the conclusion to this essay.

HETEROSEXUAL PRIVILEGES

Like maleness, heterosexuality should be critically examined. Like maleness, heterosexuality operates as an identity norm, the "what is" or "what is supposed to be" of sexuality. This is illustrated, for example, by the nature versus nurture debate. The question about the cause of sexuality is almost always formulated in terms of whether homosexuality is or is not biologically determined rather than whether sexual orientation, which includes heterosexuality, is or is not biologically determined. Scientists are searching for a gay, not a heterosexual or sexual orientation, gene. Like female identity, then, homosexuality signifies "difference"—more specifically, sexual identity distinctiveness. The normativity of heterosexuality requires that homosexuality be specified, pointed out. Heterosexuality is always already presumed.

Heterosexuals should challenge the normativity and normalization of heterosexuality. They should challenge the heterosexual presumption. But heterosexuals might be reluctant to do so to the extent that they perceive such challenges to call into question their (hetero)sexual orientation. As Lee Edelman observes in a related context, there "is a deeply rooted concern on the part of ... heterosexual males about the possible meanings of [men subverting gender roles]."[26] According to Edelman, heterosexual men consider certain gender role inversions to be potentially dangerous because they portend not only a "[male] feminization that would destabilize or question gender" but also a "feminization that would challenge one's (hetero) sexuality."[27] Edelman's observations suggest that straight men may want to preserve what I am calling the "heterosexual presumption." Their investment in this presumption is less a function of what heterosexuality signifies in a positive sense and more a function of what it signifies in the negative—*not* being homosexual.

And there are racial dimensions to male investment in heterosexuality. For example, straight black male strategies to avoid homosexual suspicion could relate to the racial aspects of male privileges: heterosexual privilege is one of the few privileges that some black men have. These black men may

want to take comfort in the fact that whatever else is going on in their lives, they are not, finally, "sissies," "punks," "faggots." By this I do not mean to suggest that black male heterosexuality has the normative standing of white male heterosexuality. It does not. Straight black men continue to be perceived as heterosexually deviant (overly sexual; potential rapists) and heterosexually irresponsible (jobless fathers of children out of wedlock). Still, black male heterosexuality is closer to white male heterosexual normalcy and normativity than is black gay sexuality. Consequently, some straight (or closeted) black men will want to avoid the "black gay [male] ... triple negation" to which Marlon Riggs refers in the following quote: "Because of my sexuality I cannot be Black. A strong, proud, 'Afrocentric' black man is resolutely heterosexual, not even bisexual. ... Hence I remain a sissy, punk, faggot. I cannot be a black gay man because, by the tenets of black macho, a black gay man is a triple negation."[28]

Assuming away the heterosexual presumption problem, assuming, in other words, that heterosexuals are willing to destabilize heterosexual normalcy by exposing their heterosexual privileges—that is, "coming out" as heterosexuals—do we want them to do so? Do heterosexuals reinforce heterosexual normativity when they come out? At first blush, the answer seems obvious: no. The notion would be that the more heterosexuals explicitly invoke their heterosexuality and "come out" as heterosexuals, the less it operates as an unstated norm. Yet, there are reasons to be concerned about heterosexuals "coming out."

These reasons are unrelated to concerns about whether individual acts of heterosexual signification undermine political efforts to establish a privacy norm around (homo)sexuality. The privacy norm argument would go something like the following: to the extent that heterosexuals are "closeted" (i.e., private) about their (hetero)sexuality, they help to send a message that (homo) sexuality is a private matter and should be irrelevant to social and political decision-making.

I am not persuaded by this sexual identity privacy argument. It is analogous to race neutrality arguments: not invoking race, ignoring race, keeping race "private," helps to delegitimize the invidious employment of race as a relevant social category. However, keeping race private, removing race from public discourses, further entrenches racism. The social realities of race derive in part from the fact that race is always already public—a status marker of difference. Race continues to matter. Therefore, we ought to talk about it—and publicly. Avoiding public discussions about sexuality is not a sensible way to address the social realities of homophobia. Sexuality matters. Thus, we ought to have public discussions about why and how it matters. We have to deal publicly with sexuality before we can get beyond it.

My concerns about heterosexuals "coming out" relate to the social meaning of that act. Individual acts of heterosexual signification contribute to the growing tendency on the part of people who are not gay or lesbian to employ the term "coming out" to reveal some usually uncontroversial or safe aspect of their personhood. Nowadays, people are "coming out" as chocolate addicts, as yuppies, as soap opera viewers, and even as Trekkies. Sometimes the "outing" is more political: "I 'out' myself as a conservative," I heard someone say recently. This appropriation and redeployment of the term is problematic to the extent that it obscures the economic, psychological, and physical harms that potentially attend the gay and lesbian coming out (or outing) process. Although context would clearly matter, there is usually little, if any, vulnerability to "coming out" as a conservative, as a yuppie, as a Trekkie, etc. Nor is there usually any vulnerability to "coming out" as a heterosexual. The assertion of heterosexuality, without something more, merely reauthenticates heterosexual normalcy.[29]

Yet, more and more heterosexuals are "coming out," and often with good intentions. This "coming out" is performed explicitly and implicitly—affirmatively and by negation. Consider, for example, the way Houston Baker comes out in a panel discussion about gender, sexuality, and black images: "I am not gay, but I have many gay friends."[30] When asked about his decision to reveal his sexual identity in the negative (Baker did not say, "'I am a heterosexual,' but 'I am not gay'"), Baker responds that in thinking about our identities, "You decide what you are not, rather than leaping out of the womb saying, 'I am this.' "[31]

The questions about whether Baker should have "come out" as a heterosexual in the affirmative or the negative obscures the fact that it is the "coming out" itself that is potentially problematic. As Bruce Ryder points out, "heterosexual men taking gay or lesbian positions must continually deal with the question of whether or not to reveal their heterosexuality." On the one hand, self-identifying as a heterosexual is a way to position oneself within a discourse so as not to create the (mis)impression of gay authenticity. Moreover, revealing one's heterosexuality can help to convey the idea that "heterosexism should be as much an issue for straight people as racism should be for white people."[32] On the other hand, "coming out" as a heterosexual can be a heteronormative move to avoid gay and lesbian stigmatization. It can function not simply as a denial of same sex desire but to preempt the attribution of certain stereotypes to one's sexual identity. The assertion of heterosexuality, stated differently, is (functionally, if not intentionally) both an affirmative and a negative assertion about sexual preferences ("I sleep with persons of the opposite, not the same, sex") and about the normalcy of one's sexual relationships ("therefore I am normal, not abnormal").

Keith Boykin, former director of the Black Gay and Lesbian Leadership Forum, maintains that "heterosexual sexual orientation has become so ingrained in our social custom, so destigmatized of our fears about sex, that we often fail to make any connection between heterosexuality and sex."[33] Boykin is only half right. The socially constructed normalcy of heterosexuality is not due solely to the desexualization of heterosexuality in mainstream political and popular culture. It is due also to the sexualization of heterosexuality as normative and to the gender-norm presumptions about heterosexuality—that it is the normal way sexually to express one's gender.[34]

Moreover, it is not simply that homosexuality is sexed that motivates or stimulates homophobic fears about gay and lesbian relationships. These fears also relate to the fact that homosexuality is stigmatized and is perceived to be an abnormal way sexually to express one's gender.[35] The disparate social meanings that attach to gay and lesbian identities on the one hand and straight identities on the other make individual acts of heterosexual signification a cause for concern.

Recently, I participated in a workshop where one of the presenters "came out" as a heterosexual in the context of giving his talk. This sexual identity disclosure engendered a certain amount of whispering in the back row. Up until that moment, I think many people had assumed the presenter was gay. After all, he was sitting on a panel discussing sexual orientation and had participated in the Gay and Lesbian section of the American Association of Law Schools. There were three other heterosexuals on the panel, but everyone knew they were not gay because everyone *knew* them; they had all been in teaching for a while, two were very senior, and everyone knew of their spouses or partners. Everyone also knew that there was a lesbian on the panel. She, too, had been in teaching for some time and had been out for many years. Apparently, few of the workshop participants knew very much about the presenter who "came out." Because "there is a

widespread assumption in both gay and straight communities that any man who says something supportive about issues of concern to lesbian or gay communities must be gay himself,"[36] there was, at the very least, a question about his sexuality. Whatever his intentions were for "coming out," whatever his motivations, his assertion of heterosexuality removed the question.

And it is the politics behind the removal of the question—the politics of sexual identity signification—that we should be concerned about. Is it an act of resistance or does it reflect an acquiescence to existing sexual identity social meanings? Consider, for example, the television situation comedy *Spin City*, in which Michael Boatman played the role of Carter Heywood, an openly gay black male character. Boatman is clearly very comfortable with the role and is "believably gay"—perhaps, for some, "too believably gay." Thus, in an article in *Essence* about Boatman we learn rather quickly that Boatman is not in fact a gay man—he just plays one on television. We learn, too, that it was not Heywood's sexuality that attracted Boatman to the role (he had not set out to play a gay man), but rather Heywood's career. The relevant text reads: "It was Heywood's job description (a civil rights attorney who joins the mayor's office) rather than his sexuality that attracted the 32-year-old actor to the groundbreaking sitcom. 'We've been exposed to the stereotype of swishy gay men,' explains the *happily married* acting veteran."[37] The text thus removes the question about Boatman's (homo)sexuality.

I became sensitized to the politics of heterosexuals "coming out" in the context of reading about James Baldwin. Try to find a piece written about Baldwin and count the number of lines before the author comes out as heterosexual. Usually, it is not more than a couple of paragraphs, so the game ends fast. The following introduction from a 1994 essay about Baldwin is one example of what I am talking about: "The last time I saw James Baldwin was late autumn of 1985, when my wife and I attended a sumptuous book party."[38] In this case, the game ends immediately. Independent of any question of intentionality on the author's part, the mention of the wife functions as an identity signifier to subtextually "out" his heterosexuality. We *read* "wife," we *think* heterosexual. My point here is not to suggest that the essay's overall tone is heterosexually defensive; I simply find it suspicious when heterosexuals speak of their spouses so quickly (in this case the very first sentence of the essay) when a subject (a topic or a personality—here, James Baldwin) implicates homosexuality.

There is no point wondering what the author was "doing" with Baldwin in Paris. The game is over. The possibility of a gay sub textual reading of the text vis-á-vis the author's relationship with Baldwin and/or the author's sexual identity is rendered untenable by the rhetorical deployment of the "wife." Her presence in the text operates not only to signify and authenticate the author's heterosexual subject position but also to signify and functionally (if not intentionally) stigmatize Baldwin's gay subject position. The author engages in what I call "the politics of the 3Ds"—disassociation, disidentification, and differentiation. The author is "different" from Baldwin (the author sleeps with women), and this difference, based as it is on sexual identity, compels the author to disassociate himself from and disidentify with that which makes Baldwin "different" (Baldwin sleeps with men).

Heterosexual significations need not always reflect the politics of the 3DS. In other words, the possibility exists for heterosexuals to point out their heterosexuality without reauthenticating heterosexuality. Consider, for example, the heterosexual privilege list that I give below. While each item on the list explicitly names—outs—heterosexuality, in none of the items does heterosexuality remain unproblematically normative.

As a prelude to the list, I should be clear that the list is incomplete. Nor do the privileges reflected in it represent the experiences of all heterosexuals. As Bruce Ryder observes: "Male heterosexual privilege has different effects on men of, for example, different races and classes. ... In our society, the dominant or 'hegemonic' form of masculinity to which other masculinities are subordinated is white, middleclass, and heterosexual. This means that the heterosexual privilege of, say, straight black men takes a very different shape in their lives than it does for straight white men."[39] My goal in presenting this list, then, is not to represent every heterosexual man. Instead, the purpose is to intervene in the normalization of heterosexual privileges. With this intervention, I hope to challenge the pervasive tendency of heterosexuals to see homophobia as something that puts others at a disadvantage and not something that actually advantages them.

Heterosexual Privileges: A List

1. Whether on television or in the movies, (white) heterosexuality is always affirmed as healthy and/or normal (black heterosexuality and family arrangements are still, to some degree, perceived to be deviant).
2. Without making a special effort, heterosexuals are surrounded by other heterosexuals every day.
3. A husband and wife can comfortably express affection in any social setting, even a predominantly gay one.
4. The children of a heterosexual couple will not have to explain why their parents have different genders—that is, why they have a mummy and a daddy.
5. (White) Heterosexuals are not blamed for creating and spreading the AIDS virus (though Africans—as a collective group—are blamed).

6. Heterosexuals do not have to worry about people trying to "cure" their sexual orientation (though black people have to worry about people trying to "cure" black "racial pathologies").

7. Black heterosexual males did not have to worry about whether they would be accepted at the Million Man March.

8. Rarely, if ever, will a doctor, on learning that her patient is heterosexual, inquire as to whether the patient has ever taken an AIDS test and if so, how recently.

9. Medical service will never be denied to heterosexuals because they are heterosexuals (though medical services may not be recommended to black people because they are black).

10. Friends of heterosexuals generally do not refer to heterosexuals as their "straight friends" (though nonblack people often to refer to black people as their "black friends").

11. A heterosexual couple can enter a restaurant on their anniversary and be fairly confident that staff and fellow diners will warmly congratulate them if an announcement is made (though the extent of the congratulation and the nature of the welcome might depend on the racial identities of the couple).

12. White heterosexuals do not have to worry about whether a fictional film villain who is heterosexual will reflect negatively on their heterosexuality (though blacks may always have to worry about their racial representation in films).

13. Heterosexuals are entitled to legal recognition of their marriages throughout the United States and the world.

14. Within the black community, black male heterosexuality does not engender comments like "what a waste," "there goes another good black man," or "if they're not in jail, they're faggots."

15. Heterosexuals can take jobs with most companies without worrying about whether their spouses will be included in the benefits package.

16. Child molestation by heterosexuals does not confirm the deviance of heterosexuality (though if the alleged molester is black, the alleged molestation becomes evidence of the deviance of black [hetero] sexuality).

17. Black rap artists do not make songs suggesting that heterosexuals should be shot or beaten up because they are heterosexuals.

18. Black male heterosexuality does not undermine a black heterosexual male's ability to be a role model for black boys.

19. Heterosexuals can join the military without concealing their sexual identity.

20. Children will be taught in school, explicitly or implicitly, about the naturalness of heterosexuality (they will also be taught to internalize the notion of white normativity).

21. Conversations on black liberation will always include concerns about heterosexual men.

22. Heterosexuals can adopt children without being perceived as selfish and without anyone questioning their motives.

23. Heterosexuals are not denied custody or visitation rights of their children because they are heterosexuals.

24. Heterosexual men are welcomed as leaders of Boy Scout troops.

25. Heterosexuals can visit their parents and family as who they are, and take their spouses, partners, or dates with them to family functions.

26. Heterosexuals can talk matter-of-factly about their relationships with their partners without people commenting that they are "flaunting" their sexuality.

27. A black heterosexual couple would be welcomed as members of any black church.

28. Heterosexual couples do not have to worry about whether kissing each other in public or holding hands in public will render them vulnerable to violence.

29. Heterosexuals do not have to struggle with "coming out" or worry about being "outed."

30. The parents of heterosexuals do not love them "in spite of" their sexual orientation, and parents do not blame themselves for their children's heterosexuality.

31. Heterosexuality is affirmed in most religious traditions.

32. Heterosexuals can introduce their spouses to colleagues, and not worry about whether the decision will have a detrimental impact on their careers.

33. A black heterosexual male does not have to choose between being black and being heterosexual.

34. Heterosexuals can prominently display their spouses' photographs at work without causing office gossip or hostility.

35. (White) heterosexuals do not have to worry about "positively" representing heterosexuality.

36. Few will take pity on a heterosexual on hearing that she is straight, or feel the need to say, "That's okay" (though it is not uncommon for a black person to hear, "It's okay that you're black" or "We don't care that you're black" or "When we look at you, we don't see a black person").

37. (Male) heterosexuality is not considered to be symptomatic of the "pathology" of the black family.

38. Heterosexuality is never mistaken as the only aspect of one's lifestyle, but is perceived instead as merely one more component of one's personal identity.

39. (White) heterosexuals do not have to worry over the impact their sexuality will have personally on their children's lives, particularly as it relates to their social lives (though black families of all identity configurations do have to worry about how race and racism will affect their children's well-being).

40. Heterosexuals do not have to worry about being "bashed" after leaving a social event with other heterosexuals (though black people of all sexual orientations do have to worry about being "racially bashed" on any given day).

41. Every day is (white) "Heterosexual Pride Day."

CONCLUSION: RESISTING PRIVILEGES

I have argued that one of the ways to contest gender and sexual orientation hierarchy is for heterosexual men to detail their social experiences on the privileged side of gender and sexual orientation. In advancing this argument, I do not mean to suggest that the role of these men is to legitimize "untrustworthy" and "self-interested" victim-centered accounts of discrimination. There is a tendency on the part of dominant groups (e.g., males and heterosexuals) to discount the experiences of subordinate groups (e.g., straight women, lesbians, and gays) unless those experiences are authenticated or legitimized by a member of the dominant group. For example, it is one thing for me, a black man, to say I experienced discrimination in a particular social setting; it is quite another for my white male colleague to say he witnessed that discrimination. My telling of the story is suspect because I am black (racially interested). My white colleague's telling of the story is not suspect because he is white (racially disinterested). The racial transparency of whiteness—its "perspectivelessness"[40]—renders my colleague's account "objective."[41]

The problem of racial status (in)credibility is quite real. Consider how Cornel West alludes to it in the following anecdote about his inability to get a cab in New York City:

> After the ninth taxi refused me, my blood began to boil. The tenth taxi refused me and stopped for a kind, well-dressed, smiling female fellow citizen of European descent. As she stepped in the cab, she said, "This is really ridiculous, is it not?"
>
> Ugly racial memories of the past flashed through my mind. Years ago, while driving from New York to teach at Williams College, I was stopped on fake charges of trafficking cocaine. When I told the police officer I was a professor of religion, he replied, "Yeh, and I'm the Flying Nun. Let's go, nigger!" I was stopped three times in my first ten days in Princeton for driving too slowly on a residential street with a speed limit of twenty-five miles per hour. ... Needless to say, these incidents are dwarfed by those like Rodney King's beating. ... Yet the memories cut like a merciless knife at my soul as I waited on that godforsaken corner. Finally I decided to take the subway. I walked three long avenues, arrived late, and had to catch my moral breath as I approached [my appointment with] the white male photographer and white female cover designer. I chose not to dwell on this everyday experience of black New Yorkers. And we had a good time talking, posing, and taking pictures.[42]

Here West is connecting two problematic episodes. His racial representations of these episodes reflect concerns about his racial credibility. His narrative suggests that he is worried about how his readers will read him (is he a trustworthy witness?) and thus *read* the events he describes (do they reflect racism?). West understands that he is (or, rather, will be constructed as) an unreliable witness to his own racial victimization. That is, he is fully aware that as a black man his racial story (like his racial identity) is suspect. Thus, he rhetorically deploys a "disinterested" witness to legitimize and authenticate his racial narrative—the woman "of European descent." She can be trusted. She is white and respectable—"well-dressed" and "smiling." To the extent that she confirms West's racial interpretation of the cab story—"This is really ridiculous, is it not?"—the notion is forwarded that West is not racially imagining things; in fact, his race is interfering with his ability to get a cab. The employment of whiteness to racially authenticate West's first story renders West's second story (in which West is called a "nigger") more believable.[43]

Men invested in exposing their privileges should be careful not to replicate the kind of authentication strategy reflected in West's anecdote. They should not perform the legitimation function that the white woman's challenge to racism performs in West's text. To the extent that male heterosexuals participate in discourses on gender and sexuality, they should not create the (mis)impression that, because they do not experience the subordinating effects of patriarchy and heterosexism, their critiques of patriarchy and/or heterosexism are more valid and less suspect than the critiques propounded by lesbians, straight women, and gay men.

Assuming that the identification/listing of privileges methodology I have described avoids the problem of authentication, one still might wonder whether the project is sufficiently radical to "dismantle gender and sexual orientation hierarchies." Certainly the lists I have presented do not go far enough. They represent the very early stages in a more complicated process to end gender and sexual orientation discrimination.

The lists, nevertheless, are politically valuable.[44] For one thing, the items on the lists reveal that men enforce and maintain their gender privileges through the personal actions they take and do not take every day. For another, to the extent that the lists focus our attention on privileges, they invite men to think about the extent to which they are unjustly enriched because of certain aspects of their identities.

To be sure, men will not be eager to learn or quick to accept the notion that they are unjustly enriched. The realization and acknowledgment of unjust enrichment carries with it the possibility of disgorgement. However, to the extent that men actually come to see their privileges as forms of unjust enrichment (and the lists help men do precisely that), they are more likely to take notice of the ways in which unjust enrichment operates systemically.

None of this is to say that awareness and acknowledgement of privilege is enough. Resistance is needed as well. But how does one resist? And what counts as resistance? With respect to marriage, for example, does resistance to heterosexual privilege require heterosexuals to refrain from getting married and/or attending weddings? It might mean both of those things. At the very least, resistance to identity privilege would seem to require "critical acquiescence": criticizing, if not rejecting, aspects of our life that are directly linked to our privilege. A heterosexual who gets married and/or attends weddings but who also openly challenges the idea that marriage is a heterosexual entitlement is engaging in critical acquiescence.

In the end, critical acquiescence might not go far enough. It might even be a cop out. Still, it is a useful and politically manageable place to begin.

NOTES

1. See *Washington v. Davis,* 426 U.S. 229, 246–48 (1976) (requiring a showing of discriminatory intent to establish an equal protection claim). For two classic critiques of the standard, see Alan D. Freeman, "Legitimizing Racial Discrimination through Antidiscrimination Law: A Critical Review of Supreme Court Doctrine," *Minnesota Law Review* 62 (1978): 1049; and Charles R. Lawrence III, "The Id, the Ego, and Equal Protection: Reckoning with Unconscious Racism," *Stanford Law Review* 39 (1987): 317.

2. See Stephanie Wildman, *Privilege Revealed: How Invisible Preference Undermines America* (New York: New York University Press, 1996).

3. See Karen D. Pyke, "Class-Based Masculinities: The Interdependence of Gender, Class, and Interpersonal Power," *Gender and Society* 10 (1996): 527 ("Conventional theoretical perspectives on power … view micro level power practices as simply derivative of macro-structural inequalities and overlook how power in day-to-day interactions shapes broader structures of inequality").

4. See Wildman, *Privilege Revealed.*

5. See Peggy McIntosh, "White Privilege and Male Privilege: A Personal Account of Coming to See Correspondences through Work in Women's Studies," in *Power, Privilege and Law: A Civil Rights Reader,* ed. Leslie Bender and Daar Braveman (St. Paul, Minn.: West Publishing, 1995), 22.

6. See Judith Butler, *Gender Trouble: Feminism and the Subversion of Identity* (New York: Routledge, 1990): 136–39 (describing the performative aspect of gender); see also Devon W. Carbado and Mitu Gulati, "Working Identity," *Cornell Law Review* 85 (2000): 1259 (discussing

identity performance as a function of a strategic response to specific institutional norms).

7. See Judith Butler, "Performative Acts and Gender Constitution: An Essay in Phenomenology and Feminist Theory," *Theater Journal* 40 (1988): 519,523 ("The body becomes its gender through a series of acts which are renewed, revised and consolidated through time"). But see Bruce Wilshire, *Role Playing and Identity: The Limits of Theatre as Metaphor* (Bloomington: Indiana University Press, 1982) (arguing that gender is not a performance).

8. For a discussion of the concept of false necessity in legal theory, see Roberto M. Unger, *False Necessity: Anti-Necessitarian Social Theory in the Service of Radical Democracy* (New York: Cambridge University Press, 1987).

9. See Carbado and Gulati, "Working Identity" (arguing that people work their identities to avoid discrimination).

10. See Brent Staples, "Parallel Time," in *Brotherman: The Odyssey of Black Men in America,* ed. Herb Boyd and Robert L. Allen (New York: One World, 1995) (discussing the author's attempts to appear harmless while walking at night by whistling Vivaldi).

11. See Carbado and Gulati, "Working Identity" (discussing the costs and burdens of working one's identity).

12. Ibid, (arguing that working one's identity is work); see also Elizabeth V. Spelman, "'Race' and the Labor of Identity," in *Racism and Philosophy,* ed. Susan E. Babbitt and Sue Campbell (Ithaca: Cornell University Press, 1999), 202–15.

13. See Barbara Flagg," Was Blind, But Now I See: White Race Consciousness and the Requirement Of Discriminatory Intent," *Michigan Law Review* 91 (1994): 953,963; McIntosh, "White Privilege and Male Privilege."

14. Flagg, "Was Blind, But Now I See," 963, 957.

15. Ibid., 970–71.

16. Ibid., 957.

17. McIntosh, "White Privilege and Male Privilege," 23.

18. See ibid., 25–26. See also bell hooks, *Feminist Theory: From Margin to Center* (Boston: South End Press, 1984), 54–55 (interrogating whiteness).

19. McIntosh, "White Privilege and Male Privilege," 6, 23.

20. Of course, not all men are empowered by patriarchy in the same way. Race, class, and sexual orientation shape the nature of men's relationships to patriarchal privilege. Perhaps it is more accurate to say, then, that patriarchy gives to (some) men (more than others) what it takes away from (some) women (more than others); the disempowerment of (some) women (more than others) is achieved through the empowerment of (some) men (more than others). See Pyke, "Class-Based Masculinities," 527, 531 ("The effects of gender on interpersonal power relations are not one-dimensional. Hierarchies of social class, race, and sexuality provide additional layers of complication. They form the structural and cultural contexts in which gender is enacted in everyday life, thereby fragmenting gender into multiple masculinities and femininities").

21. See Simone Beauvoir, *The Second Sex* (New York: Knopf, 1957 [1949]).

22. Here, too, my comments about race, class, and sexual orientation pertain.

23. Andrea Dworkin and Catharine Mackinnon, *Pornography and Civil Rights: A New Day for Women's Equality* (Minneapolis: Organizing against Pornography, 1988), 22–23,

24. McIntosh, "White Privilege and Male Privilege," 23.

25. See, e.g., Robert Vorlicky, "(In)visible Alliances: Conflicting 'Chronicles' of

Feminism," in *Engendering Men: The Question of Male Feminist Criticism,* ed. Joseph A. Boone and Michael Cadden (New York: Routledge, 1990), 275–76 (discussing universal manhood in the context of women's outrage toward men for the gang rape of a New York jogger).

26. Lee Edelman, "Redeeming the Phallus: Wallace Stevens, Frank Lentricchia, and the Politics of (Hetero)sexuality," in *Engendering Men: The Question of Male Feminist Criticism,* ed. Joseph A. Boone and Michael Cadden (New York: Routledge, 1990), 50.

27. Ibid.

28. Marlon T. Riggs, "Black Macho Revisited: Reflections of a SNAP! Queen," in *Black Men on Race, Gender, and Sexuality: A Critical Reader,* ed. Devon W. Carbado (New York: New York University Press, 1999), 307.

29. In some sense, heterosexuals are out all the time, kissing comfortably in public, sharing wedding pictures at work, announcing anniversaries, etc. These are not the practices I am referring to when I suggest that perhaps heterosexuals should develop a practice of "coming out." For none of the foregoing heterosexual significations challenge the socially constructed normalcy of heterosexuality. Further along in this essay, I provide an indication of how heterosexuals *might be* able to assert their heterosexuality without further entrenching heterosexual normalcy.

30. Houston A. Baker Jr., "'You Cain't Trus' It': Experts Witnessing in the Case of Rap," in *Black Popular Culture,* ed. Gina Dent (Seattle: Bay Press, 1992), 132.

31. Ibid.

32. Bruce Ryder, "Straight Talk: Male Heterosexual Privilege," *Queen's Law Journal* 16 (1991): 303.

33. Keith Boykin, *One More River to Cross: Black and Gay in America* (New York: Doubleday, 1997).

34. See Francisco Valdes, "Queers, Sissies, Dykes, and Tomboys: Deconstructing the Conflation of 'Sex,' 'Gender,' and 'Sexual Orientation' in Euro-American Law and Society," *California Law Review* 83 (1995): 1.

35. See ibid. See also Sylvia A. Law, "Homosexuality and the Social Meaning of Gender," *Wisconsin Law Review* (1998): 187 ("Disapprobation of homosexual behavior is a reaction to the violation of gender norms, rather than simply scorn for the violation of norms of sexual behaviors."); and Elvia R. Arriola, "Gendered Inequality: Lesbians, Gays, and Feminist Legal Theory," *Berkeley Women's Law Journal* 9 (1994): 103, up. (observing that gay identities are often theoretically connected to gender).

36. Ryder, "Straight Talk: Male Heterosexual Privilege," 303.

37. Michael Boatman, "Acting 'Out'" *Essence,* September 1997, 78 (emphasis added).

38. Leon Forrest, "Evidences of Jimmy Baldwin," in *Relocations of the Spirit,* ed. Leon Forrest (Emeryville, Calif: Asphodel Press/Moyer Bell, 1994), 267.

39. Ryder, "Straight Talk: Male Heterosexual Privilege," 292.

40. See Kimberlé Williams Crenshaw, "Foreword: Toward a Race-Conscious Pedagogy in Legal Education," *Southern California Review of Law and Women's Studies* 4 (fall 1994): 33, 35 (employing the term "perspectivelessness" to describe the ostensibly race-neutral way in which law is taught).

41. Peter Halewood comments on this problem from a white heterosexual male perspective: "Because I am white and male, the Article is more likely to be accepted (or ignored) by colleagues as a scholarly application of scholarly ideas than it would be if written by a black female professor. A black female author of this piece would probably encounter more skepticism

about the method, claims, and motives of the article and would probably be viewed, at least by some, as being oversensitive and making trouble for her mostly white and male colleagues" (Halewood, "White Men Can't Jump: Critical Epistemologies, Embodiment, and the Praxis of Legal Scholarship," *Yale Journal of Law and Feminism* 7 [1995]: 1,6 n.14). To avoid contributing to this authentication of whiteness and delegitimation of blackness, Halewood argues that "rather than approaching the subject of law and subordination as neutral, theoretical experts or as political vanguardists, white male legal academics must recognize the legitimacy—even the superiority—of certain 'outsider' perspectives on these issues, and assume the role of secondary contributors to the development of scholarship in these areas" (7).

42. Cornel West, *Race Matters* (Boston: Beacon, 1994), xv–xvi.

43. For a very thoughtful discussion of the role of race in Cornel West's scholarship and especially in his popular book, *Race Matters*, see Dwight A. McBride, "Trans-disciplinary Intellectual Practice: Cornel West and the Rhetoric of Race Transcending," *Harvard BlackLetter Journal* 11 (1994): 157–82.

44. See McIntosh, "White Privilege and Male Privilege."

4

Welcome to Your Gender Workbook

By Kate Bornstein

From the moment we take our first breath (and sometimes even before that, what with sonic imaging technology), the cry "It's a boy" or "It's a girl" ushers us into this world. As we grow into adulthood, everything about us grows and matures as *we* grow and mature. Everything except gender, that is. We're supposed to believe that our gender stays exactly the same as the day we were born. Our genders never shift, we're told. The genders we're assigned at birth lock us onto a course through which we'll be expected to become whole, well-rounded, creative, loving people—*but only as men or as women.* From where I stand, that's like taking a field of racehorses, hobbling the front legs of half of them and the rear legs of the other half, and expecting them to run a decent race: it doesn't work. Gender, this thing we're all seemingly born with, is a major restraint to self-expression.

That doesn't make sense to me. Why should we be born with such a hobble? Does that make sense to you? Well, this is a workbook about questioning things like that, so let's get right to work and start questioning things, shall we?

DISCOVERING YOUR GENDER APTITUDE

Would you like to know more about your own gender and how it's been affecting your life? Just how freewheeling and open are you when it comes to the subjects of gender and sexuality? Do you have much flexibility when it comes to grasping the mechanics of *changing* genders? How about the people who are questioning their own genders these days? Are they a little crazy for doing that? Here's a series of questions that will give you a good idea of exactly where you stand when it comes to gender.

This isn't a quiz or an exam to see how good you are at this. There are no right or wrong answers. Just take your time and check off the answers that *most nearly match* the way you feel about each question. When you're done, you'll know your GA–your Gender Aptitude–and from there, we'll go on a little journey together through previously unexplored and underexplored areas of gender, identity, sexuality, and power. Now, doesn't that sound exciting? I should think so! All right, let's begin.

YOUR GENDER APTITUDE, SECTION I: ASSUMPTIONS

Which of the following most accurately describes you?

> __A. I'm a real man.
> __B. I'm a real woman.
> __C. I'm not a real man or a real woman, but I'd like to be.
> __D. None of the above. I'm something else entirely.

Give yourself 5 points if you checked A, 3 paints if your checked B, 1 point for C, and no points for D.

Write your score for this section here.

SO ... ARE YOU A REAL MAN? A REAL WOMAN?

I'm not attempting to look like a man, but there are a whole lot of the straight folks who mistake me for one. It's real hard being a butch little kid, and being beat by boys who thought I was a boy wearing girls clothes. Sometimes it's hard being a grown up and being told you're going to the wrong washroom, or get called sir by a whole lot of folks. When I was 9 months pregnant, and in maternity clothes, I was still called sir. I sure don't feel like a man.

-Tammy Potter

At first glance, that seems to be a simple pair of questions. Most people when asked those questions would smile and say, "Of course I'm a real man," or ''Of course I'm a real woman." It's not something most of us question. The difficult part comes when we're asked to remember the times we've been made to feel we're not quite as manly or as womanly as we could be or should be. Maybe it was the day we found ourselves deeply afraid or weeping uncontrollably, and we (or someone else) questioned how much of a man we really are. Maybe we've not been able to get pregnant, or maybe we haven't wanted to, and we (or someone else) questioned how much of a woman we really are. There are so many qualifications for those categories, aren't there? We make jokes like "Real men don't eat quiche," or admonitions like "A real woman would be married by now." Not that anyone has ever written *all* these qualifications down, mind you. People have tried, but there's been too much disagreement about what constitutes a "real man," and what constitutes a "real woman" for there to be one acceptable document containing the absolute definitions of either of those categories of identity. So by trial and error we learn the reality of our real manhood and real womanhood. We build our own definitions for these, and we're very pleased to know people who agree with our definitions. When enough people agree with us, we begin to assume it's *natural*.

Well, here's a question: If gender is so natural, then why hasn't it been written down and codified? Most everything else that's considered "natural" has been codified. Why isn't there some agreed-upon manual we could hand our children and say, "Here, honey. This is what a real man is. Learn this well." Why do we mystify these categories to such a degree that we assume "everyone knows" what real men and real women are?

Let's keep looking at your Gender Aptitude when it comes to the subject of these categories called "real men" and "real women."

YOUR GENDER APTITUDE, SECTION II: PERCEPTIONS

1. ***Do you stand up to pee?***
   A. Yup, most of the time.

B. No, never.

C. Well, I've tried it a few times.

D. It all depends on the effect I want to create.

2. ***Have you ever worn the clothes of "the opposite sex?"***

A. Hey, give me a break. No way!

B. Yes, but when *I* wear them, they're for the *right* sex.

C. What sex in the world would be opposite of *me?*

D. Several of the above.

3. ***Do you shave?***

A. Yup. Except when I'm growing my beard or mustache.

B. Depends. I go back and forth on the hairy armpit thing.

C. Where?

D. Yes, but not myself.

4. ***When you go into a department store to buy yourself clothing, do you shop mostly in a department labeled for your assigned gender?***

A. Well, duh! Where else?

B. No, because sometimes the other departments have stuff that fits me better.

C. Yes, because it's very important to me to do that.

D. I will shop in *any* department for *anything* that's Fabulous.

5. ***Are there things you* can *do in the world because of your gender that others can't do because of theirs?***

A. Yes, but that's just the way the world is.

B. Yeah, but *they* get paid well for doing what *they* can do.

C. I used to think so.

D. Honey, I've never let a little thing like gender get in my way.

6. ***Are there things you* can't *do in the world because of your gender that others can?***

A. No. Well, maybe I can't have a baby, but who wants to? Ha ha ha!

B. Well, duh. Of course!

C. I used to think it was because of my gender, yeah.

D. Maybe a long time ago, back before I met the Scarecrow, the Tin Man, and the Lion.

7. ***When the store clerk asks, "How can I help you, sir," you***

A. Smile.

B. Wince.

C. Curse.

D. Curtsy.

8. ***When the store clerk looks up at you inquiringly and says, "Yes, ma'am?" you***

A. Wish you'd grown that mustache after all.

B. Smile.

C. Purr.

D. Brightly exclaim, "Gee I'm sorry … would you like to try for Door Number Three?"

9. ***Basic black looks best …***

A. On my new BMW.

B. With pearls.

C. With anything.

D. Well, dip me in honey and throw me to the Goth chicks.

10. ***Have you read the book*** Gender Outlaw ***by Kate Bornstein?***

A. Nope. Is it a Western?

B. I'd say what I really think about that book, but I'm nervous about how that might effect my aptitude score.

C. Yes, and I loved it!

D. I could've written it better.

Give yourself 5 points if you checked A, 3 points if your checked B, 1 point for C, and no points for D.

Write your score for this section here.

THE ELUSIVE "REAL ME"

I'm thinking we live in the latter days of what might as well be called the "Age of Identity." The part of ourselves we show to others might be called an identity. Ideally, our identities are an accurate reflection of who we feel we are. Some people give this identity a name; they call it "The Real Me."

There are books, television shows, college-level courses, tapes, videos, focus groups, cults, all promising that we can learn to be an identity called "the real me." Why, I'm wondering, would we need to learn to be that, unless there was so much pressure coming from the rest of the world, making us *not* be "the real me." There are obviously enough people in the world who think they're *not* being "the real me" to keep all these other people in business trying to teach them. People who recover from alcoholism become "the real me." Lesbians, gays, and bisexual people coming out of the closet and embracing their desires become "the real me." Men who learn to cry discover another kind of "real me." People born-again into anything from fundamentalism to feminism claim to have discovered "the real me." More to the point, some transsexual people believe when they've gone from one gender to another that they've arrived at "the real me." Well, what is that identity? And what's "the real me" got to do with being a "real man" or a "real woman?" And most importantly, does your gender (identity) match up with who you feel yourself to be? Do you think your gender is an accurate reflection of everything you are? Everything you could possibly be? Does your gender match up with the real you? Let's see.

YOUR GENDER APTITUDE, SECTION III: INTEGRITY

1. *Has someone else ever accused you of being not really a man, or not really a woman?*

A. No.
B. Yes.
C. No, but I've felt that myself.
D. Yes, and I've had to agree with them.

2. *You're in the middle of the sidewalk, in broad daylight. Your lover leans over and kisses you hard and long on the mouth. Do you*

A. Kiss back and lose yourself in the moment?
B. Start to panic about who might be watching and what might happen to you?
C. Thank heaven for Max Factor more-or-less permanent lipstick?
D. Offer to sell tickets to gawking passers-by?

3. *Has it ever happened that you've been in a group of people who are similarly gendered to you, and you find yourself behaving in a way that's gender inappropriate?*

A. No.
B. No, I'm very careful about that.
C. Yes.
D. Yes, it happens all the time.

4. *You receive an invitation to a concert. The top of the invitation reads, "All Genders Welcome." Do you …*

A. Wonder why they phrased it like that.
B. Get nervous about who or what might show up.
C. Feel defensive.
D. Feel included.

5. *Have you ever been mistaken for being a member of a gender other than that which you think you're presenting?*

A. No.
B. Yes.
C. Yes, but not as frequently as before.
D. I intentionally try to confuse people.

6. *Have you ever agonized over your appearance to the point of canceling a social obligation because you feel you don't look right or won't fit in?*

A. No.

B. Yes, I've agonized, but I haven't canceled.

C. It doesn't have to be some social obligation; sometimes it's just easier not to leave the house.

D. Yes.

7. ***Have you ever been discriminated against, harassed, or attacked because of your gender presentation***

A. No.

B. No, I've been careful.

C. Yes, and it happens to women every hour of the day.

D. Yes.

8. ***Is acceptance by or membership in some men's or women's organization important to you?***

A. Not really.

B. Yes.

C. Yes, but I don't hold out much hope for that.

D. No, we're starting our own.

9. ***Which of the following most nearly matches your definition for the word transgender?***

A. It's some disorder that results in men cutting off their penises.

B. Being born in the wrong body, or having the wrong sex for your gender.

C. Changing from one gender to another, or just looking like you've done that.

D. Transgressing gender, breaking the rules of gender in any way at all.

10. ***Which of these phrases describes you most accurately when it comes to rules about personal behavior and identity?***

A. I pretty much make up the rules to suit my needs, and I follow those rules as long as I'm getting something out of it.

B. I think many social and cultural rules governing individual behavior and identity are necessary.

C. I'm trying to figure out which rules to follow and which rules to ignore.

D. Rules? Honey, the Identity Police have arrested me so many times, I've got a cell with my name on it.

Give yourself 5 points for each A answer, 3 points for every B, 1 point for a C, and no points for any D answers.

Write your score for this section here.

WHY IT'S ME WHO GETS TO ASK THESE QUESTIONS

> I don't know who discovered water, but I'm pretty sure it wasn't a fish.
> —*posted on the Internet*

This is a book about gender, because gender is what I know inside and out. It's what I've been questioning and researching all my life because that seems to be the journey I was given to make this time around. I'm what's called a transsexual person. That means I was assigned one gender at birth, and I now live my life as something else. I was born male and raised as a boy. I went through both boyhood and adult manhood, went through a gender change, and "became a woman." A few years later, I stopped being a woman and settled into being neither. I wrote a book about gender-as-neither, and I travelled with several plays and performance pieces about gender-as-neither. On the personal side of things, my lesbian lover of over three years decided to become a man. We lived together for a few more years as a heterosexual couple, then we stopped being lovers. He found his gay male side, and I found my slave grrrl side. What a whacky world, huh? I can't think of a day in my life when I haven't thought about gender. I think what I've found is a pretty interesting hole in the theory that there's actually such a thing as a real man or a real woman. And that's what this workbook's about and why I got to write it.

But enough about me, let's get back to you.

AND JUST WHO DO YOU THINK YOU ARE, ANYWAY?

You're *not* the same person you were ten minutes ago.

None of us is.

Each of us makes dozens if not hundreds of minor decisions in the space of ten minutes. And unless we're truly hermits, each of us is subject to influences by and connections with the world around us that change the course of our lives. No, they're not dramatic changes, but they are changes nonetheless.

Maybe someone smiled at you on the street this morning and made you feel good. Maybe you heard something on the news just now that made you wonder how much say you have in our government. Perhaps it was a phone call from a long-lost friend. It could have been a bit of email, or some passage or question in this book, or a piece of poetry, or just a bird landing on your windowsill that made you change your mind about the state of your life. Interactions of most every type have a tendency to change us; that's what growth is all about. We're so used to these mini-changes that we give them no thought, but the fact is we're not the same people we used to be.

I've gone through some pretty dramatic changes. I've changed my gender, several times in fact. But I think the question we should be asking ourselves is: "Why is that

so dramatic?" I'm not saying it's not dramatic. I think it is. I'm just asking what is it that the culture taught me to make me think that changing gender is dramatic?

We change our attitudes, our careers, our relationships. Even our age changes minute by minute. We change our politics, our moods, and our sexual preferences. We change our outlook, we change our minds, we change our sympathies. Yet when someone changes hir gender, we put hir on some television talk show. Well, here's what I think: I think we all of us *do* change our genders. All the time. Maybe it's not as dramatic as some tabloid headline screaming "She Was A He!" But we do, each of us, change our genders. In response to each interaction we have with a new or different person, we subtly shift the *kind* of man or woman, boy or girl, or whatever gender we're being at the moment. We're usually not the same *kind* of man or woman with our lover as we are with our boss or a parent. When we're introduced for the first time to someone we find attractive, we shift into being a different *kind* of man or woman than we are with our childhood friends. We all change our genders. I'm just saying it's time we knew exactly what we are doing and why. So, let's get on with the next section of our Gender Aptitude questionnaire and see just how flexible your gender might be. Hang on, we're going to dig a bit deeper now.

YOUR GENDER APTITUDE, SECTION IV: FLEXIBILITY

1. *When the kind of person to whom you are normally attracted begins to flirt heavily with you, you*
   A. Envision the great sex you're going to have later tonight.
   B. Try to get to know this person a bit better.

C. Panic because it's been so long and you wonder if you know how to do it right any more.

D. Flirt right back, matching move for move.

2. ***When the kind of person that normally turns you off begins to flirt heavily with you, you***

    A. Hit the person.

    B. Leave.

    C. Tell them, "Honey, you flirt with this hand."

    D. See if there's anything about it you can enjoy as long as it's only flirting.

3. ***When was the last time you were aware of something about your gender that was holding you back in the world?***

    A. I can't recall a time like that.

    B. Do you want that in minutes or seconds?

    C. Do you mean the times I did something about it, or the times it overwhelmed me?

    D. It was just before I changed my gender the last time.

4. ***How many genders do you really think there are?***

    A. Two.

    B. Well, there are two sexes. Is that what you mean?

    C. I'm going to guess there are lots of genders and two sexes.

    D. When do you want me to stop counting?

5. ***Do you feel it's possible for someone to change hir gender?***

    A. No. And what does "hir" mean. Flake-o?

    B. I think people can try, but no. Not really, no.

    C. Yes, with proper supervision, surgery, and hormones. I think so.

    D. How many times?

6. ***What do you believe the essential sign of gender to be?***

    A. The presence or absence of a penis.

B. A combination of genitalia, secondary sex characteristics, hormones, and chromosomes.

C. It's an energy thing. People have male or female energy.

D. Whatever.

7. ***If someone tells you they're neither a man nor a woman, and you find out they mean it, you think to yourself***

    A. This person is either kidding or is really, really sick.

    B. The poor, brave dear!

    C. Whoa! What a trip!

    D. I found another one at last!

8. ***If you meet someone who you think is one gender, but you find out they used to be another gender, you think to yourself***

    A. Is this some costume party?

    B. The poor, brave dear!

    C. Wow, and I didn't even know!

    D. Yeah, yeah. But can you do a good Elvis?

9. ***If you see someone on the street whose gender is unclear to you, do you***

    A. Dismiss that person as a freak?

    B. Try to figure out if it's a man or a woman?

    C. Mentally give them a makeover so they can pass better as one or the other?

    D. Notice they're staring at you, trying to figure out what *you* are?

10. ***Is the male/female dichotomy something natural?***

    A. Well, duh. Of course.

    B. It's probably a combination of nature and nurture.

    C. Probably, but there are a lot of exceptions walking around!

    D. There's a male/female dichotomy? On what planet?

Give yourself 5 points for each A answer, 3 points for every B, 1 point for a C, and no points for any D answers.

Write your score for this section here.

A WORD ABOUT COMFORT

I want to say this pretty early on in the book: some of this exploration of gender might make you uncomfortable. That's what I heard from early readers. I'm sorry. I really am. It's an uncomfortable subject, I know. I've tried to be as compassionate as I can be about the discomfort this book is going to cause some people, but as hard as I try to make you comfortable, the real comforting is going to have to come from inside yourself. It's taken me a long time to learn that one.

I had very little compassion for the part of myself that couldn't live up to being either a real man or a real woman, and also little reason to be *willing* to be compassionate with myself. When I finally started to come to grips with this gender stuff of mine, I ran into the odd position of discovering people who were much more willing than I to simply let me experience my gender quandary.

A Catholic priest taught me the value of compassion for myself. I was in Alcoholics Anonymous at the time, still a guy and still afraid of dealing with my transgender stuff. I went on a men's retreat to a Catholic monastery. We did all the standard retreat-type workshops and meetings, but the last thing we each had to do was sit down with a priest and go over our "personal issues." The priest assigned to me was an older man; I'm guessing he was in his seventies, a real nice father-type guy. He asked me what the "big issue" in my life was, and I figured oh fuck it, I'd tell him. So for about a half an hour, I spilled out my transgender story. At the end of my

tale, this priest looked at me—maybe his eyebrows were a little further up on his forehead—and he said "Well, I'm certainly not qualified or experienced enough to give you any specific advice about a sex change, but I can tell you this: your comfort level is somewhere down around your ankles, and you need to do something about that." He went on to tell me that I should do at least three things a day to make myself more comfortable, and then he said, "Al, you need to learn to treat yourself like you would treat an honored guest in your house." That was about twelve years ago, and it's still some of the best advice I've ever received. Whenever I'm beating myself up about gender stuff or anything else, I can usually get back to the point of treating myself like an honored guest.

EXERCISE: Has there ever been a time in your life that you haven't been treated like a real man or a real woman? If so, did you give yourself any negative messages about that? If you did, write them down here.

I don't know about you, but I grew up with the idea that you simply do not write in books. Well, I wrote this book to be written in, okay? And don't worry ... there are no right or wrong answers to any of these questions and exercises, okay?

Now, what if a dear friend of yours were to come to your house. Ze sits down and tells you that ze is exploring hir gender identity with the idea of maybe changing genders, but ze tells you ze has reservations about doing it. Ze lists out all the reasons in the box you just filled in above. How would you counsel your dear friend?

Was there any difference between the way you counsel yourself and the way you would counsel your dear friend? Think you could treat yourself the way you treat a friend?

EXERCISE Do three simple things for yourself today to make yourself more comfortable. Anything at all that makes you comfortable, and doesn't place a lot of stress or guilt on yourself for doing it. Repeat this exercise daily for at least a week. At the end of the week, write down any changes you notice in the way that you feel about yourself.

If we don't show ourselves the same amount of compassion we show others, we'll eventually come to resent the compassion we have for others. I think there's little enough compassion in the world right now, so we need to grow our own to compensate for that.

All right, I'll be checking on your comfort level from time to time. But now that you've got the idea, let's get into some deeper questions so we might better assess your Gender Aptitude.

YOUR GENDER APTITUDE, SECTION V: LOVE AND SEX

1. ***Do you have a "type" of person you regularly fall for?***
   A. Definitely, yes.
   B. I try to keep my mind open about this sort of thing, but I usually fall for one type.
   C. I seem to fall for lots of "types" of people, but usually they're all the same gender.

D. What? You want to know if I fall for typists? What a silly question. I fall for people I can connect with and who connect with me.

2. ***If you fell in love with a heterosexual woman, you would be***
   A. Pleased as punch.
   B. Really confused.
   C. Nervous as hell.
   D. Curious, curious, curious.

3. ***If you fell in love with a heterosexual man, you would be***
   A. Reassuring yourself that the old Greeks had friendships like that.
   B. Pleased as punch.
   C. Nervous as hell.
   D. Curious, curious, curious.

4. ***If you fell in love with a lesbian woman, you would be***
   A. Apprehensive, but titillated.
   B. Nervous as hell,
   C. Pleased as punch.
   D. Curious, curious, curious.

5. ***If you fell in love with a gay man, you would be***
   A. Reassuring yourself that the old Greeks had friendships like that.
   B. Resigned to your fate.
   C. Pleased as punch.
   D. Curious, curious, curious.

6. ***If you fell in love with a woman who used to be a man, you would be***
   A. Concerned how well she would pass in public.
   B. Wondering why you couldn't have met her *before* her change.
   C. Nervous as hell.
   D. Curious, curious, curious.

7. ***If you fell in love with a man who used to be a woman, you would be***
   A. Convinced that he's really a woman and you're not really a faggot.

B. Really confused.

C. Nervous as hell.

D. Curious, curious, curious.

8. ***Who's ultimately responsible for birth control?***

   A. She is.

   B. He is.

   C. I am.

   D. Honey, I haven't had to worry about that one for *years!*

9. ***I like it …***

   A. On the bottom.

   B. On the top.

   C. In the middle.

   D. Yes I do!

10. ***Who's ultimately responsible for keeping sex safe during this time of the AIDS epidemic?***

    A. I am.

    B. I am.

    C. I am.

    D. All of the above.

Give yourself 5 points for each A answer, 3 points for every B, 1 point for a C, and no points for any D answers.

Write your score for this section here.

NO GENDER, NO CRY

Warning Label: This workbook gets into the subject and area of something we can call for lack of a better (or any) term "no gender." That's how I see myself: I live pretty much without a gender, which paradoxically means I can do many genders.

Signs of impending no-genderedness might include but are not limited to vertigo, light-headedness, confusion, revulsion, whimsy, gut-wrenching angst, giggles, nausea, or all or none of the above.

Disclaimer: This workbook is not intended as a cure for the above symptoms, or for any other symptoms for that matter. Should these or any other symptoms persist, CALL A DOCTOR! Or call a friend.

Ha ha ha! Just kidding. No-gender is an interesting place for me to live. I made this point in my first book, *Gender Outlaw,* and received quite a bit of correspondence that boiled down to, "Okay Kate, you say you live without a gender. How exactly do you do that?" Well, there's a real easy answer to that one. Honest, it's simple. This is the key to the whole workbook. Really. Ready?

The way you live without gender is you look for where gender is, and then you go someplace else.

If you've got that, you don't need to read any further. Give me a call, and let's go out for tea or something. If, however, it's not that easy to spot where gender is or if once you've spotted it, it's difficult to find a place where gender isn't, then maybe reading and doing the exercises in this book would be a good idea. Let's see how you fare on the final criteria of your gender aptitude: issues of no gender whatsoever.

YOUR GENDER APTITUDE, SECTION VI: NO GENDER

1. ***Which one of the following statements most nearly matches your Idea of gender?***

   A. Gender simply is. If you don't like yours, get over it.

   B. I've been working on my own gender for a long time, and I'm getting to the point where I may actually have made it my own.

   C. I think there's a lot about gender that we don't know about yet, and I wonder why that might be.

   D. Gender is what happens to me when I get dressed in the morning.

2. *Which one of the following statements most nearly matches your feelings about gender?*

A. My *what* about gender?

B. I guess my feelings range anywhere from anger and frustration to happiness and exhilaration.

C. Gender confuses me. I don't know why it is the way it is.

D. I feel … I feel … I feel a song coming on!

3. *Has there been any time when you've felt you have no gender?*

A. No, I'm never really aware of my gender anyway.

B. No, I'm very aware of my gender nearly all the time.

C. Maybe sometimes when I'm alone or I'm in some situation where gender doesn't matter.

D. Lots of genders, no genders. What's the difference?

4. *Have you ever questioned the nature of gender itself?*

A. No, it's not polite to question Mother Nature.

B. I question the nature of my own gender, but gender itself? No.

C. I question gender, but I get the spooky feeling I'm not supposed to do that.

D. The nature of gender? Isn't that an oxymoron?

5. *If there were no more gender, do you think there'd be any more desire?*

A. Well of course not! That's why it's impossible to reach a point of no gender.

B. That's a good question. I'll have to ask my group.

C. My head says no, but my heart says yes.

D. Oh dear. You really think a little thing like no gender is going to get in the way of *my* sex life?

6. *If you woke up one morning and discovered you were neither a man nor a woman, you would*

A. Kill yourself, or stay in hiding the rest of your life.

B. Discuss this new development with your group.

C. Read the rest of this book as fast as you could.

D. Yawn and get dressed.

7. *Do you think there's some sort of connection between your gender and your spirituality?*

A. My gender and my *what?*

B. Well yes, it's all about *yin* and *yang* and the inherent duality and non-duality of the universe, isn't it?

C. Perhaps gender is part of our spiritual challenge.

D. My *what* and my spirituality?

8. *Have you ever killed off part of yourself you didn't like?*

A. There's really nothing about myself I don't like.

B. I've *let go* of parts of myself I haven't liked, yes.

C. Sometimes. Are you saying that applies to gender?

D. Oh baby, wanna see where I stashed the bodies?

9. *Why are you reading this book?*

A. I certainly didn't *choose* to read it, that's for sure.

B. I think it's important to try to understand what it is that other people experience.

C. It's been dawning on me that maybe these might sort of be, well, my issues too.

D. Because *nearly* everything else about gender has been positively *dreary*, darling.

10. *If you thought this book was leading you into some sort of radical gender change, you would*

A. Stop reading and throw the book away.

B. Finish reading the book, then sell it at the used book store.

C. Put the book up on the shelf and read it a whole lot later.

D. Hahahahahaha. Kate would never lead anyone into that unless they wanted to be led there!

Give yourself 5 points for each A answer, 3 points for every B, 1 point for a C, and no points for any D answers.

Write your score for this section here.

OKAY, BOYS AND GIRLS! ON THE COUNT OF THREE, CHANGE YOUR GENDER! ONE ... TWO ...

No, no. The goal of this workbook is *not* for you, dear reader, to completely change your gender from male to female or from female to male. I'm not asking you even to ponder the idea of doing that unless that's something you've had in the back of your mind to do anyway. This is not a book for and about transsexuals only. I'm not going to ask you to join some massive underground movement. I'm not recruiting rebels to "The Cause." I'm not going to exhort you to stop being a man or a woman. Why should I do that if that's what you enjoy being? This is simply a book about gender, and who hasn't got one of those? Transsexual or not, you've got a gender, don't you? Well, have you looked at it recently? I mean really really looked at it? Well, take a deep breath, because here we go.

THIS IS YOUR GENDER APTITUDE!

Congratulations! You've finished your gender aptitude questions! Now, go back and collect up all your subtotalled scores for each section. Write the total of your score for all six sections here:

You have a range of possible scores from zero to 255, and if you haven't guessed it by now, when it comes to your Gender Aptitude (GA), smaller is better. But don't fret, please. It's just an aptitude, and like any other part of human potential, with a little or a lot of work you can always improve. Let's see what the numbers translate into.

If your GA was: Then your Gender Aptitude Level is:

0–60 Gender Freak. Whoa! This stuff must seem like kid's play for you. Either that or water in the desert, huh? Have fun reading the book any ol' way you want to. It's going to make you feel a lot less alone in the world. Call me and let me know if I got this stuff right, will you?

61–100 Gender Outlaw. You've been working not only on your own gender, but the subject of gender itself for quite some time, huh? I'm willing to bet things are still a bit scary and a bit serious for you in your life. If I were you, I'd read this book with the intent to get the most fun out of it. Have a ball!

101–175   Gender Novice. Gee, it's like you have one hand in respectability and the other hand someplace where both of you like it. You're not always taken for "normal," are you? In fact, you probably get an infrequent but regular bout of the gender willies from time to time, don't you? Fret not. You've got a very rewarding journey ahead of you. All it's going take is some practice. Read on, read on. Make sure you do all the exercises, okay?

176–235   Well Gendered. Hiya, Mister Man! Hello, Ms. Lady! I'm guessing you're not reading this book to learn anything about yourself, am I right? Maybe you're reading it as a class requirement, or maybe a friend or family member wanted you to read it. Well, I think that's very commendable. Keep on reading, and do what's comfortable for you to do. I promise I'll be gentle.

236–255   You're Captain James T. Kirk! Omigod, I've always wanted to meet you! Can I have your autograph, please? Ah, Captain, you finally get to truly go where no man has gone before.

There. Now you know more about yourself and your relationship to gender than most people in the history of the world. Isn't that neat?

No, there's no further significance to your Gender Aptitude than that. (Yes, it's accurate, but no, it's no big deal). Let's keep going.

Part II
Organizing Identity

5

Introducing Organization
Organizing the Self

By Dustin Bradley Goltz and Jason Zingsheim

How is your identity organized? Take a moment to reflect on all the ways you might, in any given circumstance, complete the sentence "I am …" How do differing discourses work to shape and dictate how you define yourself? What is your gender identity, racial identity, or national identity? How does your employment or role as student organize and shape who you are, or more pointedly, who you have come to understand yourself to be? What meanings come to mind when you hear someone is a doctor, a lawyer, a salesperson, a politician, a barista, or unemployed? What does a college sweatshirt or ball cap from your college bookstore say about you and your identity? What does your major or academic institution say about you (or how have discourses circulating around your major worked to shape how you see yourself in relation to your institution)?

This section of the text looks at how varying discourses work to organize identity, ranging from workplace organizations and academic institutions, to broader organizing systems such as race, nation, and religion. For example, social convention and cultural norms have made the question, "what do you do?" a commonplace and expected inquiry when we are first introduced to a new person. This question is a familiar script used for small talk and "getting to know someone." However, if someone were to respond with the answer, "I eat three meals a day," "I listen to music," or "I watch television," their answer would likely be understood as evasive, sarcastic, or ridiculous. While we "do" an infinite number of things, we understand that this question is specifically inquiring about work or workplace identity. What we do for a living, how we earn money, and the title we have in the workplace are highly valued and considered foundational in our cultural understandings of one's identity. Who you are is closely tied to what you do for work. The answer to this question also allows us to organize our new acquaintances. Similarly, college students are socialized to ask each other, "What is your major?" With both questions, we are able to begin categorizing people based on the organizations they are a part of.

On a broader level, you may live in the United States of America as a citizen and fall under the category of "legal citizen" according to governmental laws, but national identity is much more complicated than this. Discourses surrounding national identity, patriotism, your understandings of the role of the USA in the global community, political affiliations, familial affiliations, religious beliefs, the news outlets you rely upon, and multiple other factors will work to shape and define how you understand what it means to "be American." These factors will shape how rigidly or fluidly you understand yourself in relation to citizens of other countries, other "legal citizens," or individuals living in the U.S. without government-sanctioned citizenship. These various institutions discursively construct what being an American means, what an American should think, feel, do and not do.

ORGANIZATIONAL IDENTITIES: THE SELF AT WORK

> "Throughout this century the relationship between a person's sense of who they are—their personal identity—and the paid work they perform for a living has been a source of regular, if almost always implicit, concern to nearly all those engaged in theorizing about modern work organization and behavior" (Du Gay, 1996, p. 9).

Since the majority of our lives are spent in organizational contexts, such as schools, businesses, and workplaces, organizational identity has been the subject of much research in organizational communication. Initially, this research focused on the command and control model of "organizing" employees; in other words, how upper levels of management ruled lower-level employees. Eventually, this approach shifted to analyzing the process of **organizational identification**—getting employees to think as a "we" instead of an "I" or "them" (Cheney 1983a, 1983b). In the field of organizational communication, many critical scholars are ambivalent about this focus on identification. On one hand, it does move away from models of overt coercion and domination and toward more participatory and

democratic forms of organization. On the other hand, the exertion of power is still present (though not as explicit) and may be even more totalizing as it is internalized through identification. This can make it easier to maintain a hegemonic relation that serves the interests of the owning class with the consent of the organizationally marginalized who now identify with the organization.

Critical organization scholars look to organizations to understand how identity is produced, negotiated, and resisted and how this also influences identity construction both inside and outside of "work." Robin Patric Clair (1996) analyzes the expression "a real job" to illustrate how we use communication to construct meanings for work and for ourselves. This phrase is often used to devalue certain forms of labor ("that's not a real job") and to undercut the significance of current enterprises and privilege a future goal ("I'm going to school now so I can get a real job later"). We use language to create a binary between what we consider "real" and what is deemed "fake," with one side clearly privileged over the other. We use communication to frame "real" jobs just like we create "real" selves, and in both cases we limit and cheapen our experiences. Recall from the first chapter how Tracy and Trethewey (2005) work to rescript "real" self and "fake" self dichotomies in everyday discourses with the concept of a crystallized identity. Rather than conceive of workplace identity as false or less real than any other identity, the crystallized self makes space to think of identity as multifaceted and fluid. Similarly, workplace organizations have been examined as distinct cultures where workers are consistently being socialized and assimilated into the specific norms, values, and expectations of the organization. However, organizational cultures are not isolated or discrete from other social systems, nor are the identities that are navigated and shaped through the organization. In other words, beyond looking at distinct organizational cultures, critical organizational theorists work to examine how differing subjectivities within an organization (e.g., gender, race, class, age) are negotiated, engaged, and organized differently.

Using the example of gender, many critical organizational scholars look to understand how gender differences in an organization shape and constrain organizational identity, advancement, and perceptions. Trethewey (1999) examines the relationship between "organizational discourse and women's professional embodied identities" (p. 427), marking how discourses of the professional body reinforce a masculine bias in the workplace, which is reproduced and enacted by male and female workers. The professional female body is a fit body, one that is disciplined and assumed to be more competent and efficient (p. 430), although "the parameters for men's bodies are much wider and more forgiving" (p. 434). Her research suggests that the female body in the workplace is faced with unique obstacles, specifically the mappings of excessive sexuality as an organizational threat (437), suspicion and lack of commitment attributed to the pregnant or potentially pregnant body (438–9), and excessive emotionality (441). "The female body is always a potential professional liability" (445), forcing women to navigate a gender-specific tightrope in how they dress (one must look attractive, but not "too sexy"), act, feel, and perform their work—disciplining their bodies in the name of a masculine-biased construction of "professionalism."

Approaching the traditionally feminine-gendered career of nursing, Joan Evans and Blye Frank (2003) examine the experiences and perceptions of men who enter this field of work and resist social norms of gender. In this study, the authors suggest masculinity works to discipline male nurses for entering a traditionally feminine profession, while at the same time, traditionally hegemonic masculinity also benefits and mobilizes male nurses in workplace interactions and advancement. Alongside and within the complexity of gendered systems shaping the experiences of male nurses, additional axes of difference, such as sexuality and race, further complicate and shape how identities are organized within this specific occupation.

A final example of the relationship between discourses of gender and organizational discourse comes from the growing body of research on work–life. Caryn Medved and Erika Kirby (2005) analyze online support groups and self-help books for stay-at-home mothers and discover the pervasive influence of corporate discourse in shaping identities for these women. Medved and Kirby's work reveals four subject positions that are available and promoted as desirable for stay-at-home moms: the professional, the manager, the productive citizen, and the irreplaceable worker. In each case, women are encouraged to adopt the ideologies and practices of the workplace as a superior approach to their parenting; this includes crafting mission statements and viewing their work as productive because they are producing children. While the use of a corporate mentality to accomplish the tasks of stay-at-home parenting may be useful for some parents, particularly those transitioning from full time paid employment, Medved and Kirby caution against the wholesale colonization of the home by the hierarchal, classist, and often racist ideologies of managerialism and corporate discourse.

POLITICIZED IDENTITY AND IDENTITY POLITICS

As we have already seen in the first unit, identity is messy work. In order to organize identities into any coherent or distinguishable categorization, the messiness of identity must, understandably, be somewhat reduced. The danger lies in taking this reduction too far and making identities oversimplified. **Stereotypes** become one problematic strategy for organizing identity, where a set of prescribed and generalized traits is assigned to a group of people. Discourses of identity have historically tended to address one axis of identity at a time, working to draw divisions within populations based upon a singular subjectivity, for example gender (though this is often conflated with sex in our cultural discourse). To look at the world through the lens and division of gender and sex is riddled with problems. First, dividing the population into male and female (sex) fails to account for intersex or transsexual populations. In addition, much of our understandings of sex are informed by gender, which refers to a fluid spectrum of cultural meanings and assumptions about what it means to be masculine and/or feminine that span across sexed experiences. Furthermore, the arbitrary organization of identity via sex and gender erases a multitude of additional factors and complications, both assuming that "all men" and "all women" somehow share some innate and essential characteristics or experiences. **Essentialism**, as a concept, marks this limited logic where it is assumed that everyone within a particular subjectivity shares the same set of traits, beliefs, experiences, or commitments. What are the dangers of placing an affluent disabled heterosexual white female and a working-class Chicana lesbian under a generic category of "women" or representative of "women's experience?"

While the underlying logics of essentialist arguments are fictive (or completely false), limiting and problematic, some social theorists point to their necessity and effectiveness for organization. Why invest in such a reductive argument? Essentialist claims, despite their shortcomings, can be effective for advancing political identity work (i.e., women's rights, gay rights, and the civil rights movements). Without the stable and essential notion of the female identity, gay and lesbian identity, or African American identity, there is no way to organize and mobilize identities for political change and visibility.

Such a deployment of essentialized identity, not for the purposes of claiming a universal female or lesbian or Black experience, but for the purposes of political organizing has been termed **strategic essentialism**. The organizing of identity is a tricky and potentially reductive business, which has led to the increasingly complex and intersectional models for theorizing identity introduced in chapter one. This section of the text considers several ways that scholars have sought to interrupt, interrogate, and rethink the ways discourses of identity work within organizational, cultural, national, and international contexts.

ORGANIZING IDENTITY: A PREVIEW

The first reading in this section, Brenda Allen's "Black Womanhood and Feminist Standpoints" examines Allen's situated experiences as an African American female in higher education. Her essay brings to light the distinct and sometimes contradictory ways that discourses of race and gender complicate and uniquely shape a social reality of being a professor in her university, narrating experiences and understandings often overlooked or unknown to her differently-situated colleagues. Organized in and through these differences, Allen provides a grounded and provocative theoretical account for how discourses of race and gender weigh upon the negotiation and construction of organizational identities. As you read through the chapter, consider:

- How does Allen navigate between the individual and social levels of identity?
- How does Allen's location in the matrix of domination within this organizational context influence the possibilities for her identity?
- Where do you see examples and evidence of Allen's belongings? How is her identity

relational and how does she respond to those belongings?

Also focused on a specific organizational site, Chapter Seven, Alexandra Murphy's "The Dialectical Gaze: Exploring the Subject—Object Tension in the Performances of Women Who Strip," offers a qualitative study of identity negotiation in a female strip club. Complicating previous and simplified accounts of power and identity in the stripping profession, Murphy offers a close examination of how management, patrons, and performers navigate economic, gendered, and organizational discourses of power on and off the dancer's stage. Rejecting an either/or formation, where strippers are either helpless victims to sexploitation or active entrepreneurial agents, Murphy argues these women navigate identities that both want to be viewed, and yet are "constrained by [their] own visibility" (p. 94, this volume). The study provides a complex discussion of organizational power, gender systems, and worker identity, while offering a grounded and nuanced case study for discussing stigmatized organizational identity performances.

- Murphy argues that the strippers' negotiation of power within the club is more complicated than rigid a subject/object distinction. How does she support this claim?
- What factors within and outside of the strip club work to produce the women's "stripper" identity?
- While organizational positions and gender are at the center of the study, what other subjectivities further complicate discussions of identity in the club?

In his chapter, "Born to Belonging," Tim Wise expands the scope of our exploration by interrogating how histories function to simultaneously grant us access to organizations and to organize our identities. Histories exert influence over our selves because when we are born we do "not emerge onto a blank slate of neutral circumstance" (p. 99, this volume). Instead, he argues, we are born into particular belongings that locate us within specific relationships to social organizations and institutions. In his case, as a white male, he was born into privileged relationships with governmental organizations and banking institutions, which allowed him access to educational and political institutions, as well as a host of other socially privileged positions and opportunities.

- In what ways is Wise's identity organized without his comprehension or compliance?
- How have your own families' histories influenced possibilities for your identity?
- Reflecting on Carbado's chapter "Privilege," where might Wise's discussion be further informed by his gender and sexuality?

Shifting from personal histories to national histories and how identity is organized through nation and nationalist rhetoric, Lane Bruner's "The Rhetorical Dimensions of National Identity" offers an introduction to the discursive production of citizenships. Exploring how national collectivity and community are erected and maintained through rhetorical devices, with specific attention to national memory and memorials, Bruner calls for us to critically reflect upon how speeches, memorials, and sites of nationalist identity production work to promote specific histories, memories, and investments at the expense of multiple others.

- What is your national identity? What messages, events, and rituals work to shape and inform your understanding of your self as a citizen?
- What national memorials have you visited or experienced? How do they work to construct and shape national identity?

- Considering current national events, how is the ideal citizen constructed? What additional identities or subjectivities are highlighted or assumed? Who is excluded or erased?

Extending from Bruner's introduction, Chela Sandoval's "Dissonant Globalizations, Emancipatory Methods, and Social Erotics" invites us to rethink and re-imagine notions of national identity, borders, and discourses of belonging through an oppositional consciousness shaped through third world feminism. In this speech delivered to the Queer Globalization Conference in 1998, Sandoval calls for us to examine the limitations of nationalist and identity-based rhetoric, both for the violences that they impose and reproduce, and also for the coalitional potentials and possibilities they actively foreclose. Rethinking how discourses and identities work to organize and sever modes of belonging, she boldly asks us to re-envision who are our country-people and who it is we do (and might) belong to. Sandoval reclaims a method of differential consciousness and invites her audience to investigate how systems of power, in the name of identity and nation, work to conceal potential affinities within and across geographical, gendered, racial, and sexual difference.

- In relation to Bruner, how is Sandoval inviting us to rethink or reorganize our understandings of identity beyond nation?
- Where do you see connections between Sandoval's call for reconsidering kinship and Carrillo-Rowe's relational and coalitional models of subjectivity?
- How do mainstream media work to constrain and foreclose Sandoval's call for us to rethink our country people and our possible connections across borders? How might new media technologies work to resist or rework these messages?

Moving from the global to a situated case study, the final chapter in this unit—Dustin Bradley Goltz's sarcastically titled "[Insert Scholarly Title Here]: Contested Identities in the Performance of *X-Communication*"—provides a performative account of competing identities surrounding his performance of his one man show *Banging the Bishop: Latter Day Prophecy*. The performance, chronicling his experiences as a gay Jewish male who converted to Mormonism in his late teens, was contested and postponed at his university due to a complex web of academic, economic, and religious organizational pressures. As academic and artist, gay Jew and ex-Mormon, Goltz seeks to bridge heated and seemingly incommensurable worldviews across difference through a personal and performative engagement. Emerging in his account is a conflicted narration of how differing systems work to organize his personal experience, how identity is strategic and contested, and how faith, truth, and self move and shift through time and space.

- How do organizational, religious, sexual, and religious discourses shape and constrain the identities at the center of the "Banging the Bishop" controversy?
- How are all personal accounts of experience, inevitably, a "crank call?"
- What are the temporal (situated within and over time) dimensions of identity organization? How can "truth" of self be bound and located within the past? Where have you experienced a change in the "truth" of your identity?

REFERENCES

Cheney, G. (1983a). On the various and changing meanings of organizational membership: A field study of organizational identification. *Communication Monographs, 50,* 342–362.

Cheney, G. (1983b). The rhetoric of identification and the study of organizational communication. *Quarterly Journal of Speech, 69,* 143–158.

Clair, R. P. (1996). The political nature of the colloquialism, "A real job": Implications for organizational socialization. *Communication Monographs, 63,* 249–267.

Du Gay, P. (1996). *Consumption and identity at work.* Thousand Oaks, CA: Sage.

Evans, J., & Frank, B. (2003). Contradictions and tensions: Exploring relations of masculinities in the numerically female-dominated nursing profession. *Journal of Men's Studies, 11,* 3, 277–292.

Medved, C. E., & Kirby, E. L. (2005). Family CEOs: A feminist analysis of corporate mothering discourses. *Management Communication Quarterly, 18,* 435–478.

Tracy, S. J., & Trethewey, A. (2005). Fracturing the real-self ↔ fake-self dichotomy: Moving toward "crystallized" organizational discourses and identities. *Communication Theory, 15*(2), 168–195.

Trethewey, A. (1999). Disciplined bodies. *Organization Studies, 20,* 423–450.

ADDITIONAL SUGGESTED READINGS

Allen, B. J. (2007). Theorizing communication and race. *Communication Monographs, 74,* 259–264.

Ashcraft, K. L., & Mumby, D. K. (2004). *Reworking Gender: A Feminist Communicology of Organization.* Thousand Oaks, CA: Sage.

Buzzanell, P. M., & Turner, L. H. (2003). Emotion work revealed by job loss discourse: Backgrounding–foregrounding of feelings, construction of normalcy, and (re)instituting of traditional masculinities. *Journal of Applied Communication Research, 31,* 27-58.

Clarke, K. M., & Thomas, D. A. (Eds.) (2006). *Globalization and Race: Transformation in the Cultural Production of Blackness.* Duke University Press.

Cohen, C. J. (2005). Punks, bulldaggers, and welfare queens: The radical potential of queer politics? In E. P. Johnson & M. G. Henderson (Eds.), *Black queer studies* (pp. 21–51). Durham, NC: Duke University Press.

Deetz, S. A. (1992). *Democracy in an age of corporate colonization: Developments in communication and the politics of everyday life* (pp. 65–90). Albany, NY: SUNY Press.

Duggan, L. (2002). The new homonormativity: The sexual politics of neoliberalism. In R. Castronovo and D. D. Nelson (Eds.), *Materializing democracy: Towards a revitalized cultural politics* (pp. 175–194). Durham, NC: Duke University Press.

Erikson, R. J. (2005). Why emotion work matters: Sex, gender and the division of household labor. *Journal of Marriage and Family, 67,* 337–350.

Fuss, D. (1989). *Essentially speaking: feminism, nature & difference.* New York: Routledge.

Golden, A. G. (2007). Fathers' frames for childrearing: Evidence toward a "masculine concept of caregiving." *Journal of Family Communication, 7,* 265–285.

Kirby, E. L., Golden, A. G., Medved, C. E., Jorgenson, J., & Buzzanell, P. M. (2003). An organizational communication challenge to the discourse of work and family research: From problematics to empowerment. *Communication Yearbook 27* (pp. 1–43). Thousand Oaks, CA: Sage Publications.

Kirby, E. L., & Krone, K. J. (2002). "The policy exists but you can't really use it": Communication and the structuration of work–family policies. *Journal of Applied Communication Research, 30,* 50–77.

Medved, C. E. (2007). Investigating family labor in communication studies: Threading across historical and contemporary discourses. *Journal of Family Communication, 7,* 225–243.

Mumby, D. K. (2005). Theorizing resistance in organization studies: A dialectical approach. *Management Communication Quarterly, 19,* 19–44.

Mumby, D. K. (1998). Organizing men: Power, discourse, and the social construction of masculinity(s) in the workplace. *Communication Theory, 8,* 164–183.

Nadesan, M. H., & Trethewey, A. (2000). Performing the enterprising subject: Gendered strategies of success (?) *Text and Performance Quarterly, 20,* 223–250.

Sotirin, P., Buzzanell, P. M., & Turner, L. H. (2007). Colonizing family: A feminist critique of family management texts. *Journal of Family Communication, 7,* 245–263.

Tracy, S. J., & Rivera, K. D. (2010). Endorsing equity and applauding stay-at-home moms: How male voices on work–life reveal aversive sexism and flickers of transformation. *Management Communication Quarterly, 24,* 3–43.

Trethewey, A. (2001). Reproducing and resisting the master narrative of decline: Midlife professional women's experiences of aging. *Management Communication Quarterly, 15,* 183–226.

Trethewey, A. (1997). Resistance, identity, and empowerment: A postmodern feminist analysis of a human service organization. *Communication Monographs, 64,* 281–301.

Trethewey, A., Tracy, S. J., & Alberts, J. (2006). Crystallizing frames for work–life. *Electronic Journal of Communication, 16* (3&4).

Tyler, M. (2004). Managing between the sheets: Lifestyle magazines and the management of sexuality in everyday life. *Sexualities, 7,* 81–106.

Urrieta, L. (2005). "Playing the game" versus "selling out": Chicanas and Chicanos relationship to whitestream schools. In B. K. Alexander, G. L. Anderson, & B. P. Gallegos (Eds.), *Performance theories in education* (pp. 173–196). Mahwah, N.J.: Lawrence Erlbaum Associates.

Black Womanhood and Feminist Standpoints

6

By Brenda J. Allen

At the intersection of race and gender stand women of color, torn by the lines of bias that currently divide white from nonwhite in our society, and male from female. The worlds these women negotiate demand different and often wrenching allegiances. As a result, women of color face significant obstacles to their full participation in and contribution to higher education. (Moses, 1989, p. 1)

On certain dimensions, Black women may more closely resemble Black men; on others, white women; and on still others Black women may stand apart from both groups.

(Collins, 1991, p. 207)

Being Black and woman engenders complex ways of knowing and being. In this article, I discuss challenges and consequences of being a member of two historically oppressed groups in the United States. To frame the discussion, I rely on feminist standpoint theory—a distinctive element of contemporary feminist thought about how we construct knowledge (Longino, 1993). I focus on U.S. academe as a discursive site for constructing identity. I recount some of my experiences as a tenure-track faculty member to illuminate issues and to afford the reader a glimpse of my everyday reality. Although my experiences do not necessarily represent those of other Black women or women of color in predominantly White institutions, numerous others have described similar experiences and perspectives (e.g., Etter-Lewis, 1993; Jones, 1994; Moraga & Anzaldua, 1983; Moses, 1989; Nieves-Squires, 1991; Olivas, 1997).

I begin with an overview of feminist standpoint theory, after which I describe my standpoint. Next, I discuss examples and interpretations of my

Brenda J. Allen, "Black Womanhood and Feminist Standpoints," *Management Communication Quarterly: An International Journal*, vol. 11, no. 4, pp. 575-586. Copyright © 1998 by Sage Publications. Reprinted with permission.

experiences as a Black woman academic. Finally, I discuss implications of the issues that I have raised.

FEMINIST STANDPOINT THEORY

Proponents of feminist standpoint theory contend that we should solicit women's perspectives on social reality to construct knowledge and to critique dominant knowledge claims (which usually are based on White men's lives). Socialist feminists developed this concept as an extension of Marxist notions of the standpoint of the proletariat: "Like the lives of proletarians in Marxist theory, women's lives in Western capitalist societies also contained possibilities for developing a critique of domination" (Hartsock, 1997, p. 168). Feminist standpoint theory enjoins us to view women as "strangers" or "outsiders" whose experiences might provide insight that is invisible to "natives" (usually White men) who are too immersed within dominant institutions to detect the patterns and behaviors that comprise reality (Hennesey, 1993).

Feminist standpoint theory does not essentialize the category "woman." Rather, it encourages us to solicit stories from many types of women (Buzzanell, 1995). Due to the interlocking web of oppression that stems from belonging to two disenfranchised groups, women of color may enact the role of outsider or stranger differently from White women (e.g., Beale, 1970; Bell, 1992; Dill, 1979; Higginbotham & Weber, 1992; hooks, 1984; Houston, 1994; Spelman, 1988). Therefore, women of color should prove to be valuable resources for acquiring a variety of perspectives and narratives about how oppression operates and about how women resist oppression.

Consistent with general feminist goals, feminist standpoint theory focuses on gender differences and strives to emancipate women. Researchers assess women's historically shared group experiences, and they emphasize social conditions that construct oppressed groups (Collins, 1997; Harding, 1991). Thus, feminist standpoint situates women's lived, concrete experiences in local contexts, while also linking them with broader social and institutional issues (Allen, 1996). It goes further, however, by seeking to expose oppression and to highlight acts of resistance. As a result, women who verbalize their struggles and victories may experience "consciousness raising" (Smith, 1987).

Thus, feminist standpoint theory holds great promise for feminist studies and activism. When we privilege the knowledge of the oppressed or outsiders, we reveal aspects of the social order that previously have not been exposed. Consequently, we might gain information and insights that will help us to describe and theorize about how we construct and maintain social order. Moreover, we can envision and begin to enact more just social practices (Hartsock, 1997).

MY STANDPOINT

I am an African American woman.[1] I place primacy on these socially constructed aspects of my identity because of (a) their physical salience, (b) the accompanying likelihood that I will encounter oppression and discrimination based upon how others see me, and (c) my acute awareness of having been socialized into Black womanhood. Although space constraints prevent me from extensively describing my identity and background, to adhere to tenets of feminist standpoint theory, I offer a brief autobiographical sketch to contextualize this essay.

I am a heterosexual, first-generation college graduate who was raised by my Black mother in the 1950s and 1960s in a lower-class, Black, midwestern U.S. community. When I was almost 40 years old, I earned a doctoral degree in communication at Howard University, a historically Black university.

In 1989, I was the first person of color to be hired in the tenure track of a department of communication at a predominantly White, Western research institution that was actively seeking to increase the numbers of faculty women and members of racial-ethnic plurality groups. My "only" status has not changed during my 8 years in the department.

Finally, I view myself as an "outsider within" the academy, as Collins (1991) explains:

> The exclusion of Black women's ideas from mainstream academic discourse and the curious placement of African-American women intellectuals in both feminist and Black social and political thought has meant that Black women intellectuals have remained outsiders within in all three communities. ... The assumptions on which full group membership are based—whiteness for feminist thought, maleness for Black social and political thought, and the combination for mainstream scholarship—all negate a Black female reality. Prevented from becoming full insiders in any of these areas of inquiry, Black women remain outsiders within, individuals whose marginality provides a distinctive angle of vision on the theories put forth by such intellectual communities. (p. 12)

I agree with Collins (1991) that "the marginality that accompanies outsider within status can be the source of both frustration and creativity" (p. 233). My solitary and often lonely position as outsider-within and as the only person of color or Black woman in my department presents numerous challenges and consequences. Next, I share stories and insight from my intellectual autobiography to illustrate this point.[2]

CHALLENGES/CONSEQUENCES OF BLACK WOMANHOOD IN ACADEME

CONFLICTUAL ENCOUNTERS

I have experienced numerous situations that reflect the interlocking nature of racism, sexism, or both. For instance, I have encountered the attitude that I was a "twofer," someone hired because administrators could count me as a female hire and as a racial minority. Not long after I assumed my tenure-track position, one of my colleagues told me that someone said I was an affirmative action hire and not qualified for my job. Yet another person reported that someone in my department said I was not a good writer. Just about every sister scholar (woman of color academician) I know has a story of being mistaken in an academic setting for anyone but Dr. So-and-So, and I am no exception. These flagrant and subtle messages reveal oppressive attitudes that question my credibility as a member of the academy.

I have endured countless interactions in which I found myself second-guessing the other person's intentions (i.e., I wondered if he or she was being racist, sexist, both, or neither). For example, the first day that I convened an introductory course in organizational communication, a White male student informed me that he was going to drop the course because, he said, "I have already taken a course to fulfill my ethnic studies requirement." In providing an overview of the course, I had never said a word about ethnicity. Then there was the time that I shared what I thought was a great idea with the chair of my department, who barely acknowledged it. However, when a White male colleague made the same suggestion, the chair immediately put it into effect. Once, a White woman at a social gathering of academics asked me to sing a Negro spiritual that she loved. Another time, a White store clerk blatantly avoided touching my hand as she handed me change. As a final example, in a local grocery store, a White woman grabbed her purse from her shopping cart both times that I entered a section where she was browsing.

Of course, I never will know these persons' actual intentions. Some White persons discount my interpretations of these types of encounters by observing that they have had similar experiences. However, I do not think they understand how I feel as someone who repeatedly deals with these types of exchanges across numerous contexts, and who finds herself spending valuable mental and emotional energy trying to process them.

Due to tokenism, I frequently endure demands on my time that other faculty members in my department do not face.[3] People seem to expect that I can or should provide insight as a representative of women, people of color, women of color, Black people, or Black women. Thus, I sometimes feel more like a symbol or representative than an individual. When I was hired, the chair of my department warned me that I would be asked to "sit on every damned committee," and he was right. I have learned to be more discerning about when to say yes, but I still spend time deciding whether I should accept an invitation.

I also expend energy monitoring my emotions, masking them, or both. For instance, a high-ranking administrator told what I considered to be a derogatory joke about football players. I was the only person of color at the meeting, and the only person who did not crack a smile at his joke. I wanted to tell him that I was insulted, but I held my tongue. I often am careful not to display negative emotion (e.g., sadness, despair, anger, disagreement) because I do not want to enact negative stereotypes. For instance, I might suppress my anger because I do not want to be seen as a militant Black person or as a domineering, loud Black woman, or as a bitchy woman. As Marshall (1993) observes:

Sensitivity to context is imperative to allow women to survive in an alien world, and yet it marginalizes and disempowers them. They are often trying to anticipate difficulties and to screen out unacceptable aspects of their heritage of female values, or trying to manage the disturbance they create. (p. 135)

Being both woman and Black compounds these tensions for me, particularly when it seems that other people do not seem to be sensitive to my feelings or to my value systems.

Collins (1991) notes that a dialectic of identity can occur when women of color have to negotiate the contradictions of dual membership. Moreover, "they can even experience pressure to choose between their racial identity and their womanhood" (Moses, 1989, p. 1). I experienced this type of conflict when one of my former students, an African American man, was accused of rape. Some members of the Black community wanted me to support the student when he was barred from campus subsequent to his trial, whereas women's groups wanted me to support their position that the student should not be allowed on campus.[4] I sidestepped the situation by not doing anything.

Fortunately, the rape example depicts an extreme case. However, I often confront less distressing situations in which I feel torn between being identified because of my race-ethnicity or my gender. For instance, when I was the only Black woman on a job search committee, the lone Black man often sought my support on racial matters, and the White woman often looked to me for support regarding issues related to female applicants.

DIALECTIC TENSIONS IN THE ETHIC OF CARING

Collins (1991) asserts that material conditions of oppression may generate some uniformity in the epistemologies of subordinate groups. For instance, she propounds a particularly acute convergence in Black women of an ethic of caring that African Americans (see also Cox & Nkomo, 1990; Foeman & Pressley, 1987) and women (see also, Buzzanell, 1994; Marshall, 1993; Wood, 1993) often exhibit. Collins (1991) cites three interrelated components of this ethic of caring: (a) an emphasis on individual uniqueness, (b) freedom to express emotions, and (c) a capacity for empathy. I often epitomize this convergence during interactions with others and as I develop myself as a feminist scholar.

I usually assign students to write an autobiography, so that I can view each person as an individual (as opposed to entertaining a common stereotype at the university that they are rich, White kids who only want to party). I am expressive, and I frequently use humor. I allow my enthusiasm to show, and I also express anger and disappointment. Basically, my approach to teaching stems from the Golden Rule: "Do unto others as you would have them do unto you." As a Black woman, I do not want to be stereotyped. I wish to be treated as an individual, even as others recognize that I come from a *different* (not deficient) cultural background than most of them.

In the classroom, I employ an interactive style, somewhat similar to the "call and response" tradition of Black churches. I also take a collaborative, cooperative approach to teaching and learning. However, I run a "tight ship," displaying an attitude described in a saying from my Black neighborhood: "I joke, but I don't play." Although students (especially White ones) tend initially to struggle with my style (I often am their first Black teacher), after a couple of sessions most of them get into it. Often, they tell me that my class is the only one that they

attend regularly, and many students have expressed gratitude for how I challenge them to think for themselves.

I also display an ethic of caring by spending a lot of time in one-on-one interaction during office hours with students, who often discuss personal problems. Students of color who are not in my classes also visit me to discuss their personal as well as school-related concerns. Some of my colleagues also visit me to discuss various issues. My mother calls me Mary Worth (after the character in the funny papers who always helps others, including strangers) or Ann Landers because I am always trying to assist other people with their life problems.

This propensity toward an ethic of caring holds negative and positive consequences for my advancement as an academician. I realize that I may have shortchanged other aspects of my role when I was an assistant professor, particularly research and writing. Moreover, those persons who evaluate me for reappointment, merit raises, or promotion are not likely to know, care about, or credit these activities. However, based on cards, letters, and gifts from students, as well as departmental and university-wide teaching awards, I am certain that I have made a positive difference in many students' lives, and this gratifies me.

I also am giving myself the benefit of the ethic of caring. Following the lead that feminist standpoint theory furnishes, I have begun to look for (and create) acts of resistance in my intellectual autobiography. The most obvious example is my decision to change my area of study from computer mediated communication to feminism. By centering my research efforts on Black women, I have given myself permission to focus my career on a marginal, potentially volatile area of study. I also allow myself to feel and sometimes express the emotions that arise from delving into this area of study.

Furthermore, although I certainly do not deny that I am oppressed because of my gender, my race-ethnicity, and their intersection, I conscientiously reject the status of "victim," and "stigmatized other" (see Buzzanell, 1994; Moraga & Anzaldua, 1983). Rather, I celebrate the positive consequences of having been socialized as Black and woman, and I am determined to help other women of color to view and value themselves similarly. I believe that I am blessed and I am a blessing. Thus, the process of using a feminist standpoint to speak my intellectual autobiography has been transformative.

IMPLICATIONS

Although the issues I raise only begin to reveal the complexities and challenges of Black womanhood, my preliminary efforts elicit numerous practical implications for organizational communication processes—not only in academe but also in other professional settings. In a comprehensive report on Black women students, administrators, and faculty members in higher education, Moses (1989) makes several recommendations that relate to this essay. For instance, she encourages readers to acknowledge Black women's comments or suggestions because we often feel that others ignore our input. I have felt slighted to the point of being discouraged from sharing my ideas, which can be detrimental not only to my morale but also to the growth of my academic unit, which will not reap benefits that my ideas might generate.

Moses (1989) also cautions university employees to "assume the best when colleagues work together. Too often, interchanges between male and female colleagues are viewed as sexual liaisons, collaboration among women in general is seen as 'plotting,' and collaboration among Black women is seen as 'separatist'" (p. 14). She further suggests that administrators endorse support networks among women of color, although she warns them not to expect that every woman of color would want to be involved. Finally, she encourages personnel committees to engage in rigorous job searches and to let others know that a Black woman is qualified for her position.

I recommend that concerned individuals should not assume that a woman of color is interested in dealing with diversity issues. Even when she is, acknowledge her other skills and areas of expertise. In addition, recognize that addressing and valuing diversity should be everyone's responsibility: Do not burden us with the task. For instance, identify and use resources (on your campus and from other sources) that are designated to assist faculty, students, and staff with understanding diversity. Also, strive to incorporate diversity issues into your curriculum. However, do not reserve your attention for a separate unit within your courses. Rather, seek examples (e.g., case studies, films, illustrations, guest speakers) that depict people of color in a variety of positive roles that do not always concentrate on their race, gender, or both.

I also encourage you to check yourself for stereotyping and assumptions. Recognize that Black women and other women of color are not all alike. Try to strike a balance between viewing us as individuals while realizing that, due to our shared histories, many Black women in professional situations endure similar sexist and racist attitudes and interactions. Related to this, try to understand that women of color experience varying types and degrees of sexism and racism, according to their racioethnic background (e.g., people might expect Asian women to be quiet and subservient).

I hope that I have illuminated the issues that Moses (1989) and Collins (1991) raise in the opening quotes of this essay. I also hope that my stories and recommendations inspire and guide you toward creating and maintaining work climates where every person feels valued and validated.

NOTES

1. I use Black and African American interchangeably, although the current politically correct term seems to be African American. Black connotes an important time in my life and in U.S. history, when many Negroes (or colored people) began to assert pride in their racial background. Thus, I prefer to refer to myself as Black.

2. For more examples and analyses of some of my experiences, please see Allen (1996).

3. See Kanter (1977) for a discussion of characteristics and professional consequences of being a token (i.e., a representational figure of a particular group).

4. Rape is a particularly controversial topic between Black and White feminists because of complex sexual politics that stem from the U.S. historical legacy of slavery, where White men routinely raped Black women and viewed them as animals (see Collins, 1991). In contemporary society, Black women are socialized to view their bodies negatively, to be concerned more about the welfare of family and community than themselves, and to protect Black men from the criminal justice system's propensity to severely punish Black men. Statistics reveal that Black women are more likely than White women to be rape victims, less likely to report rape, and less likely to see their accused attacker convicted of the crime (Joseph & Lewis, 1986).

REFERENCES

Allen, B. J. (1996). Feminist standpoint theory: A Black woman's (re)view of organizational socialization. *Communication Studies, 47,* 257–271.

Beale, F. (1970). Double jeopardy: To be Black and female. In T. Cade (Ed.) *The Black woman anthology* (pp. 90–100). New York: Penguin.

Bell, E. L. (1992). Myths, stereotypes and realities of Black women: A personal reflection. *Journal of Applied Behavioral Science, 28,* 363–376.

Buzzanell, P. (1994). Gaining a voice: Feminist organizational communication theorizing. *Management Communication Quarterly, 7,* 339–383.

Buzzanell, P. (1995). Retraining the glass ceiling as a socially constructed process: Implications for understanding and change. *Communication Monographs, 62,* 327–354.

Collins, P. H. (1991). *Black feminist thought: Knowledge, consciousness, and the politics of empowerment.* New York: Routledge.

Collins, P. H. (1997). Comment on Hekman's "Truth and method: Feminist standpoint theory revisited": Where's the power? *Signs, 22,* 375–381.

Cox, T., & Nkomo, S. (1990). Invisible men and women: A status report on race as a variable in organization behavior research. *Journal of Organizational Behavior, 11,* 419–431.

Dill, B. T. (1979). The dialectics of Black womanhood. *Signs, 4,* 543–555.

Etter-Lewis, G. (1993). *My soul is my own: Oral narratives of African American women in the professions.* New York: Routledge.

Foeman, A. K., & Pressley, G. (1987). Ethnic culture and corporate culture: Using Black styles in organizations. *Communication Quarterly, 35,* 293–307.

Harding, S. (1991). *Whose science? Whose knowledge?* Ithaca, NY: Cornell University Press.

Hartsock, N.C.M. (1997). Comment on Hekman's "Truth and method: Feminist standpoint theory revisited": Truth or justice? *Signs, 22,* 367–374.

Hennesey, R. (1993). Women's lives/feminist knowledge: Feminist standpoint as ideology critique. *Hypatia, 8,* 14–34.

Higginbotham, E., & Weber, L. (1992). Moving up with kin and community: Upward mobility for

Black and White women. *Gender and Society, 6,* 416–440.

Hooks, b. (1984). *Feminist theory: From margin to center.* Boston: South End Press.

Houston, M. (1994). When Black women talk with White women: Why dialogues are difficult. In A. Gonzalez, M. Houston, & V. Chen (Eds.) *Our voices: Essays in culture, ethnicity, and communication* (pp. 133–139). Los Angeles: Roxbury.

Jones, J. (1994, November). *Sista docta.* Performance at the convention of the Speech Communication Association, New Orleans, LA.

Joseph, G. I., & Lewis, J. (1986). *Common differences: Conflicts in Black and White feminist perspectives.* Boston: South End.

Kanter, R. M. (1977). *Men and women of the corporation.* New York: Basic Books.

Longino, H. E. (1993). Feminist standpoint theory and the problems of knowledge. *Signs, 19,* 201–212.

Marshall, J. (1993). Viewing organizational communication from a feminist perspective: A critique and some offerings. In S. Deetz (Ed.), *Communication Yearbook 16* (pp. 122–143). Newbury Park, CA: Sage.

Moraga, C., & Anzaldua, G. (Eds.). (1983). *This bridge called my back: Writings by radical women of color.* New York: Kitchen Table, Women of Color Press.

Moses, Y. T. (1989). *Black women in academe: Issues and strategies.* Washington, DC: Project on the Status and Education of Women, Association of American Colleges.

Nieves-Squires, S. (1991). *Hispanic women: Making their presence on campus less tenuous.* Washington, DC: Project on the Status and Education of Women, Association of American Colleges.

Olivas, M. R. (1997, February). *Two peas in a pod: A dialogue toward understanding the intersection of race, class, and gender.* Paper presented at the convention of the Western States Communication Association, Monterey, CA.

Smith, D. (1987). *The everyday world as problematic: A feminist sociology.* Boston: Northeastern University Press.

Spelman, E. V. (1988). *Inessential woman: Problems of exclusion in feminist thought.* Boston: Beacon.

Wood, J. T. (1993). Gender and moral voice: Moving from woman's nature to standpoint epistemology. *Women's Studies in Communication, 15,* 1–24.

Brenda J. Allen (Ph.D., Howard University) is an Associate Dean in the College of Liberal Arts and Sciences, and a Professor in the Department of Communication at the University of Colorado Denver.

AUTHOR'S NOTE: *I presented a version of this paper at the Speech Communication Association convention in 1995. I am grateful to Cynthia Stohl and Dennis Mumby for their assistance and support. Thanks to Patrice Buzzanell for her suggestions on earlier drafts of the manuscript. I also appreciate the efforts of other panel members (Anna Spradlin, Karen Ashcraft, Maryanne Wanca-Thibault, and Phil Tompkins) and our respondent, Linda Putnam. This research was made possible in part by funding from the University of Colorado, Boulder's Implementation of Multicultural Perspectives and Approaches in Research and Teaching (IMPART) program.*

The Dialectical Gaze
Exploring the Subject–Object Tension in the Performances of Women Who Strip

By Alexandra G. Murphy

Much of past research on female exotic dance has characterized strippers as deviant workers who are either passive, objectified victims of a sexploitation system that trades on their bodies for financial gain or as active subjects who work the exchange for their own benefit. Drawing on theories of power, performance, and communication, this work complicates the subject–object tension, showing how power circulates through a system of competing discursive relationships forming a dialectic of agency and constraint in which strippers are simultaneously subjects and objects. The author presents ethnographic data of how strippers discursively negotiate the ambivalence and contradictions they experience during their interactions with customers, management, and their families. Finally, this work concludes that given the need for all women to perform their prescribed gender in the course of their everyday lives, the occupation of the exotic dancer may not be as deviant as previously defined.

Keywords: *exotic dance; ethnography; power; organization; communication; gender*

A football game on a big-screen TV silhouettes a half-nude woman dancing for a row of cheering men. Waitresses wander through the club in white lace G-string lingerie. One asks what I want to drink. Her name is Ilona, and she speaks with a soft Spanish accent. $4.50 for a Miller Lite! "PUT THE GREENERY ON THE SCENERY," I hear an amplified voice ring out over the sound of Madonna singing, "Like a Virgin." "COME ON GENTLEMEN, THESE WOMEN DON'T GET A SALARY FROM THIS ESTABLISHMENT. THEY RELY ON GENEROUS TIPS FROM YOU!" Though stimulated by vision, the customers are controlled by sound. A dancer performs a table dance for the man next to me. He is alone. She is called the "Polynesian Queen." In this dark room full of smoke, he can pretend to be her king. Her breasts appear too round. Are they real? He doesn't seem to care. He watches her body move to the beat as Janet Jackson sings "Nasty Girl." She leans forward and presses her perfectly round breasts together—in his face. She bends down—her head in his lap. Her hair *hides what she is not doing—mock fellatio. She turns around. With her back to the patron, she bends over again. This time I see her face. She looks disinterested. He looks impressed. I'm impressed with her ability to walk in four-inch heels. Music pounds so loudly it vibrates my chair. "Welcome to Paper Dolls," a sign out front declares, "The Hottest Show on Earth."*

Paper Dolls[1] is a "first-class" strip joint nestled between a Shell gas station and a Budget rental car shop. The "hottest show on earth" depends on the manufacturing of a seamless performance where outside men in tuxedos park cars and inside women in G-strings take off their clothes for money. As such, Paper Dolls is a "sexploitation organization, where sexuality is exploited for the benefit of the managers and owners" (Hearn and Parkin 1987, 68). As members of "sexploitation organizations," striptease dancers are categorized as sex workers along with prostitutes, erotic models, and erotic film stars: their work is based on a sexual trade.

Sexploitation organizations, and in particular strip clubs, have been the subject of academic interest and controversy.[2] The majority of literature on stripping, whether male or female, professional or amateur, defines the activity as deviant (Calhoun, Fisher, and Cannon 1998; Ronai and Cross 1998; Wood 2000). They question why strippers are drawn to the "stigmatized" profession (Skipper and McCaghy 1970; Carey, Peterson, and Sharpe 1974) and consider the justifications they make to rationalize their choices (Thompson and Harred 1992). They analyze the types of relationships the strippers develop (and often fake) with the customers (Enck and Preston 1988; Ronai and Ellis 1989) and with each other (McCaghy and Skipper 1969; Carey, Peterson, and Sharpe 1974; Reid, Epstein, and Benson 1995). And they explore the consequences for self-esteem and identity for the women and men working in this industry (Reid, Epstein, and Benson 1994; Ronai and Ellis 1989;

Dressel and Peterson 1982). While most of the literature focuses on professional female strippers, a few studies have emerged distinguishing between male and female strippers (Peterson and Dressel 1982; Margolis and Arnold 1993; Montemurro 2001; Tewksbury 1994) and professional and amateur shows (Calhoun, Cannon, and Fisher 1996; Calhoun, Fisher, and Cannon 1998; Cannon, Calhoun, and Fisher 1998).

At the heart of feminist investigations into sex work is a concern about the degree of agency women have within an industry that positions them as objects. Feminist responses, however, are divided (Bell 1987; McCormick 1994). Radical feminists have directed their energies toward eliminating the sex work industry, arguing that it contributes to a continued objectification that harms all women—not just the sex trade workers (e.g., Barry 1995). Liberal feminists, on the other hand, believe sex workers are active participants in a social system—exploiters who trade on their own sexuality for commerce. Some seek to increase the amount of power that women in these roles have through unions and increased protective regulations (Hanna 1998; St. James 1987). Other liberal responses reveal how dancers are more subjects with power than objects of power (Ronai 1992; Ronai and Ellis 1989; Wood 2000). Ronai and Ellis (1989), for example, wrote about the types of strategies female dancers use to control the customer–dancer interaction and to capitalize financially. Wood (2000) also closely examined the gendered power evident in female strip clubs. She took issue with the radical anti-sex work position that places the strippers solely as the object of the male gaze. Focusing on the interactions between the customers and the dancers, she found that the dancers gain agency and subjectivity through their discourse and are therefore more than mere sexual objects of a masculine gaze. She said, "Rather than understanding power as a monolithic social force oppressing women … power is understood to be a contested, negotiated social resource that is constantly being enacted during interpersonal encounters" (p. 7). Ronai (1992) wrote about the complexity of her own stripper subjectivity as she worked through her simultaneous and often conflicting roles of exotic dancer, researcher, and wife.

In this vein, this study will maintain that female professional stripping cannot be viewed as either entirely liberating or entirely constraining: strippers are neither completely with nor completely without power. I will explore the resources and constraints these women encounter and the rhetorical and performative tactics they enact as they negotiate power relationships both in and out of the workplace. First, I draw on relevant theories of power, performance, and communication. I focus on how expressions of power through performance complicate the subject–object tension; it is a dialectic rather than a dichotomy. Second, I present data from ethnographic observations and interviews of how power is performed and negotiated during interactions between customers and dancers, management and dancers, and the dancers and their families. Throughout, I argue that it is not about whether strippers are object or subject, or whether they have power or not. It is about how they discursively negotiate the ambivalence and contradiction inevitable when competing expressions of power are culturally and socially constructed and performed. Finally, I conclude that stripping may not be as deviant a profession for women as it has been previously defined. Whether through expression or suppression, for many professional women, sexuality is a spoken or unspoken component of work. Their jobs do not have to require them to take off their clothes for them to feel that to be successful they must shape and discipline their bodies toward a prescribed feminine image (Nadesan and Tretheway 2000; Tretheway 1998).

EXPRESSIONS OF POWER AND PERFORMANCE

At first glance, female strippers provide extraordinary examples of what Bell (1993) has described as the "female body as object and situated in performance as display of that object" (p. 352). Indeed, for centuries the female body has been the object of public surveillance and desire. She is displayed for popular consumption in films, paintings, television, and stage where heterosexual men can desire her and women can desire to be like her. Unlike their male counterparts, female performers are marked for sexual appropriation, availability, and sexuality (Dolan 1993; Tannen 1994).

Slavoj Žižek (1992) helped us understand why watching is such a pleasure. He believed that watching is the embodiment of unfulfilled desire. For the male customers, the strippers represent the "object á" or the object-cause of their desire. The object of desire eludes our grasp no matter what we do to attain it; yet "the final purpose of our demand for an object is this, not the satisfaction of a need attached to it, but confirmation of the other's attitude toward us" (p. 5). In light of this, male customers may believe they are attempting to satisfy their desires by attaining the object á. To attain it, however, eliminates the desire, and subsequently the spectators lose their subjective control. Žižek described this as the paradoxical relationship between the gaze and the object of desire. The object can only be perceived by a gaze that is "distorted" by desire. Without the distortion of desire, the object does not exist. So, the objectified female body only exists in the subjective desire of the male spectator. As a "sex object" in itself, she does not exist, "since [she] is nothing but the embodiment, the materialization of his very distortion, of this surplus of confusion and perturbation introduced by desire into so-called 'objective reality'" (p. 12).

Therefore, while the male customer exerts power over the stripper by constructing her as the object á of his subjective desire, the man is controlled by his very spectatorship. Calling this the "dialectic of the gaze," Žižek (1992) stated,

> The gaze denotes at the same time power (it enables us to exert control over the situation, to occupy the position of the master) and impotence (as bearers of a gaze, we are reduced to the role of passive witnesses to the adversary's action). (p. 72)

From this perspective, the male customers experience the dialectic of the gaze as they are simultaneously in control (they occupy the position of the master) and yet are impotent (both figuratively and literally in this case); as bearers of the gaze, they are reduced to the role of passive witnesses of the adversary's action.

In strip clubs, however, it is not always so clear who is watching whom. As numerous researchers describe, the female dancers watch the customers as much as they are watched (e.g., Ronai and Ellis 1989; Ronai 1992; Wood 2000). Management watches customers and dancers, and dancers watch management. Jill Dolan (1993) recognized the more complex manifestations of gaze in both performances on stage and everyday life. According to Dolan, women have the ability to resist the passive position as the object á of the gaze. The gaze is not unidirectional but instead fraught with exchanges of desire "among performers, spectators, and audiences in particular, historicized, localized contexts" (p. 130). The strippers, then, also experience the dialectic of the gaze, positioning them as mistress[3] and yet rendering them impotent.

Central to this work is how this control/impotence tension translates into creative and constraining dialectic forces of individual action. Giddens (1979), Wentworth (1980), and Eisenberg and Goodall (2001) each described how individuals are molded, formed, and controlled by social forces and institutions, while simultaneously these same individuals shape, create, and reinforce society and social systems of meaning. Giddens called this the duality of structure in which individuals are bound by the governing rules and regulations while open to the possibility of shifting or changing those rules, or even creating new ones. De Certeau (1984) further explored how power is expressed in this dialectical relationship. He distinguished between strategies and tactics. Strategies are dominant forces of power in institutionalized sites such as patriarchy, organizations, and families. They create constraints by dictating what is "proper" within each institutionalized site. For example, in an organization it is proper for an employee to defer to the authority of an employer; in a family, a child defers to a parent. Tactics, on the other hand, are the "art of the weak" (p. 37). Tactics take form as creative guises, trickery, and deception. An employee may defer to the authority of an employer while siphoning money from organizational accounts. The child may return home for a midnight curfew, only to sneak out of a window later in the night. As Wentworth stated, "We are rule and system users and rule and system breakers as well" (p. 40). In light of this, the dancers at Paper Dolls can be seen to tactically negotiate and break the rules that they are simultaneously molded, controlled, and ordered to follow to maintain a "proper" performance when watched by their customers, their managers, and their families.

METHOD

To explore the stripping performances at Paper Dolls, I spent three months (120 hours) observing the practices in the club, including time watching the front-stage activities and hanging out backstage in the dancers' changing room and in the manager's office. Field notes were taken whenever possible, and as discreetly as possible, so as not to draw too much attention to my presence as a researcher. Extensive field notes were written after each observation period. During observations, I informally interviewed dancers, waitresses, bartenders, and floor managers. These interviews were conversational and were not tape-recorded, but notes were taken and the interviewees were aware of the study. I formally interviewed ten dancers, the general manager, two assistant managers, a doorman, a waitress, and the housemother (the person who helps the dancers put on makeup and change clothes). Interviewees were selected to provide a cross section of day—and night—shift workers, ages (ranging from eighteen to thirty-nine), and dancing experience (from two months to nine years). Each person approached agreed to be interviewed for the study and was promised confidentiality in exchange. These formal interviews lasted between one hour and four hours and were all tape-recorded and transcribed. The interviews followed a moderately scheduled format that asked the same questions of each party but allowed for flexibility to follow up interesting tangents. Five of the formal interviews with the dancers, the general manager, the two assistant managers, and the doorman took place privately in the manager's back office. The housemother, waitress, and three of the dancers were interviewed in the dancers' changing room. The final two dancers were formally interviewed in a restaurant. Afraid of how the customers would react to questions, the general manager requested that I not interview them. Following prescribed research methods, field notes and interviews were all analyzed according to prevalent themes of power and resistance (Bantz 1993).

Several characteristics of Paper Dolls merit mention as a context for the research presented here. First, the club sells alcohol and is therefore regulated by the state to follow specific policies. For example, the dancers are only allowed to strip to G-string underwear and must wear pasties over their nipples. Legally, customers are only allowed to touch the dancers on their arms and hips. Second, the club has a policy that no single women are allowed to enter alone as management views them as competition for the dancers. Therefore, throughout this research a male companion or off-duty dancers accompanied me. Third, the dancers are considered employees of the club. They do not have to pay an independent contractor fee for dancing. They do, however, have to tip out the DJ and the housemother.

Prior to this research, I had never been to a topless bar. As a naive participant, I was a woman experiencing a space primarily created for the fantasies of men. Callaway (1992) noted the implications of gender in fieldwork: simultaneously constrained and enabled by gender, researchers will "experience" their fieldwork differently (p. 29).[4] Clearly, my experience of life at Paper Dolls cannot be identical to others. Indeed, Clifford (1986) stated, "Ethnographic writings can properly be called fictions in the sense of 'something made or fashioned'" (p. 6). In this spirit, throughout this analysis I provide italicized ethnographic fictions drawn from interviews and field note data to help provide more contextual narratives for my findings.

DIALECTICAL GAZE: DANCING ON CENTER, ORGANIZATIONAL, AND PRIVATE STAGES

As stated earlier, strippers are molded, controlled, and ordered to maintain a "proper" performance in front of their customers, their managers, and their families. Goffman (1959) noted that a performance is usually given in highly bounded regions. These front regions can be as obvious as dancing on a center stage or as subtle as an evening dinner with family. In either case, in the front region, there are spoken or unspoken "proper" expectations guiding the behavior of the performers and audience members. The "back region," on the other hand, "may be defined as a place, relative to a given performance, where the impression fostered by the performance is knowingly contradicted as a matter of course" (p. 112). Accordingly, for Goffman, it is only in the back region that the vital secrets of the show are supposed to be revealed, where we may discover the discursive tactics such as complex webs of self-presentation, trickery, and deception that help strippers create new rules for power. The following sections detail the front and back regions of the center, organizational, and private stages on which strippers dance. It is important to remember, however, that for strippers, the front and back regions are not so discrete. They must negotiate the competing performance demands associated with their different audiences. For example, performing a table dance for a customer is a front region for that customer but may be a back region for their families. The very tactics that render them powerful in one region may render them impotent in another.

Dancing on Center Stage: Customer and Dancer Relations

"GET THOSE DOLLARS READY, GENTLEMEN, 'CAUSE HERE THEY COME," the DJ screams over Aerosmith singing "Girls, Girls, Girls." Part of the stage is lifted, and thirty dancers descend to infiltrate the main floor. Some men wait by the stage to get first choice for a table dance; others sit back and allow the dancers to come to them. In front of us is a long speaker on which unsolicited dancers are forced to stand. Like an auctioneer, the DJ calls out to the customers to take "one of these fine-looking ladies" until eventually all the dances have been sold. Soon the whole room becomes a faceless mass of bodies moving to the beat of Snoop Doggie Dog. The scene is unnerving and alive with naked bodies moving in synchronicity. They are rhythmic—spellbinding. The second song breaks in, and a whiny voice declares, "I don't like Mondays." Not only is the song undanceable, it is depressing. The awkward move ruptures the rhythm of the room and breaks the spell. The formless bodies once again have a face, some laughing, some glaring at the DJ as they try to move to the music—their hips not able to catch the halting rhythm of the song. I feel uncomfortable in this place—conspicuous. I sit next to my husband, and there are naked breasts everywhere. All sizes. Some real, some not. I mock the women who have fake boobs, yet I wonder why the flat-chested women don't get boob jobs. Small and even average-sized breasts seem out of shape and out of place.

On the surface, the center stage presents an image of dancers as powerless victims in a system that objectifies their sexuality for commerce. Although the chairs in the bar lounge are arranged around a strobe-lighted center stage, the majority of customer–dancer interactions takes place at the guests' individual tables. During these interactions, the customer is released from any traditional expectations—there are no promises of commitment or long-term relationships—he does not have to be witty, nice, or smart for these female bodies to serve and entertain him. To make money in this occupation, dancers must stand almost naked in front of fully clothed men and tolerate their insulting and degrading comments, daily sexual propositions, roving hands, and even some physical threats. Strippers do perform the "proper" performance in front of their customers. As one dancer explained,

"You become whatever they [the customers] want you to be." This is an important statement as she is not saying that the strippers *are* what the customers want them to be. They become or they *perform* what the customers want them to be. To do this, they cannot remain as passive objects of male desire. They must devise creative discursive tactics that simultaneously enable their own active subjectivity yet allow them to appear in the proper form, that of the passively observed.

There is no formal guidebook to teach strippers these strategies. Instead, they rely on informal socialization methods to discuss tips and tactics ranging from how to tell if a man has money to how to handle an obnoxious customer. As noted in stripping literature, some form friendships and mentoring relationships[5] (e.g., Calhoun, Fisher, and Cannon 1998; Carey, Peterson, and Sharpe 1974; Dragu and Harrison 1988; Sweet and Tewksbury 2000). For example, Annie started working at Paper Dolls four months ago. She did not make any money for a week until Kit showed her how to talk to guys and ask them for table dances. "Kit took me under her wing," she says. "It was really nice." Debbie has been at the club only two months. Her friend Stacie recommended the job. Although Stacie no longer works at the club, she has become Debra's mentor, teaching her valuable lessons, such as putting all her money in a safe deposit box and running it through money orders so that it is not traceable by the Internal Revenue Service, explaining how to make the most money on stage, and insisting that she always personally thank a customer who tips her on stage so that she is set up for a table dance. Not all of the dancers at Paper Dolls describe having a mentor or a friend show them the ropes. Jennie explains, "When you first start working, no one is going to tell you what to do because they don't want you to make their money." Phoenix agrees,

You learn by watching; you take a move from one girl, a phrase from another, and a head tilt from that one over there; then after a while you have your own thing. And I have to admit, I do my country act really well.

Whether taught through mentoring friendships or by watching others, knowing how to use the center stage for her own benefit is perhaps the most important tactic a dancer can learn. As documented in other studies on professional and amateur stripping, many of the dancers expressed joy and pride in their performances on stage (Calhoun, Fisher, and Cannon 1998; Carey, Peterson, and Sharpe 1974; Forsyth and Deshotels 1998; Skipper and McCaghy 1971). For example, when Stacie goes out on the main stage, she "wants all eyes on her." She is in her own words "a bit of an exhibitionist." While some of them told me that they "love their time" on the main stage, others admitted they considered it "doing their time." Debbie, for example, hates to dance on the main stage. She said, "I don't have any floor work and it seems like they always have me following the girl who can put her ankles behind her ears."

Despite their different feelings, all agree that the main stage is their opportunity to check out the room. So, just as the strippers are watched, they also watch—from their vantage point on the main stage, they use their nonverbal reading skills to assess where the money is (Ronai and Ellis 1989). A couple of the dancers explained to me that they look for the man who is alone, wearing khaki pants, a button-down oxford shirt, and expensive loafers. One dancer, Jennie, went to a local department store to study what expensive shoes and watches look like so that she would be prepared. "Either a guy has money or he doesn't," she said. "And," she continued, "you don't waste your time on someone who doesn't."

Though the center stage is a critical vantage point for the dancers to shift the power of the gaze, they make little of their money while dancing there. They must try to gain the attention of the customers who they believe have the money to purchase individual table dances. As Wood (2000) noted, customers tend not to approach the women—the dancers typically ask individual customers if they would like a table dance. Several dancers explained that they find it difficult to just walk up to a customer and ask for a dance. Instead, they try to break the ice while on the main stage by trying to make eye contact with a potential "money" customer from the stage. Jennie states, "My gimmick is that I smile." Men tell her that they chose her because she is the "only one who has smiled all night." She explains that she may look like she is having fun, but it is a "fake smile." She said,

> It is not like I am having fun. Most of the time it is just work. I put in my time and get out of there, but you still gotta smile, act like you are having so much fun, and that you are practically falling in love with them.

For her performance to be successful, the dancer must convince a guest that he is the only one she is smiling for. "Confronting man, woman is always play-acting," explained Simone de Beauvoir (1952). "She lies when she makes believe that she accepts her status as the inessential other, she lies when she presents to him an imaginary personage through mimicry, costumery, studied phrases" (p. 543). Enck and Preston (1988) described this deception as "counterfeit intimacy." Through counterfeit actions such as the "fake smile," the dancer can maintain an imaginary relationship with the customer so he is more likely to keep buying table dances from her. She is also able to control the interaction without the customer realizing it. At times, men will attempt to assert their masculine control by becoming more physically aggressive. Although they violate the established rules of touching, men often sit with their legs apart and pull the dancer into them, making them rub up on them. "It makes you so mad," Debra states. "You want to just slap them." But Debra knows she cannot do this without risking the relationship. Rather than directly combat them, the stripper can covertly control the situation by maintaining and even enhancing her performance (Ronai and Ellis 1989). Annie describes the situation like this:

> It is really easy to control. Let's say your back is facing them and they are touching you, you just turn around and step back. Or, if a guy puts his hands on your behind, I just grab his hands and smile, like we are having fun here. I am being friendly by grabbing his hands. I am not being rude like, don't touch me.

The counterfeit performance continues even when the dancing stops. Before or after a table dance, the entertainers will sit and talk with the guests. Jennie laughs as she explains her use of studied phrases.

> When you talk to a guy you have to make them believe you are totally into them. You lean forward and say, "That is *so* interesting." Or, when they tell you about their job you say, "You must be *so* responsible."

The trick is to make the audience feel like they are somehow special or unique. Jennie became so practiced in this counterfeit intimacy that one of the bartenders would imitate her from across the room, mouthing the words, "You must be *so* responsible."

The stripper seduces the customer by manufacturing a believable relationship. They pose as sexual objects to control their audience. While at work in their club, their secrets are "strategic" (Goffman 1959), where their audience expects and desires that there be secrets kept to maintain the performance. Their audience does not want these secrets revealed to them because then they will no longer be able to play in the performance frame that Turner (1988) called "let us make-believe." He will continue to pay as long as he and the stripper can continue to play "make-believe." Stacie states, "I've had guys tell me they love me. One guy gave me his credit card and told me I could have anything I wanted" (she made $3,500 that night).

As the dancers perform the sexual object á of the male desire, they do it from a position of subjective power. Jennie states, "I am making so much money off these guys that are stupid enough to spend it. That is power. What is more power than that?" Annie explains to me, "If I were a guy, I would never come into a place like this. For one thing it costs way too much money. And what do they get for it?" Annie continues, "One time there was this guy who really thought I was going to go out with him." She had been playacting an intimate role with him and was incredulous when he "really" believed her. She continues with an incredulous sadness in her voice: "He said, 'You mean you aren't really going to go out with me?' I couldn't believe he really believed me. I felt so sorry for him." Debra remarks, "The first time I got a drunk guy to give me all his money, I had to go home and call Stacie. I know that is a terrible thing, but [in] there that is the game."

These examples clearly show that the stripper is not solely the passive object of the masculine gaze. She maintains agency through her own watchful eye. Just like the men, however, this position renders them simultaneously in control and controlled. Dancers are not immune from the societal constraints defining their profession as deviant. For example, after calling Stacie to tell of her financial victory, Debra cried all night "from shame." She said, "I couldn't believe that this is how I was going to make a living." They also reveal their own vulnerability in the face of rejection. Kit explains,

It is very bad for your self-esteem. You go to one customer and say, "Hi, would you like a dance?" And they say, "No, I don't have any money." You are like, "No problem," and you leave. Then he buys a dance from every other single woman but you. Tips every other woman but you. Then that brings your self-esteem down and makes you feel ugly.

Again, the dancers are simultaneously in control because they watch and are controlled because they are watched. Their identities are not defined purely as the object of desire of the masculine gaze, nor are they totally immune from it. The next two sections explore this conundrum of control as it plays out in the performative personas of the working stripper and the woman in her private life.

Dancing on an Organizational Stage: Management and Dancer Relationships

Sitting in a small, cluttered office in the back of the club, Bob explains how he came to work for a strip club. "When I turned eighteen, my brother took me to my first titty bar. Just as I was taking a bite out of my cheeseburger, a naked woman stood on the table with her legs on either side of my head." As Bob continues to talk, I can hear the club music playing in the background of our conversation. Jimmy Buffet croons, "Cheeseburger in paradise, paradise." "That was my first naked woman," Bob explained. "Ever since then I have been going to clubs or have been affiliated with them. Not to sound conceited or anything, but I have opened six clubs already and I have worked with some of the best people, knowledgeable. I know how to run entertainers, how to speak to guests, and the floor men. I know exactly what the DJ needs to do. I know what kind of advertising we need to do, what kind of clientele we need in here."

Paper Dolls is a corporation, and as such, in addition to the center stage, the performance of exotic dance takes place on an organizational stage. As in many corporations, the dominant or preferred organizational practices are determined so that all employee actions serve corporate interests. Furthermore, previous research has found that given the morally "tainted" position of strip clubs, they are subject to more scrutiny than other mainstream organizations, and accordingly, managers maintain even closer control over their employees (Ashforth and Kriener 1999; Montemurro 2001). Dancers, therefore, are watched not only by the customer but also by management. During my time at Paper Dolls, I was exposed to the managerial "party line" through my interactions with James, a new assistant manager, and Bob, the new general manager. Proud of his new position, James provided me with his seventy-seven page managerial handbook. The handbook continually reinforces how the manager is the "most important single individual" in the entire organization. James had highlighted the following lines: "The buck stops with the manager. He is the one held accountable for the bottom line." The bottom line is of primary importance to Bob as well. Recently recruited from a sister club as the new general manager in charge of operations at Paper Dolls, Bob is pleased with the club's increased profit margins since his arrival.

Bob's efforts are directed toward a strategic plan to establish Paper Dolls as an "upscale adult entertainment club." De Certeau (1984) reminded us that "as in management, every 'strategic' rationalization seeks first of all to distinguish its 'own' place, that is, the place of its own power and will, from its 'environment'" (p. 36). Paper Dolls has to be distinct from any other club right from the beginning. For Bob, this means the performance must be strictly scripted and starts from the moment the guests walk through the front door. The front door hostess has to be as bubbly and as full of energy and as genuine as you can possibly find. He tells me,

> She should say, "Hey, how are you doing? Welcome to the world-famous Paper Dolls. Where are you guys in town from?" They all have to be with it. It starts right there, and goes all the way down the line to the entertainers.

Bob acknowledges that the entertainers are the center of the business. "Without them, none of us would have a job," he explains. He does not, however, seem to see them as employees; they are viewed as sexual objects to be manipulated and controlled for managerial gain. To do this, Bob says,

> There are times you have to be their brother. There are times you have to be their father. There are times where you have to be, I won't say lover, but intimate. You have to compliment them; you just can't go in and treat them like they are children. That just doesn't work.

His use of intimacy masks a classical, patriarchal management style. He further explains, "Communication is the key to everything. I tell the employees exactly how to do their jobs." During nightly staff meetings, Bob goes over a list of items the entertainers need to pay attention to. Although the show revolves around the entertainers, Bob explains, "They cannot control it. They don't know how to run the show."

In a recent memorandum, Bob laid out the ground rules for employee behavior in the club. "This is my favorite part," he says as he reads the memorandum to me. "Be aware that even though you may not see me, or you know that I am not in the building, it does not mean that I am not conscious of how the club is being run." In saying this, Bob tries to establish his own power through a managerial gaze. He exercises control through unpredictable surveillance. He never tells employees what his hours are or when he might come into work. "That way," he says, "they never know when the boss is going to be around." Foucault (1977) described this as the panoptic gaze in which the major effect of the "panopticon [is] to induce in the inmate a state of conscious and permanent visibility that assures the automatic functioning of power" (p. 200).

Employees functioning under a panoptic gaze do not know when they are being watched. Therefore, they may participate in self-regulation and choose to reproduce organizational policies to avoid disciplinary action.

Bob has been met with ambivalent reviews by the dancers. Some think he is "just what the club needs," that he is "bringing in a more upscale clientele," and that "he is more professional and it is better since he got here." Others state that "this place really blows now," "he is way too corporate and inflexible," and "he is a control freak." Accepting, even if not liking, the masculine power characteristic of sexploitation organizations (Hearn and Parkin 1987), Jennie, a dancer, claims that "dancers know their place. We are dancers and these people are for some God-given right, or by virtue of them being men, managers."

Dancers do appear to know their place. They regulate their behavior and perform a subordinate role on the organizational stage much in the same

way they perform the role of sexual object on the center stage. Participating in self-regulation, however, does not completely strip dancers of their subjectivity or agency. Indeed, the very action of self-regulation demonstrates a level of subjective agency that opens possibilities of resistance (Ashcraft and Pacanowsky 1996; Ferguson 1984). McPhee (1985) further stated, "The capacity to resist gives [people] some degrees of control over the conditions of reproduction of the system" (p. 168).

Most prevalent at Paper Dolls are subtle resistant practices that interfere with the organizational preferred practices. One of the biggest problems facing the managerial staff is that the dancers do not identify with the organizational goals and values. The dancers are not in the business to make money for the club. Therefore, there are a number of entertainers who do not show up for their shifts. Maintaining a resistant air of plausible deniability, they will manufacture excuses to cover up their absences. According to Bob, it is common for a dancer's grandmother to die one week and then be very sick the next. One dancer explains,

> Most of the girls do not consider this a job. They think of it as another part of their social life. So, when they don't show up for a shift, they don't think about it as being unprofessional. They just figure they aren't going out that night.

For these women, their work is not taking their clothes off for money; their play is. This finding is similar to the motivations associated with amateur stripping and male professional stripping rather than female professional stripping (Calhoun, Fisher, and Cannon 1998; Dressel and Peterson 1982; Tewksbury 1993). Sweet and Tewksbury (2000) found that though most women enter the professional stripping profession for money, that is not, however, the only reason that they stay. They claimed that the "party dancer" is one of three different types of women in the stripper occupation. Unlike the "career dancer," whose motivation for stripping is to make money, or the "power dancer," who obtains psychological rewards by being desired by others, the party dancer uses the club as an outlet to enact a lifestyle of alcohol and drug consumption. Regardless of their type of individual motivation, the point here is that motivation is not organizationally driven. By constructing their own meanings for their performances at the club, the dancers defy managerial preferred meanings and practices.

Furthermore, dancers use tactics of trickery and deception to maximize their own profits. Often, these tactics are in opposition to managerial goals. For example, management is not concerned that a particular dancer makes money. It is only necessary that customers remain happy and continue to spend money. The club makes most of its profit margin off the inflated cost of drinks, and a customer must continue to buy drinks for a dancer to remain sitting with him. The dancers' drinks cost the same as regular club drinks. They come, however, in a smaller glass and are made with only half the alcohol content as a regular drink. Dancers have learned to use their drinks for their own profits—to save their spots for a customer with money. Rather than finish an entire drink (something that management wants them to do so that the customer will have to purchase another one), the dancers will sip their drinks and leave them partially full on the table with the customer to mark their spot should they have to leave for any reason. This is important because the dancers make most of their money during personal interactions with the customers, but they are also on a strict rotation schedule to dance on the main stage. For management, nothing is more financially harmful than an empty stage. Therefore, when the dancer's name is

called, she must leave whomever she is with and get ready for her turn on stage. Dancers are forbidden by management to "mark a spot" with a customer when they must leave since management wants the customer to continue spending money by buying drinks for another dancer. The practice, however, was prevalent at Paper Dolls.

Dancers will also attempt to maximize their own profits at the expense of other dancers through tactics such as "blocking." Blocking occurs when one dancer leaves a guest momentarily, either to take her turn on the main stage or to use the bathroom, and another dancer purposefully takes her place. The second dancer may "block" the first one by manufacturing stories about her. She may tell the guest that the first dancer has emotional problems, has a large boyfriend or husband, or hates dancing. Concerned for customer satisfaction, Bob claims he will not tolerate any "blocking" over guests. The policy is not to protect the dancers but to protect the club's financial interests. Knowing that blocking will not stop simply because there is a managerial policy forbidding it, dancers have devised buddy system tactics to counteract blocking. Phoenix explains,

> Let's say I am sitting with a guest and I recognize that he has a lot of money to spend. I will call Kit, a friend, over to sit with them. We will both work together to "drain" him and cover for each other when one of us has to go on the main stage.

Exotic dance is a site of work, and strippers must perform on an organizational stage. Stripped of their voice in decision-making practices, dancers appear powerless as management determines the dominant or preferred organizational practices. Like disempowered workers in a variety of industries, strippers "bargain with the company to accept conditions of subordination for the sake of financial payoffs" (Deetz 1998, 167). And through their own strategies and tactics, dancers undercut managerial authority and determine their own hidden organizational practices and meanings to maximize that financial payoff. The relationship between management and the dancers also reveals that the performance of intimacy is not reserved for the patrons and the dancers. While Bob claims a need to be "intimate" with the dancers to control them, Stacie explains how she uses her sexuality to control Bob. Once she was walking in the mall with her sisters. At the time, none of them knew that she takes her clothes off for a living. She was due in for her shift in thirty minutes, so she slipped away from her sisters to find a phone and call the manager. He was unsympathetic to her plight, saying, "If you don't come in, then find another job." Caught in an impossible dilemma, Stacie chose to risk her job rather than tell her sisters the truth. She told me, "I went to work the next day. Bob looked at me and said, 'Hey, didn't I fire you?' I smiled big at him and said really sweetly, 'Yeah, but I figured you didn't mean it. I brought you cookies.'" Stacie's story shows the dialectic of control and subordination possible in the stripper as employee discourse. She plays off the very means of her subordination to control the situation and to get her job back. Her story also shows the third stage on which strippers must perform—the private stage.

Dancing on a Private Stage: Family and Dancer Relationships

No one in Stacie's family knew she had been stripping for almost a year. Every night before she left for work, she would call her mother. "That way," she explained, "she would have talked to me once a day, and wouldn't be likely to call later that night."

Stacie's system of lies was working. Due to the nightly phone calls, her mother had no reason to wonder where she was. But one night she wanted to talk to someone, so she called her sister. "I felt so isolated and alone. So I told my sister." Stacie thought she could tell her anything and really wanted to share it with her. "My mother told me she found out because someone saw me," Stacie said with resignation. "But nobody would have seen me there. I mean, nobody that she knows. They are all church people and they wouldn't have been there." Stacie's parents were so upset that her mother told her, "We know we are going to find you lying dead in a gutter somewhere." Her parents stopped talking to her for three months. Then they began calling the club and asking for her by her stage name. When she would get on the phone they would tell her she was going to "burn in hell." She had to continually change her stage name so that her parents wouldn't know whom to ask for. I am struck by the ironic life of the stripper: privately she must hide what publicly she exposes. She can't tell her family or close friends what she does; yet she can sit in a crowded restaurant and tell her secrets to me.

Throughout Western history and in numerous cultures, women have been paid to be attractive or to provide men with sexual gratification. If these women do so in traditional, heterosexual ways such as wife and mother, they are considered "Madonnas" or "good girls" (McCormick 1994, 83). However, if they are heterosexual women with multiple partners, or sex workers who exchange sexual services for money, they are "bad girls," promiscuous, and "despised as 'whores'" (McCormick 1994, 83). The good girl–bad girl dichotomy reflects cultural judgments regarding the (de)sexualization of women. To be good means to suppress one's sexuality; to be bad means to express and embody sexuality. Strippers are caught among competing institutionalized forces regarding these bad girl–good girl performances (de Certeau 1984). The gaze of the center and organizational stages requires and legitimizes "bad girl" practices. Private relationships, including families, however, require them to maintain a "good girl" performance.

As noted in previous research (e.g., Reid, Epstein, and Benson 1994a, 1994b; Ronai and Ellis 1989), the strippers at Paper Dolls employ identification tactics to resist the "bad girl" image. For example, they commonly referenced their own work in opposition to the strippers at another local club. "I thought these clubs were all prostitutes and drug addicts, dark walls and red lights," Kit admits. "But it isn't like that here," she continues. "It's not like the club down the street." Other typical distinguishing comments are, "If you are going to prostitute yourself then you should just go to [other club]." "We are 'good girls' here; if you want 'that,' you better go to the [other club]." "If guys come in looking for action like that, I send them to the [other club]." By projecting the "bad" characteristics associated with sex work on the other clubs, the strippers at Paper Dolls maintain their own "good girl" image in relation to the others.

The strippers define themselves as a group when comparing their "higher class" version of dance to that of other strippers. There is also research support indicating that strippers will rely on this group outside of the club and form a "family" of sorts as a means of negotiating the potentially isolating and deviant occupation (e.g., Thompson and Harred 1992). Many of the dancers at Paper Dolls, however, claim they do not want to maintain a group identity or even associate with any coworkers outside of the club. "I'm sorry," Kit says, "when we are working I will be your best friend, but I can't socialize with girls that will *act like a dancer*

after work." Acting like a dancer outside of the club jeopardizes the rationalization many use for dancing in the first place. Strippers try to separate their "working" identities from their "real" ones (Ronai 1992; Thompson and Harred 1992). They make comments such as "I am really a college student," "I am different than the other girls here," and "I am only doing this for a little while to make some fast cash." Kit sums up this distinction: "I put the wig on and I am a dancer; I take it off and I am me." "When I leave this place, I leave it all behind me," Phoenix says. "It doesn't impact my home life; I won't let it." Though she makes less money, Phoenix works the day shift so that she can more easily present the "proper" image to her two sons who believe she works as an executive secretary.

All the strippers I spoke with were keeping their stripping a secret from someone important in their lives. Like Phoenix, some were hiding it from their children. "My daughters only know that I work in a big people's place," Annie says. Others were hiding it from parents: "I was raised with conservative midwestern ideals. I will never tell my parents what I am doing," explains Debra. In this way, many dancers engage in "defensive strategies" to maintain their secret identities (Goffman 1959). They ambiguously tell people that they dance, that they are entertainers, or that they "work in a bar." Annie, whose father is the deacon of a church, says, "When people ask me directly, I don't lie. I mean I *am* a dancer. They don't need to know that I take my clothes off." Others employ more extensive defensive practices. Kit tells people she is a teacher (she does teach children physical fitness part-time at a local community center). All but three of Debra's family and friends believe she is a nurse's aide. She says,

I lie. I am a liar now. I have become a liar. I can honestly say that before [this job] I was a very honest person. But now I lie.

I lie about my lies. I can't remember who I told what or where I am supposed to be on this night.

Through her secrets and lies, the stripper is not only on stage while she is dancing; she is on stage in her private life as well. However, unlike the strategic secrets she keeps from the customers where she and the patrons play "let us make-believe," the secrets she keeps in her personal relationships are dark. Goffman (1959) described a dark secret as one kept in a relationship in which there are no expectations that any secrets should be kept. The audience does not know or expect that any secret is being kept so the performance is framed in what Turner (1988) would call "let us believe." If her dark secrets are discovered, her carefully constructed "good girl" image is destroyed, as stripping is incompatible with the image of self that she attempts to maintain before her private audience.

Making their dark secrets difficult to maintain is the way their bodies become marked as "strippers." The "stripper look," according to the club manager, is "tanned, thin, and in shape." Strippers manipulate their bodies to achieve the "stripper look," going on crash diets and laying in tanning booths—sometimes twice a day. The most drastic form of bodily manipulation is breast augmentation. Annie states, "Most girls get boob jobs if they are going to strip for any length of time." They spend much of their private time preparing for their public performance.

She may be able to remove a wig or change her clothes, but the bodily manipulations are not something the stripper can remove once she leaves the club. In fact, Jennie claims she can pick out a stripper anywhere by the way she walks and the way she looks. Similar to an experience related by Ronai (1992), Jennie explained that once when a man stared at her in the mall, she wanted to scream, "If you are going to look at me, then you better give me money!" She may not have been in a strip club, but her body still had the look.

Foucault (1977) claimed that the manipulation of the body, the molding it into the wanted as opposed to leaving its natural form, is the turning point in the creation of power relations. It is through the body that women in our culture learn their own particular forms of self-surveillance. Sandra Bartky (1998) identified the "panoptical male connoisseur" in women's consciousness (quoted in Wolff 1990, 127). Women learn how to monitor their own appearances and conform to what the culture presents as the ideal for femininity. In this way, "the discursive practices that produce 'femininity' are in the culture and within women. It is through the body that women collude in their own oppression" (Wolff 1990, 127). Strippers provide an obvious example of feminine collusion as they manage their appearances by disciplining and manipulating their bodies to fit an ideal feminine image. Yet it is also through their bodies that strippers enable themselves and construct their own subjectivity. They are both subject and object in the process. Ashcraft and Pacanowsky (1996) explained that it is important to recognize that women are active agents in their own oppression. As is the case with their self-regulation on the center and organizational stages, their agency in private performances allows the capacity for resistance. Through the lives of strippers, we can see that people can be caught in contradictions that they simultaneously resist and reproduce, challenging meanings as they also undermine those challenges.

CONCLUSION: SEXUALITY, PERFORMANCE, AND WOMEN'S WORK

Fumbling for a match, Kit finally lights a cigarette, takes a long drag, and with smoke still emerging from her lips says, "I have always been a dancer. When I am up there, I usually wear a wig and I am a whole different person. I am more theater than anything. I am not the typical 'here are my boobies, here is my butt.' No, I am going to show you aerobics, gymnastics, ballet, and theater all at once. And I do. … The younger guys go for the big-boobed, blonde-haired, dream-looking girl. I have natural boobs, and they are big enough to where I can make money off them." Later in the interview she tells me, "But, the job screws with your outside relationships. It ruins you. I used to have a fiancé and when I would get home from the club he would say 'I love you.' I told him, 'I know you love me; hell, so does everybody else, give me something.' Eventually he started throwing thousands of dollars on the bed and that would turn me on. It was money."

Separating the center, organizational, and private stages is an effective analytical tool to understand the different stages on which strippers must perform. As has been shown, there are clearly defined and conflicting requirements for what constitutes a "proper" performance of self for the various viewing audiences. The dancers negotiate the constraints of the "proper" performance with their own creative actions. They do this through discursive tactics that range from nonverbal displays (holding hands and laughing, while moving the customer's hands away from their bodies), strategic secrets (counterfeiting

an intimate relationship with the customer and/or the manager to control the relationship), and dark secrets (lying to family and friends about their occupations).

Considering all three stages together contributes to the growing literature on stripping by extending the theories used to understand the performance of self. For example, several studies compare Hochschild's work on the emotional management of flight attendants to performance of emotion by strippers (e.g., Montemurro 2001; Ronai 1992; Wood 2000). Drawing on Goffman's (1959) theory of impression management, Hochschild created dichotomies between public and private selves that are used interchangeably with false and true selves (Wouters 1989). Like putting on and taking off masks, workers are seen as presenting a false self in public, while a true self is expressed only in private. This image works well for flight attendants to explain how they are required to sell their smiles as part of their service (Hochschild 1983; Murphy 1998, 2001). The comparison to strippers does not hold up as well when you consider how in practice, the boundaries among the stages and between false and true selves are much more blurred.

For example, in the excerpt above, Kit displays a sense of pride in her center-stage performance. She claims to be a "whole different person" when on the center stage. She also, however, explains how her working performance interferes with her private relationships. In this case, Kit's "bad girl" or stripper identity is not separate or any less real than her personal identity. Although numerous studies, including this one, show that strippers attempt to keep them distinct (i.e., "in my 'real' life, I am a college student") as a way of coping with their sexualized and stigmatized profession, the idea of a "real" self and a "performative" self is arbitrary, and keeping them separate is a rational ideal. Strippers may claim to take on a different persona when working. If they could, however, really see their occupation as role-playing, as distinct from their "real" selves, then it would not affect their self-esteem. Furthermore, though she may not wear a wig to disguise herself in her private interactions, many dancers keep dark secrets from their families, performing a self that is no more real than the characters they play on stage.

Accordingly, an analysis of women who strip is about more than regional impression or emotional management. Identity is more complex than either an objective or even subjective presentation of self for different audiences. As Dolan (1993) stated, "Identity becomes a site of struggle, at which the subject organizes and reorganizes [within the constraints of] competing discourses as they fight for supremacy" (p. 88). This is particularly evident in the case of women who strip as they simultaneously exist in and with conflicting requirements for their displays of self. In her analysis of her own conflicting roles as stripper and researcher, Ronai (1999) described this process as "drawing, erasing, drawing again, composing, and destroying narratives of the self within contexts that are constantly in flux (p. 128)." As such, strippers are neither pure object nor pure subject but negotiate their own agency resources and constraints within each of these conflicting fields.

Blurring the boundaries between work and home, public and private realms, this work also provides a lens into more than the world of sex work. It offers a magnification of the sexualized and intimate roles that many working women perform, showing that sex work may not solely lie in sexploitation organizations. Sex work has been viewed as an oxymoron. We are taught to think of organizations as "pure products" (Clifford 1988) where work does not encompass sex and sex does not encompass work. Feminine sexuality, however, is a spoken or unspoken component in all workplace settings. As a category, women are marked (Tannen 1994). To be unmarked is to be without descriptors. In Western culture, white, heterosexual males constitute the unmarked category. As the norm, it is assumed that the unmarked category is present unless otherwise indicated. Therefore, any other deviation must be marked with a qualifying descriptor: a lady doctor, a female manager, a woman lawyer. Accordingly, every woman's life, whether she is a stripper or not, is a sexual performance (Butler 1990; Dolan 1993).

Speaking about the gendered strategies of mainstream working women, Nadesan and Tretheway (2000) stated, "In short, the literature indicates that the woman with the entrepreneurial spirit is able to manage her life and career successfully through shaping and disciplining her very body, in terms of its image, sexuality, and nonverbal displays" (p. 237). Clearly, it is not just in the sex work industry where sex works in women's lives. And it is not just strippers who must live with and negotiate the ambivalences associated with a subject–object dichotomy. Waggoner and O'Brien Hallstein (2001) turned the research lens back on themselves and other feminist scholars by considering what they called the agency/constraint conundrum of feminists who love clothes. They find that although feminist scholars realize that the fashion industry objectifies the female body, making "no distinction between a woman and her attire," they still desire and embrace the idea of being fashionable (p. 27). And, like the strippers, they are neither fully object nor fully subject, neither complete agents nor completely constrained. To negotiate this ambivalence, they even display role-playing and identity distancing tactics very similar to those used by strippers. Nadesan and Tretheway continued,

> Despite the emotional and physical labor that must be expended to successfully perform an exemplary identity, many women may feel that they have little choice in this matter as organizational performance measures increasingly focus

on the employee's ability to embody and enact a highly prescribed image. (p. 223)

Given the need for all women to perform their prescribed gender in the course of their everyday lives, the occupation of the exotic dancer may not be as deviant as previously defined.

Much past work on female exotic dance has characterized strippers as either passive, objectified victims of a sexploitation system that trades on their bodies for financial gain or as active subjects who work the exchange for their own benefit. By considering (and blurring) all three stage performances, this work shows that it cannot be one or the other. Power circulates through the system of discursive relationships forming a dialectic of agency and constraint in which strippers are simultaneously subjects and objects. The strippers at Paper Dolls empower themselves through performative tactics that do not confront reified power structures (whether masculine, organizational, or familial) head-on. Instead, they role-play, lie, and distort their images to aid their own agendas. At the same time, a sense of ambivalence emerges through the visual representation as strippers negotiate their own identity resources and constraints. Indicating a level of subjective desire, there is a sense of pride that arises from the identity implications for a woman dancing on a stage: as part of her identity, she wants to be watched. She is, however, constrained by her own visibility. And given the sexualized visibility of all working women, there is no "off stage" for the stripper to go.

NOTES

1. The names of the club and the employees have been changed to provide confidentiality.
2. For a more complete review of stripping literature, see Calhoun, Fisher, and Cannon (1998).

3. "Mistress" is used here as the female equivalent to "master" used in the previous paragraph. The sexualized connotation of mistress should not be ignored.
4. During these initial visits, I felt uncomfortable, conspicuous. I felt like I had entered a male fantasy cliche: football played on a gigantic television screen adjacent to a main stage where a topless woman danced around a pole filled with bubbling water. My fourth visit marked a turning point in my research. At one point in the evening, Bob, the manager of the club, came over and told me to take a seat in a chair he had retrieved from a nearby table. In front of me was a blonde woman wearing a black Lycra bra and G-string bottoms and holding a tray full of shots in test tubes. "What do you want, sex on the beach?" Bob asked as I tried to figure out what was going on. "Sex on the beach is fine," I replied, still not knowing the full implications of that response. The woman took one of the liquid-filled test tubes off her tray and with her head tilted back lowered the test tube down her throat and back up again; then, with the end of the tube still in her mouth, she leaned over me putting the other end in my mouth, forcing the alcohol down my throat. Cheers rang out as I finished the shot. I was no longer watching the spectacle; I had become a part of the show. Later, I realized the importance of that shot. If I had turned it down, I would have rejected the lifestyle of the organizational members I was trying to understand. After that evening, I had open access to the club.
5. Past studies on professional stripping have found that relationships can turn romantic or sexual. See, for example, McCaughy and Skipper (1969), Ronai and Ellis (1989), and Calhoun, Fisher, and Cannon (1998), who all discussed the prevalence of lesbianism in strip

clubs. Although this may have been prevalent for the strippers at Paper Dolls, it was not a finding in this study.

AUTHOR'S NOTE: I would like to thank Chris Green, Mark Neumann, Elizabeth Bell, and my writers' group for their valuable feedback and encouragement on this work. I am also grateful for the critical and constructive insights offered by Rob Benford and the two anonymous reviewers of the Journal of Contemporary Ethnography.

REFERENCES

Ashcraft, Karen L., and Michael E. Pacanowsky. 1996. "A woman's worst enemy": Reflections on a narrative of organizational life and female identity. *Journal of Applied Communication Research* 24:217–39.

Ashforth, B.E., and G. E.Kriener. 1999. "How can you do it?" Dirty work and the challenge of constructing a positive identity. *Academy of Management Review* 24:413–34.

Bantz, Charles. 1993. *Understanding organizations: Interpreting organizational communication cultures.* Columbia: University of South Carolina Press.

Barry, Kathleen. 1995. *The prostitution of sexuality.* New York: New York City Press.

Bartky, Sandra. 1988. Foucault, femininity, and the modernization of patriarchal power. In *Feminism and Foucault: Reflections on resistance*, edited by I. Diamond and L. Quinby, 61–86. Boston: Northeastern University Press.

Bell, Elizabeth. 1993. Performance studies as women's work: Historical sights/sites/citations from the margin. *Text and Performance Quarterly* 13:350–74.

Bell, L. 1987. Introduction. In *Good girls, bad girls: Feminists and sex trade workers face to face*, edited by L. Bell. Seattle, WA : Seal Press.

Butler, Judith. 1990. *Gender trouble: Feminism and the subversion of identity.* New York: Routledge.

Calhoun, Thomas C., Julie Ann Harms Cannon, and Rhonda Fisher. 1996. Amateur stripping: Sexualized entertainment and gendered fun. *Sociological Focus* 29:155–66.

Calhoun, Thomas C., Rhonda Fisher, and Julie Ann Harms Cannon. 1998. The case of amateur stripping: Sex codes and egalitarianism in a heterosocial setting. In *The American ritual tapestry*, edited by Mary Jo Deegan, 47–61. Westport, CT: Greenwood.

Callaway, Helen. 1992. Ethnography and experience: Gender implications for field-work and texts. In *Anthropology and autobiography*, edited by Judith Oakley and Helen Callaway, 29–50. London: Routledge.

Cannon, Julie Ann Harms, Thomas C. Calhoun, and Rhonda Fisher. 1998. Amateur stripping and gaming encounters: Fun in games or gaming as fun. *Deviant Behavior* 19 (4): 317–37.

Carey, S. R., R. A. Peterson, and L. K. Sharpe. 1974. A study of recruitment and socialization in two deviant occupations. *Sociology Symposium* 11:11–24.

Clifford, James. 1986. Introduction: Partial truths. In *Writing culture: The poetics and politics of ethnography*, edited by J. Clifford and G. Marcus. Berkeley: University of California Press.

———. 1988. *The predicament of culture: Twentieth-century ethnography, literature, and art.* Cambridge, MA: Harvard University Press.

de Beauvoir, Simone. 1952. *The second sex.* New York: Knopf.

de Certeau, Michel. 1984. *The practice of everyday life.* Berkeley: University of California Press.

Deetz, Stanley A. 1998. Discursive formations, strategized subordination and self-surveillance. In *Foucault, management, and organizational theory*, edited by A. McKinlay and K. Starken, 151–72. London: Sage.

Dolan, Jill. 1993. *Presence and desire*. New York: Routledge.

Dragu, M., and A. S. A. Harrison. 1988. *Revelations: Essays on striptease and sexuality*. London: Nightwood Editions.

Dressel, Paula, and David Peterson. 1982. Becoming a male stripper: Recruitment, socialization, and ideological development. *Work and Occupations* 9:387–406.

Eisenberg, Eric M., and H. L. Goodall Jr. 2001. *Organizational communication: Balancing creativity and constraint*. 3d ed. New York: St. Martin's.

Enck, Graves E., and James D. Preston. 1988. Counterfeit intimacy: A dramaturgical analysis of an erotic performance. *Deviant Behavior* 9:369–81.

Ferguson, Kathy E. 1984. *A feminist case against bureaucracy*. Philadelphia: Temple University Press.

Forsyth, Craig, and Tina H. Deshotels. 1998. A deviant process: The sojourn of the stripper. *Sociological Spectrum* 18 (1): 77–92.

Foucault, Michel. 1977. *Discipline and punish: The birth of a prison*. New York: Pantheon.

Giddens, Anthony. 1979. *Central problems in social theory*. London: Hutchinson.

Goffman, Erving. 1959. *The presentation of self in everyday life*. New York: Doubleday.

Hanna, Judith. 1998. Undressing the First Amendment and corseting the striptease dancer. *Drama Review* 42 (2): 38–69.

Hearn, Judith, and Wendy Parkin. 1987. *Sex at work: The power and paradox of organization sexuality*. New York: St. Martin's.

Hochschild, Arlie R. 1983. *The managed heart: The commercialization of human feeling*. Berkeley: University of California Press.

Margolis, M. L., and M. Arnold. 1993. Turning the tables? Male strippers and the gender hierarchy in America. In *Sex and gender hierarchies*, edited by B. D. Miller, 334–50. Cambridge, UK: Cambridge University Press.

McCaghy, Charles H., and James K. Skipper. 1969. Lesbian behavior as an adaptation to the occupation of stripping. *Social Problems* 17:262–70.

McCormick, N. B. 1994. *Sexual salvation: Affirming women's sexual rights and pleasures*. Westport, CT: Praeger.

McPhee, Robert D. 1985. Formal structure and organizational communication. In *Organizational communication: Traditional themes and new directions*, edited by R. D. McPhee and P. K. Tompkins. Beverly Hills, CA: Sage.

Montemurro, Beth. 2001. Strippers and screamers: The emergence of social control in a noninstitutionalized setting. *Journal of Contemporary Ethnography* 30 (3): 275–304.

Murphy, Alexandra G. 1998. Hidden transcripts of flight attendant resistance. *Management Communication Quarterly* 11 (4): 499–535.

———. 2001. The flight attendant dilemma: An analysis of communication and sensemaking during in-flight emergencies. *Journal of Applied Communication Research* 29 (1): 30–53.

Nadesan, Majia H., and Angela Tretheway. 2000. Performing the enterprising subject: Gendered strategies for success(?). *Text and Performance Quarterly* 20 (3): 223–50.

Peterson, David, and Paula Dressel. 1982. Equal time for women. *Urban Life* 11:185–208.

Reid, Scott A., Jonathon A. Epstein, and D. E. Benson. 1994. Role identity in a devalued occupation: The case of female exotic dancers. *Sociological Focus* 27:1017.

———. 1995. Does exotic dancing pay well but cost dearly? In *Readings in deviance*, edited by Alex Thio and Thomas C. Calhoun. New York: HarperCollins.

Ronai, Carolyn R. 1992. The reflexive self through narrative: A night in the life of an erotic dancer/researcher. In *Investigating subjectivity: Research on lived experience*, edited by C. Ellis and M. Flaherty. Newbury Park, CA: Sage.

———. 1999. The next night sous rapture: Wrestling with Derrida's mimesis. *Qualitative Inquiry* 5 (1): 114–30.

Ronai, Carol R., and Rebecca Cross. 1998. Dancing with identity: Narrative resistance strategies of male and female stripteasers. *Deviant Behavior* 19 (2): 99–119.

Ronai, Carol R., and Carolyn Ellis. 1989. Turn-ons for money: Interactional strategies of the table dancer. *Journal of Contemporary Ethnography* 18:271–98.

Skipper, James K., and Charles H. McCaghy. 1970. Stripteasers: The anatomy and career contingencies of a deviant occupation. *Social Problems* 17 (3): 391–405.

———. 1971. Stripteasing, a sex oriented occupation. In *The sociology of sex*, edited by J. Henslin, 275–96. New York: Appleton-Century-Crofts.

St. James, M. 1987. The reclamation of whores. In *Good girls, bad girls: Feminists and sex trade workers face to face*, edited by L. Bell. Seattle, WA: Seal Press.

Sweet, N., and Richard Tewksbury. 2000. Entry, maintenance, and departure from a career in the sex industry: Strippers' experiences of occupational costs and rewards. *Humanity and Society* 24 (2): 136–61.

Tannen, Deborah. 1994. *Talking from nine to five: Who women's and men's conversational styles affect who gets heard, who gets credit, and what gets done at work*. New York: William Morrow.

Tewksbury, Richard. 1993. Men objectifying men: The case of male strippers. In *Doing women's work: Men in nontraditional occupations*, edited by Christine L. Williams, 168–81. Newbury Park, CA: Sage.

———. 1994. A dramaturgical analysis of male strippers. *Journal of Male Studies* 2 (4): 325–42.

Thompson, William E., and Jackie L. Harred. 1992. Topless dancers: Managing stigma in a deviant occupation. *Deviant Behavior* 13:291–311.

Tretheway, Angela. 1998. Disciplined bodies: Women's embodied identities as work. *Organization Studies* 20 (3): 423–50.

Turner, Victor. 1988. *The anthropology of performance*. New York: PAJ.

Waggoner, Catherine E., and D. Lynn O'Brien Hallstein. 2001. Feminist ideologies meet fashionable bodies: Managing the agency/constraint conundrum. *Text and Performance Quarterly* 21 (1): 26–46.

Wentworth, W. 1980. *Context and understanding*. New York: Elsevier.

Wolff, J. 1990. *Feminine sentences: Essays on women and culture*. Los Angeles: University of California Press.

Wood, Elizabeth A. 2000. Working in the fantasy factory: The attention hypothesis and the enacting of masculine power in strip clubs. *Journal of Contemporary Ethnography* 29 (1): 5–31.

Wouters, C. 1989. The sociology of emotions in flight attendants: Hochschild's *Managed Heart*. *Theory, Culture, and Society* 6:95–123.

Žižek, Slavoj. 1992. *Looking awry: An introduction to Jacque Lacan through popular culture*. Cambridge, MA: MIT Press.

Alexandra G. Murphy received her Ph.D. in communication from the University of South Florida. She is an associate professor of communication at DePaul University where she teaches a variety of courses in organizational communication, including gender, culture, power, and politics in the workplace. Her current research explores the cultural feminization of occupations such as flight attendants, nurses, and exotic dancers as it relates to understandings of organizational identity and power.

Born to Belonging

By Tim Wise

8

> *"People who imagine that history flatters them (as it does, indeed, since they wrote it) are impaled on their history like a butterfly on a pin and become incapable of seeing or changing themselves, or the world. This is the place in which it seems to me, most white Americans find themselves. Impaled. They are dimly, or vividly, aware that the history they have fed themselves is mainly a lie, but they do not know how to release themselves from it, and they suffer enormously from the resulting personal incoherence."*
>
> —James Baldwin,
> "THE WHITE MAN'S GUILT,"
> *Ebony,* August 1965

It is nothing if not difficult to know where to begin when you first sit down to trace the story of your life. Does your life begin on the day you came into this world, or does it begin before that, with the lives of your family members—your parents and grandparents and such—without whom you would never have existed?

For me, there is only one possible way in which to answer the question. My story has to begin before the day I entered the world, October 4, 1968,

for I did not emerge onto a blank slate of neutral circumstance. My life was already a canvass upon which older paint had begun to dry, long before I arrived. My parents were already who they were, with their particular life experiences, and I was to inherit those experiences, for good or ill, whether I liked it or not.

What I'm trying to say is that when we first draw breath outside the womb, we inhale tiny particles of all that came before, both literally and figuratively. We are never merely individuals; we are never alone; we are always in the company, as uncomfortable as it sometimes can be, of others, the past, of history. We become part of that history just as surely as it becomes part of us. There is no escaping it, merely different levels of coping. It is how we bear the past that matters, and in many ways it is all that differentiates us.

I was born amidst great turmoil, none of which had been of my own making, but which I could hardly have escaped in any event. My mother had carried me throughout all of the great upheavals of that tumultuous year, 1968,—perhaps one of the most explosive and monumental years in twentieth century America. She had carried me through the Tet Offensive in Vietnam, through the assassinations of Martin Luther King Jr. and Robert Kennedy, through the decision by President Johnson not to seek reelection in the midst of the unfolding murderous quagmire in Southeast Asia, and through the upheaval in the streets of Chicago during that year's Democratic Party convention. I think that any child born in 1968 must, almost by definition, be especially affected by the history that surrounded him or her upon arrival—there was too much energy floating around, good and bad, not to have left a mark.

Once born, I inherited my family and all that came with it. I also inherited my nation and all that came with that. And I inherited my "race" and all that came with that, too. In all three cases, the inheritance was far from inconsequential.

More than that, all three inheritances were intimately connected, intertwined in ways I could not possibly have understood at the time, but which are all too clear today. To be the child of Michael Julius Wise and Lucinda Anne (McLean) Wise meant something; to be born in the richest and most powerful nation on earth meant something; and to be white, especially in the United States, most assuredly meant something—a lot of things, truth be told.

What those inheritances meant, and still mean, is the subject of this inquiry; it is the theme that will be revisited again and again in these pages, with special emphasis on the last issue: What does it mean to be white, especially in a nation created for the benefit of people like you?

We don't often ask this question, mostly because we don't have to. Being a member of the majority, the dominant group, allows one to ignore how race shapes one's life. For those of us called white, whiteness simply *is*. Whiteness becomes, for us, the unspoken, uninterrogated norm, taken for granted, much as water can be taken for granted by a fish.

In high school, whites are sometimes asked to think about race, but rarely about whiteness. In my case, we read John Howard Griffin's classic book, *Black Like Me,* in which the author recounts his experiences in the Jim Crow South in 1959, after taking a drug that turned his skin brown and allowed him to experience apartheid for a few months from the other side of the color line.

It was a good book, especially for its time. Yet I can't help but find it a bit disturbing that it remains one of the most assigned volumes on summer reading lists dealing with race. That it continues to prove so popular signifies the extent to which race is considered a problem of the past—the book, after all, is more than four decades old, and surely there are some more contemporary racial events students could discuss—not to mention the degree to which race is still viewed as something that can only be understood from the perspective of "the other." Whites are encouraged to think about race from the perspective of blacks, which is nice. Indeed, whites *should* listen to and learn from the stories of black and brown peoples—real black and brown peoples, not white men pretending to be black until the drugs wear off. But Black Like Me leaves another aspect of the discussion untouched: namely, the examination of the white experience.

Although whiteness may mean different things in different places and at different times, one thing I feel confident saying up front, without fear of contradiction, is that to be white in the United States, whether from the South, as I am, or from the North, West, or Midwest, whether one is rich or poor; male or female; Jew or Gentile; straight or gay, is to have certain common experiences based solely upon race. These experiences have to do with advantage, privilege (in the relative sense, vis-á-vis people of color), and belonging. We are, unlike people of color, *born* to belonging, and have rarely had to prove ourselves deserving of our presence here. At the very least we can say that our right to be here hasn't been questioned, in the most part, for a long time.

While some might insist that whites have a wide range of experiences, and so, presumably, it isn't fair to make generalizations about whites as a group, this is a dodge, and not a particularly artful one at that. Of course we're all different, sort of like snowflakes, which come to think of it are also white. None of us have led the exact same life. But irrespective of one's particular history, all whites were placed above all persons of color when it came to the economic, social, and political hierarchies that were to form in the United States, without exception. This formal system of racial preference was codified in law from the 1600s until at least 1964, at which time the Civil Rights Act was passed, if not 1965, with the passage of the Voting Rights Act, or 1968 (that year again), when our nation finally passed a law making racial housing discrimination illegal.

Prior to that time we didn't even pretend to be a nation based on equality. Or rather we did pretend, but not very well; at least not to the point where the rest of the world believed it, or to the point where people of color in this country ever did. Most white folks believed it, but that's simply more proof of our privileged status. Our ancestors had the luxury of believing those things that black and brown folks could never take as givens: all that stuff about life, liberty, and the pursuit of happiness. Several decades later, whites can, indeed *must,* still believe it, while people of color have little reason to join the celebration, knowing as they do that there is still a vast gulf between who we say we are as a nation and people, and who we really are.

In other words, there is enough commonality about the white experience to allow us to make some general statements about whiteness and never be too far from the mark. Returning to the snowflake analogy, although as with snowflakes, no two white people are exactly alike, it is also true that few snowflakes have radically different experiences from those of the average snowflake. Likewise, we know a snowflake when we see one, and in that recognition we intuit, almost always correctly, something about its life experience.

CLIMBING THE FAMILY TREE AND SURVEYING THE PRIVILEGED LAND BELOW

At first glance, mine would not appear to have been a life of privilege. Nor would it seem that I had been born to any particularly impressive set of inherited advantages. Far from affluent, my father was an on-again, off-again stand-up comedian and actor, and my mother has worked for most of my life in marketing research. While I was growing up, my parents' income would have fallen somewhere in the range of what is politely considered working class, even though their jobs were not traditional working-class jobs. Had it not been for the financial help of my grandparents, it is altogether likely that we would have been forced, at certain points along the way, to rely on food stamps. Most certainly we would have qualified for them in several of my years as a child.

I spent the first eighteen years of my life in a perfectly acceptable but inadequately maintained 850-square-foot apartment with spotty plumbing, a leaky air conditioner, certainly no dishwasher or washing machine, and floorboards near the sliding glass door in my bedroom that were perpetually rotting, allowing roly-polies or slugs to occasionally find their way inside. The walls stand out in my mind as well: thin enough to hear every fight my parents ever had, and to cave in easily under the weight of my father's fists, whenever the mood struck him to ventilate the plaster.

But before the busted-up walls or the leaky faucets at the Royal Arms Apartments (funny how folks always try to make the most average places sound palatial), there had already been quite a bit of family water under the proverbial bridge.

Examining the source of that stream provides substantial insight into the workings of privilege, and the ways in which even whites who lived, as I did, in modest surroundings, had been born to belonging nonetheless.

Even if one does not directly inherit the material advantages of one's ancestry, there is something empowering about the ability to trace one's lineage back dozens of generations, as so many whites but so few persons of color can. In 1977, when my third grade teacher would encourage the students to trace our family trees—inspired by the miniseries *Roots,* and not cognizant of how injurious it might be for black students to make the effort, only to run head-first into the crime of slavery and its role in their family background—it was apparent that the white kids, who could go back much further and with less pain than the black kids, had gained a sense of pride, even *rootedness,* as a result.

Genealogy itself is something of a privilege, coming far more easily to those of us for whom enslavement, conquest, and dispossession of our land has not been our lot. Genealogy offers a sense of belonging and connectedness to others, with firm, identifiable pasts—pasts that directly trace the rise and fall of empires, and which correspond to the events we learned about in history classes, so focused were they on the narratives of European peoples. Even when we personally have no desire to affiliate ourselves with those in our past about whom we learn, simply knowing from whence you came has the effect of linking you in some great chain of mutuality. It is enabling, if far from ennobling. It offers a sense of psychological comfort, a sense that you belong in this story known as the history of the world. It is to make real the famous words, "This land is *my* land."

As I sat down recently to examine my various family histories, I have to admit to a sense of excitement as I peeled back layer upon layer, generation after generation. It was like a game, in which the object was to see how far back you could go before hitting a dead end.

Sure enough, on several branches of my family tree, I had no trouble going back hundreds, even thousands of years. In large measure this was because those branches extended through to royal lineage, where records were kept meticulously, so as to make sure everyone knew to whom the spoils of advantage were owed in each new generation.

Make no mistake, my claim to royal lineage here—including the Capets in France and the Stuarts in England, not to mention some random and assorted German princesses, and ultimately William the Conqueror, Julius Caesar, Cleopatra, and King Herod—means nothing. After all, since the number of grandparents doubles in each generation, by the time you trace your lineage back even five hundred years (assuming generations of roughly twenty-five years each), you will have had as many as one million grandparents at some remove. Even with pedigree collapse—the term for the inevitable overlap that comes when cousins marry cousins, as happened with all families if you go back far enough—the number of persons to whom you'd be connected by the time you got back a thousand years would still be several million.

That said, I can hardly deny that as I discovered those linkages, even though they were often quite remote—and despite the fact that the persons to whom I discovered a connection were often despicable characters who stole land, subjugated the masses, and slaughtered others in the name of nationalism or God—there was still something about the process that made me feel more *real,* more alive, and even more purposeful. To explore the passing of time as it relates to world history, and the history of your own people, however removed from you they may be, is like putting together a puzzle, several pieces of which had previously been missing. That is a gift, and one that cannot, should not, be underestimated.

And for those of us prepared to look at the less romantic side of it all, genealogy also makes it possible to uncover and then examine one's inherited advantages.

Going back a few generations on my mother's side, for instance, we have the Carter family, traceable to one John Carter, born in 1450 in Kempston, Bedfordshire, England. It would be his great- great-great-grandson, William, who would bring his family to the Virginia Colony in the early 1630s, just a few of 20,000 or so Puritans who came to America between 1629 and 1642, prior to the shutting down of emigration by King Charles I at the outset of the English Civil War.

The Carters would move inland after their arrival, able to take advantage in years to come of one of the New World's first affirmative action programs, known as the "headright" system, under which male heads of household willing to cross the Atlantic and come to Virginia were given fifty acres of land that had previously belonged to one of at least fourteen indigenous nations whose members had lived there, foremost among them the Powhatan.

Although the racial fault lines between those of European and African descent hadn't been that deep in the earliest years of the Virginia Colony—race-based slavery wasn't in place yet, and among indentured servants there were typically more Europeans than Africans—all that would begin to change in the middle of the seventeenth century. First, beginning in the 1640s, the colony began to assign blacks to permanent enslavement. Then in the 1660s, they declared that all children born of enslaved mothers would be slaves, in perpetuity, themselves. That same decade, Virginia announced that no longer would Africans converted to Christianity be immune to enslavement or servitude. Then, in the wake of Bacon's Rebellion in 1676, which witnessed both European and African laborers joining forces to overthrow the government of Governor Berkeley, elites began to pass a flurry of new laws intended to limit black freedom, elevate whites, and thus divide and conquer any emerging cross-racial alliances between the two groups.

In 1682, the colony codified in law that all whites, no matter their condition of temporary servitude, were to be seen as separate and apart from African slaves, and that they would enjoy certain rights and privileges off limits to the latter: among these, due process in disputes with their masters, and the right to redress if those masters in any way abused them. Furthermore, once released from terms of indenture, white servants would be able to claim up to fifty acres of land with which to begin their new lives as free laborers. Ultimately, indentured servitude would be abolished in the early eighteenth century, replaced by a dramatic upsurge in chattel slavery. Blacks, along with "mulattoes, Indians and criminals" would be banned from holding any public or ecclesiastical office after 1705, and the killing of a rebellious slave would no longer be deemed murder. Rather, according to Virginia law, the event would be treated "as if such accident had never happened."

The Carters, as with many of the Deans (another branch of my mother's family), lived in Virginia through all of this period—the period in which whiteness was being legally enshrined as a privileged space for the first time. And they were there in 1800, too—like my great- great- great- great-grandfather, William M. Carter—when a planned rebellion by Thomas Prosser's slave Gabriel, in Henrico County, was foiled thanks to other slaves exposing the plot. As a result, Gabriel was hanged, all free blacks in the state were forced to leave, or else face reenslavement, and all education or training of slaves (even hiring them out to persons other than their owners) was made illegal. Paranoia over the Prosser conspiracy, combined with the near-hysterical reaction to the Haitian revolution under way at that point, which would expel the French from the island just a few years later, led to new racist crackdowns and the extension of still more advantages and privileges to whites like those in my family.

Then there were the Neelys, the family of my maternal great-grandmother, who can be traced to Edward Neely, born in Scotland in 1745, who came to America sometime before the birth of his son, also named Edward, in 1770.

The Neelys would move from Ulster County, New York, in the Hudson Valley, to Kentucky, where Jason Neely, my great- great- great- grandfather was born in 1805. The land on which they would settle, though it had been the site of no permanent indigenous community by that time, had been hunting land used in common by the Shawnee and Cherokee. Although the Iroquois had signed away all rights to the land that would become Kentucky in the Treaty of Fort Stanwix in 1768, the Shawnee had been no party to the treaty, and rejected its terms. Not that their rejection would matter much, as ultimately the area came under the control of whites, and began to produce substantial profits for farmers like Jason Neely.

By 1860, three years after the Supreme Court, in its *Dred Scott* decision announced that blacks could never be citizens, even if free, and "had no rights which the white man was bound to respect," Jason had accumulated eleven slaves, ranging in age from forty down to two—a number that was quite significant by local and even regional standards for the "Upper South."

And then we have the two primary and parental branches of my family, the McLeans and the Wises.

The McLeans trace their lineage to around 1250, and apparently at one point were among the most prosperous Highland clans in Scotland, owning as many as five islands in the Hebrides. But having allied themselves with Charles Edward Stuart (claimant to the thrones of England, Ireland, and Scotland), they ultimately lost everything when Stuart (known as Bonnie Prince Charlie) was defeated at the Battle of Culloden in 1746.

The McLeans, as with many of the Highlanders, supported the attempt to restore the Stuart family to the thrones from which it had been deposed in 1688. Once the royalists were defeated, and the Bonnie Prince had been forced to sneak out of Scotland dressed as an Irish maid, the writing began to appear on the wall for the McLeans, and many of the Highland Scots who had supported him.

With that, family patriarch Ephraim McLean (my great- great- great- great- great-grandfather) set out for America, settling in Philadelphia before moving south in 1759. Once there, Ephraim would ultimately be granted over 12,000 acres of land in North Carolina and Tennessee—land that had previously belonged to Catawba and Cherokee Indians, and much of which had been worked by persons of African descent for over a century, without the right of the latter to own so much as their names.

Although the family version of the story is that Ephraim received these grants deservedly, as payment for his service in the Revolutionary War, there is something more than a bit unsatisfying about this narrative. While Ephraim served with distinction—he was, in fact, wounded during the Battle of King's Mountain, recognized as among the war's most pivotal campaigns—it is also true that at least 5,000 blacks served the American Revolution, and virtually none of them, no matter the distinction with which they served, received land grants. Indeed, four out of five blacks who served failed to receive even their freedom from enslavement.

In fact, Ephraim's ability to fight for the revolution was itself, in large part, because of white privilege. Although the Continental Congress authorized the use of blacks in the army beginning in 1777, no southern militia with the exception of that in Maryland allowed them to serve. The Congress, cowed by the political strength of southern slaveowners and threats by leaders in South Carolina to leave the war if slaves were armed and allowed to fight, refused to press the issue. This meant that blacks would be kept from service, and denied whatever postwar land grants for which they might otherwise have been eligible.

In the early 1780s, Ephraim became one of the founding residents of Nashville, and served as a trustee and treasurer for the first college west of the Cumberland Mountains, Davidson Academy. On the board with him were several prominent residents of the area, including a young Andrew Jackson, in whose ranks Ephraim's grandson would later serve, during the 1815 Battle of New Orleans, and alongside whom his great-nephew, John, would serve during the massacre of Creek Indians at Horseshoe Bend.

Ephraim's son, Samuel (my fourth great-grandfather), was a substantial landowner, having inherited property from Ephraim. Although the records are unclear as to whether Ephraim had owned slaves (the odds, however, are good), Samuel most certainly did; he had at least a half-dozen by the time of his death in 1850.

Down through the generations the McLeans would pass on the land they had accumulated, and the good name and reputations that came along with it, taking full advantage of their whiteness and what it had come to mean over the years.

In contrast to this tale, in which European immigrants come to the new country and are almost immediately welcomed into the emerging club of whiteness, we have the story of the Wises (not our original name), whose patriarchal figure, Jacob, came to the United States from Russia escape the Czar's oppression of Jews. Theirs was similar to the immigrant stories of so many other American Jews from Eastern Europe. You've heard the drill: They came here with nothing but three dollars and a ball of lint in their pockets; saved and saved, worked and worked, and eventually climbed the ladder of success, achieving the American dream within a generation or two.

Whether or not it had really been as bleak as all that, it certainly hadn't been easy. Jacob's arrival in 1907 (or 1910, it's not clear which) was not actually his first time to make it to the United States. He had entered New York once before, in 1901, but had the misfortune of cruising into the harbor only ten days or so after an American of Eastern European descent, Leon Czolgosz, had made the fatal decision to assassinate President William McKinley. McKinley had lingered for a week after the shooting, and died just a few days before the arrival of my great-grandfather's boat. As the saying goes, timing is everything—a lesson Jacob would learn, sitting in steerage and coming to realize that he had been literally just a few days too late.

So back he went, along with the rest of his shipmates, turned away in the shadow of Lady Liberty by a wave of jingoistic panic, anti-immigrant nativism, hysteria born of bigotry, and a well-nurtured, carefully cultivated skill at scapegoating those who differed from the Anglo-Saxon norm. That Czolgosz claimed to be an anarchist, and thus his shooting of McKinley came to be seen as a political act, and not merely the lashing out of a madman, sealed Jacob's fate for sure. To the authorities, all Eastern Europeans were to be viewed for a time as anarchists, as criminals, and later as communists, Czolgosz was to be executed, and tens of thousands of Eastern Europeans and other "undesirable" ethnics would be viciously oppressed in the following years.

The mind of a well-fed twenty-first-century American is scarcely equipped to contemplate just how long the trip back to Russia must have been, not merely in terms of hours and days and weeks, but as measured in the beating of one's heart, the slow and subtle escape of all optimism from one's tightened lungs. How painful it must have been, how *omnicidal* for Jacob, meaning the evisceration of everything he was, of everything that mattered to him—the extermination of desire, of hope. Though not of the same depth, nor coupled with the same fear as that which characterized the journey of Africans in the hulls of slave ships (after all, he was still a free man, and his journey, however aborted, had been voluntary), there must have been points where the magnitude of his cynicism and despair was intense enough to make the distinction feel as though it were one without much meaning.

So he returned to Minsk, in modern-day Belarus, for nearly another decade, it taking that long for him to save up enough money to make the journey again. When he finally came back, with family in tow, it would be for keeps. His desire for America was that strong: borne of the belief that in the new world things would be different, that he would be able to make something of himself and give his family a better life. The Wise family continued to grow after his arrival, including, in 1919, the birth of Leon Wise, whose name was later shortened to Leo—my grandfather.

Jacob was the very definition of a hard worker. The stereotype of immigrants putting in eighteen hours a day is one that, although it did not begin with him in mind, surely was to be kept alive by him and others like him. There is little doubt that he toiled, and sacrificed, and in the end there was a great payoff indeed. His children all became moderately successful, at least comfortable—my grandfather would graduate from a prestigious university, Vanderbilt, in 1942; and the family liquor business would grow into something of a fixture in the Nashville, Tennessee, community that the Wise family would ultimately come to call home.

But lest we get carried away, perhaps it would do some good to remember a few things about Jacob Wise and his family. None of these things, it must be stressed, take away from the unshakeable work ethic that was a defining feature of his character. But they do suggest that a work ethic is rarely, if ever, enough on its own to make the difference.

After all, there had been millions of black folks with work ethics at least as good a as his; millions of peoples of color—black, brown, red, yellow, and all shades between—had lived and toiled in this land, typically for far longer than him, and yet with few exceptions, they could not say that within a mere decade they had become successful shop owners, or that one of their sons had gone on to graduate from one of the nation's finest colleges.

Jacob was able to move south and, even as a religious minority in the buckle of the Bible Belt, find opportunity that was off limits to anyone of color. He may have been a Jew, but his skin was the right shade, and he was from Europe, so all suspicions and religious and cultural biases aside, he had only to wait and keep his nose clean a while, and then eventually he and his family would become white. Assimilation was not merely a national project; for Jacob Wise, and for millions of other Jews, Italians, and Irish, it was an implicitly racial one as well.

Even before assimilation, in fact, he had been able to gain access to jobs and opportunities that were off limits to African Americans. His very arrival in the United States—as tortuous and circuitous as was the route that he had been forced to take in order to achieve it—was nonetheless made possible by immigration policies that at that moment (and for most of our nation's history) have favored those from Europe over those from anywhere else. The Naturalization Act of 1790, which was the very first law passed by the U.S. Congress after the ratification of the Constitution, made clear that all free white persons, and *only* free white persons, were to be considered citizens, almost as soon as they arrived. Meanwhile, during the period of both of Jacob's journeys—the one that was aborted and the one that finally delivered him to his new home—there had been draconian limits on, for example, Asian immigration. These restrictions would remain largely in place until 1965, the year his grandson, my father, would graduate from high school.

If that's not white privilege—if that's not affirmative action of a most profound and lasting kind—then I dare say neither concept has much meaning any longer. And if that isn't relevant to my own racialization, since it is the history into which I was born, then the notion of inheritance has lost all meaning as well.

THE MODERN LEGACY OF WHITE BELONGING

Looking backwards in time, it becomes possible to see whiteness playing out all along the way in the history of my family, dating back hundreds of years. The ability to come to America in the first place, the ability to procure land once here, and the ability to own other human beings while knowing that you would never be owned yourself, all depended on our European ancestry.

Nonetheless, one might deny that this legacy has anything to do with those of us in the modern day. Unless we have been the direct inheritors of that land and property that our families accumulated so long ago, then of what use has that privilege been to us? For persons like myself, growing up not on farmland passed down by various branches of my family, but rather, in a modest apartment, what did this past have to do with me? And by extension, what does your family's past have to do with you?

In my case, race and privilege were every bit as implicated in the time and place of my birth as they had been in the time and place of my forbears. I was born in a nation that had only recently thrown off the formal trappings of legal apartheid. I was born in a city, Nashville, that had, just eight years earlier, been the scene of some of the most pitched desegregation battles in the South, replete with sit-ins and boycotts and marches, and white backlash to all three.

Nashville was a city where, eleven years prior to my birth, opponents of desegregation had placed a bomb in the basement of one of the city's soon-to-be integrated schools. And although the bombers in that instance galvanized opposition to terrorist tactics, opposition to integration delayed any meaningful movement in that direction until 1971, when busing was finally ordered at the high-school level. It would be 1974, the year I began first grade, before busing would filter down to the elementary level. This means that the class of 1986, my graduating class, was the first that had been truly desegregated throughout its entire educational experience. That's how far the reach of so-called past racism extends, right into the life of someone like myself, not even forty years of age. It is not, in other words, ancient history.

But when it comes to understanding the centrality of race and racism in the society of my birth, perhaps this is the most important point of all: I was born just a few hours and half a state away from Memphis, where six months earlier, to the day, Dr. King had been murdered.

I experienced the King assassination in a real if indirect way, as I suppose is always the case when one is in utero at the moment of a national catastrophe. At thirteen weeks gestation, of course, I could hardly have known that the world was burning down around me, that the bonds of human community were being ripped apart even as I sucked my thumb and fed from the umbilical cord connecting me to my maternal host.

My mom had been working that evening (not early morning, as mistakenly claimed by Bono in the famous U2 song), when King stepped onto the balcony of the Lorraine Motel, only to be felled a few seconds later by an assassin's bullet. Upon hearing the news, the managers of the department store where she was employed decided to close up shop. Fear that black folks might come over to Green Hills, the mostly white and relatively affluent area where the Castner-Knott's store was located, so as to take out vicarious revenge on whitey (or at least whitey's shoe department), had sent them into a panic. A small riot had occurred in Nashville the year before, sparked by the infamous overreaction of the Nashville police, and particularly Captain John Sorace, to a visit by radical activist Stokely Carmichael (Kwame Ture). Although the violence had been limited to a very small part of the mostly black North Nashville community around Fisk University—and even then had been totally unrelated to Carmichael's presence, contrary to the claims of then Governor Beverly Briley—by the time King was killed, white folks were on high alert for the first signs of trouble.

That I experienced my mother's bodily reaction to King's murder, as well as the killing of Bobby Kennedy two months later (at twenty-two weeks in utero) may or may not mean anything. Whether or not cell memory and the experiences of one's parent can be passed to the child as a result of trauma, thereby influencing the person that child is to become, is something that will likely never be proven one way or the other. Even the possibility of such a thing is purely speculative, and more than a bit romantic. But it makes for a good story.

Even discounting the role of cell memory, and even if we disregard the possibility that a mother may somehow transmit knowledge to a child during gestation, my experience with race predated my birth, if simply because being conceived into a white family meant certain things about the experiences I was likely to have once born: where I would live, what jobs and education my family was likely to have had, and where I would go to school.

On my third day of life I most certainly experienced race, however oblivious I was to it at the time, when my mother and father moved our family into an apartment complex in the above mentioned Green Hills community. It was a complex that, four years after completion, had still never had tenant of color, and this was not by accident. This was by design, and for those same four years it had been perfectly legal, too, as there had been nothing

unlawful until 1968 about discriminating, even blatantly, against persons of color looking to purchase or rent a place to live.

And so in we went, because it was affordable and it was a step up from the smaller apartment my folks had been living in prior to that time. More than that though, in we went because we could. Just as we could have gone into any other apartment complex anywhere in Nashville, subject only to our ability to put down a security deposit, which as it turns out was paid by my father's father anyway. At least as early as Monday, October 7, 1968, then, I was officially receiving white privilege.

The only reason you are reading this book right now, the only reason this book exists, the only reason this story is being told, is because of white privilege. You are not reading this book because I am a great writer or because I am particularly smart. There are lots of folks, especially persons of color, who know a lot more about racism than I do, people who have forgotten more about the subject since breakfast than I will likely ever know. But you're not reading their book right now; you're reading mine, and that has everything to do with privilege.

After all, how does one come to be taken seriously as an antiracist activist, writer, and lecturer by their midthirties, as I was, or even before then really, since I've been doing this work professionally, on a national level since I was twenty-one?

For one thing, it helps to know the right people.

When I graduated from college, my first job catapulted me into this work at a highly visible level. I was hired as a Youth Coordinator for the Louisiana Coalition Against Racism and Nazism, the largest and most prominent of the various groups formed to oppose the candidacy of neo-Nazi political candidate David Duke, who was running for the United States Senate. Over time, and during his bid for governor of Louisiana, I would move up the ranks of the organization, finally becoming associate director, and one of a handful of the public faces associated with the anti-Duke effort. I was, by the time Duke had fizzled and the coalition folded, all of twenty-three. Sweet work if you can get it, but most won't. I did though, which begs the question, How?

Well, I got it the old-fashioned way, which is to say that I knew the two guys who started the organization. One was a professor of mine at Tulane, Larry Powell, and the other was an activist ally and Tulane grad student at the time, Lance Hill. Even before I graduated, Larry had asked if I might want the job, and for several months I had said no. I honestly didn't think Duke was going to do all that well, and so I repeatedly turned him down, planning as I was to return home for the summer, spend whatever small amount of graduation money I would have, and then cast about for some kind of job, or possibly just float for a year, maybe going to grad school myself, or law school in a year or so.

But then as the summer dragged on and it became apparent that Duke was indeed a threat in the Senate race, I committed to returning to New Orleans and doing whatever I needed to do to insinuate myself into the anti-Duke campaign. I figured, and I was right in this, that since I knew the principals and they had offered me work before, I would probably have no problem landing a position even several months after the campaign had swung into high gear.

Had I not known Larry and Lance, there is no way I could have gotten that job, in which case I could never have built up a reputation for doing anti-racism work as I did, in which case I would never have been able to land on the lecture circuit, as I would a few years later, in which case no one would know who I am, and I surely wouldn't have been asked to write this book. But it goes deeper than that, because there is then the question of how I managed to know these two men, who were in a position to offer me such a job in the first place.

Well, I knew them, of course, because I had gone to school at Tulane; but how had I gotten there?

After all, my family was far from wealthy, and even then Tulane was extremely expensive. Although its cost is far greater today, as with all colleges and universities, in 1986, with tuition at $12,950, and all costs combined coming in at around $20,000, it was far pricier than anything my folks could afford. Complicating things further, I am notorious for procrastination—something that can be confirmed by anyone who knows me (my wife, my parents, my teachers, former bosses, the editor of this book, everyone)—and so I screwed around and didn't get my financial aid forms in on time. Since being late with financial aid forms means that one won't get as much assistance as might otherwise have been offered, how does one get to go to a place like Tulane?

It helps—and this is surely an understatement of some significance—when one's mother is able to go down to the bank and take out a loan for $10,000 to fill the gap between what the school was offering in assistance and the overall costs for my freshman year.

But how does one's mother get such a loan? Especially when, as was true for mine, she has never owned a piece of property? When she (and by extension you) have been living paycheck to paycheck, driving cars until they stopped running, taking few if any vacations because you just can't afford them?

It helps (again an understatement) if one's mother's mother can cosign for the loan. After all, banks don't typically lend money to folks without collateral like my mom, but they are very willing to lend the same money to someone *with* it, like grandmother, who was able to use her house as collateral against the loan.

The house, in which she still lives, was the fourth house that she and my grandfather, Ralph Carter McLean (who had been dead for six years by then) had owned. Although they had been of merely middle-class income—my grandfather having been in the military and then civil service for his entire adult life—they nonetheless were able to afford several nice homes, in "nice" neighborhoods, all of which had been entirely white, and again, as with the apartment complex where I grew up, not by accident. Although the Supreme Court, in 1948, had outlawed restrictive covenants barring blacks from living in these neighborhoods, it remained legal to discriminate in other ways until the late sixties, and even then, there was little real enforcement of the Fair Housing Act until teeth were added to the law in 1988.

So in a very real sense, my grandmother's house—without which I could not have gone to Tulane, met Larry and Lance, gotten the job against Duke, built up a reputation as an antiracist, and gotten out on the lecture circuit—was there to be used as collateral because we were white. Not only did we have a house to use for this purpose, but it was a house in a "desirable" neighborhood, seen as a good investment by the bank, which would continue to appreciate each year. In other words, it was a good bet that we'd be able to make good on the loan, and if we defaulted, so what? The bank would have a nice piece of property, worth more than the ten bills they were giving my mom, so in a real sense they couldn't lose, and neither could I.

The upshot of all this is simple: I am where I am today, doing what I am doing today, in large part because I was born white. I say this not to detract from whatever genuine abilities I may have, nor to take away from the hard work that helped my family in previous generations afford certain homes, but simply to say that ability and hard work alone could not have paved the way for me, just as they have not paved the way for anyone in isolation. Just as they did not pave the way, in isolation, for the millions of white families that got FHA and VA loans for homes from the 1930s to the 1960s—over $120 billion in equity in fact—at a time when such loans were essentially off limits to persons of color. We always have help along the way, some of us a lot more than others. My help came color-coded, and that has made all the difference.

Although not every white person's story is the same as mine, any white person born before 1964, at least, was legally elevated above any person of color, and as such received directly the privileges, the head start, the advantages of whiteness as a matter of routine. This goes for all whites, not merely some, but all. Even poor whites received the benefit of being considered superior to black people, for example. Even the poor whites received the benefit of public sympathy, as with the mostly positive, heart-rending portrayals of farmers in the Dust Bowl drought years of the 1930s, or the Appalachian poor in the early sixties. This, in contrast to the equally hostile images of the black and brown poor presented for the past forty-five years, via print and broadcast media.

Even whites born after the passage of the various civil rights acts of the 1960s have reaped the benefits of our skin color, since parents and grandparents don't tend to bury their accumulated assets, or "cultural capital" (itself the residue of material advantage) in a big hole in the backyard. In other words, it doesn't matter that today's whites weren't around "back then." It doesn't matter that today's whites never owned slaves, never killed any Indians, and never stole land from Mexico. We are here now, and so are the black and brown descendants of those persons of color whose ability to accumulate assets, professional credentials, education, and homes, was restricted for so long.

We are all here now, and the past has come with us into the present, whether or not we put out a welcome mat. The past may be an unwanted guest, but just like those family members you'd rather not have over for the holidays, the past is coming in the front door anyway—mine, and yours. It finds a window if the door is closed, and although the past is quite capable of sucking one's blood, or, even worse, of draining one's self entirely, quite unlike a vampire, it doesn't need an invitation in order to enter. Pity, that.

9

The Rhetorical Dimentions of National Identity

By M. Lane Bruner

Nations do not have stable or natural identities. Instead, national identity is incessantly negotiated through discourse. What the nation is at any given moment for any given individual depends on the narrative accounts and arguments they bring to bear on the subject. These characterizations vary widely from state to state and from political group to political group and have radically unequal effects on cultures, institutions, economic policies, and laws. Tensions prompted by changes in economic conditions, state authority, real or imagined domestic and international threats, and/or significant changes in cultural markers of national belonging continually cause new groups to become alienated from dominant characterizations of collective belonging, preventing the process of national identity construction from ever being completed.

There is, therefore, a never-ending and politically consequential rhetorical struggle over national identity, and, because national identities are incessantly negotiated, nation building continually requires the services of advocates offering accounts of national character. State representatives and those who publicly contend with them compete for the national imagination of citizens, particularly in times of social unrest, by appropriating available cultural materials to create visions of public belonging. They artfully (and not so artfully) appropriate history and stress economic, civic, cultural, and ethnic dimensions differently for a variety of purposes.

Because characterizations of national identity have various effects on human community, the services of rhetorical critics are also required. Given our historical role as physicians of the state and of human character, rhetoricians are broadly familiar with the various means by which discourses influence communities. Drawing on theories related to persuasion and identity, questions of concern to rhetoricians would include the following: How are different types of national identities generated? What are the constraints imposed on those who speak on behalf of the nation? What or who is omitted from widely accepted conceptualizations of the national character, and what are the material consequences of those omissions? What are the "healthiest" articulations of national character in a given case? Such questions are important, for as Erik Ringmar has observed, "The conception of a community makes a certain kind of person possible, and the conception of a person makes a certain kind of community possible. How we represent our community also determines who can represent it in the sense of 'standing for it,' 'speaking in its name.' Each representation will make certain kinds of political representation possible and others impossible." It is arguably nothing less than the character of nations ultimately, that guides the development of economic, cultural, and civic states' policies, which in turn influence the trajectory of international relations and world history.

However, central as national identities are to the unfolding geopolitical world order, the rhetorical dimensions of national identity construction remain relatively obscure. While there are numerous studies providing theories and histories of nationalism and while almost all scholars recognize the essential role of discourse in the construction of collective identity, analyses of their actual articulation are rare. Although the role of discourse in the construction of identity has been thoroughly explored theoretically in recent years and the phenomenon of national identity in particular has been analyzed from a variety of scholarly perspectives, comparative analyses of contemporary examples of national identity construction do not exist. To remedy this absence the goal here is to analyze recent examples of the public articulation of national identity in West Germany, Russia, and Quebec from a rhetorical perspective.

The rhetorical dimensions of national identity are politically significant because different types of collective identities lead to different forms of community. International relations theorist Rodney Bruce Hall notes that "change in the international system occurs with changes in the collective identity of crucial social actors who collectively constitute the units from which the system is comprised." Different national identities lead to different interstate (and intrastate) relation. If West Germans collectively imagine that any surviving National Socialists are now East German communists, then they will view capitalism quite differently from East Germans, who imagine that any surviving National Socialists are now capitalists in West Germany. If citizens of Quebec view themselves as colonized descendants of the New French, then they will treat their federal agreements differently than if they imagine themselves as citizens of a bilingual and multicultural Canada. If Russians imagine themselves as historically repressed democrats, then they will consider Western economic reforms in a manner quite distinct from Russians who imagine themselves as anticapitalist defenders of socialism.

Some characterizations of national identity and the rhetoric that supports them tend to foster democratic communities based on rights, laws, and duties negotiated by a wide range of relatively well-informed citizens. Other characterizations tend to foster authoritarian communities based on xenophobic patterns of identification, the suppression of important historical and political realities, and the maintenance of asymmetrical forms of state power. While there are as many variations on the themes as there are states and while individual states are constantly transformed through discourse, the distinctions indeed make a real political difference. Here, therefore, much of the task will be to isolate unfolding characterizations of national identity, to identify any suppression of important historical and political realities, and to explore the potential social and political implications of those characterizations.

There are several premises guiding the approach to national identity construction taken here. First, national identities are not only assumed to be expressed concretely in property, institutional infrastructures, economic policies, and laws; but they are also assumed to be malleable fictions, assembled out of available historical resources and incessantly negotiated between state and public representatives offering competing accounts of national character. Second, controversial public speeches articulating national character are taken to be useful sites for analyzing the rhetorical strategies involved in competing characterizations of the nation or the people. Third, different strategies of remembrance (politicized forms of public memory) are thought to have different consequences for the character of nations and the quality of international relations.

Fourth, strategies of remembrance have both unique and universal dimensions. On the one hand, strategies are unique in their form and function, directing the critic's focus both toward and away from public discourse. They can become highly complex, particularly in countries with considerable public discourse coupled with a seriously motivated repression—as with Germany and the repression of National Socialism—requiring the critic to engage in close textual analysis to determine the subtle nuances of a developed set of strategies. At other times, as with Russia, the public sphere is so underdeveloped that strategies become the simple and blunt instruments of naked political power. Then the focus tends to be on the nuances of the political context more than on the nuances of the discursive strategies. On the other hand, rhetorical strategies are universally situated in historical, legal, cultural, ethnic, and economic contexts. The critic must always, therefore, thoroughly examine those contexts to fully appreciate the unique functions of competing strategies. Having identified the functions, critics are better positioned to critique the strategies and their likely impact on state formation and international arrangements.

In support of these premises, chapters 2 through 4 analyze the recent pubic articulation of national identity in three states: West Germany from 1985 to 1988, in the years leading up to the fall of the Berlin Wall; Russia after the collapse of the Soviet Union and during its transition from a planned economy to a market economy in the early 1990s; and Quebec during the vote for independence from Canada in 1995. Together, they support the claim that national identities are based on characterizations that serve widely different purposes and have serious political consequences.

To frame these studies, the following is a brief overview of the history of national identity that introduces its economic, cultural, civic, and ethnic dimensions, followed by an equally brief summary of relevant theories related to the approach taken here to national identity construction. This is not intended as an exhaustive account of the history of nationalism or identity theory, tasks adequately dealt with elsewhere. The goal is simply to introduce readers to the general perspective that guides the case studies. The chapter then concludes with an introduction to the studies themselves. Each is ultimately based on the analysis of controversial speeches related to national identity delivered by state leaders and the public responses to those speeches within the given state's unique historical/ political context. By identifying competing narrative accounts within their historical/political contexts, different strategies of remembrance are identified and critiqued.

THE EMERGENCE OF NATIONAL IDENTITY AND ITS VARIOUS DIMENSIONS

The emergence of national identities and the globalization of the nation-state system were the result of a number of complex factors. The rise of representative government and industrial capitalism, imperialism and colonialism, the territorial identification that accompanied the expansion and development of state bureaucracies and official state languages, defensive reactions of local elites to the encroachments of interstate commerce, and romantic nostalgia for quickly evaporating folk cultures each played a role. Territorial-sovereign states ruled by monarchs whose legitimacy was derived from "divine right" and whose relative worldly status depended in large part on the development of trade eventually gave way to national-sovereign states governed by thriving merchant classes whose legitimacy depended on the production of national identities. State leaders were increasingly compelled to consolidate local economic and cultural resources to defend themselves against more economically developed states. Simultaneously, merchants began investing in the states. These events initially led to a number of progressive social policies pursued by monarchs who recognized the value of securing the general welfare and approbation of subjects, particularly as a counterweight to the rising influence of the propertied classes, and later included progressive social democratic policies such as Franklin Roosevelt's New Deal. The economic nation, therefore, was the product of a wide range of state policies, from protective tariffs to social security, designed to protect the interests and secure the allegiance of subjects. This, in turn, led to greater public identification with the state.

While early forms of state identification began to emerge in the monarchial states of Europe several centuries ago, it was the nineteenth and twentieth centuries that witnessed the global triumph of the nation-state principle. The collapse of the Ottoman and Austro-Hungarian empires, the retreat of military colonial powers, the creation of the League of Nations and the United Nations, and the later dissolution of Yugoslavia and the Soviet Union further instantiated the nation-state principle. The idea that states represent nations has justified a variety of foreign policy measures in the United States since at least the time of Woodrow Wilson; and by the dawn of the twenty-first century, the primary public justification for the construction of new sovereign states was the declared need to protect a historically oppressed people.

Just who these oppressed people are at any given moment in time, however, is not only an economic relation but also a rhetorical construction, and dominant characterizations of nations have life-and-death consequences for the "peoples" of the world. Simply comparing the estimated eight thousand spoken languages and the real and imagined histories of those who speak them to the two hundred odd states currently in existence shows us that not all potential "peoples" enjoy "self-rule." Instead, as Ernest Gellner has observed, most linguistic groups "go meekly to their doom … dissolving into the wider culture of some new national state." Conversely, it is equally clear that the steady fragmentation of the globe into smaller and smaller "national" units could easily continue for some time, given the rich linguistic and cultural resources still to be mined from humankind.

An important corollary of the economic nation is the *cultural* nation, which is composed of folk, ethnic, and civic elements. Subjects of states reap the benefits and suffer the consequences of economic policies differently, and most are unaware of those policies; whereas the cultural dimensions of a nation are generally shared. Citizenship usually requires that subjects speak the nation's language, obey the nation's laws, honor the nation's traditions, "believe in" the nation, and be willing to make personal sacrifices on behalf of the nation. In addition to these cultural and civic markers, in some states citizenship remains openly based on ethnic criteria, and those failing to meet those criteria are de facto aliens.

Most of these cultural, civic, and ethnic conceptions of national identity were not possible before the rise of economic nationalism, the expansion of the bureaucratic state, and the development of official state languages. For example universal literacy, enabled by state-provided education, had profound effects on increasingly urbanized workers who, having been drawn to industrial centers from rural regions, found themselves thrown into relatively anonymous and impersonal societies. Local forms of identity based primarily on interpersonal relationships were irreversibly transformed through the acquisition of official state languages and participation in collective state institutions such as public schools and conscripted armies. By the middle of the nineteenth century this gradual transformation from preliterate and interpersonal forms of community to literate and imaginary institutional forms of community, coupled with the progressive distribution of wealth and privileges to state-educated workers, led to increasing identification with the state.

The operations of the global economy, the rise of state bureaucracies, the development of state languages, and urbanization have shaped, and continue to shape, national identities. Furthermore, the various historical and economic paths taken by different states have resulted in the creation of national identities with widely different cultural, civic, and ethnic components. Civic nations are based on narratives that justify the construction of a political community with common institutions, rule of law, a bounded territory, and a sense of legal solidarity. Ethnic-cultural nations, conversely, are based on narratives that emphasize shared historical memories, myths of common ancestry rule by law, and a sense of ethnic or cultural solidarity. While each nation's ever-unfolding identity is composed of some unique combination of these economic, cultural, civic, and ethnic elements, all are based on discursive accounts of who "the people" are and the place of "the nation" in the world. It is here that rhetorical theories related to the construction of publics, as well as critical theories related to the social construction of identity, are helpful.

MAPPING STRATEGIES OF REMEMBRANCE

Collective identities are negotiated through the clash of multiple and conflicting discourses, including battles over memory, over domestic and foreign policy, and over constitutions and the meaning of laws. State and public representatives provide accounts of national character, but only particular kinds of accounts are consistent with the imagined communities preferred by publics. There are more and less popular national characterizations—and many fail dramatically—but competition over national identity is a permanent feature of domestic politics.

A national identity is not simply a narrative or set of narratives that subsequently prompts and justifies a wide range of actions; it is also an ongoing rhetorical process. Accordingly, the rhetorical approach adopted here is designed, not to uncover *the* identity of a nation, but to analyze moments in time when competing articulations collide in the ongoing discursive negotiation of what it imaginatively means to be a member of a nation. The approach is based in part on Friedrich Nietzsche's theory of history, Michel Foucault's notion of a limit attitude (an ethic of permanent resistance against the limits imposed by consensus), and Ernesto Laclau and Chantal Mouffe's notions of hegemony and radical democracy. Within this rhetorical-philosophical framework, collective identities are assumed to be political inasmuch as they are always a choice between narratives; and while subjects are never hostage to the effects of a single narrative or identity (e.g., national identity), it is nevertheless the case that many particularly influential narratives entail politically consequential exclusions oftentimes invisible to those who identify with them.

This theoretical approach is based on the analysis of controversial discourse, for it is through transgressions, or resistance, that the "limits" of identity are revealed. The approach can perhaps best be understood as a response to William Connolly's plea for an "agonistic ethic" in which "people strive to interrogate exclusions built into … entrenched identities." It is an attitude toward consensus based on the assumption that all forms of identification and the narratives that accompany them simultaneously create a field of absence, an Other, and/or forms of forgetfulness, and that only through a reflective appreciation of these limits can the emancipatory potential of collective identity by maximized. As a critical rhetorical approach, it seeks to identify narrative limits and the absences/ omissions they entail, which in turn makes them available for emancipatory purposes. As a method, it is the contextual analysis of controversial speech.

The analysis of controversial public discourse in West Germany reveals that the articulation of national identity was based on the rhetorical strategy of identifying West Germans as "victims" of National Socialism and erasing National Socialist perpetrators from public memory. In Russia it was based on the strategy of identifying Yeltsin and his economic policies with "democracy," coupled with erasing from public memory the lingering influence of the collapsed Soviet system and the general absence of democratic features such as compromise, the separation and balance of political power, and the institutional infrastructures required for effective competition. And in Quebec the public articulation of national identify was based on the strategy of "multiculturalism" and the erasure from public memory of ethnic/cultural motives for secession, when in fact the historical motivation for Quebec secession had always been based on the protection of French Canadien culture from English Canadian hegemony.

Nietzsche informs this approach by distinguishing among three types of history: monumental, antiquarian, and critical. Those who engage in *monumental history* construct a past "worthy of imitating" and "use history as an incentive to action." Such use of the past is always "in danger of being somewhat distorted, of being reinterpreted according to aesthetic criteria and so brought closer to a fiction." State and public leaders, eager to acquire or maintain a general consensus among citizens in order to gain compliance in relation to the exercise of the means of violence, monumentalize history in order to interpellate the "ideal citizen." Those who engage in *antiquarian history* supposedly love history for history's sake and wish to preserve it rather than use it. Antiquarian history is perhaps best described as the pure chronological record (e.g., at what time a person arrived, the clothes he was wearing, what she said, etc.). Even antiquarian histories, however, are highly selective, for it is impossible to record every possible detail relevant to a given historical event. *Critical history* finally relates to those who critique monumental and antiquarian histories in order to right perceived injustices in how and what they exclude.

Competing characterizations of national identity, according to such a scheme, constitute battlegrounds of interests. State and public leaders intent on fabricating a commonly held account of who are "the people" that can be called upon in times of crisis to mobilize publics, engage in monumental history to suppress contradictory aspects of a nation's history and to create widespread support for preferred policies. These monumental histories are likely to be more pernicious than the less politically motivated antiquarian histories and we have only chronological records (and personal memories) with which to compare those monumental histories for their veracity. Though all identities have a fictional dimension, relatively accurate antiquarian histories do quite well in revealing the significant historical absences required of monumental histories.

The approach used here functions as critical history inasmuch as it isolates dominant articulations of national identity and the narrative omissions they entail in order to make them available for reflection. By contextually analyzing controversial public speeches, critics can determine more precisely the kind of national identity being constructed in a given state and significant things that cannot be said lest the narrative account unravel. Initially, the rhetorical critic identifies a controversial speech or speeches disseminated in some form to a nationwide audience. The speech or speeches should include an articulation of what it means to be a citizen of the given state, who "the people" are, or what the state stands for and should provoke a broad spectrum of negative reactions. Then, by analyzing these reactions, the critic seeks to identify patterns of responses to the speeches, paying particular attention to the discourse cited as being especially offensive. Reasons usually accompany such reactions, and patterns of reasons constitute competing accounts of the nation's character and help to reveal the "unspeakable" in a given monumental history. After having simultaneously explored the relevant historical, economic, cultural, ethnic, and legal contexts for those addresses and responses, strategies of remembrance and their functions can be mapped.

STRATEGIC MEMORY IN WEST GERMANY, RUSSIA, AND QUEBEC

No history can be a completely honest history. All concepts, all identities, and all narratives necessarily leave out many things. This is not to say, however, that all are equally dishonest or that they leave equally important things out. It is to say, instead, that characterizations of national identity can be distinguished by what they do not say; and the following studies show that recent characterizations of national identity in West Germany, Russia, and Quebec were indeed accompanied by very different kinds of politically significant absences. As

noted, in West Germany those absences concerned the causes for, continuities of, and responsibility for, National Socialism. In Russia those absences related to the general lack of concrete democratic processes, the battles over state power and economic control in the wake of the Soviet collapse, and how those battles influenced the construction of the new Russian constitution. And in Quebec those absences centered on an ethnic nationalism that had outlived its usefulness.

Chapter 2 examines how state leaders in West Germany and the United States characterized the German people as victims rather than perpetrators of the Second World War. The dominant characterization was that the West German nation had suddenly become "democratic" at the end of the Second World War. The fascist roots of the German state were displaced onto communist East Germany, and the remembrance of the Holocaust was turned into an exercise in forgetfulness and forgiveness. Chapter 3 discusses the construction of the post-Soviet Russian constitution, and how the dominant characterization of both the legislative and executive branches of government was that they alone were "truly democratic." In fact, neither branch was particularly democratic. The struggle for power between the executive and legislative branches, which itself mirrored the federal struggle between the center and the periphery and between the "Russian" regions and the "ethnic" republics, was actually the main issue during the construction of the constitution. Chapter 4 examines how the *"peuple Québécois,"* historically characterized as French Canadien, were recharacterized as a multicultural people. Even though the main purpose behind secession was purportedly to protect French-Canadien culture from dissolving into English Canada, that purpose failed to inspire a large enough percentage of the population to secure Quebec's independence. Therefore, there was a shift in strategy from ethnic nationalism to civic multi-culturalism.

The studies collectively show that national identity is indeed the ever-changing product of a constant rhetorical struggle in which different factions use history in different ways to achieve different ends. Ronald Reagan, Helmut Kohl, and Richard von Weizsäcker characterized the German people as victims in order to dissociate fascism from "democratic capitalism" and to erase the memory of the perpetrators of National Socialist crimes. George Bush, Bill Clinton, and Boris Yeltsin each characterized Russia as a democracy. However, behind the democratic discourse was a concerted effort not to create a viable constitutional democracy based on a clear balance and separation of powers, but to ensure that certain market reforms were implemented and that a "strong" presidency be constitutionally established. Jacques Parizeau and Lucien Bouchard characterized the people of Quebec as the descendants of the New French because historically the French Canadians have called for secession in order to protect their culture. Lucien Bouchard, however, recognizing that secession would not be possible without a new strategy, embarked on an incompatible path of strategic multiculturalism to persuade a larger number of people to identify with the state in order to achieve greater economic leverage within the federation.

All in all, the three studies show how varied, how politically consequential, and how potentially dangerous are the rhetorical games that surround the construction of national character and how they influence economic policies, laws, and forms of imagined community. They show that characterizations of both one's own nation and other nations shift with time and circumstance and that the process continues unabated. They also suggest that similar studies could be done of any state, especially when an advocate characterizes the people in a way that is dramatically rejected.

This is a start. Since it is unlikely that national identities are going away any time soon, it is in our best interest to understand as fully as possible how they are articulated through public discourse. The analysis of controversial speech is a fruitful approach to that task.

10

Dissident Globalizations, Emancipatory Methods, Social-Erotics

By Chela Sandoval

The erotic is the nurture ... of all our deepest knowledges.

—Audre Lorde, 1978

Being the supreme crossers of cultures, homosexuals have strong bonds with the queer white, Black, Asian, Native American, Latino and with the queer in Italy, Australia and the rest of the planet. We come from all colors, all classes, all races, all time periods. Our role is to link people with each other. ... it is to transfer ideas and information from one culture to another.

—Gloria Anzaldúa, 1987

FOUR DISSIDENT GLOBALIZATIONS

Since 1969 Native American activist/scholar Bea Medicine has begun her public speeches with the greeting, "All my kinspersons, with a good heart, and strong hands, I welcome you."[1] The aim of this greeting is to interpellate connection-by-affinity: to call up the proximities-of-being that can ally individual citizen-subjects into collectivity. These are coalition politics, and they function on a profoundly different register than those politics that similarly network and link citizen-subjects in the great global exchange of capital.

Like the coalition politics of Bea Medicine, twenty-first-century transnational capitalism is conducted through linking-transactions. But globalizing capital links through a politics of transgression that crosses all bodies (with a hungry desire) while murmuring vanilla reassurances: "Just relax." "Have fun." "This is easy, it's all for the best."[2] There are, of course, the expected resistances: the tightening up, the defensiveness, the denials, the efforts to clamp down roving global energies. Nationalism thus exerts the true vanilla erotics: no transgressions permitted, border crossings monitored and militarized, and within these limits "only our kind allowed," a homogenization that disciplines the passions—puts them under control. But if postmodern globalization is polymorphous, taking on all comers, and if its resistances monitor and control the passions, then it is possible to identify an optional force, another and dissident kind of globalization that eroticizes differently, that tattoos its citizen-subjects with *amor en Aztlán,* with love drawn from mythical and forbidden territories come-to-life. When Bea Medicine welcomes a diverse community as "kinspersons" to whom she offers "heart," "hands," "goodness," and "strength," it is this community she is calling up, new citizen-warriors of alternative, decolonizing, and dissident global forces.

The afterlife of colonialism shimmers with this new dissident mode of global cosmopolitics. Dissident globalization depends on the activism of an internationalist citizen-warrior who is able to call upon the transformative capacities of consciousness and of the collective body. In this essay, I will schematize the principles on which such a dissident mode of globalization becomes embodied in the social erotic. I begin by summarizing three historically prior modes of dissident globalization (Marxism, third world liberation, and U.S. third world feminism).[3] I conclude by positing the queer, postcolonial, and feminist *method* that is necessary for bringing into being the fourth, emancipatory, mode of globalization I have already described as "dissident." This method has been articulated across ethnic, women's, queer, and subaltern interdisciplinary studies since the 1960s. In this essay, its most salient potential for liberatory globalization is emphasized: This method generates the social-erotics necessary for activating the "coalitional" global future of Bea Medicine's imaginary.

RELOCATING CITATIONS

At the turn of the previous century, an internationalist movement attempted to associate the working classes across nations into an economic, moral, and political union that would dehierarchize and transform the world. But by the 1950s that location of political insurgency and of emancipatory and collective will had relocated away from the site of the working classes, the "proletariat," to that of another social body, which was identified by Sartre, Fanon, and Barthes as being comprised of "non-European" peoples of color. This shift in the location from which an emancipatory global consciousness might arise represented a fundamental challenge to Marxism, and introduced the possibility of a new kind of transnational alliance and revolutionary class formation. "Today," Barthes wrote in 1957, "it is *colonized* peoples who assume to the full the ethical and political condition described by Marx as being that of the proletariat."[4] At that historic moment, Barthes was right.

Nineteenth- and twentieth- century geopolitical struggles for decolonization had generated a new form of global network among peoples of color that culminated during the 1950s in a transnational/transcultural slogan—and demand for "third world liberation." This term signified solidarity among new masses of peoples who were differentiated by nation, ethnicity, language, race, class, culture, sex, and gender demarcations but who were allied nevertheless by virtue of similar sociohistorical, racial, and colonial relations to dominant powers. Third world liberationists of this period imagined a new decolonizing coalition of resistance that would cross national as well as racial and cultural borders—a dissident, internationalist citizenry. This fresh sense of alliance profoundly influenced the transforming identities of U.S. peoples of color, especially the participants of the great social movements of the 1950s, 1960s and 1970s. Activists of color involved in the civil rights, antiwar, Black, Chicano, Asian, Native American, student, women's, and gay liberation movements saw themselves as bonded, despite distinct and sometimes contrary aims and goals, in a coalitional form of "third world" consciousness opposed to dominating powers and oppressive racial and social hierarchies.

During the late 1960s and early 1970s a new feminist U.S. social movement took up these class, third world, and internationalist genealogies, and extended their trajectories to include the imperatives of gender and sex. The name selected for this new radical social movement linked two apparently contradictory world power geographies in the phrase "U.S. third world feminism," as if the "U.S." and the "third world" could together represent a single political locality.[5] In a sense simply voicing this name enacted an untried revolution: a geopolitical upheaval of nation-state and its social imaginaries, and an innovative pulling together again of what leaders and visionaries of the movement hoped would become a trans-national, -gendered, -sexed, -cultured, -raced, and coalitional political site. If the dissident global imaginary that was Marxism became momentarily eclipsed by the radical notion of "third world liberation" during the sixties, then the global imaginary that was third world liberation also waned during the seventies. U.S. third world feminism, however, took up their trajectories and extended them by agitating for a unique politics of inclusion that would stand in direct relief to the predominant politics of exclusion that defined U.S.-based ethnic, race, gender, and sex liberation

movements during that period. For the purposes of this conference on "Queer Globalization/Local Homosexualities: Citizenship, Sexuality, and the Afterlife of Colonialism," it is useful to point out that the coalitional Utopian imperatives of this globalizing version of "U.S. third world feminism" were in large part formulated and guided through the leadership and vision provided by U.S. activists who were self-identified lesbians of color.

Today, few scholars are unfamiliar with the (often infamous) texts that were produced by this particular cohort of lesbian activist who, by 1975, had organized into a unique U.S. collectivity under the rubric of "radical women of color." Even this highly abbreviated list of names, Barbara Smith, Cherríe Moraga, Paula Gunn Allen, Barbara Noda, Audre Lorde, Merle Woo, Janice Gold, and Gloria Anzaldúa, recalls the political and aesthetic influence of their activism. Whether examining texts such as *This Bridge Called My Back* (1981), *Homegirls* (1982), *Borderlands* (1987), *Sister Outsider* (1983), the journal *Conditions* (1976), or Third Woman (1979) and Kitchen Table (1982) Presses, one encounters a constantly applied force that was aimed at creating a social movement that would be capable of organizing on behalf of *all* people. The U.S. third world feminist writings of this period invite citizen-subjects who had previously been separated by gender, sex, race, culture, nation, and/or class into a trans-difference coalition, inviting them to become "country people" of an unprecedented psychic terrain. This trans-difference citizenship, it was argued, would come about through a shared and specific form of oppositional consciousness, constructed through what U.S. third world feminists dared to theorize in 1981 as an embodied "politics of love."[6]

The great theorist of history, sex, and power, Michel Foucault, wrote in 1980 that to creatively enter the new millennium we must "refuse what we have been trained to become, that we must promote new forms of subjectivity."[7] The idea is to call up subjectivity with an erotic panache, suggested the lesbian and U.S. third world feminist intellectual Audre Lorde in 1976, to recognize that the "erotic" itself comprises a mode of political power.[8] But simply being "homosexual," they both believed, was not sufficient grounds on which to call up this new, emancipatory mode of oppositional praxis. Rather, a shared social-erotics is necessary, or as Fredric Jameson later pointed out, what is required is a specific *methodology* that can be used as a compass for self-consciously organizing consciousness, praxis, coalition, and resistance under late capitalist cultural conditions.[9] Examination of the feminist texts developed by U.S. third world feminist activists between 1965 and 1990 reveals their combined insistence on a structured theory and method of consciousness-in-opposition to U.S. social hierarchy that is capable, when all actors can agree to its methods, of aligning a variety of oppositional social activists with one another across differing gender, sex, race, culture, class, or national localities. This theoretical and methodological compass was developed, represented, and utilized by U.S. lesbians and feminists of color because, as lesbian Native American theorist Paula Gunn Allen put it in 1981, so much has been taken away that "the place we live now is an idea"—and in this place new forms of identity, theory, practice, erotics, love, and community become imaginable.

In 1981, Chicana lesbian Gloria Anzaldúa described these new terms of exchange in a "collection of writings by radical women of color," where she wrote, "we are the queer groups, the people who don't belong anywhere, not in the dominant world, nor completely in our own respective cultures. We do not have the same ideologies, nor do we derive similar solutions, but these differences do not become opposed to each other."[10] Instead, Audre Lorde explained in 1979, each and every difference, all tactical positions are recognized as

"a fund of necessary polarities between which our creativities spark like a dialectic. Only within that interdependency" she insisted, each ideological position "acknowledged and equal, can the power to seek new ways of being in the world generate," along with "the courage and sustenance to act where there are no charters."[11] In 1987 Anzaldúa continued by defining this "queer" consciousness as born of a life lived in the "borderlands" between races, nations, languages, genders, sexualities, and cultures. *La conciencia de la mestiza* is a form of Chicana consciousness, she wrote, but is also a learned subjectivity capable of transformation and relocation, movement that must be guided by a specific methodology she calls *la facultad,* the capacity to read, renovate, and make signs on behalf of the dispossessed. That same year philosopher Maria Lugones maintained that only nomadic "travel" across "worlds of meaning" could create the type of "loving perception" required in the political activism and social-erotics these women named U.S. third world feminism. And in 1984 Gayatri Spivak suggested "shuttling" between meaning systems in order to enact the "strategic essentialism" that would be necessary for intervening in power on behalf of the marginalized. Put together, these different quotes describe a political practice that Alice Walker dared to define in 1983 as "womanism." This was a political hermeneutic, she argued, a social movement theory that would depend on and construct a new social-erotics—"love" in the postmodern world.[12]

These voices were connected in their insistence on the recognition of a specific mode of oppositional consciousness and behavior, a social-erotics, an eccentric theory, method, and politics that had evolved from those who, as Audre Lorde put it in 1977, must "live at the shoreline" between sex, gender, race, language, culture, class, and social locations.[13] This shoreline, or "borderlands," consciousness and politics generated a method for redefining identity, community, and love ("love" understood as a mode of political action—as social-erotics). This method is utilized not only within racialized and feminist forms of so-called minority discourse. It is a methodology capable of mobilizing queer and other oppositional modalities into a coalitional and dissident-global-praxis.[14]

TO REMEMBER THE METHOD

We can remember this method by examining 1970s U.S. third world feminist theory and practice. U.S. third world feminism apprehended oppositional forms of consciousness, aesthetics, and politics as organized around five points of resistance to U.S. social hierarchy: (1) the "equal rights" (or "liberal") mode; (2) the "revolutionary" mode; (3) the "supremacist" (or "cultural-nationalist") mode; (4) the "separatist" mode; and (5) the "differential" (or "womanist," "Sister Outsider," *"mestiza,"* "strategic essentialist," "third force") mode.[15] It was this last differential mode that enabled U.S. third world feminists during the 1970s to understand and utilize the previous four, not as overriding strategies, but as tactics for intervening in and transforming social relations.[16] Under the auspices of the U.S. third world feminist form of social movement *understood as a differential oppositional practice,* the first four modes were *performed* (however seriously) only as forms of "tactical essentialism."[17] The differential praxis of U.S. third world feminism understood, wielded, and poetically deployed each mode of resistant ideology as if it were only another potential *technology of power.* The cruising mobilities required in this effort demanded of the differential practitioner commitment to the process of metamorphosis itself: This is the activity of the trickster who practices subjectivity-as-masquerade, the oppositional agent who accesses differing identity, ideological, aesthetic, and political positions.

This nomadic "morphing" was not performed only for survival's sake, as in earlier, modernist times. It was a set of *principled conversions* that require movement through, over, and within any dominant system of resistance, identity, race, gender, sex, class, or national meanings.

This form of differential consciousness recognizes and identifies all technologies of power as consensual illusions. When resistance is organized as integrationist, revolutionary, supremacist, or separatist in function, the differential mode of consciousness reads and interprets these technologies of power as transformable social narratives that are designed to intervene in reality for the sake of social justice. The differential maneuvering required here is a *sleight-of-consciousness* that activates a new space, a *cyberspace,* where the transcultural, transgendered, transnational leaps necessary to the play of effective stratagems of oppositional praxis can begin (a process recently theorized by Judith Butler as "the performative").[18] It was this 1970s U.S. third world form of feminism that advocated for a specific form of politics that was not assimilationist, revolutionary, supremacist, or separatist, but that utilized and activated all these and more in a differential form of politics. This eccentric politics is a powerful paradigm for generating coalition between oppositional groups, for accessing horizontal comradeship, for carrying out effective collaborations between divided constituencies, for making interdisciplinary connections.

As Bea Medicine hopes, this differential consciousness and social movement permit *affinities inside difference* to attract, combine, and relate new constituencies into transnational coalitions-of-resistance. But successful practice of the differential can occur only when it is activated by particular guiding principles. When utilized together, these principles function as a procedure, as a set of techniques I have elsewhere identified as the "methodology of the oppressed," but they are techniques perhaps better described as a "method-ology of emancipation."[19] The four principles of this method guide the founding precepts of such intellectual and practical inventions as cyborg feminism, genealogical analysis, subaltern studies, U.S. third world feminism, and radical *mestízaje,* and they have energized the ongoing development of feminist, queer, postcolonial, American, and global studies. Indeed, these principles create and circulate a social-erotics; they cast queer love across the postmodern world.

QUEER LOVE ACROSS THE POMO WORLD

At the turn of the twenty-first century the zones are clear: postmodern globalization is a neocolonizing force. Meanwhile, decolonizing alliance forces are mobilizing under eclectic, mobile, and presentist banners that are only too similar in structure and function to postmodern globalization. Such equivalencies, however, remain de-colonizing when their substance, values, and degrees of force are guided by what can be recognized across disciplines as a methodology of emancipation. Its function is to develop the kinds of oppositional powers that are *analogous* to but at the same time *homeopathically resistant* to postmodern transnationalization, along with peoples who are skilled enough to wield those powers. Like U.S. third world feminists, practitio-ners of this methodology act as interventionists, negotiators, assimilationists, radical transformers, separatists, and so on. They can be unified as cadres into a dissident form of cosmopolitics, however, when practitioners enact the following principles:

1. To develop sign-reading skills, reading power everywhere and always.
2. To engage interventionary tactics that are designed to shift the powers that operate

inside any sign system: The choices on the level of the sign are (a) to deconstruct, or (b) to meta-ideologize.

3. To willingly inhabit an eccentric conscious-ness that permits its practitioner to carry out any of these techniques by moving within, between, or through meaning *differentially.*

4. To enact any of these principles with the purpose of equalizing power among inter-locutors. This *democratizing aim* directs all other techniques toward the goal of egalitarian redistributions of sexed, gendered, raced, physiological, social, cultural, and/or economic powers.

Each of these principles can be operated indepen-dently. But when utilized as a single apparatus they become what a dissident globalization must insist upon as a social-erotics, an interrelated hermeneutics of "love," a methodology *for* the oppressed and *of* emancipation. Commitment to this methodology is what permitted 1970s–1980s lesbians of color to ally across their own racial geographies and to envision a coalition politics that extended beyond their own identity politics and cultural differences. Moreover, this shared methodology can generate other kinds of cross-national coalitions as well. For, like Sea Medicine's greeting, its guerrilla operations call new kinspeople into being: country-women, -men, and -children of the same psychic terrain. Their aim? To carry on irresistible revolutions, to wage love across the postmodern world.

NOTES

This essay was delivered as a plenary speech for the conference on "Queer Globalization: Sexuality, Citizenship, and the Afterlife of Colonialism," held in April 1998 at the Graduate Center of the City University of New York, CLAGS. My thanks to conference organizers Amaldo Cruz-Malavé and Martin F. Manalansan IV, who asked me to contextualize my previous work around queer and postcolonial studies; to plenary speaker Norma Alarcón for the Broadway *Chicago* experience; and to Lisa Biddle for her incisive comments on an earlier draft of the speech.

1. Bea Medicine, in *Two Spirit Peoples* and as cited in *Haciendo Coras,* ed. Gloria Anzaldúa (San Francisco: Aunt Lute Foundation, 1990) 55.
2. See, Pheng Cheah and Bruce Robbins, eds., *Cosmopolitics: Thinking and Feeling beyond the Nation,* (Minneapolis: University of Minnesota Press, 1998) and, *The Politics of Culture in the Shadow of Capital* Lisa Lowe and David Lloyd, eds., (Durham: Duke University Press, 1997).
3. The mystery of the academic erasure of U.S. third world feminism as a critical apparatus for decolonizing race, sex, and gender studies is a disappearing trick. Its exemption from academic canon short-circuits knowledge, but secures the acquittal of a "third," feminist "force" (about which Derrida said, "it should not be named"). Not named, he thought, in order that what is performative and mobile never be set into any place: freedom, he believed, could thus reside everywhere. It is out of this mobile terrain that the 1970s social movement named U.S. third world feminism called up countrypeoples of a new territory. For these country people today, who are no longer "U.S. third world feminist," the game begins again. New names (queer theory this time), new rules, new players.
4. Frantz Fanon, *Black Skin, White Masks,* trans. Charles Markmann (New York: Grove, 1967); Roland Barthes, *Mythologies,* trans. Richard Miller (New York; Hill and Wang, 1972), 148.
5. The contemporary social movement called "U.S. third world feminism" arose in recent times, though there are long histories of alliance between women of color in the United States. Examples range from the councils held by Seminole, Yamassee, and African women during times of territorial colonialism and slavery, to the coalitions made among Chinese, Chicana, and African women in protective leagues and labor movement straggles during the 1920s, 1930s and 1940s. The most cited examples of U.S. feminists of color arguing for a specific method called "U.S. third world feminism" can be found in Cherríe Moraga and Gloria Anzaldúa's collection *This Bridge Called My Back: Writings by Radical Women of Color* (New York: Kitchen Table/Women of Color Press, 1981). See also Chandra Talpade Mohanty's renowned collection and her essay "Cartographies of Struggle: Third World Women and the Politics of Feminism," in *Third World Women and the Politics of Feminism,* eds. Chandra Talpade Mohanty, Anne Russo, and Lourdes Torres (Bloomington: Indiana University Press, 1991). Also see Chela Sandoval, "Comment on Susan Krieger's 'Lesbian Identity and Community,'" in *Signs* (spring 1983). For histories of U.S. women of color in struggle, see Antonia Casteñeda's prizewinning essay "Women of Color and the Rewriting of Western History: The Discourse, Politics, and Decolonization of History," *Pacific Historical Review* 61 (1992); Asian Women United of California, ed., *Making Waves: An Anthology of Writings by and about Asian American Women* (Boston: Beacon, 1989); Paula Giddings, *When and Where I Enter. The Impact of Black Women on Race and Sex in*

America (New York: W. Morrow, 1984); Ellen DuBois and Vicki Ruiz, eds., *Unequal Sisters: A Multicultural Reader in U.S. Women's History* (New York: Routledge, 1990); Gretchen Bataille and Kathleen Mullen Sands, eds., *American Indian Women, Telling Their lives* (Lincoln: University of Nebraska Press, 1984); Rayna Green, ed., *Native American Women* (Sloomington: Indiana University Press, 1983); Paula Gunn Allen, ed., *Spider Woman's Granddaughters,* (Boston: Beacon, 1989); Albert Hurtado, *Indian Survival on the California Frontier* (New Haven: Yale University Press, 1988); Nobuya Tsuchida, ed., *Asian and Pacific American Experiences* (Minneapolis: University of Minnesota Press, 1982); Toni Cade Bambara, preface to Moraga and Anzaldúa, *This Bridge Called My Back.* For excellent work on third space feminism, see Emma Pérez, "Feminism-in-Nationalism: Third Space Feminism at the Yucatan Feminist Congresses of 1916," in *Between Women and Nation: Transnational Feminisms and the State,* ed. Norma Alarcóm, Caren Kaplan, and Minoo Moallem (Durham; Duke University Press, forthcoming). The work on *la conciencia de la mestiza, la facultad, coatlique,* and *nepantla* is by Gloria Anzaldúa in *Borderlands/La Frontera: The New Mestiza* (San Fransisco: Spinsters Aunt Lute, 1987). See also Pat Mora, *Borders* (Houston: Arte Público Press, 1986) on *nepantla.* For the relationship of the differential and *la conciencia de la mestiza* to "cyberspace," see Chela Sandoval, "Re-Entering Cyberspace: New Sciences of Resistance" in the journal *Dispositio: Subaltem Studies,* ed. José Rabasa et al. (1996). This definition appears as "U.S. Third World Feminism" in the *Oxford Companion to Women's Writing in the United States,* ed. Cathy Davidson and Linda Wagner-Martin (New York; Oxford University Press, 1995) 880–82. For an excellent discussion and analysis of this definition, see Katie King, *Theory in Its Feminist Travels: Conversations in U.S. Women's Movements* (Bloomington: Indiana University Press, 1994).

6. Merle Woo, "Letter to Ma," and many of the other essays in Moraga and Anzaldúa, *This Bridge Called My Back.* For an excellent overview of U.S. third world feminist politics, see King, *Theory in Its Feminist Travels.*

7. Michel Foucault, "The Subject and Power," in *Michel Foucault: Beyond Structuralism and Hermeneutics,* ed. Hubert Dreyfus and Paul Rabinow (Chicago: University of Chicago Press, 1983), 212.

8. Audre Lorde, "Uses of the Erotic: The Erotic as Power," in *Sister Outsider* (New York; Crossing Press, 1984).

9. Fredric Jameson, *Postmodernism, or the Cultural Logic of Late Capital* (Durham: Duke University Press, 1991). See especially the sections on "Cognitive Mapping."

10. Gloria Anzaldúa, "La Prieta," in Moraga and Anzaldúa, *This Bridge Called My Back,* 209.

11. Audre Lorde, "Comments at the Personal and the Political Panel" {"Second Sex Conference," New York, September 1979), in *Sister Outsider.*

12. Paula Gunn Allen, "Some Like Indians Endure," In *Living the Spirit* (New York: St. Martin's, 1987); Anzaldúa, *Borderlands;* Maria Lugones, "Playfulness, 'World'-Traveling, and Loving Perception," *Hypatia* 2 (1987); Patricia Hill Collins, *Black Feminist Thought: Knowledge, Consciousness, and the Politics of Empowerment* (New York: Routiedge, 1990); Gayatri spivak, "Criticism, Feminism and the Institution," *Thesis Eleven* 10–11 (1984–85 and "Explanations of Culture," in *The*

Post-Colonial Critic (New York: Routledge, 1990), 156; and Alice Walker, *In Search of Our Mothers' Gardens: Womanist Prose* (New York: Harcourt Brace Jovanovich, 1983).

13. *Audre Lorde, The Black Unicorn* (New York: Norton, 1995).

14. Note here already the implication of another "third space" gender, which today is being theorized as the category of the decolonizing "queer" as conceived by scholars of color. See, for example, the works of Cherríe Moraga, Gloria Anzaldúa, Emma Perez, Audre Lorde, Kitty Tsui, Makeda Livera, and Paula Gunn Allen. Yvonne Yarboro-Sejerano, *The Last Generation* (Boston: South End, 199S); Emma Perez, "Sexuality and Discourse: Notes from a Chicana Survivor," in *Chicana Lesbians,* ed. Carla Trujillo (Berkeley: Third Woman, 1991); Lorde, *Sister Outsider,* Kitty Tsui, Nelly Wong, and Barbara Noda, "Coming Out, We Are Here in the Asian Community: A Dialogue with Three Asian Women," *Bridge,* spring 1979; Asian Women United of California, *Making Waves;* Paula Gunn Allen, "Beloved Women: The Lesbian in American Indian Culture," *Conditions* 7 (1981); Makeda Livera, ed., *A Lesbian of Color Anthology: Piece of My Heart* (Ontario: Sister Vision, 1991); Deena Gonzáles, *Chicana Identity Matters* (Oxford: Oxford University Press, 2002); Sandoval, "Comment on Susan Krieger's 'Lesbian identity.'" Judith Butler's work on the performative develops parallel structures with the forms of U.S. third world feminism and its differential *mestiza* consciousness discussed here.

15. For in-depth descriptions and analyses of the social movement theory of U.S. third world feminism, see "U.S. Third World Feminism: The Theory and Method of Oppositional Consciousness in the Postmodern World,"

Genders 10 (spring 1991). The following schema provides its fundamental premise, which is structured to understand resistance as coalescing around the following five responses to social hierarchy:

1. The Equal Rights Mode. Within the first "equal rights" enactment of consciousness in opposition, members of the subordinated group argue that those differences—for which they have been assigned inferior status—lay only in appearance, not reality. Behind only *exterior* physical differences from the most legitimated form of the human is a content, an essence that is the same as the essence of the human-in-power. These oppositional actors thus argue for civil rights based on the philosophy that all humans are created equal. Aesthetically, this mode of consciousness seeks duplication; politically it seeks integration; psychically it seeks assimilation.

2. The Revolutionary Mode. Whereas the "equal rights" tactic insists on profound similarities between social, cultural, racial, sexual, or gender identities across their (only) external differences, the second ideology-as-tactic identifies, legitimizes, claims, and intensifies its differences—in both form *and* internal content—from the category of the most-human. Practitioners of the "revolutionary" form believe that assimilation of such myriad and acute differences is not possible within the confines of the present social order. Instead, the only way society will be able to affirm, value, and legitimate the differences they represent is if the categories by which society is ordered are fundamentally transformed.

3. The Supremacist Mode. Under "supremacism" not only do the oppressed claim their differences, but they also assert that those differences have lifted them to a higher evolutionary level than those against whom they fight. Whether practitioners understand their superior-differences as originating biologically or as developed through a history of social conditioning is of little practical concern. What matters is their effect: the subordinated group understands itself as functioning at a higher state of psychic and social evolution than do its protagonists.

4. The Separatist Mode. This is the final tactic of resistance of the four most commonly mobilized under previous capitalist modes. As in the previous three forms, practitioners of separatism recognize that their differences are branded as inferior with respect to the category of the most-human. Under this fourth mode of agency, however, the subordinated do not desire an "equal rights" type of integration with the dominant order. Neither do they seek its "revolutionary" transformation, nor its leadership through history. Rather, this form of political resistance is organized to protect and nurture the differences that define its practitioners through their complete separation from the dominant social order.

5. The Differential Mode. See text above.

16. These strategies were understood and utilized as tactics for intervention by U.S. women of color in 1960s–1970s ethnic liberation movements as well as in women's liberation movements. For explication of these usages, see Adaljiza Sosa Riddell, "Chicanas en el Movimiento," *Aztlan* 5 (1974); Moraga and Anzaldúa, *This Bridge Called My Back;* Barbara Smith, "Racism in Women's Studies," in *All the Women Are White, All the Blacks Are Men, but Some of Us Are Brave,* ed. Gloria Hull, Patricia Bell Scott, and Barbara Smith (New York: Feminist Press, 1982); Bonnie Thornton Dill, "Race, Class, and Gender: perspectives for an All-inclusive Sisterhood," *Feminist Studies* 9 (1983); Mujeres en Marcha, eds., *Chicanas in the '80s: Unsettled Issues* (Berkeley: Mujeres in Marcha Colectiva, 1983); bell hooks, *Feminist Theory: From Margin to Center* (Boston: Beacon, 1984); Alice Chai, "Toward a Holistic Paradigm for Asian American Women's Studies: A Synthesis of Feminist Scholarship and Women of Color's Feminist Politics," *Women's Studies International Forum* B (1985); Cynthia Orozco, "Sexism in Chicano Studies and the Community," in *Chicana Voices: Intersections of Class, Race, and Gender,* ed. Teresa Cordova, Norma Cantú, Gilberto Cardenas, Juan Garcia, and Christine Sierra (Austin: Center for Mexican American Studies, 1986); Chela Sandoval, "Feminist Agency and U.S. Third World Feminism," in *Provoking Agents: Gender and Agency in Theory and Practice,* ed. Judith Kegan Gardiner (Urbana: University of Illinois Press, 1995), and "U.S. Third World Feminism."

17. See Gayatri Spivak's famous essay on strategic essentialism, "Criticism, Feminism, and the Institution," and "Explanations of Culture."

18. Judith Butler, *Gender Trouble: Feminism and the Subversion of Identity* (New York: Routledge, 1990).

19. Chela Sandoval, *Methodology of the Oppressed* (Minneapolis: University of Minnesota Press, 2000).

11

[Insert Scholarly Title Here]
Negotiating Contested Identities Through
X-Communication

By Dustin Goltz

As a child, I was always cast as the "bad seed" of the neighborhood. Parents, including my own, were wary of me. Whenever a group of us were caught ding-dong-ditching or blowing up mailboxes with acid bombs, I was assumed to be the ringleader, the troublemaker, and the bad influence. "You need to stop hanging out with 'that Dusty boy!' He's always getting into trouble!" I refuse to confirm or deny these charges. When my friends and I would crank call someone, back in those blessed days before caller ID, we would all huddle around the phone, each listening in, feeding each other the next line, while holding our hands over each other's mouths to muffle our laughter. I'll start with this metaphor as a point of entry to this essay. This essay is a crank call into academia. While on one end of the phone, this may read like a coherent and stable person speaking to you, there are over a dozen of us (Deleuze and Guattari 3), slowly feeding the words and ideas that construct the "I" in this essay. Not all of us are laughing. One is gesturing right now to hang up the phone, not finding this funny at all. Another is afraid we'll get in trouble. The metaphor of the crank call is by no

means perfect, but it is a place to begin. It provides a way for me to start writing, in hopes that a better metaphor will develop along the way.

Vivian Gornick argues that constructing a well-crafted narrative with clear intent places two burdens upon the narrator. The narrator, or teller, needs to know *who* is speaking and *why* they are speaking (6). At the opening of the second paragraph of this story, I have already failed to meet her first criterion. The "I" in this story is suspect. It is a fictive construction, which at any moment, could be exposed through a burst of laughter from a dozen kids typing words onto these pages. It's a joke, but not in the sense that it is funny. It's a lie, but not in the sense that some form of truth is purposefully being withheld. It's a choice, because there is a story "I" want to tell.

In *Giving an Account of Oneself*, Judith Butler argues that, "the 'I' has no story of its own," as the "I" is always in relation to norms of discourse (8). All narrative marks a site of struggle, an assertion or action of claiming and defining the "I." Kristin Langellier extends Butler's concept of performativity as the action of the narrative, the political articulation and "struggle over personal and social identity rather than the act of a self with a fixed, unified, stable, or final essence" ("Voiceless" 208). Frederick Corey demonstrates this tension in his discussion of the personal versus the master narrative, I which he argues personal narrative "defixes" the master narrative's truth, posing a challenge to hegemonic discourse (250). In performativity, this struggle marks the site of potential to challenge discursive structures and attempts to understand the world in new ways. Langellier's work is steadfast in situating any discussion of personal narrative within a discussion of power and context. The personal narrative is a construction; something made, not found, and continually begs the question "who's interested in this/whose interest is this?" ("Two or Three" 127). She asserts that all narrative is political, serves a political function, and marks an active site of discursive struggle for personal identity ("Voiceless" 208). In order for this story to be told, for the next sentence to be written (as it has been rewritten over ten times already), I ask you to place faith in this fiction of the "I," this teller of this story, even if, in the background you hear ruptures of our muffled amusement, chatter, and conflict.

The following essay is not the story of *Banging the Bishop: Latter Day Prophecy* (Goltz, "Banging"; "Forgive"). This is my version of the controversial events surrounding *Banging the Bishop: Latter Day Prophecy* at a southwestern university[1] in the fall of 2004, a local incident that speaks to broader issues of performance scholarship in the academy, the politics of differing approaches to research, and the influence of institutional power in determining what forms of knowledge are deemed legitimate. This is one way to frame the story, although there are many others, as the events created a performance (con)text (Strine) that generated a multitude of pedagogical opportunities for discussion and interrogation. My narrative begins with the larger controversy, but chooses one (con)textual extension of the events, the performance of *X-Communication*, as its primary

focus. I create a narrative of my research and my performance of *X-Communication* in the wake of the *Banging the Bishop* postponement, offering an interrogation into the oversimplified ways that fixed or coherent identities were constructed and asserted within these events. As a gay male, a novice academic, and a former member of the LDS church, I was faced with navigating multiple and seemingly contradictory identities. I created the performance of *X-Communication* as a tool to generate dialogue within a tense and polarized community, but also as a space where I could assert my own understandings of self, challenging the simplistic identity categories that worked to lay claim on my experiences.

This essay takes the form of a quilt, an assemblage of textual fragments and identities from shifting contexts that are laced together to construct a deceptive sense of coherence. The performance text from *X-Communication* is woven throughout this essay[2] to disrupt the ease of this narrative. The jagged chaos of identity and events are filed down with temporal distance, an effect of telling and retelling our stories into clarity. These textual ruptures work to resist this coherence and draw attention to the false stability of the crank caller. I also piece together letters, emails, and journal entries from the controversy to further destabilize the authority of a singular teller, the "me" that is seated in my bathrobe in front of my computer, three years after the event, in some ways a stranger to the performances I once wrote.

"BANGING THE BISHOP": MORE THAN A EUPHEMISM FOR MASTURBATION

It was the fall of 2004. My master's degree was in performance art from a private art school, and so academia was a mystery I was just starting to piece together. On the last day of orientation, just before classes began, I was rushed to the hospital because my liver was failing. I was ordered by my doctors to "take it easy" for the next four months (my first semester as a doctoral student) and forbidden to drink any alcohol. It's okay to laugh. I did. I was back on the same campus where I started as an eighteen year old newly-converted Mormon undergraduate in 1993, took classes in the LDS institute, prepared for my Mormon mission, returned as a failed missionary, accepted a gay identity, and began doing solo performance work. I was an active member of the LDS community at one point, and so I was aware of the substantial LDS presence on this particular campus. However, this LDS presence and the speculated influence of LDS ideologies had consistently grown over the last decade, as the university's single largest benefactor was now a prominent local LDS businessman (Watson).

The story begins on 4 October 2004. I had survived a month and a half with yellowed jaundiced skin and no alcohol when I handed out the first flyer for *Banging the Bishop: Latter Day Prophecy* (hereafter *BTB*). The performance was scheduled to open in a week. The promotional flyer and press release read:

> This man will make it to heaven. All he has to do is honor his temple covenants, serve a two year mission, marry a good Mormon girl, have a ton of kids and keep smiling till it hurts … But he's Jewish … and gay … and he masturbates A LOT! *Banging the Bishop* is a multimedia performance, combining video, sound, movement, musical theater, and narrative into one absurd journey. "Goltz and [Director] expect that some audience members won't be amused by a tale that mixes synagogues, temples, bedrooms, and gay bathhouses," says [theater critic for state newspaper]. "The work is both harsh and tender in its honesty," says

[director], "Any time you reveal those kind of truths there is a risk." [Theater critic for local weekly] calls *Banging the Bishop: Latter Day Prophecy* a "slapstick journey through love, religion, sex, and hockey" that's "rowdy," "relentlessly hip," with "compelling video work." He warns you, however that "You'll never hear the hymn 'Come come yea saints' the same way again!"

On October 5th, I receive a phone call from the director of *BTB*. "We need to cancel rehearsal." In response to our publicity, a letter was sent to the director of the school of communication, the director of the performance studies area, and members of the administration. Doors were closed. Emergency meetings were taking place. Several weeks later, I was finally given a copy of this letter, which was written by an associate faculty member who was a member of the LDS church.

> *Banging the Bishop*. Its very title revolts me, and reeks of Hate Speech aimed not to elucidate one's personal experience, but to incite hatred and fear against a religion and a people who have suffered hatred, persecution, and oppression all its days … *Banging the Bishop*, in all its connotations, is an aggressive sexual act of violence akin to rape. It not only dehumanizes and objectifies the men called to serve as Bishops of my faith, but ignites violence against them. On a campus that boldly asserts: "HATE—NOT IN THIS HOUSE," how can we turn about-face and condone, even promote, such a hate-filled show? Were another, in a fit of vengeance, to propose a show entitled *Banging the* (insert any number of groups: Homosexuals …

Jews … Muslims) I am confident the humane [department] would censure, and prohibit the request. As well they should! … Others have urged me to speak decidedly, encouraging a direct address to [university president]. … yet I hesitate … I entreat you with the energy of my soul. Cancel the show. Cancel the show. Show your compassion, and cancel that show (Watson 26).

A second letter, by a second LDS faculty member, was sent directly to the university president.

> I trust that you will be sensitive to the feelings of [university's] Latter-day Saint community and seek to preserve its dignity. I trust that you will continue to maintain a campus environment where provocative ideas can be explored with respect, and where blatant provocation is not considered a legitimate substitute for critical exploration … In that light, I request that you exercise your office to censure and cancel the October 15–17 performances of *Banging the Bishop* (Watson 26).

I arrive at campus on October 5th. No one in the department is talking to me, yet I feel like everyone is staring at me. Faculty members, whom I have yet to meet, are whispering to each other, but quickly silence themselves as I walk by. Their smiles look painful on their faces. Do I still hand out flyers? I feel ashamed to be holding them, unsure of what I have done. With only two rehearsals left before curtain, I opted to go to The Empty Space and run the show by myself, even though the official rehearsal was cancelled. I sat in the theater, reading the flyer over and over. I thought about all the things I might have done wrong. The silence of the space was exaggerated by my own paranoia. I sat in judgment before an empty audience, facing accusations I had to both supply and then defend. Although I didn't know what the specific problem was, I knew that the thing I had been running away from for over a decade had just caught up with me.

I sit on a solid black cube, and talk directly with the front row.

PERFORMER. There are questions I have avoided for a long time, because I've been afraid. October 5th, I walked into this space, The Empty Space, with a bag of Wendy's and a Diet Coke. I sat right here on a box, with my hockey stick, and I performed the show, from beginning to end, by myself, as dialogue, as prayer. (*Looking to the sky*) Help me understand what it is I'm doing wrong. I don't point fingers. I don't judge. I own all of it. Please let me know because I am tired. I'm tired of waking up in the middle of the night to read scriptures, wondering if I have failed somehow. I'm tired of reading my patriarchal blessing[3] and trying to find something in there that even resembles who I am, or who I was supposed to be. I'm tired of reading Bryce's letter saying, "get back on your mission because you don't know what it's like and I do, and so you can't possibly understand what you're missing." I'm tired of wondering if I failed, if I just wasn't strong enough. Why won't these questions go away? The Mormon Church saved my life. It did. I owe my life to the Mormon Church. I'd be dead now, and I remember the calm that rushed through me every time I tried to end it, a peace, a resolution. I've been exhausted ever since.

BTB was my story, about my body, and my experiences. This highlighted my obvious personal connection to the text, but more so, an inner conflict. I wasn't standing up for the work of Larry Kramer or a distant author whose words I chose to embody, such as with the controversies surrounding *The Ghetto* and *The Normal Heart* (Roach; Strine). The text was my assertion of self, my claiming of an "I" in relation to existing discourses, and so I was responsible, if not suspect. Upon immediate attack, my first reaction was to doubt the text. I felt "I" was wrong, "I" was unfair, and "I" was now going to be punished. Ironically, the entire performance of *BTB* was about feeling guilt and shame for one's body and one's experiences, searching desperately for some form of forgiveness. Standing in the theater where I had once felt completely safe, I ran the words of the text through my body, interrogating myself for a confession or some evidence of my crime.

As I performed the words of the text, guilt turned to anger. I grew frustrated with myself for allowing their complaints to cast doubt in my mind, furious that the shame I had fought to exorcise from my life still had such power. I felt a deep connection to the text that had been absent through the rehearsal process, a fury and an urgent passion that I hadn't felt since I pounded those words into my computer years before. I remembered why I wrote this show.

> PERFORMER. I stood right there, and faced God, and I performed the monologue in the show that means the most to me. It's about a friend whom I love, a man who is gay, a man who has spent his entire life destroying himself in shame. Watching someone you love hate themself, hurts. Watching someone you love torture themself, hurts. He's sick, and that's no one's fault, and yet, it's everyone's fault. I stand here on stage and

> I pray for him, because he thinks God doesn't love him. But I love him. I love him, and that love is good. And this show is for that boy. It's about forgiveness. It's about finding forgiveness for our selves, and our bodies, and our loves.

I left the theater resolved. I felt, with a burning certainty, that *BTB* would be performed this next week because it was the right thing to do. To apologize or cower away from this performance because of LDS pressure could not be an option. Only then should I feel ashamed, because running away in fear would mean the story "I" tell in the text is a lie.

That night, I received the call from the director of the performance. The next morning, ticket reservations on the website were shut down, announcing that *Banging the Bishop: Latter Day Prophecy* was indefinitely postponed. I was never asked to be a part of the meetings that took place. The script of the performance was not read by anyone except the show's director, nor was it requested in the decision-making process. I found out that the discussions surrounding the performance extended from the president's office, to the provost, to the dean, to the department chair, through my director and collaborator, but the final decision was relegated to the performance studies faculty, with a vague directive to "cancel or postpone the show or face the consequences." (Park-Fuller, "Socio").

I didn't understand the criteria for the decision, nor the politics and power structures that placed performance studies in such a tenuous and uncertain position. To put it simply, there was much more at stake in this controversy than a few complaint letters and the questionable promotion of a performance. Over the previous summer, the university went through major restructuring, and the communication department had just landed in a new college with a new dean, as well as a newly hired departmental director. In a climate of anxiety and adjustment about the future of communication within a new college, the department was just beginning to sort through "the way we do things now" from "the way they've always been done." Needless to say, when this issue landed on the desk of the college dean, who had to answer to the provost, who was responsible for communicating with the university president, it was not an ideal situation to begin articulating the scholarly or pedagogical merits of performance research. In fact, many key stakeholders in this discussion were unfamiliar with the field of performance studies at all, as it was a brand new addition to their college. Had these events taken place in a fine arts college, which are more likely to have clear procedures or mechanisms in place for handling a controversial production, these events may have taken a much different turn. However, as our department was newly housed in a college more familiar with social scientific research and our adjustment phase was suddenly burdened with a growing controversy, a giant spotlight was shined upon performance studies expecting some explanation. This was exacerbated due to the much more strict policy within our new college for getting official permission from the dean prior to using the college or university name on any form of posting, which we had failed to do. The anxieties, adjustments, and frustrations that accompanied this institutional restructuring were already in place, further complicating the simple narrative of one flyer and two complaint letters. Transition quickly shifted to crisis. Still, as I was shut out of the discussion, my knowledge was limited to the flyer and two formal complaints. My naïve faith in a clear line that divides a "right" from a "wrong" decision reared its head. At that time, I felt they made the wrong choice. Three years later, as I have slowly gained more knowledge of these events, I have come to believe that nothing was as simple as it might have seemed at the time.

Violating doctor's orders, I indulged in a bottle of self-pity, a performance I know all too well. An odd impatience lingered around me, watching me, expecting me to do something, to respond. After sobering up from my victim status, fellow graduate students and faculty eased me into the realization that I was not powerless in this situation. As a graduate student, I was far more protected from the institution than the faculty or the administration. However, my peers argued that my framing of the events needed to be reconsidered. If I chose to respond or protest, then I needed to perform a very specific identity. I was not an artist. This was not about being a former member of the LDS church or a gay man. If I were to be taken seriously, I needed to be an academic, a performance identity for which I had yet to rehearse or embody. My complaint was about "scholarly inquiry," not "free speech." Don't mention "art" or "censorship," as these terms are irrelevant in the social sciences. It wasn't about "a performance" it was about "research." I suddenly landed in academic boot camp, the fight for legitimizing different ways of knowing through strategic use of language. The "I" that I assert in the following letter, which was sent out over the department listserv, stands in the place of a dozen peers and friends, who were equally unsettled by the events of that past week. However, it needed to come from "me."

Dear Colleagues,

Given our collective concern in the pursuit of scholarly research, some important questions need to be addressed: What are the implications of this decision, specifically in regard to power and private discourse in the university? Who is allowed to tell their story? Who has the power to silence one's story? Who is held responsible? How is it that a complaint about a research project is given serious consideration without any knowledge or investigation of the research itself? What impact do the complaints of religious organizations have on the silencing of scholarship? How does this impact your own work and the integrity of the [university] academic and artistic community? I send these questions to you to begin a dialogue. These are questions that I cannot answer because the discussions take place behind closed doors. However, I firmly believe that these questions impact many of us and need to be asked, regardless. I want to strongly encourage you to think about these questions, discuss these questions, and continue asking these questions until you, yourself, can feel satisfied with the answers.

Over the next two days, the listserv was flooded with discussion and debate. As soon as a group of graduate students and concerned faculty entered the discussion, local TV news stations, print media, CNN, and the ACLU all made efforts to contact me. While some attempted to explore the potential reasoning for the postponement, others were quick to name and define the events. Homophobia, right wing religious influence in the university, the tenuous position of performance studies, the changing role of the American university, academic freedom, and censorship became framing devices to discuss this situation, each highlighting broader issues that were already in existence on campus. Within each of the narratives my identity was constructed in distinct and often contradictory ways. I was the gay victim of homophobia, the citizen denied free speech, the reckless graduate student, the blasphemous pervert, a necessary example to mark the limits of college campus tolerance, the impassioned young scholar, the naïve artist, and the gay guy who had sex with his LDS bishop.

Mary Strine argues for an "expanded conception of the artistic performance text," or (con)text using the examples of the controversial productions of *The Ghetto* at Ball State University and *The Normal Heart* at Southwest Missouri State University (391). She examines how these productions are embedded within larger social dramas, and how these dramas point to extend performance as a potential strategy for political interference. In each of these performance (con)texts, the public controversy surrounding the productions "assumed a character of its own" (392). In a similar fashion, the postponement of the performance became a vehicle, a situation to be appropriated to discuss a myriad of issues that lacked a defining event to articulate. For this reason, the performance postponement became an opportunity for multiple interventions, broadening the (con)text far beyond the scope of a performance nobody had seen or read. As communication scholars in performance, many members of the faculty urged the graduate population to reframe this potentially damaging situation as an excellent opportunity for education and inquiry. Dialogue was happening. The attacks on performance studies' legitimacy were answered instantly through the rapid dissemination of ideas, opinions, thoughts, and perspectives on the issue (Park-Fuller, "Socio"). While theatrical performance is a vehicle for consciousness-raising and social intervention, in this case, it was the (con)text, rather than the performance, which created the intervention.

The pedagogical opportunity afforded by the performance (con)text was capitalized on in a number of settings. The closed-door discussions, which initiated the action, were broadened out to faculty-student departmental meetings, a graduate student response committee, and public forums for debate. On this level, the protection of scholarship and the visibility of departmental procedures came into question. The role of performance scholarship entered the larger discussion, providing visibility for the discipline, and created an environment that forced the importance of this work to be articulated and expanded (Park-Fuller, "Socio"). The student and local press carried this discussion to the broader community, highlighting the issues of LDS funding to state institutions and freedom of expression in the university (Watson 24). Class discussion explored, dissected, and debated the topics unearthed in the (con)text. The university hosted a public forum on academic freedom, exploring issues of power, private funding, and the role of academia in the freedom of expression (Goodall). In this situation, communication was flourishing. Articles and opinions from all sides of the discussion were featured on queer, LDS, masturbation, and art websites, and extended beyond to multiple discussion boards, and blogs.[4]

While I was cast as a character in multiple narratives, some very negative and others overly positive, these disseminated stories had very little to do with my own experience and understanding of the events. I remember walking out of a meeting with the administration and a peer asked me, "So, what do you think this is all about?" I shrugged my shoulders, unsure how to answer the question in a declarative sentence. Bothered by my pause, he corrected, "It's about homophobia. It's that simple." I remember thinking to myself, "I wish it were."

> PERFORMER. Why should this show not take place? It's a good question. It's a hard question, and more complicated than many can know, on either side. Sides, two opposing sides. This was not the intention. I stand in the middle.

Supportive friends and colleagues continually framed the story as "Dusty is being silenced by the Mormons." But the problem was, it wasn't "the Mormons," which implies some collective and unified body. Some Mormons voiced complaint, but it was the institution that postponed the show, and more specifically it was my own professors, who did so under unspecified pressures. Rather than "the Mormons," it was academia that stripped me of a voice in this situation, as it was demanded I perform a role I wasn't capable of playing. I knew the power of performance in my body. I felt performance, but was not prepared, at that time, to sit in a stuffy seminar room behind institutional tables and articulate, in their terms, a convincing argument for the defense of performance scholarship. I felt inadequate to make the arguments that needed to be made. Three years later, I have those arguments ready at a moment's notice, citing the well-crafted words of Conquergood, Schechner, Turner, Langellier, Denzin, Taylor, Madison, Pollock, and Pelias at the first sign of attack. However, at that time, I only had what I knew in my body, and that was not enough.

As the academy and the role of the academic silenced me in these events, I was equally frustrated by the ways the LDS church was being framed. *BTB* was all about my negotiation of Judaism, Mormonism, and homosexuality, and yet these events, from the initial complaint letter stripped me of any LDS affiliation, history, or experience. I was constructed as "the Mormon-hater" and the "anti-Mormon." It was assumed that my gay identity somehow cancelled out my Mormon past, and blanket statements and totalizing assessments about Mormons were thought to be acceptable in my presence. Statements like "you were Mormon" place a temporal assignment on my identity that implies I am no longer Mormon. This model of "once was, but no longer" articulates identity in terms that fails to grasp its complexity. Whenever I haven't eaten for a good part of the day and my stomach begins to growl with hunger, I am instantly taken back to Sunday fasts and the strength that I felt for enduring hunger in the name of obedience and sacrifice. I will find myself spontaneously singing "Oh Lord, My Redeemer" in my car, on the freeway, late at night. Sometimes, when I pray, I fold my arms and begin with the words, "Dear Father, who art in Heaven. I come to thee on this night." Sometimes I don't. I have experienced living as an LDS undergrad at this university. Daily, my beliefs were mocked in my classrooms and in the dorms. While I am not Mormon, at the same time, I'm not not Mormon. As people would make jokes or statements about Mormons, I felt a frustration when their beliefs were misrepresented. I resented having to take on the role of defender of Mormon beliefs, for several reasons, yet the ways LDS beliefs are constructed in popular discourses is often oversimplified or over-exoticized.

As the events unfolded, who I was in this whole discussion became less and less clear to me. Even worse, the discussion became a talking within "camps" rather than a discussion across. I was satisfied that the decision to postpone was made visible and not tucked away. Still, I failed to see the productivity in several of the strategies proposed by my peers, such as protesting the LDS Institute or speaking to news media. I knew the media would likely sensationalize the sexual elements of the performance and misrepresent performance studies. Additionally, I had several personal issues I was struggling with, as I didn't know how or where "I" had a voice amidst this whole controversy.

GAY AND MORMON (BUT NEVER HAD SEX WITH MY BISHOP)

Performance became the one way I felt I could respond to the events, one space where I could figure out who "I" was in the middle of this controversy.

PERFORMER. I walked into the Empty Space Theater over ten years ago. I guess it would be fair to say I left the church and came here. I love the name "Empty Space" because it lacks definition. It says nothing about what happens here, nothing but possibility. This space is sacred to me: as a site of inquiry, as an exploration of identity, of truth, of sites of knowledge. So many bodies, ideas and truths have used this Empty Space to ponder, to pray, to reflect, to declare. It's a safe space. Ghosts and remnants of past and futures float around this small room. I did my very first solo piece here. It was called "His Image" and the entire show was about allowing myself the space to be angry. [Two treasured mentors from my undergraduate program] allowed me that space. My twenty-year old body in black jeans and my naked twenty-year old chest smeared with mud still linger in this space amidst all of the other voices.

The *X-Communication* performance project sought to interrogate how the different "sides" of the controversy failed to account for my own identities and identifications. I wanted to explore and problematize the clear lines that were being drawn between "us" and "them," as I struggled to locate myself within/across this binary frame. I started with a series of questions. Based on my understanding and experiences within the Mormon Church, why should this production *not* take place in academia? Why should this production take place within academia? How might I attempt to engage this issue in a productive dialogue with the LDS community when their worldview is radically challenged by my queerness? How might I attempt to negotiate these diverse worldviews that exist within my own body?

Why is *BTB* at the center of this discussion? Why is it feared? Why is it (if it is, in fact) relevant?

> PERFORMER. We attended a church fireside earlier this evening, and no one was ready to go home. We drove up here, on top of this mountain.[5] Wow! Guys, check this out. Look out over the city lights, past the mountains. It's perfect, huh? It's beautiful. Peter, Morgan, Mike, this world is our gift tonight. The spirit is within us, swirling around us, can you feel that? It's overpowering. You guys are literally glowing. What a world. (*In prayer*) Heavenly Father, tonight, on this mountain, we promise we will be forever faithful and true. We will obey your word and honor you with our actions. Thank you, Father. We say these things in His name, amen. (*To audience*) I will remember this night for years to come. I will remember who I am, and the truth I hold as I stand here. I am God's child, and I am blessed with this knowledge, with this testimony. I would never write that show. Standing here, that show would never happen. Peter, Mike, Morgan and I, we would fight it, like warriors, because that's the right thing to do. And so, ten years later, I've returned to scripture, walked back into church, trying to get back to that mountain that amazing night, to remember why I would have fought me.

X-Communication is a personal investigation into the "I" that is asserted and constructed within the narrative of *BTB*. My relationship to the LDS Church was more complicated than many seemed to understand. During the entire explosion, following the postponement, I remained, technically, a member of The Church of Jesus Christ of Latter Day Saints. While I was in the process of removing my name from church records, I had taken my endowments in the Mormon Temple and engaged in sacred rituals, which are closely guarded and discussion of them is strictly prohibited outside of the temple walls. Mormonism is not some distant and abstract evil, but a piece of me with lingering remnants in my photo albums, my bookshelf, my memories, and my daily life. My mind and my body have experiences that the LDS church claims to own. I was LDS, and there is a part of me that will always be, or, at least, not not be LDS. I know, through lived experience, prayer, fasting, and daily struggle and negotiation, the work it requires to live the life of a faithful Mormon on a daily basis.

> PERFORMER. We stood on that mountain. Our reasons would not have made sense to anyone other than ourselves. Wrong is wrong. God's truth is more powerful than the academy, or free speech, or even logic. Spirit, that which carries and claims truth. To see that flyer, the charred text, the charred mission call, the temple ... Standing on that mountain, we would understand with the utmost certainty that this was the work of the lost, the misguided. Why would you do this? In that moment, I would have approached my play and myself with disgust, but mostly pity.

At eighteen years old, I "came out" as a gay male, taking that identity upon myself. I was terrified of what that meant, ashamed of what that made me, and what my life would become. It was an identity I could not manage, and I grew depressed, disgusted with myself, and eventually wanted to die. The church was at my door when no one else was.

PERFORMER. The LDS church embraced me. For the first time I could remember I knew, with all my heart, I was a good person. I had a mission. I had something divine inside of me. The discovery of this, the nurturing of this, living with this, as I woke each day … I had a knowledge, a spirit, and a testimony of the truth of this church, and a desire to love. I wished my friends could understand. I wished my family could understand. They couldn't. They thought I was nuts. But I wasn't. I was home. For the first time in my life, I was home.

When I "came out," for the second time, I forced myself to deny much of my Mormon self. These differing identities that existed inside of me refused to dialogue with each other, feeling as if one must lay dormant for the other to exist.

PERFORMER. I remember the night I was baptized. I believed I was starting over. I remember changing my clothes after the baptism and watching my friend change, and the desire I felt made me so sad. I thought that desire would be lesser. I believed it would be gone. As much as you may hate the idea of this play, I felt the same way about my body. I wanted it to be quiet. I wanted it to have some respect. I loathed its perversion, its reckless freedom, and its violation of all I held sacred.

The *X-Communication* project adopts an autoethnographic/autobiographical/personal narrative approach to the construction of the performance text. The placement of these three concepts next to each other is not intended to dismiss their differing historical developments in the academy but seeks to challenge the problematic ways they are often set apart from one another. The construction of autobiographical personal narrative, as exemplified in the controversy surrounding BTB, inescapably implicates the broader cultural backdrop (Corey; Langellier, *Two or Three*), as the effort to designate domains of the personal from the cultural is "somewhat absurd" (Gingrich-Philbrook 299). Gingrich-Philbrook interrogates the legitimizing claims that autoethnography offers a cultural critique absent from autobiography, arguing that this limited representation of autobiography serves to obscure autoethnography's mediocre claims to artistry and aesthetic commitment (301). I wish to work within these three concepts, as my project is informed by literature written under each of these terms (Corey; Ellis and Bochner; Gingrich-Philbrook; Langellier, *Two or Three*; Park-Fuller, *Absence*; Ronai). My goal was to face my fear about the questions, concerns, guilt, and shame that I felt by writing the text of *BTB*. I wanted to bring myself closer to the person I was ten years before, this Mormon convert who had absolute faith in scripture to answer any question he faced.

I placed myself in situations I had avoided for years, believing that specific sites, specific encounters, and specific situations would provide some form of connection to my past, this person I used to be. Peter[6] was my best friend for several years, as well as the man who baptized me twelve years ago. Unbeknownst to him, and maybe myself, I was in love with him for the majority of our friendship. When I left the church, our friendship faded immediately. I cut ties with him, immersed myself in gay friends, gay bars, and gay identity. The pain that drove me away from Peter was a composition of unrequited love and guilt for my broken covenants to the church, to which he was a witness. At that point in my life I was afraid to face him, fearing the way his eyes would study my overcompensating narratives that worked to justify my new life, a life

I was just beginning to reconcile and negotiate. We had not spoken more than ten minutes in a decade when I called Peter, asking him to meet me for dinner on 17 November 2004.

My anticipated responses and defenses were in overdrive. I projected potential narratives onto Peter in a preemptive effort to prepare my counter-response. I cast him as the devout Mormon who would self-righteously judge my life, my choices, and my performance. I cast myself as the queer artist who has the right to tell his story. I later realized that I was complicit in the very discourses I thought I was challenging. My anticipated scripting of our meeting was not only inaccurate, but also unfair. I was just as bad as all the people I had criticized in the performance controversy; the ones who unfairly reduced me to a singular identity stereotype. I projected this simplistic identity onto Peter, but my actions were less forgivable. Peter was my friend. A person I spent every day with for over three years, and yet somehow I filed and shaped him in my mind into something less than human. His only response to the whole performance drama was, "well, those people just don't know you. I know who you are. You'd be fair." We spent the majority of the dinner talking about the career trajectories of U2 and R.E.M., our families, and the friends we've lost touch with. We weren't the same people we once were. Some of Peter's idealism had been tarnished, his eyes tired from working long hours to support his wife and two daughters. Still, we knew each other in ways that are more complicated than saying "we once knew each other." I located a part of me that was unique to my interactions with Peter, a relational identity (Jackson) that reemerged very easily after a decade over a burger and fries. While not fully contingent on this relational identity I have with Peter, Mormonism was inescapably tied to this self. Long ago, I had convinced myself that the "Mormon me" was a performance that was somehow less authentic or accurate (Tracy

and Trethewey). I dismissed my entire life, from that time, as if it was all a lie. For clarity of self, I lumped friendships, basketball, Louis L'Amour books, Jimmy Stewart movies, and dozens of other identifications into an overstuffed bag that I labeled "Mormon" and tucked it away. What scared me was that I wasn't as different now as I wanted to believe. My identity was as contingent on physical space and relational interaction as it was on religious or sexual categorizations. The lines between then and now, the "me back then" and the "me now," lost some coherence.

My boyfriend dropped me off at the church sacrament meeting on the morning of 21 November 2004. I wore a dress shirt and a tie, shaved, and combed my hair for the first time in years. My goal was not to fit in, but to not stand out. For years I have been receiving mail and missionary visits requesting I return to church. I chose a different ward from the one I used to attend, wanting to focus on how the physical and spiritual space felt in my body without facing the pressure of explaining myself to others. Upon entering the building, I feared two different reactions. I was afraid I would feel guilty and ashamed; paranoid that everyone there would sense my transgressions like a spiritual branding across my forehead. What if they recognize me from my picture in the paper? I was equally afraid that it would feel too comfortable, too right, demanding I go through the seemingly never ending process of questioning my choices, my broken promises, and my failures.

Throughout the ceremony, I experienced both reactions. People were friendly. There were many kind smiles and handshakes. I remembered how humbled I felt during sacrament meetings years ago, and the deep shame of not feeling worthy to partake in the blood and body of Christ. I remember that person, that emptiness and humility squeezing within my stomach. However, it was less of a memory, in the sense of temporal distance, than an embodied history that challenges the logics of linear historical mapping (Taylor). My body seemed to work in different ways, negotiate differing meanings or pathways of sensation. I felt a certain sense of power in not taking the sacrament. It wasn't out of shame, but a choice, one that sat comfortably in my body as a defining action of the "me, now." I sang hymns I somehow managed to hold onto in the back of my mind. I was humbled by the prayers and missed having a regular space in my life that was set apart for spiritual reflection. I enjoyed the lessons and the speakers with a generous removal from the doctrine through a logic of "this works for you." It didn't, however, work for me. I walked out of the ward building, turned a corner, and lit a cigarette. It was a small, petty, and satisfying act of distancing myself and claiming myself. I laughed, feeling like a teenager all over again, enjoying the tiny rebellions that carve out points of departure from the identities imposed upon us. I do share something with everyone in that room, and yet, I made a choice not to live it, perform it, and place faith in it. I've placed my faith elsewhere, but we're not complete strangers, not in that space. My body still feels that space, understands its energy, and recovers a piece of me within it.

On the evening of 28 November 2004, I prayed after I finished reading the "Book of Moroni," the final section of *The Book of Mormon*. It contains a scriptural passage that is commonly used by missionaries, which asks readers to pray on the truth of the testament. It was how I came to the church many years ago, after Peter gave me a copy of *The Book of Mormon*. I realized that I'd been going about this completely wrong. This was my truth. I remember how deeply I felt this, the warmth, the conviction, and the hope that stemmed from praying on these words. How can truth be in the past tense? The next morning, I woke up and watched my boyfriend sleeping. I was listening to Sinéad O'Conner in the background and watching his face as the sun

slowly inched across the room. I had been mining my guts for everything I could feel, and watching him sleep was the most peaceful resolute sensation I had experienced in months. I remember, when I returned from my mission, I received a barrel full of letters from Mormon friends at the Missionary Training Center. They were on a campaign to save me from my "choices." One particular letter always stuck with me. It came from a close friend, who argued, "There is a difference between happiness and pleasure." That phrase haunted me for years. Looking at my partner sleep, listening to Sinéad, some of the pain of that phrase was eased.

In asking "who am 'I,'" the question perpetuates the illusion of a fixed and stable self to be located or found (Butler; Tracy and Trethewey). To approach identity in terms of intersectionality (Crenshaw), creates a space to articulate the ways multiple identities cross over one another, as religious, sexual, gendered, or academic identities do not function on "mutually exclusive terrains" (357). However, intersectional models of identity run the risk of reducing the messy nature of identity "into a formulaic grid" (Puar 128), "stabilizing identity across time and space" (128). An assemblage identity model "is more attuned to interwoven forces that merge and dissipate time, space, and body against linearity, coherency, and permanency" (128). Assemblage challenges identity formations that emphasize naming and create the illusion of timelessness (128), as identity moves and shifts through special and temporal locations.

By placing myself in these contexts and interactions, I watch my identities morph and shift, emerge and dissolve, through time and space. There are no clean breaks defining the "once was" to the "now am," as "I" continue to be negotiated, leaving open the space for an identities that are always becoming and emerging (Puar 128). For several days after I met Peter, attended church, and reread scriptures, I caught myself continually singing hymns when I was not paying attention. I found myself editing out swear words I would usually ramble off. These remnants still sit in my body, and the performances of these identities are familiar, but my personal truths have changed. These truths, much like contexts and relationships, call for different performances and forefront different identities. Watching my partner's face, as he sleeps, testifies a truth just as the spirit does when I pray.

X-COMMUNICATION: FACE-TO-FACE AND BODY-TO-BODY

Dear Colleagues,

I would like to personally invite you to a performance discussion event at The Empty Space Theater on Thursday, December 9th at 4:30 P.M. This event will attempt to create an open and civil discussion surrounding the postponed production of *BTB*.

The events surrounding this production have created a troubling and silencing polarization within the community. I firmly believe that this was not the intended result of any of the individuals involved in this situation. My hope is that a safe and respectful dialogue will assist all of us in growing to understand divergent worldviews and belief systems that differ from our own, as well as provide a forum for each of your voices to be heard, pondered, and experienced. The event proposed is designed as follows:

There will be a brief twenty-minute performance to help facilitate the discussion. This performance examines contradictory internal arguments for why *BTB*

should and should not be performed. In light of recent events, I have chosen to return to scripture, church, and LDS friends from years ago in order to explore any of my own reservations regarding this production. I offer this piece as an honest gesture of self-exploration, attempting to investigate contradictions of faith and worldview that exist inside of me, as well as within our academic community. The performance is designed for an LDS audience, and I guarantee there will be no profanity, nudity, or content that would intentionally alienate anyone in the audience.

Following the performance, a facilitated discussion will take place, opening the dialogue to the entire audience using the "Civil Discourse" model.[7] Everyone invited is asked to respect the diversity of the audience. First and foremost, my goal is to create a space where everyone involved can feel comfortable to speak on this complicated matter. I understand many of you may feel apprehension about this forum, and I am going to great lengths to prevent anyone from feeling silenced, attacked, or mocked in any way.

I organized this performance event with the hope of generating dialogue, sharing experiences, and problematizing the ways the controversy had constructed polarized positions. The performance was a tool to bridge differing perspectives (Fouss, Kistenberg and Rosenfeld) and trigger intercultural discussion (Valentine and Valentine). Using personal narrative, my objective was to give voice to diverse experiences in the audience, create mutual vocabularies, and construct productive dialogues within various positions of audience (Goodwin). This project approaches autobiographical personal narrative as a pedagogical and political act (Park-Fuller, Absence), identifying the blurred boundaries of culture and self in autoethnographic/autobiographical research to facilitate a discussion of binary positions.

In crafting the piece, I needed to decide which "I" was relevant or productive in this discussion. I have always been suspect of performance work that stands outside of structures and points fingers at the oppressive institutions, as if the performer and text were exempt from socialization and cultural production. Additionally, given the controversy, I knew there would be an audience expectation for me to assert "what really happened" (Park-Fuller, "Absence" 21), although there was no way to tell the whole story (24). The narrative was not a given, but a creation (27), one I hoped would not diminish the ambiguity of my experience and could promote an ethic of partiality and misunderstanding (Langellier and Peterson 239–240). The performance event's objectives were "to open up possibilities for learning about difference and the operations of identity rather than didactically prescribe or reinscribe particular identity configurations" (236). I believed, if well executed, X-Communication had the possibility (Madison) "To transform us. To transform others. To create change" (Martin, xviii).

In crafting the text for X-Communication, I felt frustrated with the ways LDS considerations, institutional pressures, and my own fears were monitoring every word I wrote. I was afraid to speak, terrified of the repercussions of my voice, as my story was now contextualized within, and reflective of, a larger institutional hierarchy. In addition, the discourses surrounding the events were highly charged, overly vague, and closely monitored. I did not have a clear understanding of what had happened that first week in October, and it is likely that I never will. Still, as I crafted the text of X-Communication there was a tangible sense of risk, weight, and power looking over my shoulder as I wrote. Was there any

merit to the speculation that the LDS church had direct influence over the workings of the university? Would there have been recourse if the show went on? Was communication or performance studies placed in a tenuous position because of BTB? I can't answer these questions. However, there was an accepted awareness that these risks and speculations could have merit and have real consequences. This potentially tenuous position within the institution placed performance studies in a defensive climate where it became necessary to fight for its legitimacy, "dotting each 'i' and crossing each "t"" (Park-Fuller, "Socio"). Every word that followed my deployment of "I" in the text of X-Communication was guarded, strategic, and quivering in hesitation.

As an additional consideration, I've found myself uncomfortable when I audience narratives that instruct me how I should think, feel, and engage, potentially trapping audience identification and asserting definitional authority (Langellier and Peterson). I resist performances where the subtext begs the audience to "love me," "hate them," or "please, pick me," further perpetuating the illusion of a fixed self in the narrative (Hantzis). I approach my own work as self-interrogation, self-criticism, and perhaps self-deprecation, working from an ethic of "messiness," and embracing the act of "skin-scraping." I interrogate myself. I am implicated in the very "monsters" (Park-Fuller, "Absence") I unmask, as they also live and breath in my body as a socialized being.

In constructing my arguments for why the BTB should not be performed, I realized that neither the charges of academic policy, nor hate speech, supplied a strong argument for canceling the show once the script was considered. Additionally, these arguments fail to account for, what I felt was, the larger problem the LDS church had with the production. The underlying tension seemed to be the prospect of a gay male discussing temple rituals and church doctrine alongside discussions of masturbation and gay bathhouses, potentially mocking, exposing, or violating sacred practices. In many ways, I felt the dialogue I wanted to engage in with the LDS members was a discussion of spirituality, more specifically the church doctrines on free agency and sacred covenants.

> PERFORMER. Yes, I talk about the temple[8] in the show. No specifics, but enough that I believe I am breaking my word. In this show, I break covenants with God. I speak and witness that which I swore I would not. If there is a reason this show should not be performed, it is because I'm going back on my word, my word to God, my relationship with God.

As there is no clear cut "I" (Butler 8) who is positioned against the master's (Corey) or monster's (Park-Fuller, "Absence") discourse, I chose to represent a fragmented identity on stage, occupying multiple positions through staging, physical choices, and media. In the narrative, time and physical context were continually blurred. In some scenes, my voice is prerecorded, disembodied from onstage movement. I prerecorded myself on video, delivering lines and timing pauses, to construct a simulated natural exchange with my body on stage.

> TV. I know I cannot convince those who pity or reject me to embrace my truth. I know that if I tell you I bear witness to God and he embraces me, you must, you have to, find some way to qualify or dismiss this.
> PERFORMER. One truth. One true church. One true prophet.
> TV. I can even respect that.
> PERFORMER. You broke covenants.
> TV. I accept those consequences, and they are mine to accept.

> PERFORMER. Standing here, on this mountain, no. No. No, Dust.
> TV. There is no hate in this show.
> PERFORMER. Your words hurt. Your words hurt me.
> TV. Truth hurts. I flinch at passages of this show, but it is my agency. It is my free will to do so.
> PERFORMER. What would have happened if you stayed in Utah?
> TV. Your truth hurts as well.
> PERFORMER. What would have happened if you were stronger?
> TV. My best friends in the world, who have loved me and cared for me and taught me more about God than anyone, they are the weak and lost to others.
> PERFORMER. There is a difference between happiness and pleasure.
> TV. My heart is mocked everyday.
> PERFORMER. This I understand.

The theater was filled with tremendous history, pressure, and opinion before I stepped onto the stage. The (con)text was overpowering. Who was in the audience? Peter Benson, whom I reference in the baptism monologue, revealing my sexual desires for him for the first time. Why did I invite him? The LDS faculty members were seated in the audience, men I have never met but who have made public statements about the offensiveness of my work, my "lurid portrayal," the violence I conjure, the irrelevance of my experiences, and the viciousness of my intentions. How do I "go there" in this performance? What was I thinking? I look out to the audience before I stand to deliver my first lines. I see members of the administration and departmental faculty. I imagine snickers and doubt about the scholarly integrity of this project. Should I have put citations on the video? Scribbled them in marker across my arm? I need to breathe. This is going to be a mess. Breathe. Okay, I see my boyfriend's face, along with some friends, thankfully, to support me. Everything felt loaded. Shed your usual sarcastic delivery, which could be misconstrued as defensive, if not aggressive. Still, don't force the sincerity either because that makes me gag. Go back to the day rehearsal was cancelled. Explore the text with my body and trust it as my guide. Humor was my usual way to connect with an audience up front, but I couldn't take that risk. I was afraid of it in this space. Language and content were under close inspection. The text is so scaled down, so direct, lacking the complexity of form and language I am accustomed to. I barely even use sound or video, which are primary to my aesthetic. I've never felt so confined and alienated on stage. Performing has always been my site of freedom, of exploration, and now the restrictions were suffocating. Did I warm up enough? I know I smoked too much. Now there's no way I'll be able to sing the higher notes. My mother was right. I should have stuck with musical theater. I was good at musical. … Crap! That's my cue. Get up. Just take it one line at a time. I delivered my first line. Then, I delivered my last. "And this is where I write from, and this is where I perform from. I don't point fingers. I don't judge. I just scrape away at my own skin."

As I held the final moment of the performance, my nerves raced back into my body. I fought off impulses of flight long enough to announce a short break prior to the discussion and left the stage. What happened in those twenty minutes? I don't know. Thank God for that blessed escape into "the moment" on stage that takes me there, away from my head, and off onto the mountain, into the temple, and into my past. I promised, as I stood in that temple, so many years ago, that I would cut my throat before revealing certain truths. I swore to slice my belly before I would speak. Now they claim my work is violent, and I suppose it is. I tear

away at skin, my own skin; acts of mutilation as a method for finding my own versions of "truth."

The discussion that followed the performance drifted back to the comfortable land of abstraction and academic jargon, rarely addressing the performance directly. In fact, any discussion of *X-Communication* seemed to be avoided, particularly by the LDS members who were present. During the break, a faculty member, who is an ex-Mormon himself, said to me, "There really isn't any discussion to be had after that [the performance]. That's it." He believed that *X-Communication* identified my intentions for writing *BTB*, dispelling the numerous "hate" charges that were launched against the production. However, the gentlemen who protested the performance of *BTB* did not change their previous complaints. These men felt attacked by the advertisement, and they stood firmly on this point. What I found interesting was how "the attacker" became abstracted in their current narratives. It was no longer "I" attacking them, my "lurid portrayal." Their narrative shifted to an unnamed attacker, an abstract and anonymous force that made them feel attacked. This is how I felt about my attackers two months ago, these anonymous men whom I'd never met who so quickly judged me. Things had changed.

On the surface, the dialogue remained fairly stagnant. The explanation of my intentions behind the *BTB* seemed irrelevant to these men in that particular space and time, and they simply restated their position repeatedly. The facilitator asked, "now that you've seen this performance, do you still feel that *BTB* was a direct attack?" The question was avoided, asked again, but never answered. Explanations or justifications did not matter. They wanted an apology, although my name was never spoken by any of these men. In over an hour of discussion, the dialogue never progressed beyond this point. The gentlemen also avoided commenting to the fact that the text of *BTB* had been read by the administration and was found to be free of any potential hate speech. I found out that the man who wrote the original letter was told the meaning of the phrase, "banging the bishop" before he wrote the initial complaint. A day before crafting his letter, in a meeting with the director of *BTB*, he was informed that it was a euphemism for masturbation and that there was no content in the show dealing with sexual activity or violence against bishops. Still, he wrote the letter. It was never about "hate speech" and, it seems, everyone knew that from the beginning. When *BTB* was finally staged in April 2005, one member of the administration, who was integral in the postponement, attended the performance. After the performance, I said to this administrator, "See, no hate." Her/His response was, "We never really thought there was in the first place. It was never about the show."

So did this performance matter? If the LDS faculty members were impervious to the piece, what was the point of all this? The performance created a context for discussion. Dialogue occurred, handshakes were exchanged, and people came together in a face-to-face unmediated presence that "cannot be denied" (Madison as cited in Park-Fuller, "Absence" 35). "For now we see through a glass, darkly; but then face to face" (1 Cor. 13:12).[9] We shared space, heard each other's stories, and hopefully demystified the "other" in some ways. Both the performer and audience were placed in a position of risk (Jones; Park-Fuller, "Absence"), as we all were asked to stand in the position of the other and negotiate those locations. It was no longer possible to simply cast anyone in this controversy in clear-cut positions. We had to own our positions while facing each other, and I believe all perceptions were altered for the better. Tensions were aired publicly, and I believe that this communication offered great assistance in tempering the controversy. The LDS gentlemen suggested that canceling *BTB* was not their objective, but felt they had a right to speak

their own position. The polarized positions that characterized the early voices of the controversy seemed more reasoned, less sure, and more open to the ideas of another. Greater understanding was achieved, or at least, we've heard each other out, body to body. I do believe *X-Communication* helped problematize the anti-LDS sentiment that was rampant among those "in my camp." I hope it raised some more questions for the LDS faculty as well. Perhaps it was too soon after the performance to expect these ideas to sink in, be exchanged, and take hold of each of us. Performance sits in our bodies long after we leave the performance space. The rush to verbalize the experience might undercut the bodily experience. I'd like to think that I became a little more human to these men in that space, and that is why their attacker became abstract. This I cannot know for sure.

The greatest testament to the efficacy of *X-Communication* is that when we restaged *BTB* in April of 2005, there was no further protest. The performance was successfully staged without any visible opposition. However, *BTB* can never be the same performance it would have been if it had been performed on 15 October 2004. The performance has changed, and continues to change. The words mean something else. Audiences attended the piece expecting to find controversy, hate speech, the story of a boy having sex with a church leader, or some justified fuel that started the fire a semester before. In November 2005, two days before I performed the piece in a small downtown art gallery space, I received an anonymous letter at my home address that insured me that I will get what's coming to me in the next life for the evil I do. In March of 2006, the campus newspaper ranked the controversy the second most controversial event in recent university history, although the story inaccurately reported that the "play" was "banned." As the (con)text expands, *BTB*, the events surrounding the production, and my identity will continue to shift through the negotiation of multiple and differing voices, never static or agreed upon.

This story sought to document the controversy surrounding *Banging the Bishop: Latter Day Prophecy*, which provided a (con)text for multiple pedagogical and political discussions. Although I never could have (or would have) believed this to be the case in October of 2004, the postponement of the production, and the (con)text surrounding it, became a vehicle to fulfill many of my initial hopes and objectives for *BTB*. It generated discussion, reached several audiences, and worked to push ideas forward. One of these (con)textual extensions was the performance of *X-Communication*, examining the ways Mormon, academic, and gay identities were negotiated through my personal experience within the controversy. In turn, the *X-Communication* project further investigates potential applications for educational performance and performance as a tool for triggering intercultural dialogue. I strongly disagreed with the decision to postpone the performance and still struggle with how some of the events unfolded. However, "I" find myself looking back on the events with an increasing faith that there was a guiding logic and an emergent productivity at work, which continue to give shape to the chaos.

I have asserted an "I." The context of the *BTB* controversy placed my Mormonism and gayness in the forefront of the discourse, constructing an overly simplistic tension between two marginalized and seemingly incongruent identities. However, there is much that remains remarkably absent from this construction of identity and continues to remain absent in my own crank call to academia. My voice claims a Mormon, gay, and academic self, but this narrative has been shaped through an assemblage of identities, and each of them continues to feed me lines. Simultaneously they speak in unison, in harmony, in conflict, in turn, and in relation to one another. These identities collaborate with and resist each other in infinite and indecipherable formations, shifting in time and across various contexts. Extending outside of the messy assemblage of my gay, not not Mormon, and academic self, the reader should know that my whiteness, masculinity, middle-class privilege, age and a multitude of other voices have also been speaking to you, feeding lines to the "I" that you have come to know through this conversation. I can't begin to parse out their contributions, except to tell you that they were always present, never leaving the room, speaking to you throughout this entire essay. I know this because they are the ones that usually feel the most privileged to speak at all, fueling my Mormon, gay, and academic performances with a sense of entitlement and authority. They don't take turns speaking and who "they" are is always changing. Thus, the crank call metaphor is limited in what it can offer the theorizing of identity. Then again, so are the words I have at my disposal. The ones I am typing into my computer while I munch on stale trail mix before sneaking outside for another cigarette.

The complaint letters, my responses, the entire documentation of events, and the *X-Communication* performance are much noisier, congested, and indecipherable than I have put forth. It's why live performance, bodies in the physical space with other bodies, can extend beyond some of the limitations of the crank call, this disembodied essay about identity. Sure, the spoken text will always create false illusions of coherent identities, but in live performance the words will always speak with, through, and against the body. Bodies speak to one another in space, affording much greater risk of multiple exposures and contradictions in the presence of a speaking subject claiming their "I" before an audience. Performance has the potential to cross, dislodge, and complicate identities and identity boundaries, creating identifications between audience and performer that rupture the ways discourse constructs rigid binaries. Peter claimed the LDS complaints were launched because, "They just don't know who you are." My hope is that they did get to know "me" a little more fully, as deceptive and suspect of a practice as that may be.

WORKS CITED

Butler, Judith. *Giving an Account of Oneself.* New York: Fordham UP, 2005.

Corey, Frederick C. "The Personal: Against the Master Narrative." *The Future of Performance Studies: Visions and Revisions.* Ed. Sheron J. Dailey. Annandale: National Communication Association, 1998. 249–53.

Crenshaw, Kimberlé. "The Intersection of Race and Gender." *Critical Race Theory: The Key Writings That Formed the Movement.* New York: The New Press, 1995. 357–83.

Deleuze, Gilles, and Félix Guattari. *A Thousand Plateaus: Capitalism and Schizophrenia.* Minneapolis: U of Minnesota P, 1987.

Ellis, Carolyn, and Arthur P. Bochner. "Autoethnography, Personal Narrative, Reflexivity: Researcher as Subject." *Handbook of Qualitative Research.* Eds. Norman K. Denzin and Yvonna S. Lincoln. 2nd ed. Thousand Oaks: Sage, 2000. 733–68.

Fouss, Kirk W., Cindy J. Kistenberg, and Lawrence B. Rosenfeld. "'Out Art' Reducing Homophobia on College Campuses through Artistic Intervention." *Text and Performance Quarterly* 12 (1992): 349–61.

Gingrich-Philbrook, Craig. "Autoethnography's Family Values: Easy Access to Compulsive Experiences." *Text and Performance Quarterly* 25 (2005): 297–314.

Goltz, Dustin. "Banging the Bishop: Latter Day Prophecy." *Text and Performance Quarterly* 27 (2007): 237–66.

—. "Forgive Me Audience, For I Know Not What I Do: An Artist's Statement." *Text and Performance Quarterly* 27 (2007): 232–6.

Goodall, H. Lloyd. "The Controversy and Issues (Supposedly) of Academic Freedom at [University]." [University] Academic Freedom Symposium. [university, state], 7 Dec. 2004.

Goodwin, Janna L. "The Productive Postshow: Facilitating, Understanding, and Optimizing Personal Narratives in Audience Talk Following a Personal Narrative Performance." *Theater Topics* 14 (2004): 317–38.

Gornick, Vivian. *The Situation and the Story.* New York: Farrar, Straus and Giroux, 2001.

Hantzis, Darlene M. "Reflections On 'A Dialogue with Friends: 'Performing' the 'Other'/Self' OJA 1995.'" *The Future of Performance Studies: Visions and Revisions.* Ed. Sheron J. Dailey. Annandale: National Communication Association, 1998. 203–06.

Jackson, Ronald L. "White Space, White Privilege: Mapping Discursive Inquiry into Self." *Quarterly Journal of Speech* 85 (1999): 38–54.

Jones, Joni L. "Personalizing HIV Personal Narratives: An Aesthetic and Political Imperative." *HIV Education: Performing Personal Narratives.* Ed. Frederick. C. Corey. Tempe: Arizona State University, 1993. 23–29.

Langellier, Kristin M. "Personal Narrative, Performance, Performativity: Two or Three Things I Know for Sure." *Text and Performance Quarterly* 19 (1999): 125–44.

—. "Voiceless Bodies, Bodiless Voices: The Future of Personal Narrative Performance." *The Future of Performance Studies: Visions and Revisions.* Ed. Sheron J. Dailey. Annandale: National Communication Association, 1998. 207–13.

Langellier, Kristin M., and Eric E. Peterson. *Storytelling in Daily Life: Performing Narrative.* Philadelphia: Temple UP, 2004.

Madison, D. Soyini. "Performance, Personal Narratives, and the Politics of Possibility." *The Future of Performance Studies: Visions and Revisions*. Ed. Sheron J. Dailey. Annandale: National Communication Association, 1998. 276–86.

Martin, Annette. "Keynote Address: The Power of Performance." *HIV Education: Performing Personal Narratives*. Ed. Frederick C. Corey. Tempe: Arizona State University, 1993. xii–xviii.

Park-Fuller, Linda. "Sociopolitical Performance of Literature." Defense of Poesie: The Art of Activism Panel, National Communication Association, Hilton, Chicago, 13 Nov. 2004.

—. "Performing Absence: The Staged Personal Narrative as Testimony." *Text and Performance Quarterly* 20 (2000): 20–42.

Puar, Jasbir K. "Queer Times, Queer Assemblages." *Social Text* 84/85 (2005): 121–40.

Roach, Joseph. "Normal Heartlands." *Text and Performance Quarterly* 12 (1992): 377–84.

Ronai, Carol Rambo. "The Reflexive Self through Narrative." *Investigating Subjectivity*. Eds. Carolyn Ellis and Michael G. Flaherty. London: Sage, 1992.

Strine, Mary S. "Art. Activism, and the Performance (Con)Text: A Response." *Text and Performance Quarterly*.12 (1992): 391–94.

Taylor, Diana. "Performance and/as History." *The Drama Review* 50.1 (2006): 67–86.

Tracy, Sarah, and Angela Trethewey. "Fracturing the Real-Self/Fake-Self Dichotomy: Moving Toward "Crystallized" Organizational Discourses and Identities." *Communication Theory* 15 (2005): 168–95.

Valentine, Kristin Bervig, and D. Eugene Valentine. "Facilitation of Intercultural Communication through Performed Literature." *Communication Education* 32 (1983): 303–07.

Watson, Joe. "Quid Pro [university president]." *New Times* [city] Nov. 18–24 2004: 17–29.

NOTES

1. The fact that this story takes place in the southwest United States at a university with a unique relationship to the Mormon community is vital to contextualizing these events. However, the specificity of the names involved or the various names relating to institution have been omitted or changed, as the objectives of this essay are not contingent upon these specific details. As these events were highly controversial, and this account is admittedly my own version of the story, my hope is not to incite further accusations or characterizations of individuals or institutions. One of my objectives is for this account to problematize any simplistic framing of these events, and to continue the promotion of mutual respect and productive dialogue. There is one name missing from my story whose absence is deeply regrettable—a member of the performance studies faculty, the show's director, and a dear friend—who made multiple sacrifices and contributions for *Banging the Bishop*. I would never take the liberty to speak for her, as we walked through this experience together at moments and separate at others. Still, it feels wrong to not see her name in these pages, as this experience was very much ours.

2. Unless specifically noted, all set apart text in the essay is from the performance script of *X-Communication*.

3. A patriarchal blessing is an extended blessing in the Mormon Church. The blessing is recorded and then typed up, so one can refer to it throughout one's life. The blessing contains information about the individual's entire life on earth, and serves as a guide for keeping them on the correct spiritual path.

4. The postponement of the show was reported and discussed on a multitude of local websites,

such as the university press webpage, local Jewish organizations, city newspapers, and the local Humanist chapter. Additionally, the story was discussed on sites of broader national and international interest, for example queerday.com, jackinworld.com, blogs on livejounal.com, lincolnplawg.blogspot.com, affirmation.com, as well as LDS-themed discussion boards.

5. Some sections from the "mountain" portion of the *X-Communication* text were later added to the revised script of *Banging the Bishop* in 2005. In this research, I crafted new text that I felt offered an important voice to the script, a voice that I felt was absent when I revisited the original script months later.

6. The name Peter is a pseudonym.

7. The Civil Discourse discussion model, designed by John Genette, places five seats in front of an audience. A statement is presented, from which the audience takes various positions. In our dialogue, one statement was "*Banging the Bishop* should not be performed in academia."

The five chairs range from "strongly agree," to "agree," to "neutral," to "disagree," to "strongly disagree." Once five members of the audience agree to participate, the rest of the audience observes the discussion. During the discussion, participants are encouraged to shift their chairs if their position towards the statement shifts within the dialogue.

8. The Mormon temple and the rituals conducted inside are highly secretive. The mere discussion of the temple, outside of temple walls, especially with non-members is absolutely forbidden. Covenants are made in the temple, where an individual promises to cut their own throat and belly before revealing the details of these rituals. The breaking of this covenant is the basis for my spiritual argument against my show.

9. The biblical passage is from Corinthians 13:12, as Paul addresses the infantile perspective through which we engage in our affairs. It is not until the coming of Christ that our perspectives will be clear.

Part III
Representing Identity

12

Introducing Representation
Politics of the Popular and Crisis of the Personal

By Dustin Bradley Goltz and Jason Zingsheim

As illustrated in the previous unit, organizing identities—the differentiating, disciplining, and structuring of identities—is an ongoing and negotiated process. Consider for a moment all the messages you continually receive regarding who you are and who you are not. Where do you find messages at work to define what it means to be you, or what it means to be a better you? Which identities should be admired? Feared? Desired or rejected? This unit of the text will examine some of the different ways identity is represented and the political dimensions at work in those representations. Ranging from broader representations of various identities in popular media and online environments to the process of representing the self in personal ads and scholarly writing, this section asks you to consider the ways representation, as a rhetorical and political process, works to uphold and/or resist the ways identity is organized.

What did life look like in the 1950s? Create a picture in your mind. What do you see, who is there, and what are they wearing? Admittedly, the question is utterly flawed and ridiculous. First of all, many readers of this text were not born until several decades later. Secondly, even if you have lived experience from the 1950s, the question

must be clarified. Whose life in the 1950s? What country? The question is so absurdly vague, and yet, how many of you could easily formulate a picture in your mind? Do you see drive-in burger joints? Servers on roller skates? Perhaps you picture James Dean or Brando-esque men with leather jackets, pompadours, and white T-shirts, or something more in line with the cast of *Grease*. Maybe you picture it in black and white, based on a film or a photograph. The point of this absurd inquiry is that even though many of us were not alive at this time in history, representations of this time period have worked to shape and define our reality of the 1950s (in the absence of lived experience). Do you picture a Norman-Rockwell type soda fountain scene with a young heterosexual couple sharing a malt, or do you picture a society violently segregated along racial lines? Do you picture a high school sock hop, or gay men being arrested for dancing with one another in underground meeting spaces? Consider the 1920s, the 1970s, or the 1980s. Did your picture of these different decades exist in the U.S.? Were the characters in your picture white, able-bodied, middle-class, and assumed to be heterosexual? Why or why not? Now consider all the experiences you have never had, places across the globe and within your own country you have never been, and all the people and different types of people you have never met. In the absence of experience, how do mediated representations of these places, people, and identities work to "fill in" your lack of experience?

POPULAR CULTURE AND THE POLITICS OF REPRESENTATION

The concept of **normativity** and the process of normalization are central to this discussion of the politics of representation. Normativity refers to that which has come to be constructed for us as normal and natural, or more simply, the perceived "norm." No one person is "the norm," as this is a theoretical concept that works to account for a complex process where identities are organized in relation to the invisible and idealized center. Those individuals whose subjectivities are closer to the center are assumed to be "normal," and those identities that violate normative systems are relegated to the margins and discursively constructed as "abnormal" or different. In broader U.S. discourses, being white has been constructed as normative, as have other subjectivities such as heterosexuality, the able-bodied, the middle-class, and Christians. Imagine for a moment playing a trivia game in the car on a roadtrip, and you are trying to get your driving companion to guess a famous actor or actress. Your first clue is "he is straight." Your second clue is "he is white." Your third clue is "able-bodied." Likely, this will not be very helpful is assisting the game to proceed. However, were you to substitute any of the clues with a non-normative identification, these clues would likely be very helpful. Why? Because we rarely mark the norm, but we consistently utilize the norm to distinguish and differentiate that which falls outside its domain.

In the area of rhetoric, cultural studies, and media criticism, there are large bodies of research that work to examine the political implications and workings of mediated representations and the construction of normativity. These scholars endeavor to investigate the ideological functions of representations—how they work to construct, confine, and shape identities across a broad range of diverse texts. Some of these discussions might be very familiar to you, such as the ways Barbie works to construct a hegemonic, unhealthy, and unattainable standard of female beauty. Or perhaps you have grown more critical of how action films often construct male characters as unemotional, ruggedly independent, and excessively violent.

How are your identities represented in the media you consume? How do media inform your understanding of attractiveness? What mediated representations do you remember idolizing as a child? What posters did you have hanging on your walls near your bed (or did you have posters)? What values and ideologies are embedded in the construction of these figures? These questions work to explore not just how you come to "know" or think about experiences different from your own (different places, people, or times), but also how representation plays a part in how you come to understand and assign meanings to your own multiple identities. Using the example of race, we can examine how whiteness as a normative construction is enlisted and perpetuated in popular media. Consider films and television shows, from your experience, that you would categorize as interrogating racialized experiences; in other words, which shows were "about race"? *The George Lopez Show*? *Living Single*? *The Cosby Show*? Perhaps *Ugly Betty* or *Modern Family*, to reference popular programs at this historical moment. Why these shows? Why not *Frasier*, *The Brady Bunch*, or *Dexter*? Historically, unless a program introduces a non-white character, where racial topics are then addressed and examined, the program is often audienced as "not about race." Yet programs that regularly represent nonwhite bodies are almost always discussed for their racial implications. This trend highlight the ways whiteness in media, as in broader discourses in the U.S., is often not seen as a racial category, but rather is constructed as the absence of race. The interrogation of how whiteness is represented in media, however, works to broaden the discussion of racism from examining only overt acts of prejudice to highlighting and unearthing the silent privileges associated with whiteness.

Looking at the film *City of Joy*, Raka Shome (1996) examines how whiteness is rhetorically constructed in relationship to notions of civilization, individualism, and rationality, where nonwhite bodies are represented as uncivilized, often in a pack or collective grouping, and are depicted as irrational and primal. Kelly Madison's (1999) concept of the "white savior" extends this work, where the white man or woman is often constructed as the noble helper and hero, coming to the aid of the racially marginalized. The concept of the white savior is productive in reading the common narrative of the white teacher in lower income school who brings knowledge, such as Michelle Pfeiffer in *Dangerous Minds*, Goldie Hawn in *Wildcats,* or more recently the film *Freedom Writers*. Sandra Bullock's Oscar-winning performance as Leigh Anne Tuohy in *The Blind Side* can be read as a white savior narrative, in that the broader socioeconomic conditions that led to the disenfranchised state of "Big Mike" are obscured in the narrative, but what is fore-fronted is the heroic selflessness of an upper-middle-class white woman who graciously takes in and saves Big Mike from his impoverished existence. This common "white savior" narrative functions rhetorically to perpetuate white heroism and ignore white privilege, while simultaneously erasing the work of racially marginalized individuals in the fight for racial and economic justice.

When looking at popular culture and considering/critiquing the politics of representation, the application of different theories and concepts will illuminate diverse dimensions of the text. Gender theories will draw attention towards subject/object construction, the positioning of male and female bodies, how power is linked to masculine or feminine traits, and many other dimensions at the heart of gendered analyses. However, the same exact text can be read through theories of race (or sexuality, class, etc.) to bring to light entirely different dimensions and understandings. In this respect, we can think of the theory or theoretical concepts enlisted in the analysis of representation like a pair of glasses with distinct lenses. **Polysemy** marks the multitude of potential meanings and perspectives available in the consideration, study, or reception of a text. Expressed another way, we can say that all texts are **polysemic**. No one read or interpretation of a given text is more correct, but from a critical perspective, some reads are more productive, emancipatory, or enlightening (for more on polysemy, see Fiske, 1986; Cloud, 1992; Ceccarelli, 1998).

The readings in this section make no effort to examine the most current texts and trends, as popular culture moves quickly, and many of the texts that are all the rage today will be obsolete in the near future. At the time of this writing, *Glee* is the new breakout hit, *LOST* just completed its final season, and *True Blood* and the *Twilight* films seem to dominate many discussions of representation. Rather than chase the trend of the day, this anthology works to provide you with a series of voices and tools whose concepts and discussions have remained relevant for many years. The texts shift, and the fads move rapidly, but the discourses around race, gender, sexuality, and class in the media are far more resilient to change. In reading these chapters, consider the media you are currently consuming and reflect upon how these concepts, arguments, and offerings still inform the contemporary media landscape. How have things changed? How have they remained the same?

CRISIS OF REPRESENTATION

As we have already broken apart and complicated fixed and stable illusions of identity, the latter part of this chapter (and unit) moves to reflect and consider the writing of identity. Extending beyond mediated representations, this chapter also explores how identities are crafted, negotiated, and constructed in the writing of experience: How we represent our own identities in the writing process. Critical researchers face what has been labeled a "crisis of representation" in scholarship (Denzin & Lincoln, 2005, p. 19). Critical research operates under an epistemological assumption that there is no knowledge outside of systems of power; all knowledge is situated, partial, discursive, and requires contextualization. Assertions of capital "T" truth are looked upon with skepticism, and smaller "t" truths are always produced through and within specific raced, gendered, national, economic, and sexualized subjectivities. In short, your truth (and thus your knowledge) is tied to a multitude of identities related to your social position. This foundation for critical scholarship problematizes distanced, third person accounts of "what happened" and calls for researchers to be reflexive about the social conditions that shape and enable their claims of experience.

Critical frameworks of identity are messy and shifting, and so critical accounts of experience work to represent the ways differing subjectivities shift, bleed, and intersect within multiple contexts and temporal locations. Identity, or the narration of self, is not something that is found, but is something that is made. In other words, how we represent ourselves works to (re)create the very thing we are trying to represent. Identity becomes a construction, assembled through previous experiences, existing discourses, and various social locations. In terms of research, when a scholar works to assert a claim (e.g., "this happened"), we come to understand that the researcher is not an objective observer of a phenomenon, but is an active participant in the creation and representation of experience ("this is my representation of events as I experienced and understand them").

REPRESENTING IDENTITY: A PREVIEW

This unit navigates these various approaches to representation and identity, moving from popular media representation to the navigation and challenges of self-representation. In chapter thirteen, an excerpt of Stuart Hall's work titled "The Whites in Their Eyes: Racist Ideologies in the Media," Hall provides a foundation for theorizing the relationship between mediated representation and ideology. Outlining key concepts of inferential racism and mediated grammars of race, Hall provides a critical framework for locating and critiquing the "base-images" of African-American representation in mainstream media. While reading this chapter, consider:

- According to Hall, why is it important to be critically conscious of the ideological workings of mainstream representation? What is at stake in this discussion?
- As Hall focuses primarily on African American representations, what are the base-images or grammars of race for additional racialized subjectivities? Sexual subjectivities? Aged, classed, gendered, and religious subjectivities?
- Do you see white representations falling into such rigid typologies in popular culture? Is there a grammar to white representation? How do these representations differ?

Extending on Hall's discussion, Jan Pieterse's "White Negroes" offers a historical examination of how mediated representation and biological discourses have been used to construct and "naturalize" race. Enlisting examples from the Irish and the Chinese, Pieterse works to uncover how political investments, rather than essential biological differences, have been utilized to construct racial discourses and promote racial hierarchies. Herein, race as a discursive production is traced through politically motivated representations, shaping attitudes, meanings, and identities of difference and inferiority/superiority under the false premise of biology. His examination of Irish identity, which is now commonly subsumed under the umbrella of whiteness in contemporary U.S. discourses, draws attention to the temporal, discursive, and political dimensions of representations of racial difference.

- According to Pieterse, how are "biological facts" of identity and difference produced through politicized discourses?
- How are the Irish constructed in contemporary representation? How are the Irish racialized? How have these discourses shifted over time? Why do you think this has happened?
- Where in contemporary culture do you see political discourses of identity enlisting biology and nature to justify and promote hatred and intolerance of difference? Superiority of one group above others?

In the next chapter, Clint Wilson and Félix Gutiérrez take a historical look at advertising strategies in the U.S. to examine how racially marginalized identities have been crafted, stereotyped, targeted, and negotiated in mainstream representation. "Advertising and People of Color" traces the use of overtly stereotypical representations in marketing (to assumed normative white consumers) for the purposes of bolstering and normalizing white racist mainstream value systems through problematic characterizations such as "Frito Bandito" and "Aunt Jemima." Under growing awareness of the economic power and financial opportunities often ignored in marginalized markets, they chronicle the increasing courtship of racially marginalized consumers through targeted marketing strategies. Through the lens of advertising, this chapter examines how advertising practices and strategies both reflect hegemonic systems of race and class, and work as an active site of identity production to rhetorically craft consumer identities in and across racialized systems.

- In contemporary advertising, how do you see differing racial subjectivities targeted and constructed as consumers? What are the current practices at work that use race as a marketing strategy?
- Which of the historical marketing representations were shocking to you? Where do you still see stereotypes being used in advertising campaigns? For which subjectivities are they more socially permissible? Why do you think this is?

Jay Clarkson's "Contesting Masculinity's Makeover: *Queer Eye,* Consumer Masculinity, and 'Straight-Acting' Gays" continues our discussion of consumer identity through a specific look at Bravo's 2003–2007 series *Queer Eye For the Straight Guy.* As a highly visible representation of gay male culture, the reality series worked to uphold and bolster definitions of gay male identity as cosmopolitan, upper class, and consumer-driven. Furthermore, Clarkson argues how the series worked to complicate traditional definitions of hegemonic masculinity, giving masculinity a commodified and hyper-consumerist "makeover." In short, traditional models of hegemonic masculinity, which worked in and through oppositional relations to homosexuality and femininity, are renegotiated in *Queer Eye*'s version of the skilled "straight guy" consumer. In the second part of this study, Clarkson turns to the website straightacting.com to show how a community of gay men, defining their identities as "straight-acting," reject *Queer Eye*'s representation of gay male culture, asserting and defining their identities through traditional modes of hegemonic masculinity. This study provides a complex negotiation of identity within gendered and sexual hierarchies; competing capitalist efforts to craft and articulate ideal consumers work to rescript masculinity, while straight-acting gay males work to assert and reclaim a privileged gay masculinity through traditional strategies of anti-femininity and hegemonic masculine dominance. Centralizing representation within the negotiation of identity construction, Clarkson's work demonstrates how shifting and contested categories of gender, sexuality, and consumer identity are part of a situated, power-laden, and intersectional process.

- What are the key characteristics of traditional hegemonic masculinity (based on Trujillo)? What are the key characteristics of Clarkson's new masculine "makeover"? How are they both hegemonic?
- In "Queer Eye," as well as in your experience in contemporary culture, how have representations of masculinity worked to reconstruct and rework idealized masculine identity through consumption?
- How are the participants in the straightacting.com discussion upholding traditional hegemonic gender identity? How is this (or is this?) complicated by their sexuality?

Lisa Nakamura's *"Where Do You Want To Go Today: Cybernetic Tourism, The Internet, and Transnationality"* shifts the discussion of representing identity to internet technologies and advertisements, wherein the Western computer user is constructed as tourist within cyberspace. Examining advertisements produced by corporations such as IBM and Microsoft, Nakamura looks at the commodification of exoticized racial, ethnic, and national cyber destinations through the construction of the Western colonialist gaze. Positioning the western tourist in the seat of borderless mobility, as the consumer of timeless, "unspoiled," and "authentic" iconography of "Third World" representations, Nakamura argues that these advertisements of a utopian cyberspace construct "a technological Utopia of difference" (p. 209, this volume). The assumed white male Western computer user is positioned in opposition to the exoticized Other, shoring up the normative non-otherness of the assumed viewer. The internet, rather than a leveling space for racial and economic differences, represents otherness as a commodity to be consumed by the normalized identity of the Western cyber tourist.

- How does the construction of the exoticized other in tourist representations work to shore up the normativity (and superiority) of the assumed Western consumer?
- How are "authentic" cultures, "unspoiled" Third World locations, and "othered" bodies constructed as commodities to be consumed?
- Reflecting on the internet and the false utopian promises Nakamura interrogates, would you still argue that the internet remains a "utopia of difference"? Has our relationship to this technology (and the world) changed? Why or why not?

Bringing together discussions of mediated representations and representation of self, David Harrison's "The Personals" recounts the experiences and interactions of a trans-identified man in navigating the representation of identity through his own personal ads. Harrison's fluid and always-in-process gendered and sexual identity works to expose the limitations of language systems to discuss gender variant experiences, as well as the ways that representations of the temporal and shifting dimensions of gender and sexuality are faced with obstacles and pose challenges to hegemonic understandings of normative sexuality and gender categories.

- What obstacles do you encounter in discussing, summarizing, and talking through Harrison's piece? Where do words fail this discussion? What does this tell us about bias and limitations within our language system?
- How does Harrison's article challenge mainstream discourses of gender and sexual identity? How does adding a temporal and shifting dimension to these identities trouble or complicate dominant understandings?

The final chapter in this section, Jason Zingsheim's "Lost in The Gap: Between the Discourses and Practices of White Masculinity," extends our discussion of representational practices in writing and scholarship through autoethnographic examination. As a white, U.S., gay male scholar attempting ethnographic research in gay bars in Dublin, Zingsheim's own conception of his identity comes unhinged as national, sexual, racial, and gendered subjectivities and assumptions fail to map and structure his experiences in the field. The certainty, temporal linearity, and coherence of the self, as writer and researcher, get lost in his navigation as tourist/researcher within Irish gay bars and clubs. Troubling fixed or static notions of representing self, and showing how identity is mapped through specific contexts and specific moments in time, Zingsheim's mobility as a white, masculine, Western traveler across "any city in the world" is troubled by shifting understandings of new-found sexual identity, unearthed rational assumptions of U.S. white masculine identity, and the loss of his identity map.

- Think about the discourses of identity that worked to shape Zingsheim's identity prior to his experiences in Dublin (gender, race, nation, sexuality, religion). How did these representations fail to provide him a map for his experiences in Ireland?
- Zingsheim marks two events that threw him "beside himself" and complicated his seemingly fixed understanding of self. Where, in your life or in your experiences with others, have you experienced or witnessed this unhinging of identity?
- How does performative writing work to trouble, disrupt, and complicate the representation of identity in writing? What does this form of writing and scholarship offer the study and examination of identity formation and negotiation?

REFERENCES

Ceccarelli, L. (1998). Polysemy: Multiple meanings in rhetorical criticism. *Quarterly Journal of Speech*, *84*, 395–415.

Cloud, D. L. (1992). The limits of interpretation: Ambivalence and the stereotype in *Spenser: For Hire*. *Critical Studies in Mass Communication, 9*, 311–324.

Denzin, N. K., & Lincoln, Y. S. (2005). *Handbook of qualitative research* (3rd ed.). Thousand Oaks, CA: Sage.

Fiske, J. (1986). Television: Polysemy and popularity. *Critical Studies in Mass Communication, 3*, 391–408.

Shome, R. (1996). Race and popular cinema: The rhetorical strategies of whiteness in *City of Joy*. *Communication Quarterly, 44*, 502–518.

Madison, K. (1999). Legitimation crisis and containment: The "anti-racist-white-hero" film. *Critical Studies in Mass Communication, 16*, 399–416.

ADDITIONAL SUGGESTED READINGS

Brookey, R. A., & Cannon, K. L. (2009). *Sex lives in Second Life. Critical Studies in Media Communication, 26*, 145–164.

Brookey, R. A. (1996). A community like *Philadelphia. Western Journal of Communication, 60(1)*, 40–56.

De Lauretis, T. (1987). *Technologies of gender: Essays on theory, film, and fiction.* Bloomington: Indiana University Press.

Dow, B. (1996). *Prime-time feminism: Television, media culture and the women's movement since 1970.* Philadelphia, PA: University of Pennsylvania Press.

Ellis, C., & Bochner, A. P. (2000). Autoethnography, personal narrative, reflexivity: Researcher as subject. In N. K. Denzin & Y. S. Lincoln (Eds.), *Handbook of qualitative research (2nd ed.,* pp. 733–768). Thousand Oaks: Sage.

Gauntlett, D. (2008). *Media, gender, and identity: An introduction (2nd ed.).* New York, NY: Routledge.

Goltz, D. B. (2010). *Queer temporalities in gay male representation: Tragedy, normativity, and futurity.* New York, NY: Routledge.

Grindstaff, D. A., & DeLuca, K. M. (2004). *The corpus of Daniel Pearl. Critical Studies in Media Communication, 21(4)*, 305–324.

Gross, L. (2001). *Up from invisibility.* New York: Columbia University Press.

Halperin, D. M. (1990). *One hundred years of homosexuality and other essays on Greek love.* New York: Routledge.

Hammers, M. L. (2005). Cautionary tales of liberation and female professionalism: The case against *Ally McBeal. Western Journal of Communication, 69*, 167–182.

Hegde, R. S. (2001). *Global makeovers and maneuvers: Barbie's presence in India.* Feminist Media Studies, *1(1)*, 129–133.

hooks, b. (1992). Eating the other: Desire and resistance. In *Black looks: Race and representation* (pp. 21–39). Boston, MA: South End Press.

hooks, b. (2004). Popular culture: Media masculinity. In *The will to change: Men, masculinity, and love* (pp. 125–134). New York: Atria Books.

Jackson, R. L. (2004). *African American communication & identities.* Thousand Oaks, CA: Sage.

Kilbourne, J. (2003). "The more you subtract, the more you add": Cutting girls down to size. In G. Dines & J. M. Humez (Eds.), *Gender, Race, and Class in the Media 2nd ed.,* pp. 258–267). Thousand Oaks: Sage.

Langellier, K. M., & Peterson, E. E. (2004). *Storytelling in daily life: Performing narrative.* Philadelphia: Temple University Press.

Mukherjee, R. (2006). The ghetto fabulous aesthetic in contemporary black culture. *Cultural Studies, 20*, 599–629.

Nakamura, L. (2008). *Digitizing race: Visual cultures of the internet.* Minneapolis, MN: University of Minnesota Press.

Nakayama, T. K. (1994). Show/down time: "Race," gender, sexuality, and popular culture. *Critical Studies in Mass Communication, 11*, 162–179.

Ronai, C. R. (1992). The reflexive self through narrative. In C. Ellis & M. G. Flaherty. (Eds.), *Investigating Subjectivity.* London: Sage.

Shugart, H. A. (2003). Reinventing privilege: The new (gay) man in contemporary popular media. *Critical Studies in Media Communication, 20*, 67–91.

Shugart, H. A. (2007). Crossing over: Hybridity and hegemony in popular media. *Communication and Critical/Cultural Studies, 4*, 115–141.

Sloop, J. (2000). Disciplining the transgendered: Brandon Teena, public representation, and normativity. *Western Journal of Communication, 64,* 165–189.

Trujillo, N. (1991). Hegemonic masculinity on the mound: Media representations of Nolan Ryan and American sports culture. *Critical Studies in Mass Communication, 8,* 290–08.

Van Maanen, J. (1988). *Tales of the field: On writing ethnography.* Chicago: University of Chicago Press.

13 The Whites of Their Eyes
Racist Ideologies in the Media

By Stuart Hall

We begin by defining some of the terms of the argument. "Racism and the media" touches directly the problem of *ideology*, since the media's main sphere of operations is the production and transformation of ideologies. An intervention in the media's construction of race is an intervention in the *ideological* terrain of struggle. Much murky water has flowed under the bridge provided by this concept of ideology in recent years; and this is not the place to develop the theoretical argument. I am using the term to refer to those images, concepts and premises which provide the frameworks through which we represent, interpret, understand, and "make sense" of some aspect of social existence. Language and ideology are not the same—since the same linguistic term ("democracy," for example, or "freedom") can be deployed within different ideological discourses. But language, broadly conceived, is by definition the principal medium in which we find different ideological discourses elaborated.

Three important things need to be said about ideology in order to make what follows intelligible. First, ideologies do not consist of isolated and separate concepts, but in the articulation of different elements into a distinctive set or chain of meanings. In liberal ideology, "freedom" is connected (articulated) with individualism and the free market; in socialist ideology, "freedom" is a collective condition, dependent on, not counterposed to, "equality of condition," as it is in liberal ideology. The same concept is differently positioned within the logic of different ideological discourses. One of the ways in which ideological struggle takes place and ideologies are transformed is by articulating the elements differently, thereby producing a different meaning: breaking the chain in which they are currently fixed (e.g., "democratic" = the "Free" West) and establishing a new articulation (e.g., "democratic" = deepening the democratic content of political life). This "breaking of the chain" is not, of course, confined to the head: it takes place through social practice and political struggle.

Second, ideological statements are made by individuals: but ideologies are not the product of individual consciousness or intention. Rather we formulate our intentions *within ideology*. They pre-date individuals, and form part of the determinate social formations and conditions in which individuals are born. We have to "speak through" the ideologies which are active in our society and which provide us with the means of "making sense" of social relations and our place in them. The transformation of ideologies is thus a collective process and practice, not an individual one. Largely, the processes work *unconsciously*, rather than by conscious intention. Ideologies produce different forms of social consciousness, rather than being produced by them. They work most effectively when we are not aware that how we formulate and construct a statement about the world is underpinned by ideological premises; when our formations seem to be simply descriptive statements about how things are (i.e., must be), or of what we can "take-for-granted." "Little boys like playing rough games; little girls, however, are full of sugar and spice" is predicated on a whole set of ideological premises, though it seems to be an aphorism which is grounded, not in how masculinity and femininity have been historically and culturally constructed in society, but in Nature itself. Ideologies tend to disappear from view into the taken-for-granted "naturalised" world of common sense. Since (like gender) race appears to be "given" by Nature, racism is one of the most profoundly "naturalised" of existing ideologies.

Third, ideologies "work" by constructing for their subjects (individual and collective) positions of identification and knowledge which allow them to "utter" ideological truths as if they were their authentic authors. This is not because they emanate from our innermost, authentic, and unified experience, but because we find ourselves mirrored in the positions at the centre of the discourses from which the statements we formulate "make sense." Thus the same "subjects" (e.g., economic classes or ethnic groups) can be differently constructed in different ideologies. ...

Let us look, then, a little more closely at the apparatuses which generate and circulate ideologies. In modern societies, the different media are especially important sites for the production, reproduction,

and transformation of ideologies. Ideologies are, of course, worked on in many places in society, and not only in the head. ... But institutions like the media are peculiarly central to the matter since they are, by definition, part of the dominant means of *ideological* production. What they "produce" is, precisely, representations of the social world, images, descriptions, explanations and frames for understanding how the world is and why it works as it is said and shown to work. And, amongst other kinds of ideological labour, the media construct for us a definition of what *race* is, what meaning the imagery of race carries, and what the "problem of race" is understood to be. They help to classify out the world in terms of the categories of race.

The media are not only a powerful source of ideas about race. They are also one place where these ideas are articulated, worked on, transformed, and elaborated. We have said "ideas" and "ideologies" in the plural. For it would be wrong and misleading to see the media as uniformly and conspiratorially harnessed to a single, racist conception of the world. Liberal and humane ideas about "good relations" between the races, based on open-mindedness and tolerance, operate inside the world of the media. ...

It would be simple and convenient if all the media were simply the ventriloquists of a unified and racist "ruling class" conception of the world. But neither a unifiedly conspiratorial media nor indeed a unified racist "ruling class" exist in anything like that simple way. I don't insist on complexity for its own sake. But if critics of the media subscribe to too simple or reductive a view of their operations, this inevitably lacks credibility and weakens the case they are making because the theories and critiques don't square with reality. ...

Another important distinction is between what we might call "overt" racism and "inferential" racism. By *overt* racism, I mean those many occasions when open and favourable coverage is given to arguments, positions and spokespersons who are in the business of elaborating an openly racist argument or advancing a racist policy or view. ...

By *inferential* racism I mean those apparently naturalised representations of events and situations relating to race, whether "factual" or "fictional," which have racist premises and propositions inscribed in them as a set of *unquestioned assumptions.* These enable racist statements to be formulated without ever bringing into awareness the racist predicates on which the statements are grounded. ...

An, example of *this* type of racist ideology is the sort of television programme which deals with some "problem" in race relations. It is probably made by a good and honest liberal broadcaster, who hopes to do some good in the world for "race relations" and who maintains a scrupulous balance and neutrality when questioning people interviewed for the programme. The programme will end with a homily on how, if only the "extremists" on *either* side would go away, "normal blacks and whites" would be better able to get on with learning to live in harmony together. Yet every word and image of such programmes are impregnated with unconscious racism because they are all predicated on the unstated and unrecognized assumption that the *blacks* are the *source of the problem.* Yet virtually the whole of "social problem" television about race and immigration—often made, no doubt, by well-intentioned and liberal-minded broadcasters—is precisely predicated on racist premises of this kind. ...

... Recent critics of the literature of imperialism have argued that, if we simply extend our definition of nineteenth-century fiction from one branch of "serious fiction" to embrace popular literature, we will find a second, powerful strand of the English literary imagination to set beside the *domestic* novel: the male-dominated world of imperial adventure, which takes *empire,* rather than *Middlemarch,* as its microcosm. ... In this period, the very idea of *adventure* became synonymous with the

demonstration of the moral, social and physical mastery of the colonisers over the colonised.

Later, this concept of "adventure"—one of the principal categories of modern *entertainment*—moved straight off the printed page into the literature of crime and espionage, children's books, the great Hollywood extravaganzas and comics. There, with recurring persistence, they still remain. Many of these older versions have had their edge somewhat blunted by time. They have been distanced from us, apparently, by our superior wisdom and liberalism. But they still reappear on the television screen, especially in the form of "old movies" (some "old movies," of course, continue to be made). But we can grasp their recurring resonance better if we identify some of the base-images of the "grammar of race."

There is, for example, the familiar *slave-figure:* dependable, loving in a simple, childlike way—the devoted "Mammy" with the rolling eyes, or the faithful fieldhand or retainer, attached and devoted to "his" Master. The best-known extravaganza of all—*Gone With the Wind*—contains rich variants of both. The "slave-figure" is by no means limited to films and programmes *about* slavery. Some "Injuns" and many Asians have come on to the screen in this disguise. A deep and unconscious ambivalence pervades this stereotype. Devoted and childlike, the "slave" is also unreliable, unpredictable and undependable—capable of "turning nasty," or of plotting in a treacherous way, secretive, cunning, cut-throat once his or her Master's or Mistress's back is turned: and inexplicably given to running away into the bush at the slightest opportunity. The whites can never be sure that this childish simpleton—"Sambo"—is not mocking his master's white manners behind his hand even when giving an exaggerated caricature of white refinement.

Another base-image is that of the "native." The good side of this figure is portrayed in a certain primitive nobility and simple dignity. The bad side is portrayed in terms of cheating and cunning, and, further out, savagery and barbarism. Popular culture is still full today of countless savage and restless "natives," and sound-tracks constantly repeat the threatening sound of drumming in the night, the hint of primitive rites and cults. Cannibals, whirling dervishes, Indian tribesmen, garishly got up, are constantly threatening to over-run the screen. They are likely to appear at any moment out of the darkness to decapitate the beautiful heroine, kidnap the children, burn the encampment or threatening to boil, cook and eat the innocent explorer or colonial administrator and his lady-wife. These "natives" always move as an anonymous collective mass—in tribes or hordes. And against them is always counterposed the isolated white figure, alone "out there," confronting his Destiny or shouldering his Burden in the "heart of darkness," displaying coolness under fire and an unshakeable authority—exerting mastery over the rebellious natives or quelling the threatened uprising with a single glance of his steel-blue eyes.

A third variant is that of the "clown" or "entertainer." This captures the "innate" humour, as well as the physical grace of the licensed entertainer—putting on a show for The Others. It is never quite clear whether we are laughing with or at this figure: admiring the physical and rhythmic grace, the open expressivity and emotionality of the "entertainer," or put off by the "clown's" stupidity.

One noticeable fact about all these images is their deep *ambivalence*—the double vision of the white eye through which they are seen. The primitive nobility of the aging tribesman or chief, and the native's rhythmic grace, always contain both a nostalgia for an innocence lost forever to the civilised, and the threat of civilization being over-run

or undermined by the recurrence of savagery, which is always lurking just below the surface; or by an untutored sexuality, threatening to "break out." Both are aspects—the good and the bad sides—of *primitivism*. In these images, "primitivism" is defined by the fixed proximity of such people to Nature.

Is all this so far away as we sometimes suppose from the representations of race which fill the screens today? These *particular* versions may have faded. But their *traces* are still to be observed, reworked in many of the modern and up-dated images. And though they may appear to carry a different meaning, they are often still constructed on a very ancient grammar. Today's restless native hordes are still alive and well and living, as guerilla armies and freedom fighters in the Angola, Zimbabwe, or Namibian "bush." Blacks are still the most frightening, cunning, and glamorous crooks (and policemen) in New York cop series. They are the fleet-footed, crazy-talking under-men who connect Starsky and Hutch to the drug-saturated ghetto. The scheming villains and their giant-sized bully boys in the world of James Bond and his progeny are still, unusually, recruited from "out there" in Jamaica, where savagery lingers on. The sexually-available "slave girl" is alive and kicking, smouldering away on some exotic TV set or on the covers of paperbacks, though she is now the centre of a special admiration, covered in a sequinned gown and supported by a white chorus line. Primitivism, savagery, guile and unreliability—all "just below the surface"—can still be identified in the faces of black political leaders around the world, cunningly plotting the overthrow of "civilisation." …

White Negroes

By Jan Nederveen Pieterse

T he interplay of race, class, and gender, the main systems of domination, ... is a well-established theme, but most discussions concern the way these systems intersect rather than the way they interact. Comparisons are rare between racism, classism, and sexism in terms of their histories, ideologies, imageries, and underlying logic; we are offered a wealth of vignettes but systematic explorations are lacking. However brief an excursion into a large and difficult area, the focus here on images and stereotypes may shed new light. ...

SITUATIONS: IRISHMEN, CHINESE, JEWS

Statements in which comparisons are made between blacks and other groups, without a reason why being given, seem to be relatively simple; presumably the comparison is in terms of status, treatment, or appearance. Thus Chamfort, in the eighteenth century: "The poor are the negroes of Europe." The British in India often referred to Indians as "niggers," mostly on the basis of skin colour. Of a similar nature is the statement ... by the Belgian socialist leader Emiel Vandervelde, who compared the way the working class was treated with the treatment of negroes.[1] John Lennon said, "Women are the niggers of the world." A little more complex is a statement by Francisco Cabral, superior of the Portuguese Jesuit mission in Japan (1570–81), about the Japanese: "After all, they are Niggers, and their customs are barbarous."[2] So to the pious Portuguese, after a hundred years of Portuguese experience in Africa, the Japanese were put in the same category as Africans.

In some cases comparison of blacks with other groups goes much further. In 1880 the Belgian essayist Gustave de Molinari noted, in a series of articles about Ireland, that England's most important newspapers and magazines "allow no occasion to escape them of treating the Irish as a kind of inferior race—as a kind of white negroes—and a glance in *Punch* is sufficient to show the difference between the plump and robust personification of John Bull and the wretched figure of lean and bony Pat."[3]

English views of Ireland display an interesting zigzag pattern. In the early Middle Ages Ireland was famed as a centre of Christian civilization: several English kings went there to be educated. Ireland's reputation declined, however, as England's interest in conquering and colonizing it increased. In the wake of the Anglo-Norman invasion and after the classic description of Ireland by Gerald of Wales in the twelfth century, which set the tone for later descriptions, Ireland was considered savage and barbarous. Down to the present this notion of the "wild Irish" has hardly changed, although there have been marked shifts of emphasis. The distinction between Celtic and Anglo-Saxon "races" in the British Isles is one of long standing, but from the mid-nineteenth century onward the British image of the Irish was recast in biological racial terms.[4] In addition, from about 1840, the standard image of the good-natured Irish peasant was revised, becoming that of a repulsive ape-like creature.

> In cartoons and caricatures as well as prose, Paddy began to resemble increasingly the chimpanzee, the orangutan, and, finally, the gorilla. The transformation of peasant Paddy into ape-man or simianized Caliban was completed by the 1860s and 1870s, when for various reasons it became necessary for a number of Victorians to assign Irishmen to a place closer to the apes than the angels.[5]

Irishmen were depicted with low foreheads, prognathous features and an apelike gait by cartoonists such as Sir John Tenniel of *Punch*. In 1862 a satire in *Punch* attacked Irish immigration under the title "The Missing Link": "A creature manifestly between the Gorilla and the Negro is to be met with in some of the lowest districts of London and Liverpool by adventurous explorers. It comes from Ireland, whence it has contrived to migrate; it belongs in fact to a tribe of Irish savages: the lowest species of Irish Yahoo."[6]

What prompted the metamorphosis of Paddy the peasant to Paddy the ape was the stream of Irish immigrants, in the wake of the famines of the 1840s, along with the mounting Irish resistance to British domination. The "Fenian outrages" of the 1860s involved anti-English acts of sabotage and subversion. Thus, English images of the Irish hardened in the context of colonialism, migration, and resistance. About this time the first apes were brought to Europe (the first live adult gorilla arrived at the London Zoo in 1860), and as they made their first appearance in zoos, they began to appear in cartoons and as a new metaphor in popular imagery. …

… What is striking is how consistent the colonizer's cultural politics are, regardless of geography or ethnicity. Like Africans and blacks, the Irish have been referred to as "savages" and likened to "apes," to "women," and to "children," just as the Celts were often described as a "feminine" race, by contrast with the "masculine" Anglo-Saxons. …

Cartoons in periodicals such as *Harper's Weekly (A Journal of Civilization)* made the hostile equation of Irishmen with blacks a routine part of American culture.[7]

These comparisons, in England between Irish people and Africans, and in the United States between the Irish and blacks, were made under the heading of race, but this only serves as a reminder that, until fairly recently, the terms "race" and "nation" (or "people") were synonymous. The peoples of Europe, within regions as well as within countries, were viewed as much as rungs on the racial "ladder" as were peoples or "races" outside Europe. Indeed, virtually all the images and stereotypes projected outside Europe in the age of empire had been used first within Europe. However, when they were *re-used* within Europe the repertoire was infused with the imagery of empire, with other, wider logics of exclusion, of which the imperial construction of "race" was one. Thus in 1885 the English physician John Beddoe devised an "index of nigrescence," a formula for identifying a people's racial components. "He concluded that the Irish were darker than the people of eastern and central England, and were closer to the aborigines of the British Isles, who in turn had traces of 'negro' ancestry in their appearances. The British upper classes also regarded their own working class as almost a race apart, and claimed that they had darker skin and hair than themselves."[8]

This profile could be extended to other minorities. An example is the Chinese who entered the western United States in the nineteenth century as a cheap labour force, following in the footsteps of blacks. Imported on a contract basis to work on the railroads, the "coolie" had in common with the black slave that both were perceived as enemies of free labour and republicanism; what ensued has been termed the "Negroization" of the Chinese.

> Racial qualities that had been assigned to blacks became Chinese characteristics. Calling for Chinese exclusion, the editor of the *San Francisco Alta* claimed the Chinese had most of the vices of the African: "Every reason that exists against the toleration of free blacks in Illinois may be argued against that of the Chinese here." Heathen, morally inferior, savage, and childlike, the Chinese were also viewed as lustful and sensual. Chinese women were condemned as a "depraved class" and their depravity was associated with their almost African-like physical appearance. While their complexions approached "fair," one writer observed, their whole physiognomy indicated "but a slight removal from the African race." Chinese men were denounced as threats to white women. ...[9]

Thus virtually the whole repertoire of anti-black prejudice was transferred to the Chinese: projected on to a different ethnic group which did, however, occupy a similar position in the labour market and in society. The profile of the new minority was constructed on the model of the already existing minority.

Americans often drew comparisons between national minorities (blacks or Native Americans) and peoples overseas. When the U.S. annexed or colonized Hawaii, the Philippines, Puerto Rico and Cuba at the turn of the century, the American popular press characterized the native populations by analogy with either "red Injuns" or blacks. The *Literary Digest* of August 1898 spoke casually of "Uncle Sam's New-Caught Anthropoids."[10] On the American conquest of the Philippines, Rudyard Kipling, the bard of imperialism, characterized the native inhabitants as "half devil and half child." The American press regularly presented Filipinos and other peoples *as* blacks—images which suggest graphically that the sensation of power and supremacy was the same, whether on the American continent or overseas, and was being expressed through the same metaphors. Again, it is not ethnicity, or "race" that governs imagery and discourse, but rather, the nature of the *political relationship* between peoples which causes a people to be viewed in a particular light.

A similar dynamic was at work during the Vietnam war. A common expression among American GIs in Vietnam was "The only good gook is a dead gook," with "gook" (the term of abuse for Vietnamese) replacing "nigger" or Indian ("Injun") in the existing formula.[11] The underlying logic of dehumanizing the enemy by means of stereotyping is the same. These examples of dehumanization and victimization illustrate what Ron Dellums has called, in a phrase, the "niggering process."[12] ...

... "What racism, classism, sexism all have in common is social inequality: the key to all the social relations discussed above is the pathos of hierarchy. While the common denominator is power—the power that arises from a hierarchical situation and the power required to maintain that situation—it is also a matter of the anxiety that comes with power and privilege. Existing differences and inequalities are magnified for fear they will diminish. Stereotypes are reconstructed and reasserted precisely when existing hierarchies are being challenged and inequalities are or may be lessening. Accordingly, stereotyping tends to be not merely a matter of domination, but above all, of humiliation. Different and subordinate groups are not merely described, they are *debased*, degraded. Perceptions are manipulated in order to enhance and to magnify social distance. The rhetoric and the imagery of domination and humiliation permeate society. They concern processes in which we all take part, as receivers and senders, in the everyday rituals of impression management, in so far as taking part in society means taking part in some kind of status-ranking.

As the negative of the denigrating images sketched above, there emerges the top-dog position, whose profile is approximately as follows: white, western, civilized, male, adult, urban, middle-class, heterosexual, and so on. It is this profile that has monopolized the definition of humanity in mainstream western imagery. It is a programme of fear for the rest of the world population.

NOTES

1. Quoted in Vints (1984, p. 26).
2. Boxer (1978, p. 23).
3. Quoted in Curtis (1971, p. 1).
4. A classic source is J. Beddoe, *The Races of Britain* (1885). See MacDougall (1982) and Rich (1986, pp. 13–20).
5. Curtis (1971, p. 2).
6. Curtis (1971, p. 100). See cartoons by Tenniel and others (pp. 55, 56, 57, 58, 59, 60, 62).

7. During a visit to America in 1881, the English historian Edward Freeman wrote: "This would be a great land if only every Irishman would kill a Negro, and be hanged for it. I find this sentiment generally approved—sometimes with the qualification that they want Irish and negroes for servants, not being able to get any other" (Curtis, 1984, p. 58).
8. Curtis (1984, p. 55) and Beddoe (1885).
9. Takaki (1980, pp. 217–218). "The 'Negroization' of the Chinese reached a high point when a magazine cartoon depicted [one of] them as a bloodsucking vampire with slanted eyes, a pigtail, dark skin, and thick lips. White workers made the identification even more explicit when they referred to the Chinese as 'nagurs.'" One may add that there were also differences between the stereotypes of Chinese and blacks.
10. See Drinnon (1980, pp. 276–277) and Jacobs and Landau (1971).
11. Lifton (1973/1985, p. 204).
12. Dellums (1978).

REFERENCES

Beddoe, J. (1885). *The races of Britain*. London.

Boxer, C. R. (1978). *The church militant and Iberian expansion, 1440–1770*. Ann Arbor, MI: Books on Demand.

Curtis, L. P., Jr. (1971). *Apes and angels: The Irishman in Victorian caricature*. London: Newton Abbot.

Curtis, L. (1984). *Nothing but the same old story: The roots of anti-Irish racism*. London.

Dellums, R. V. (1978). *The link between struggles for human rights in the United States and Third World*. Washington, DC.

Drinnon, R. (1980), *Facing west: The metaphysics of Indian-hating and Empire-building*. New York: Schocken.

Jacobs, P., & Landau, S. (1971). *To serve the devil* (2 vols.). New York.

Lifton, R. J. (1985). *Home from the war: Vietnam veterans—Neither victims nor executioners.* Boston: Beacon. (Original work published 1973)

MacDougall, H. A. (1982). *Racial myth in English history.* Montreal: Hannover.

Rich, P. B. (1986). *Race and empire in British politics.* Cambridge.

Takaki, R. T. (1980). *Iron cages: Race and culture in nineteenth-century America.* London: Oxford University Press.

Vints, L. (1984). *Kongo: Made in Belgium.* Leuven, Belgium.

15

Advertising and People of Color

By Clint C. Wilson II and Félix Gutiérrez

For years advertisers in the United States reflected the place of non-Whites in the social fabric of the nation either by ignoring them or, when they were included in advertisements for the mass audience, processing and presenting them in a way that would make them palatable salespersons for the products being advertised. These processed portrayals largely mirrored the stereotypic images of minorities in the entertainment media that, in turn, were designed to reflect the perceived values and norms of the White majority. In this way, non-White portrayals in advertising paralleled and reinforced their entertainment and journalistic images in the media.

The history of advertising in the United States is replete with characterizations that, like the Frito Bandito, responded to and reinforced the preconceived image that many White Americans apparently had of Blacks, Latinos, Asians, and Native Americans. Over the years advertisers have employed Latin spitfires like Chiquita Banana, Black mammies like Aunt Jemima, and noble savages like the Santa Fe Railroad's Super Chief to pitch their products to a predominantly White mass audience of consumers. In 1984 the Balch Institute

for Ethnic Studies in Philadelphia sponsored an exhibit of more than 300 examples of racial and ethnic images used by corporations in magazines, posters, trade cards, and storyboards.

The advertising examples in the exhibit include positive White ethnic stereotypes, such as the wholesome and pure image of Quakers in an early Quaker Oats advertisement and the cleanliness of the Dutch in a turn-of-the-century advertisement for Colgate soaps. But they also featured a late-19 th-century advertisement showing an Irish matron threatening to hit her husband over the head with a rolling pin because he didn't smoke the right brand of tobacco. Like Quaker Oats, some products even incorporated a stereotypical image on the package or product line being advertised.

"Lawsee! Folks sho' whoops with joy over AUNT JEMIMA PANCAKES," shouted a bandanna-wearing Black mammy in a magazine advertisement for Aunt Jemima pancake mix, which featured a plump Aunt Jemima on the box. Over the years, Aunt Jemima has lost some weight, but the stereotyped face of the Black servant continues to be featured on the box. Earlier advertisements for Cream of Wheat featured Rastus, the

Black servant on the box, in a series of magazine cartoons with a group of cute but ill-dressed Black children. Some of the advertisements played on stereotypes ridiculing Blacks, such as an advertisement in which a Black schoolteacher, standing behind a makeshift lectern made out of a boldly lettered Cream of Wheat box, asks the class, "How do you spell 'Cream of Wheat?'" Others appeared to promote racial integration, such as a magazine advertisement captioned "Putting it down in Black and White," which showed Rastus serving bowls of the breakfast cereal to Black and White youngsters sitting at the same table.

Racial imagery was also integrated into the naming of trains by the Santa Fe railroad, which named one of its passenger lines the Super Chief and featured highly detailed portraits of the noble Indian in promoting its service through the Southwestern United States. In another series of advertisements, the railroad used cartoons of Native American children to show the service and sights passengers could expect when they traveled the Santa Fe line.

These and other portrayals catered to the mass audience mentality by either neutralizing or making humor of the negative perceptions that many Whites may have had of racial minorities. The advertising images, rather than showing people of color as they really were, portrayed them as filtered through Anglo eyes. This presented an out-of-focus image of racial minorities, but one that was palatable, and even persuasive, to the White majority to which it was directed. In the mid-1960s Black civil rights groups targeted the advertising industry for special attention, protesting both the lack of integrated advertisements including Blacks and the stereotyped images that the advertisers continued to use. The effort, accompanied by support from federal officials, resulted in the overnight inclusion of Blacks as models in television advertising in 1967 and a downplaying of the images that many Blacks found objectionable.

"Black America is becoming visible in America's biggest national advertising medium," reported the *New York Times* in 1968. "Not in a big way yet, but it is a beginning and men in high places give assurances that there will be a lot more visibility."[1]

But the advertising industry did not generalize the concerns of Blacks, or the concessions made in response to them, to other groups. At the same time that some Black concerns were being addressed with integrated advertising, other groups were being ignored or singled out for continued stereotyped treatment in such commercials as those featuring the Frito Bandito.

Among the Latino advertising stereotypes cited in a 1969 article[2] by sociologist Tomás Martínez were commercials for Granny Goose chips featuring fat gun-toting Mexicans, an advertisement for Arrid underarm deodorant showing a dusty Mexican bandito spraying his underarms after a hard ride as the announcer intones, "If it works for him it will work for you," and a magazine advertisement featuring a stereotypical Mexican sleeping under his sombrero as he leans against a Philco television set. Especially offensive to Martinez was a Liggett & Meyers commercial for L&M cigarettes that featured Paco, a lazy Latino who never "feenishes" anything, not even the revolution he is supposed to be fighting. In response to a letter complaining about the commercial, the director of public relations for the tobacco firm defended the commercial's use of Latino stereotypes.

"'Paco' is a warm, sympathetic and lovable character with whom most of us can identify because he has a little of all of us in him, that is, our tendency to procrastinate at times," wrote the Liggett & Meyers executive. "He seeks to escape the violence of war and to enjoy the pleasure of the moment, in this case, the good flavor of an L&M cigarette."[3] Although the company spokesman claimed that the character had been tested without negative reactions from Latinos (a similar claim was made by Frito-Lay regarding the Frito Bandito), Martínez roundly criticized the advertising images and contrasted them to what he saw as the gains Blacks were then making in the advertising field.

"Today, no major advertiser would attempt to display a black man or woman over the media in a prejudiced, stereotyped fashion," Martínez wrote.

> Complaints would be forthcoming from black associations and perhaps the FCC. Yet, these same advertisers, who dare not show "step'n fetch it" characters, uninhibitedly depict a Mexican counterpart, with additional traits of stinking and stealing. Perhaps the white hatred for blacks, which cannot find adequate expression in today's ads, is being transferred upon their brown brothers.[4]

In 1970 a Brown Position Paper prepared by Latino media activists Armando Rendón and Domingo Nick Reyes charged that the media had transferred the negative stereotypes it once reserved for Blacks to Latinos, who had become "the media's new nigger."[5] The protests of Latinos soon made the nation's advertisers more conscious of the portrayals that Latinos found offensive. But, as in the case of the Blacks, the advertising industry failed to apply the lessons learned from one group to other racial minorities.

Although national advertisers withdrew much of the advertising that negatively stereotyped Blacks and Latinos, sometimes replacing them with affluent, successful images that were as far removed from reality as the negative portrayals of the past, the advances made by those groups were not shared with Native Americans and Asians. Native Americans' names and images, no longer depicted either as the noble savage or as cute cartoon characters, have all but disappeared from broadcast commercials and print advertising. The major exceptions are advertising for automobiles and trucks that bear names such as Pontiac, Dakota, and Navajo and sports teams with racial nicknames such as the Kansas City Chiefs, Washington Redskins, Florida State University Seminoles, Atlanta Braves, and Cleveland Indians. Native Americans and others have protested these racial team names and images, as well as the pseudo-Native American pageantry and souvenirs that accompany many of them, but with no success in getting them changed.

Asians, particularly Japanese, continue to be dealt more than their share of commercials depicting them in stereotypes that cater to the fears and stereotypes of White America. As was the case with Blacks and Latinos, it took organized protests from Asian American groups to get the message across to the corporations and their advertising agencies. In the mid-1970s, a southern California supermarket chain agreed to remove a television campaign in which a young Asian karate-chopped his way down the store's aisles cutting prices. Nationally, several firms whose industries have been hard-hit by Japanese imports fought back through commercials, if not in the quality or prices of their products. One automobile company featured an Asian family carefully looking over a new car and commenting on its attributes in heavily accented English. Only after they bought it did they learn it was made in the United States, not Japan. Another automobile company that markets cars manufactured in Japan under an English-language name showed a parking lot attendant opening the doors of the car, only to find the car speaking to him in Japanese. For several years Sylvania television ran a commercial boasting that its television picture had repeatedly been selected over competing brands as an off-screen voice with a Japanese accent repeatedly asked, "What about Sony?" When the announcer responded that the Sylvania picture had also been selected over Sony's, the off-screen voice ran off shouting what sounded like a string of Japanese expletives. A 1982

Newsweek article observed that "attacking Japan has become something of a fashion in corporate ads" because of resentment over Japanese trade policies and sales of Japanese products in the United States, but quoted Motorola's advertising manager as saying, "We've been as careful as we can be" not to be racially offensive.[6]

But many of the television and print advertisements featuring Asians featured images that were racially insensitive, if not offensive. A commercial for a laundry product featured a Chinese family that used an "ancient Chinese laundry secret" to get their customers' clothes clean. Naturally, the Chinese secret turned out to be the packaged product paying for the advertisement. Companies pitching everything from pantyhose to airlines featured Asian women coiffed and costumed as seductive China dolls or exotic Polynesian natives to pitch and promote their products, some of them cast in Asian settings and others attentively caring for the needs of the Anglo men in the advertisement. One airline boasted that those who flew with it would be under the care of the Singapore Girl.

Asian women appearing in commercials were often featured as China dolls with the small, darkened eyes, straight hair with bangs, and a narrow, slit skirt. Another common portrayal featured the exotic, tropical Pacific Islands look, complete with flowers in the hair, a sarong or grass skirt, and shell ornament. Asian women hoping to become models sometimes found that they must conform to these stereotypes or lose assignments. Leslie Kawai, the 1981 Tournament of Roses Queen, was told to cut her hair with bangs by hairstylists when she auditioned for a beer advertisement. When she refused, the beer company decided to hire another model with shorter hair cut in bangs.[7]

The lack of a sizable Asian community, or market, in the United States was earlier cited as the reason that Asians are still stereotyped in advertising and, except for children's advertising, are rarely presented in integrated settings. The growth rate and income of Asians living in the United States in the 1980s and 1990s, however, reinforced the economic potential of Asian Americans to overcome the stereotyping and lack of visibility that Blacks and Latinos challenged with some success. By the mid-1980s there were a few signs that advertising was beginning to integrate Asian Americans into crossover advertisements that, like the Tostitos campaign, were designed to have a broad appeal. In one commercial, television actor Robert Ito was featured telling how he loves to call his relatives in Japan because the calls make them think that he is rich, as well as successful, in the United States. Of course, he adds, it is only because the rates of his long distance carrier were so low that he was able to call Japan so often.

In the 1970s mass audience advertising in the United States became more racially integrated than at any time in the nation's history. Blacks, and to a much lesser extent Latinos and Asians, could be seen in television commercials spread across the broadcast week and in major magazines. In fact, the advertisements on network television often appeared to be more fully integrated than the television programs they supported. Like television, general circulation magazines also experienced an increase in the use of Blacks, although studies of both media showed that most of the percentage increase had come by the early 1970s. By the early 1970s the percentage of prime-time television commercials featuring Blacks had apparently leveled off at about 10%. Blacks were featured in between only 2% and 3% of magazine advertisements as late as 1978. That percentage, however small, was a sharp increase from the 0.06% of news magazine advertisements reported in 1960.[8]

The gains were also socially significant, because they demonstrated that Blacks could be integrated into advertisements without triggering a White backlash among potential customers in the White majority. Both sales figures and research conducted since the late 1960s have shown that the integration of Black models into television and print advertising does not adversely affect sales or the image of the product. Instead, a study by the American Newspaper Publishers Association showed, the most important influences on sales were the merchandise and the advertisement itself. In fact, while triggering no adverse affect among the majority of Whites, integrated advertisements were found to be useful in swaying Black consumers, who responded favorably to positive Black role models in print advertisements.[9] Studies conducted in the early 1970s also showed that White consumers did not respond negatively to advertising featuring Black models, although their response was more often neutral than positive.[10] One 1972 study examining White backlash, however, did show that an advertisement prominently featuring darker-skinned Blacks was less acceptable to Whites than those featuring lighter-skinned Blacks as background models.[11] Perhaps such findings help explain why research conducted later in the 1970s revealed that, for the most part, Blacks appearing in magazine and television advertisements were often featured as part of an integrated group.[12]

Although research findings have shown that integrated advertisements do not adversely affect sales, the percentage of Blacks and other minorities in general audience advertising did not increase significantly after the numerical gains made through the mid-1970s. Those minorities who did appear in advertisements were often depicted in upscale or integrated settings, an image that the Balch Institute's Stolarik criticized as taking advertising "too far in the other direction and created stereotypes of 'successful' ethnic group members that are as unrealistic as those of the past."[13] Equally unwise, from a business sense, was the low numbers of Blacks appearing in advertisements.

Advertisers and their ad agencies must evaluate the direct economic consequences of alternative strategies on the firm. If it is believed that the presence of Black models in advertisements decreases the effectiveness of advertising messages, only token numbers of Black models will be used,

wrote marketing professor Lawrence Soley at the conclusion of a 1983 study.

Previous studies have found that advertisements portraying Black models do not elicit negative affective or conative responses from consumers. … Given the consistency of the research findings, more Blacks should be portrayed in advertisements. If Blacks continue to be underrepresented in advertising portrayals, it can be said that this is an indication of prejudice on the part of the advertising industry, not consumers.[14]

COURTSHIP OF SPANISH GOLD AND THE BLACK MARKET

Although Soley stopped short of accusing corporate executives of racial prejudice, he contended that a "counterpressure" to full integration of Blacks into mainstream media portrayals was that "advertising professionals are businessmen first and moralists second."[15] If so, then it was the business mentality of advertising and corporate professionals that led them into increasingly aggressive advertising and marketing campaigns to capture minority consumers, particularly Blacks and Latinos, in the 1970s and 1980s.

Long depicted as low-end consumers with little money to spend, Black and Latino customers became more important to national and regional advertisers of mainstream goods who took a closer look at the size, composition, and projected growth of those groups. Asian Americans, who experienced a sharp percentage growth in the 1970s and were generally more affluent than Blacks and Latinos, were not targeted to the same extent, probably because of their relatively small numbers and differences in national languages among the groups. And, except for regions in which they comprised a sizable portion of the population, Native Americans were largely ignored as potential consumers of mainstream products.

One part of the courtship of Blacks and Latinos grew out of the civil rights movements of the 1960s, in which both Blacks and Latinos effectively used consumer boycotts to push issues ranging from ending segregation to organizing farmworkers. Boycotts had long been threatened and used by minority consumers as economic leverage on social issues. But in the 1960s Black ministers organized the Philadelphia Selective Patronage Program in which Blacks did business with companies that supported their goals of more jobs for Blacks. This philosophy of repaying the corporations that invest in the minority communities through consumer purchases was replicated in other cities. It was followed by slick advertising campaigns directed at minority consumers. In 1984 the same line of thinking led to the brewers of Coors beer attempting to end disputes with Blacks and Latinos by signing controversial agreements with the National Association for the Advancement of Colored People (NAACP) and five national Latino groups that committed the brewery to increase its financial support of the activities of those organizations as Blacks and Latinos increased their drinking of Coors beer.

A second, and more influential, element of the courtship has been the hard-selling job of advertising agencies and media specializing in the Black and Spanish-speaking Latinos. Spurred by the thinking of Black advertising executive D. Parke Gibson in his 1968 book *The $30 Billion Negro* and a steady stream of articles on Black and Latino consumers in media trade publications, national advertisers became aware of the fact that minorities were potential consumers for a wide range of products. The advertisers also were persuaded that the inattention they had previously received from mainstream products made Blacks and Latinos respond more favorably and with greater loyalty to those products that courted them through advertisements on billboards and in the publications and broadcast stations used by Latinos and Blacks.

The third, and most far-reaching, element in the courtship was a fundamental change in the thinking of marketing and advertising executives that swayed them away from mass audience media. Witnessing the success they had in advertising on radio stations and magazines targeted to specific audience segments following the advent of television as the dominant mass medium in the 1950s, advertising agencies advised their clients to go after their potential customers identified with market segments, rather than the mass audience. Advertisers found that differences in race, like differences in sex, residence, family status, and age, were easy to target through advertising appeals targeted to media whose content was designed to attract men or women, young or old, suburban or rural, Black or White, Spanish or English speaking. These media, in turn, produced audience surveys to show they were effective in reaching and delivering specific segments of the mass audience. By the mid-1980s, market and audience segmentation had become so important to advertisers that the term *mass media* was becoming an anachronism.

"It is a basic tenet of marketing that you go after markets with rifles, not shotguns. It is foolhardy—and idealistic in the worst way—to try to sell the same thing to everyone in the same way," wrote Caroline R. Junes, executive vice president of Mingo-Jones Advertising, in a 1984 article in the advertising trade magazine *Madison Avenue*.

> Good marketing involves breaking down potential markets into homogeneous segments; targeting the most desirable segments; and developing creative programs, tailored for each segment, that make your messages look different from your competitors'. All of that should be done with the guidance of thorough research on characteristics, beliefs and preferences of the people in the targeted markets.[16]

Like others who have pitched minority audiences to major corporations as ripe targets for slick advertisements, Jones advised advertising professionals reading the magazine to target advertising to Black consumers because *"there's money in it."* Among the factors she cited as making Blacks desirable customers was a reported disposable income of more than $150 million, a "high propensity for brand names and indulgence items," a high degree of "brand loyalty," a young and growing population, growing education and income, concentration in the nation's largest 25 cities, and "its own growing media network."[17]

Much the same approach has been used to sell Latinos to advertising agencies as a target too good to be passed up. A 1965 article on Latino consumers in the advertising trade magazine *Sponsor* was headlined "America's Spanish Treasure," a 1971 *Sales Management* article proclaimed "Brown Is Richer Than Black," and in 1972 *Television/Radio Age* advised readers, "The Spanish Market: Its Size, Income and Loyalties Make It a Rich Marketing Mine."[18] In addition to the characteristics that were cited as making Blacks an attractive market, Latinos have been depicted as being especially vulnerable to advertisements because their use of Spanish supposedly cuts them off from advertising in English-language media. Thus, advertisers are advised to use the language and culture that are familiar with their target audience to give their messages the greatest delivery and impact.

"U.S. Hispanics are most receptive to media content in the Spanish language," wrote Antonio Guernica in a 1982 book titled *Reaching the Hispanic Market Effectively*.[19] Guernica and others have counseled advertisers to package their commercial messages in settings that are reinforced by Latino culture and traditions. These appeals link the product being advertised with the language, heritage, and social system that Latinos are most comfortable with, thus creating the illusion that the product belongs in the Latino home.

"The language, the tradition, the kitchen utensils are different" (in a Latino home) said Shelly Perlman, media buyer for the Hispania division of the J. Walter Thompson advertising agency in a 1983 *Advertising Age* article.

> There are ads one can run in general media that appeal to everyone but that contain unmistakeable clues to Hispanics that they are being sought. It can be done with models, with scene and set design— a whole array of factors.[20]

Corporations seeking the Latino dollar also have been told to picture their products with Latino foods, celebrities, cultural events, community events, and family traditions. The goal has been to adapt the product to make it appear to be a part of the Latino lifestyle in the United States, which often requires being sensitive to the language, food, and musical differences among Latinos in different parts of the nation and from different countries in Latin America.

For both Blacks and Latinos the slick advertising approach often means selling high-priced, prestige products to low-income consumers who have not fully shared in the wealth of the country in which they live. But Blacks and Latinos, who have median family incomes well below national averages, have been nonetheless targeted as consumers for premium brand names in all product lines and particularly in liquor, beer, and cigarettes. In response, Black and Latino community groups and health organizations in the 1990s protested the targeting of alcohol and tobacco products to their communities and, in some cases, forced outdoor advertising companies to restrict the number of such billboards in these communities.

Through the 1990s, corporations making and marketing products ranging from beer to diapers tried to show Blacks and Latinos that consumption of their goods is part of the good life in America. It may not be a life that they knew when they grew up in the ghetto, barrio, or in another country. It may not even be a life that they or their children will ever achieve, but it is a lifestyle and happiness they can share by purchasing the same products used by the rich and famous. Prestige appeals are used in advertising to all audiences, not just minorities. But they have a special impact on those who are so far down on the socioeconomic scale that they are especially hungry for anything that will add status or happiness to their lives and help them show others that they are "making it." The advertisements promote conspicuous consumption, rather than hard work and savings, as the key to the good life. ...

By recognizing elements of the Black or Latino experience that may have been ignored by White Americans, the advertisers also play on national or racial pride to boost sales of their products. In the 1970s, Anheuser-Busch commissioned a series of glossy advertisements commemorating the Great Kings of Africa, and Schlitz produced a Chicano history calendar. These and similar advertising campaigns provided long overdue recognition of Black and Latino heritage, but they also prominently displayed the corporate symbols of their sponsors and were designed to boost the sale of beer more than to recognize overlooked historical figures and events. ...

The media targeted to non-Whites are eager to promote themselves as the most effective way to reach consumers of color. In 1974 one of New York's Black newspapers, the *Amsterdam News,* vigorously attacked the credibility of a New York *Daily News* audience survey that showed it reached more Black readers than the *Amsterdam News.* In a 1979 *Advertising Age* advertisement, *La Opinion,* Los Angeles's Spanish-language daily newspaper, promised advertisers it could show them how to "Wrap Up the Spanish-language Market." Advertising is the lifeblood of the print and broadcast media in the United States, and media that target people of color have been quick to promote themselves as the most effective vehicles for penetrating and persuading the people in their communities to purchase the products advertised on their airwaves and in their pages.

HOW LOUD IS THE NOT-SO-SILENT PARTNER'S VOICE?

Minority-formatted publications and broadcasters depend on advertising to support their media. They have benefited from the increased emphasis on market segmentation by promoting the consumption patterns of the audiences they reach and their own effectiveness in delivering persuasive commercial messages to their readers, listeners, and viewers. But advertising is also a two-edged sword that expects to take more money out of a market segment than it invests in advertising to that segment. Black and Spanish-language media will benefit from the advertising dollars of national corporations only as long as dollars are the most cost-effective way for advertisers to persuade Blacks and Latinos to use their products. This places the minority-formatted media in an exploitative relationship with their audience, who because of language, educational, and economic differences sometimes are exposed to a narrower range of media than Whites. Advertisers support the media that deliver the audience with the best consumer profile at the lowest cost, not necessarily the media that best meet the information and entertainment needs of their audience.

The slick, upscale lifestyle used by national advertisers is more a goal than a reality for most Blacks and Latinos. It is achieved through education, hard work, and equal opportunity. Yet advertisers promote consumption of their products as the shortcut to the good life, a quick fix for low-income consumers. The message to their low-income audience is clear: You may not be able to live in the best neighborhoods, wear the best clothes, or have the best job, but you can drink the same liquor, smoke the same cigarettes, and drive the same car as those who do. At the same time, advertising appeals that play on the cultural or historical heritage of Blacks and Latinos make the products appear to be "at home" with minority consumers. Recognizing the importance of national holidays and the forgotten minority history, they have joined with Blacks and Latinos in commemorating dates, events, and persons. But they also piggy-back their commercial messages on the recognition of events, leaders, or heroes. Persons or events that in their time represented protest against slavery, oppression, or discrimination are now used to sell products.

Advertising, like mining, is an extractive industry. It enters the ghetto and barrio with a smiling face to convince all within its reach that they should purchase the products advertised and purchase them often. It has no goal other than to stimulate consumption of the product; the subsidization of the media is merely a by-product. But owners of minority-formatted media, having gained through the increased advertising investments of major corporations, now have greater opportunities to use those increased dollars to improve news and entertainment content and, thus, better meet their social responsibility to their audience. Unlike advertisers, who may support socially responsible activities for the purpose of promoting their own images, minority publishers and broadcasters have a long, though sometimes spotty, record of advocating the rights of the people they serve. Their growing dependence on major corporations and national advertising agencies should do nothing to blunt that edge as long as the audiences they serve continue to confront a system of inequality that keeps them below national norms in education, housing, income, health, and other social indicators.

NOTES

1. Cited in Philip H. Dougherty, "Frequency of Blacks in TV Ads," *New York Times,* May 27, 1982, p. D19.
2. Tomás Martínez, "How Advertisers Promote Racism," *Civil Rights Digest* (Fall 1969), p. 10.
3. Martínez, "How Advertisers Promote," p. 11.
4. Martínez, "How Advertisers Promote," pp. 9–10.
5. Domingo Nick Reyes and Armando Rendón, *Chicanos and the Mass Media* (Washington, DC: The National Mexican American Anti-Defamation Committee, 1971).
6. Joseph Treen, "Madison Ave. vs. Japan, Inc.," *Newsweek* (April 12, 1982), p. 69.
7. Ada Kan, *Asian Models in the Media,* Unpublished term paper, Journalism 466: Minority and the Media, University of Southern California, December 14, 1983, p. 5.
8. Studies on increase of Blacks in magazine and television commercials cited in James D. Culley

and Rex Bennett, "Selling Blacks, Selling Women," *Journal of Communication* (Autumn 1976, Vol. 26, No. 4), pp. 160–174; Lawrence Soley, "The Effect of Black Models on Magazine Ad Readership," *Journalism Quarterly* (Winter 1983, Vol. 60, No. 4), p. 686; and Leonard N. Reid and Bruce G. Vanden Bergh, "Blacks in Introductory Ads," *Journalism Quarterly* (Autumn 1980, Vol. 57, No. 3), pp. 485–486.

9. Cited in D. Parke Gibson, *$70 Billion in the Black* (New York: Macmillan, 1979), pp. 83–84.

10. Laboratory studies on White reactions to Blacks in advertising cited in Soley, "The Effect of Black Models," pp. 585–587.

11. Carl E. Block, "White Backlash to Negro Ads: Fact or Fantasy?" *Journalism Quarterly* (Autumn 1980, Vol. 49, No. 2), pp. 258–262.

12. James D. Culley and Rex Bennett, "Selling Blacks, Selling Women."

13. "Using Ethnic Images," p. 9.

14. Soley, *The Effect of Black Models*, p. 690.

15. Soley, *The Effect of Black Models*, p. 690.

16. Caroline R. Jones, "Advertising in Black and White," *Madison Avenue* (May 1984), p. 53.

17. Jones, "Advertising in Black and White," p. 54.

18. Félix Frank Gutiérrez, *Spanish-language Radio and Chicano Internal Colonialism*, Doctoral Dissertation, Stanford University, 1976, pp. 312–314.

19. Antonio Guernica, *Reaching the Hispanic Market Effectively* (New York: McGraw-Hill, 1982), p. 5.

20. Theodore J. Gage, "How to Reach an Enthusiastic Market," *Advertising Age* (February 14, 1983), p. M–11.

16

Contesting Masculinity's Makeover

Queer Eye, Consumer Masculinity, and "Straight-Acting" Gays

By Jay Clarkson

This article analyzes conflicting and competing discourses about gay masculinities in and about Bravo's Queer Eye for the Straight Guy. *The author analyzes* Queer Eye's *normalization of consumer masculinity, which rejects aspects of traditional masculinity and depends on vanity consumption. The author argues that consumer masculinity is at odds with the masculinities that the gay men on StraightActing.com are attempting to uphold. Their interpretations of* Queer Eye *differ significantly from academic media critic Kylo-Patrick Hart's interpretation that* Queer Eye *is the most positive representation of gay men ever. It is in the struggle over mediated masculinity that the men of StraightActing.com find themselves paradoxically aligned with radical conservatives in fearing the impact of* Queer Eye *on heterosexual audiences but for completely contradictory reasons.*

Keywords: *gay men and television; hegemonic masculinity; consumerism; internet community*

Queer Eye for the Straight Guy (hereafter *Queer Eye*) is the latest and perhaps most flamboyant entrant into the struggle over dominant masculinity. The men of *Queer Eye* convert relatively open-minded heterosexual men into sleek, stylish, and sensitive metrosexuals in a mediated presentation of the contemporary contestation over masculine ideals. The makeovers they conduct mold straight men into hyperconsumers and model them on advertising industry's effigy of a gay male market that is assumed to have an inherent access to greater degrees of refinement and taste than straight men. Who would have thought that a reality television makeover show would depict a full frontal capitalist assault on traditional heteromasculine gender performance? In this battle, some gay men and straight men are willingly surrendering to the construction of the "new and improved" consumption masculinity. However, many other men, including the gay

Jay Clarkson, "Contesting Masculinity's Makeover: *Queer Eye*, Consumer Masculinity, and 'Straight-Acting' Gays," *Journal of Communication Inquiry*, vol. 29, no. 3, pp. 235-255. Copyright © 2005 by Sage Publications. Reprinted with permission.

men of StraightActing.com, are engaged in a last ditch effort to save traditional masculinity from what they perceive as the influences of gayness and femininity. It is in the conflicted discourses of *Queer Eye* and StraightActing.com that the ways in which gayness, femininity, and consumption are conjoined concepts in contemporary culture are readily observed.

This article analyzes conflicting and competing discourses about masculinity in *Queer Eye* in the media and on the discussion boards of StraightActing.com. First, I outline the representations of masculinity that are contested in *Queer Eye*; next, I detail the ways in which media have responded to these representations; and finally, I discuss the ways in which the gay men of StraightActing.com use their online forum to actively resist capitalism's influence by denigrating gayness as an identity and reinterpreting the meanings of masculinity. The discourse on StraightActing.com represents a site of ideological contestation where its members challenge the notion that gay men similarly respond to gay representations from a monolithic gay subject position and where gay men can be seen defending traditional masculinity by reinscribing its antifeminine and homophobic characteristics through their discussions of *Queer Eye*. The purpose of this study is not to catalog the multiplicity of potential gay male readings, but to illustrate the ways in which *Queer Eye*'s consumer masculinity and traditional masculinity represent highly conflicted discourses among some straight-acting gay men who resist any change in the contemporary gender order.

Before moving to an analysis of *Queer Eye*'s representation of masculinity and the ways in which the straight-acting gay men interpret it, a brief overview of the two forums—*Queer Eye* and StraightActing.com—in which I analyze masculinity is necessary.

QUEER EYE FOR THE STRAIGHT GUY

Queer Eye is the most high profile and perhaps flamboyant mainstreaming of gay men on television to date. The series is predicated on the basic assumption that straight men are unrefined, ungroomed, and simply need a gay man's help to attain a higher fluency of culture, charm, and sophistication. In each episode, the "fab five"—Carson (fashion), Kyan (grooming), Jai (culture), Thom (interior design), and Ted (food and wine)—inflict their areas of expertise on a hapless straight man, who, more often than not, is depicted as a clueless slob with a good heart and a woman who loves him the way he is but would like to see him improved.

Invariably, *Queer Eye* forces its "straight guys" to confront issues of physical beauty and taste to make themselves more attractive to women. Even John, the first season's straight guy and who could generally be considered attractive, at the beginning of the episode (Carson calls him a "hottie"), is forced to deal with a variety of physical improvements ranging from hair styling to eyebrow plucking. The growing pressure on men to attain virtually unattainable standards of physical perfection has been blamed for the recent dramatic increase in male drug use, cosmetic surgery, and eating disorders. Although this pressure is nothing new to women or gay men, it is a relatively new phenomenon among heterosexual men for whom hegemonic masculinity has demanded that they avoid any possibility of being perceived as feminine.

STRAIGHTACTING.COM

StraightActing.com is a privately funded Web site featuring quizzes, personal ads, home pages, a monthly cover model contest, and a discussion board. The site provides an online space for straight-acting gay men[1] to socialize, meet, and discuss a wide variety of issues and includes the Butch Boards, a discussion forum. This forum is for members only (although membership is free) and includes discussions ranging from common interests, such as entertainment, politics, religion, and sports, to topics dealing specifically with the meaning of straight acting and masculinity.

Although my analysis here is limited primarily to the members' reactions to *Queer Eye*, it is important to consider the general tone of this group. The site founders acknowledge that one should not discriminate against anyone for expressing their preference for straight-acting men, but the heteronormative and homophobic sentiments voiced by many of the members of this community remain alarming reminders that group and individual identity formation often reflect struggles for power among and within similarly situated groups. Stepen, a long-time member of the Web site, summarizes the potentially problematic nature of this community, saying, "To be honest flammers [*sic*][2] frighten me as I'm not quite sure how they tick."

I focus on this Web site because I believe that the mediated presence of this gender affinity group is appealing to these men to avoid less straight-acting gay men and also insulates them from being forced to confront the real implications of their femiphobia and their own internalized homophobia. Indeed, I focus on this particular site because, after conducting an overview of several gay-themed sites—Outsports, Just Us Boys, and StraightActing.com—this site focuses most clearly on gender issues, although simultaneously demonstrating a lack of feminist consciousness and an obvious commitment to distinguishing among gay masculinities. Functionally, the existence of this community allows for these men to come together to reinforce their own beliefs about men and masculinity and facilitates their condemnation of those men who do not conform.

Although gay men are presumably at the core of *Queer Eye*'s target audience, the members of StraightActing.com gather, albeit virtually, to validate straight-acting queer identities that seemingly are at odds with stereotypical versions of gay masculinity and the metrosexuality represented in *Queer Eye*. Before I begin to analyze their reactions to *Queer Eye*'s masculinity, I discuss the concept of hegemonic masculinity and outline the consumer masculinity constructed in the series.

HEGEMONIC MASCULINITY

Hegemonic masculinity and heteronormative masculinity (Cloud, 1998) are two key components of hegemony that often have been used to study the oppression of women in the mass media. Recently, the emerging masculinity studies have begun to focus on the process through which men come to be gendered. The study of hegemonic masculinity is the exploration of the "culturally idealized form of masculine character" (Connell, 1987, p. 83), which can most often be seen in "fantasy figures or models remote from the lives of the unheroic majority" (Donaldson, 1993, p. 646).

Kimmel (2003) argues that masculinity "is the product of historical shifts in the grounds, on which men rooted their sense of themselves as men" (p. 120). In his overview of historical masculinities, he illustrates the transition from two 18th- and early 19th-century models—the genteel patriarch and heroic artisan—to the marketplace man of the latter 19th century. Each of these masculine archetypes reflects the dominant economic system of their day. The genteel patriarch "derived his identity from land ownership ... he was refined, elegant and given to causal sensuousness. He was a doting and devoted father," whereas the heroic artisan "embodied the physical strength and republican virtue ... in the yeoman farmer, independent urban craftsman or shopkeeper" (Kimmel, 2003, pp. 120–121). Kimmel argues that these masculinities, although different, coexisted because they shared common gender ideals and because they rarely interacted. However, with the rise of modern capitalism, these archetypes were replaced by the marketplace man, who:

> derived his identity entirely from his success in the capitalist marketplace, as he accumulated wealth, power, status. He was the urban entrepreneur, the businessman. Restless, agitated and anxious. Marketplace Man was an absentee landlord at home and an absent father with his children, devoting himself to his work in an increasingly homosocial environment—a male-only world in which he pits himself against other men … Marketplace Manhood was a manhood that required proof, and that required the acquisition of tangible goods as evidence of success. (Kimmel, 2003, p. 121)

Susan Alexander (2003) argues that because of the 1950s, the marketplace man has given way to a new form of masculinity that is a consumer product that "rests on one's outward appearance rather than on the traditional male role of production" (p. 551). Mackinnon (1997) argues that this change in masculinity can be attributed to contemporary capitalism's incompatibility with the patriarchal division of traditional gendered behaviors:

> When it no longer, as it were, suits capitalism that there be two antithetical, mutually exclusive genders, the patriarchal demand for belief in them is undermined. If contemporary capitalism needs, in addition to security of production, a technology of consumption

> together with the legitimation of desire, it is fair comment that the differentiation of bodies by sex is increasingly irrelevant. (p. 26)

According to Alexander (2003), "masculinity is no longer defined by what a man produces, as in Kimmel's discussion of Marketplace Manhood, but instead by what he consumes" (p. 551). Ehrenreich (1983) argued more than 20 years ago that men began to use consumption as a form of rebellion against an increasingly bureaucratic workforce that viewed them solely as "mere earning mechanisms" (p. 6) for families. Holt and Thompson (2003) argue that men who consume are never "above suspicion that [they] are on a quest to compensate" (p. 425) for their masculine insecurities. Here, however, is the key concept: the cultural adage that "he who wins with the most toys" is no longer seen as compensating for a lack of masculinity; it is part and parcel of being masculine in contemporary society.

The shift from masculinity as a producing and providing role to a consumer role is nowhere more apparent than in *Queer Eye*. The research on masculinity has generally argued that traditional hegemonic masculinity has been marked in five ways: "(1) physical force and control, (2) occupational achievement, (3) familial patriarchy, (4) frontiersmanship, and (5) heterosexuality" (Trujillo, 1991, p. 291), but in *Queer Eye* each of these attributes of traditional masculinity gets a capitalism-sponsored makeover.

The archetype of the masculinity emerging in *Queer Eye* differs from these categories in several ways. In this series, manhood is equated with vanity consumption and labor and a fluency in a wide variety of class-inflected taste categories. Ultimately, this idealized manhood is centered on the consumption of beauty and hygiene products and services, extravagant foods, high-end couture, expensive furniture, and involvement in high culture.

For the emerging metrosexual, the quest for physical perfection replaces the need for brute force. Sheer physicality and the need to physically dominate women or other men is never mentioned as a desirable trait by the fab five, instead they focus on contouring the body through spray-on tanning and teaching these men to sculpt their physiques in the gym for cosmetic purposes, not strength. The body that ceases to be built as a form of armor, as Bordo (1999) suggests, functions to challenge the cultural gaze. The male body in *Queer Eye* is built to be looked at by women and gay men. The straight man's comfort with being looked at by gay men and women as desirable reflects his new found confidence and strength. In *Queer Eye*, it gives his agency a boost instead of objectifying him.

Occupational achievement is not eliminated but is signified through the conspicuous performance of a high level of taste literacy. Admittedly, a large amount of money would be required to maintain these performances, but the men must have sufficient leisure time to engage in home decorating, cooking gourmet meals, enjoying fine wines and liquors, and shopping for the right tea for every occasion. It alters the breadwinner model's focus on working hard to feed one's family to working hard to make enough money to afford more expensive leisure. In this formulation, occupational achievement is no longer limitedto the workplace; it is also dependent on a working knowledge of gourmet cooking, design principles, bartending, a wide variety of dance styles, and chemical engineering. It is a tacit acknowledgement that the line between leisure and labor is increasingly blurred, if indeed, it has ever been separate.

The work of being masculine in the home has traditionally been limited to ruling the roost and performing manual tasks. However, with consumer masculinity, familial patriarchy no longer consists of exerting control over women and children and serving as the sole breadwinner. *Queer Eye*'s metrosexual is expected to be an attentive and understanding partner who recognizes women as equals. Additionally, he must also contribute to the maintenance of the household and the rearing of children. Indeed, at the beginning of every *Queer Eye*, it is the men who are blamed for the disastrous living conditions that the fab five invariably arrive to find, regardless of the presence of a romantic partner or grown children.

The frontiersman is replaced with a dapper, dashing man about town who sings to his wife, knows how to handle himself at high-class urban events, and takes time to enjoy a day at the spa. Out with the Marlboro Man of the 1960s, and in with the sensitive, less misogynist everyday James Bond. The challenge to societal order that the rebellious male symbolized has been discarded as a threat to the sophisticated, affluent lifestyle that consumer masculinity requires. Indeed, nonmetropolitan locations are antithetical to the metrosexual. He is confined to urban locations where his aesthetician, tanning salon, and wine steward are only a taxi ride away. The only time he braves the elements is to treat his romantic interest to a picnic in the park.

Heterosexuality, however, is not replaced as the core of hegemonic masculinity. Even with John, a sensitive, good-looking man who was in touch with his feminine side, we are positioned to understand that he is getting fixed up to propose to his girlfriend. Thus, marriage, the ultimate signifier of heterosexuality (for now), assures us that he may be in the process of being queered, but deep down he is 100% heterosexual. However, heterosexuality in *Queer Eye* is changed in one highly significant way: it cannot be homophobic. Instead, although we are constantly reminded of the fab five's sexual identities, the straight guy must remain comfortable with homosexuality without questioning his own heterosexuality except in a humorous way. Kimmel (2003) argued that traditional masculinity has, as its "central organizing principle," a reliance on homophobia (p. 127). For Kimmel,

> Homophobia is the fear that other men will unmask us, emasculate us, reveal to us and the world that we do not measure up, that we are not real men. We are afraid to let other men see that fear ... we are ashamed to be afraid ... The fear of being a sissy dominates the cultural definitions of manhood. (pp. 127–128)

Remarkably, as the idealized, straight, White masculinity is finally being revealed as marked, socially constructed, and difficult to attain, he is expected to relinquish the fear of being perceived as weak. The adoption of metrosexuality by self-identified heterosexual men erases the imagined line between gay and straight male gender performances and results in straight men not only not fearing being perceived as gay, but enjoying their ambiguous position:

> While some metrosexuals may simply be indulging in pursuits they had avoided for fear of being suspected as gay, like getting a pedicure or wearing brighter colors—others consciously appropriate tropes of gay culture the way white suburban teenagers have long cribbed from hip-hop culture, as a way of distinguishing themselves from the pack. Having others question their sexuality is all part of the game.
>
> "Wanting them to wonder and having them wonder is a wonderful thing," said Daniel Peres, the editor in chief of *Details*, a kind of metrosexual bible. "It gives you an air of mystery: could he be?

It makes you stand out." (St. John, 2003, pp. 16–17)

To observe the ideological reaction of this blurring, one merely has to turn to reality television series such as *Boy Meets Boy* and *Playing it Straight*. Both of these shows revolve around a lone contestant's (James and Jackie, respectively) attempt to choose a potential mate from a pool of mixed heterosexual and homosexual men without knowing who is playing for which sexual side. These tests of "gaydar," which the official *Playing it Straight* Web site defines as "the intuitive sense that enables someone to identify whether another person is gay," reveal the growing discomfort with blurring lines of homo and hetero performances of masculinity. For gay people, the possibility of gaydar constitutes a sort of double-edged sword, in which locating community or potential mates may be easier, but gay people become identified by a set of characteristics that constrain the multiplicity of gay identities.

This blurring of gay and straight provides an opportunity to study contemporary gender dynamics. Connell (1992) argues that we must "explore how gender operates for those men most vehemently defined as unmasculine: how masculinity is constructed for them, how homosexual and heterosexual masculinities interact, and how homosexual men experience and respond to change in the gender order" (p. 737).

Donaldson (1993) argues that gay men always challenge the norms of hegemonic masculinity while failing to achieve it because masculinity is based on homophobia and the exclusion of femininity. However, research into how gay men who distinguish themselves as straight-acting actually construct masculine identities has remained relatively limited. The seminal study of gay masculinities is Connell's (1992) "A Very Straight Gay." Connell argues that gay men encounter hegemonic masculinity in their normal life development, but as they come to recognize a sexual desire for men, they are forced to develop masculine identities that compensate for the distance from hegemonic masculinity that their homosexuality produces.

What is interesting about the *Queer Eye* depiction of masculinity is the ways in which its straight men are expected to adjust their masculinity to the queer model of the fab five and thus distance themselves from traditional masculinity by replicating a form of imposed gayness. Previous formulations of masculine identity formation have assumed that heterosexual masculinity may inform gay masculinities, but the lived product of the incorporation of heteromasculine ideals resulted in a completely different product through its deconstruction and recombination. According to Fejes (2000),

> Gay males draw upon the various texts of heterosexual masculinity as the basis for the construction of their own identities, yet the end product is not simply a distorted mirror image of heterosexual masculinity. Rather the product is a deconstruction and recombination of its elements, reconfigured in such a way as to produce a multiplicity of identities— from the hyper-macho leather daddy to the effeminate, yet powerfully dominant drag queen—whose meanings are very different from that of heterosexual masculinity and which cannot be simply "read-off" or "read-against" the heterosexual masculine text. (p. 114)

This deconstruction and reidealization of the straight masculinity, in the form of clone, muscleman, and frat boy, have resulted in these performances in the gay community being depicted as a form of gay parody. Here, the performance of a heteromasculinity, without excess or camp, parodies and challenges the heteromasculine associations of these traits. This process of parody goes one step further in *Queer Eye*. Instead of gay men drawing on heterosexual masculinity, heterosexual men are imitating the idealized masculinity created by the advertising agency. But in the imitation of the queer guys, it is a metrosexual consumption masculinity, which openly rejects an overt, aggressive masculinity, but still relies on notions of urbane refinement, class, and taste.

Instead of the heterosexual man being the assumed audience for all products not specifically aimed at women or a marginalized group, he is now being targeted based on a set of expected characteristics. Thus, *Queer Eye* helps to create a need for men to adapt their gender performances to the consumer model created just for them. Consequently, the struggle over the definition of hegemonic masculinity is one that is waged between the conditions of capitalism that seek to transform it into a consumer model and those who seek to preserve the traditional masculine model. However, the labeling of this new masculine aesthetic as gay or queer obscures the role of contemporary capitalism in its construction and obscures the ways in which the perceived feminization of American men has been scapegoated as spurring a crisis of masculinity that has led to a variety of societal ills ranging from an increased emotional instability in men to the horrific events in Columbine.

In actuality, the increased emphasis on male consumption is spurred by marketers who salivate at the prospect of using the market-driven gay aesthetic to capitalize on an emerging type of heterosexual man. Just as advertisers have learned to tailor their advertisements to appeal to attitudes traditionally associated with homosexuality to exploit the buying power of homosexuals, they can be seen here attempting to create a consumer masculinity, or metrosexual, just as they helped to construct a hegemonic depiction of gay identity.

Analysis of *Queer Eye*'s brand of consumer masculinity is only one path to understanding the ways in which it is being contested in contemporary culture. It would be naïve to assume that everyone would unquestioningly buy the masculinity that *Queer Eye* is selling. The next section discusses gay and straight media and the StraightActing.com member's responses to *Queer Eye*.

RESPONSES TO *QUEER EYE*

The obviousness of *Queer Eye*'s textual reconstruction of heteromasculinity makes it an easy place to look for backlash against the consumer masculinity. Seemingly subversive *South Park* recently featured *Queer Eye*'s fab five as villains:

> In the episode, Stan, Kyle, Kenny and Carman turn metrosexual—trading their hooded jackets for tight T-shirts and gelled hair. At first their mothers and the women in general take a liking to this change in appearance and attitude. However, as things progress, they come to notice the dark underside of this fad. The men of South Park have become so concerned with making it to the next shoe sale and keeping up their fabulous look that they stop paying attention and lose sight of their own masculinity. The metrosexualization of the show's male population provides an opening for a group of effeminate alien creatures called Crab People, who then proceed to try and take over the planet. (Finn, 2004, ¶ 3)

In this episode, the fab five are actually "Crab People" in disguise who deliberately feminize men so that they will be unable to defend the world from invasion. In this instance, the fear of changing

male roles is decidedly conspicuous. Finn (2004) goes on to note that

> there is something decidedly unnatural about this new trend … it alters standard male behavior and propels male narcissism to new heights. … As a result, guys stop gazing in admiration of female beauty and become fixated on themselves. (¶ 4)

This, he argues, is a "dead-end on the road to rediscovering a healthy masculinity" (¶ 4), which he claims is necessary to deter a potential invasion from Crab People. Although this last sentence may be tongue in cheek, it reveals the ways in which some men (and some women) view the necessity of a particularized form of male masculinity, despite the fact that it is dependent on the objectification of women and relies on antiquated notions of a natural and prediscursive masculinity that is somehow magically attached to the male body.

Karl du Fresne (2004), of the *Nelson Mail*, argues that to find out why this generation of men has "lost confidence in their masculinity" (p. 15), one should look no further than *Queer Eye*. Indeed, he blames television for a "sustained assault" on "traditional 'maleness'" that is epitomized in the "celebration of homosexual culture," which results in men who are "confused about their sexual identities" (¶ 21–22). Thus, du Fresne equates the changing masculinity with destroying a perceived natural boundary between heterosexuality and homosexuality and, in turn, conflating sexuality and gender and re-inscribing a traditional male gender performance.

Some critics claim that the blurring of gay and straight by the evolving metrosexual consumer masculinity is a symptom of the current crisis of American masculinity. This conservative scare tactic has been widely used to demonize the women's movements and lesbian and gay rights movements and attempt to reaffirm traditional heterosexual masculinity and privilege. Although these critics tend to work for non-gay-oriented media, the contestation of this new masculinity can also be observed in gay media where *Queer Eye* has elicited widely divergent responses.

Al Rantel, a conservative but openly gay radio personality, argues that the public is "turned off by the 'really queenie [*sic*] quality that these guys have'" and believes that "a lot of people are secretly offended by it" (Lowry, 2003, p. C6). Rantel contends, "gay people dress just as badly as anybody else" (Lowry, 2003, p. C6). Conversely, gay-rights activist John Aravosis argues that these stereotypes are no longer harmful because "we're being presented as the person you wish you could have as your neighbor" (Lowry, 2003, p. C6). Aravosis may be right; these men do embrace many stereotypes about gay men that seem to construct gay male identity as affluent, witty, funny, and attractive. Accordingly, gay academic media critic Kylo-Patrick Hart (2004) argues that *Queer Eye* "consistently offers the most positive representation of gay men" (p. 242) to date because the fab five are gay men who are represented as being superior to straight men. Hart concludes that although some may suggest that *Queer Eye* feminizes gay men,

> this is certainly not the case. The widespread perception that it does so, however, contributes to the show's radically subversive potential: it appears to offer only images of gay men that are non-threatening to heterosexual viewers while at the same time it is bombarding those same viewers with representations implicitly suggesting that gay men are actually superior—rather than inferior—to heterosexuals. (p. 246)

However, Rantel is correct to fear the reduction of gay men to one essential type, which Hart (2000) has previously argued that television producers must take care to avoid. Thus, critics must continuously analyze mediated images of homosexuality to assess the diversity of genders and sexualities being depicted because some people may form their opinions about gay people based on televisual representations. Conservative ideologue Pat Buchanan (2003), in arguing that one of the goals of gay-themed shows is "social subversion, the breaking down of taboos" (p. 26), recognizes the influence of increased representation of gays and lesbians on reality television.

Here, Buchanan's (2003) statement reveals an ideologically conservative response to an ambiguous message. It is not necessarily the content of the series that Buchanan fears, but it is the potential effect that these representations will have on society. Buchanan's fear is that these representations will lead to a societal shift in attitudes toward homosexuality. Yet his assumption here is that those who consume these images are actually those for whom homosexuality is still a social taboo. Buchanan seems to share Hart's (2004) assumption that this text is potentially a subversive influence on an imagined audience who can be influenced toward greater acceptance of homosexuality. Although Buchanan (2003) and Hart (2004) seem to represent ideologically divergent positions, they ultimately fail to consider the target audience of the series. It is difficult to assume that a show about five gay men making over a straight man would have ever been targeted at a homophobic demographic, no matter how stripped of sexuality the characters may be. Indeed, it is possible that the marketing of *Queer Eye* to a primarily heterosexual audience on NBC, in addition to Bravo's gay-friendly and gay audience, merely offers them new and more acceptable homosexual representations to obscure their own dominance and assuage any concerns about their own homophobia.

The contemporary political climate illustrates a viewing public who are still uneasy with homosexuality, especially when it comes to marriage and other civil rights, but who have little trouble accepting particular forms of male homosexuality when confined to stereotypically traditional representations. It is possible that *Queer Eye* functions to reassure those heterosexual viewers who identify as socially progressive about homosexuality that the popularity of *Queer Eye* relieves them of any guilt about their own homophobia. Hart (2004) suggests that *Queer Eye* positions gay men as superior to straight men. The straight viewer's acceptance of their superiority, although limited to specific areas of expertise, may prove to themselves and the general public that they are not homophobic. In essence, the gay men of *Queer Eye* may function as the proverbial Black friend that racists claim to prove they are not in fact racist. Furthermore, the relative absence of homophobia in the show assures viewers that the struggle for civil rights for gay men and lesbians are merely symbolic and do not reflect a fear of material consequences.

Hart's (2004) analysis of *Queer Eye* is uncharacteristically optimistic about its potentially subversive power. In his rush to label the show subversive, he forgets that not all readers will negotiate the same meanings that he has in his textual analysis, and he completely ignores the gendered context of the show. This show is about making better heterosexual men. Indeed, Hart's reading of the text seems to stretch the imagination of other readers. For instance, he argues that when Carson humorously quips that people believe he looks like Ellen Degeneres, it reveals "how ludicrous it is for individuals to suggest that gay men look like women" (Hart, 2004, p.247). Although I agree with much of Hart's analysis—the show is highly enjoyable and may position gay men as superior to straight men in certain respects—I

do not agree with many of the ways that he reads the text as subversive. Carson's actual resemblance to Ellen Degeneres does not undermine any assumption about gay men looking like women; it is funny because Carson does actually look a bit like Degeneres. Carson is funny because he is often the victim of his own scathing wit. Indeed, it is the ability to laugh at these men that many may find appealing. Regardless, Hart's analysis represents only one set of readings, albeit an optimistic and celebratory one. In the remainder of this analysis, I discuss the ways in which Hart's overwhelmingly positive response is not shared by some other gay men.

STRAIGHTACTING.COM AND *QUEER EYE*

The struggle over this emerging masculinity has not been limited to heterosexual men. Analysis of the bulletin board posts of a group of straight-acting gay men reveals an array of conservative and conflicted perspectives on *Queer Eye*'s masculine representations. The discussion topic about *Queer Eye* contains many comments about how the fab five are highly stereotypical characters who not only do not represent the members of the forum but also represent the continuing symbolic annihilation (although not their language) of straight-acting gay men through the repetition of iconic gay stereotypes. Stevestr, a highly opinionated participant in this particular discussion group, argued "it appears Bravo found the most stereotypical fags in each of the fields represented. If that is not blatant patronizing then what is?" Indeed, a careful analysis of the series itself, coupled with at least a passing knowledge of male hairdressers on virtually any makeover show, would support the idea that Kyan (grooming) is not the "most stereotypical fag" in the hairdressing profession, as Stevestr would suggest. Indeed, even in this posting, not all agree, and another poster, Olympicnut, argued that Carson (fashion) is the only one "over the top."

Although this is but one example, the following discussion of these men's readings of *Queer Eye* suggests that they do not see the series as the subversive text that Hart (2004) argued it could be. Instead, these men read these performances as abnormal, suggesting that even though diversity may exist, only certain performances are acceptable to the members of this group. Specifically, these discussions revealed the belief of its members that the straight-acting gay man is not being adequately represented in *Queer Eye* and that the fab five are themselves bad representations of gay men.

TomMichigan argued the following:

> It indeed *did* perpetuate the stereotype that all gay guys are flaming fags, that part of the show I most definitely DID NOT like. Most of the "gays" represented in the mainstream media are the flamers, not regular guys. … SO in readjusting my opinion a bit, I'd say it was fun and entertaining, to a point, but disgusting because it was about the kind of gay guys I can't stand.

Again, a broader analysis of existing televisual depictions of gay men reveals a range of gay characters that does include some that this group would most likely accept as straight acting, including David and Keith on *Six Feet Under*, Ben and Dave on *Queer as Folk*, Carter on *Spin City*, and the subtly named Butch on *Normal, Ohio*. Ironically, Will from *Will & Grace* was criticized in the first three seasons by many gay activists for not being gay enough. My point, here, however, is not to prove the men of StraightActing.com wrong, but to illustrate the defensive nature with which they treat gay representations. They seem to equate better representations for gay men with representation of gay men as straight acting (i.e., less feminine or flamboyant) and with increased representations of gay men as "normal" guys. They ignore the ways in which the normal guys they see as straight acting are being redefined by the consumer masculinity of *Queer Eye* and focus solely on the performances of the gay men.

As TomMichigan noted above, only "flamers," whom he cannot stand, are represented, not "regular guys."

JS noted,

> Those guys are annoying as hell! Where did they find them on a Greenwhich [*sic*] Village Ricki Lake episode? I watched (actually suffered though) a half hour of it and had to turn it off. Still waiting for something to portray less nelly guys. … Maybe they're too boring to bring in cash for the networks?

adem_NYC agreed saying,

> Another femmy image of gay men. I didn't care for it at all. It generalizes all gay men, just like a lot of TV programs. … No offense to those of who enjoyed it, but I was put off and offended by the show, because that is the way everyone thinks gay men are supposed to act. If this show exemplifies how far we've gotten then "we" haven't gotten very far. The gay men involved with putting this garbage on TV shouldn't be praised, they're only keeping the stereotypes alive and well.

These statements, although positioning specific gender performance as desirable, also reveal an ongoing theme in these discussions best illustrated by Stevestr,

Someone who still remembers this site is called straightacting.com. Its [*sic*] impressive so many of you like a show so full of stereotypes it can send us back about 30 or 40 years. One episode of the painfully clear "Yes we're Bravo and yes we are painfully obviously catering to the 5 gay viewers we have" show was enough for me. I can imagine a straight couple now: Oh look hunny [*sic*] those silly fags are on TV again. See fags are weird. All they do is lisp, dress badly, go shopping, cook overpriced food, and furnish rooms so gaudy their own mothers wouldn't live in them. ... For those who thought the 5 gay guys were not bad?!? Well, I better not say.

To which megatron266 disagreed,

I totally disagree. Entertainment is just that. Entertainment. A way for people to relax and enjoy something other than sex or reading a book. Now watching a show that shows a few queens does not make us any less straight acting. That is like to say if a straight guy watched a chick flik and people started saying he was turning into a girl just because he saw a chick flik. Frankly I see nothing wrong with having this show on. I don't see it as a step backwards. I see it as a step forwards. We are entering the houses of the ones who hate us just by using satellite signals. How freakin smart is that. I would be like "these people are smart. These deadbolts don't work anymore." "Maybe we should listen to what they got to say." If it weren't for those "Silly Fags" then we wouldn't be where we are now. Those "Silly Fags"

got us noticed and they wouldn't back down for anybody. IF anything, I think they deserve a pat on the back for doing what they did in the past and what they still are doing. If every gay man in the world were straight acting then we would not have the little rights we have now. Because nobody would have known where to find us since we blend in with the straight guys.

Blackmet also argues,

I remember one of the guys saying in *Time* something along the lines of "if culture wants to stereotype me as someone who's stylish and can make a great some-kind-of-fancy-food, who am I to complain?" When you look at it that way, it's not as awful as it could be, I suppose.

Yet Stevestr argues,

no one wants to watch a show about fags that shows them as normal. Hell they could go next door and watch the straight dude watching a football game and drinking a beer. The drama of flamboyant queens is what brings in ratings and Bravo knows it. What is sad is when gay men themselves continue to support these so called good gay TV shows.

He continued later, in response to megatron266:

It's very damaging when the wrong signals are being sent across the satellite. If the gay community is so inclusive they need to start including some more of their straighter brethren instead of always playing to the media stereotype of a flaming queen … thanks for taking the time to at least state your views Willy. I'm not attacking you personally, I just want you to try and explore a bit beyond what the "gay community" has fed to you over the years and encouraged you to believe. You should never live life as a clone.

In one broad sweep, Stevestr acknowledges the potential role of these mediated images in constructing a hegemonic gay identity. Yet in his dismissal of the clone, he ignores the ways in which his own masculinity has been constructed. He urges this man to abandon the gay community's teaching and turn to the heteronormative community from which most men learn their own masculinity. Indeed, the real clone in this situation could be Stevestr, who has adhered to the conventional standards of masculinity and not challenged the dominant regime of gender and sexuality. Yet ironically, the masculinity being "fed" to straight men in *Queer Eye* has been modeled on the advertiser's model of gay men. Eventually, the straight men of *Queer Eye* may epitomize the same straight-acting masculinity that the men of this forum idolize.

Steverstr concluded, "I'm being exploited as a straight appearing gay man and I refuse to give endorsement to the view that all fags are lispy queens." This comment from Stevestr (as well as other members, some gay activists and some critical media scholars) seems to call for more "positive" portrayals of gay men and lesbians. Such demands for the different representations signal a new and insidious type of internalized homophobia and illustrate the pervasive ideological dominance of hegemonic masculinity and heteronormativity. As Brookey's (1996) analysis has suggested, many of these positive portrayals of homosexuality are positive only because homosexuality has been discarded. Here, it is straight-acting gay men who color their own identities as the only legitimate shade of gay

identity and enact a type of discursive violence on those who do not conform to their assumptions of gay masculinity. In turn, these assumptions are tinted by the normative assumptions of the heterosexual society about what behaviors constitute men. Although Stevestr's concerns about a media representation of gay male identities as a unified, monolithic identity, it is his pejorative labeling of the particular mediated identity as "flaming" and "lispy queens" that is particularly problematic. Additionally, Stevestr attempts to blame the gay community for promoting a feminized gay identity without acknowledging the relative lack of power that gay people have in deciding which identities are represented. Finally, Stevestr's comments reflect a lack of critical awareness of the straight masculinity that is being produced in *Queer Eye*. The show clearly blurs the line between gay and straight male gender performance, but not by making the gay men seem to be like straight men, but by making the straight men more like gay men and ultimately less like the straight-acting gay men. Ultimately, it may be more difficult for these straight-acting gay men to actually identify as straight as the economy increasingly models straight masculinity on a gay market model.

The hierarchical nature of hegemonic masculinity encourages gay men and lesbians to turn against each other in a battle for position. Nardi (2000) has argued that this focus on hypermasculinity in the gay community has resulted in a divide among gay men seeking the power and acceptance that (hegemonic) masculinity offers those who embody it, those gay men who have embraced femininity or who cannot attain the masculine ideal, and those gay men who reject the quest for masculinity.

These discussions of supposedly straight-acting men about the power of representation obscure the fundamental assumption link between men passing as straight and access to male privilege. JS argued,

Just a thought, maybe if they really need nelly drama queens to bring in viewers and ratings, can't they at least have one (or a few) non-stereotypical gay guys? I think that would help a lot with our "image" as the general public would see it and say "He's gay? I thought gay guys were all girly acting … I guess I was wrong! There really are gay guys out there who act like guys!"

Indeed, the notion that men have a specific set of behaviors that marks them as guys is especially problematic, for in their calls for inclusion these men focus on inclusion for those men who adhere to the traditional and perhaps conventional expectations of male behavior. In this discussion group, these particular men want to see a change in the ways gay men are represented. They are angered by the seeming focus on feminine gay characters and want to shift the focus to gay men who act just like normal heterosexual men, thus returning feminine gay men to a closet of symbolic annihilation. Indeed, they want to return to the privileged position of seeming to be just like heterosexual men so that they can assume some of the power that this position entails.

Butler (1993) suggests that the idea of homosexuality as a copy or inauthentic derivative of heterosexuality is problematic. To Butler, without homosexuality, heterosexuality would be without something to define itself against; thus, without the existence of homosexuality, it would be impossible to delineate what types of gender performances were considered heterosexual. Indeed, as homosexuality needs heterosexuality to define itself, it appears that straightness needs the oppositional concept of gayness to exist. Here, the very binaries that Butler critiques are recreated. According to Butler,

Gender is a kind of imitation for which there is no original; in fact, it is a kind of imitation that produces the very notion of the original as an effect and consequence of the imitation itself. In other words, the naturalistic effects of heterosexualized genders are produced through imitative strategies; what they imitate is an effect. In this sense, the "reality" of heterosexual identities is perfomatively constituted through an imitation that sets itself up as the origin and ground of all imitations. In other words, heterosexuality is always in the process of imitating and approximating its own phantasmatic idealization of itself—and failing. (p. 313)

Thus, the straight-acting gay men and *Queer Eye* straight guys are not copies, but constitute "inverted imitations, ones which invert the order of imitated and imitation, and which, in the process, expose the fundamental dependency of 'the origin' on which it claims to produce as its secondary effect" (Butler, 1993, pp. 313–314). Here, then, the question of whether gay men who identify as or fetishize straight-acting men are attempting to be heterosexual is moot, for heterosexuality has no claim to the emerging consumer masculinity because it is neither origin nor copy. It is not a gay masculinity that is modeled by straight men, nor is it a straight masculinity that has been appropriated by gay men. It is an example of the ways in which the capitalist system produces gendered bodies to fulfill its need for consumption.

Although the men of StraightActing.com certainly have the right to defend their own traditionally masculine identities, a defense that comes at the expense of other masculine performances reveals the ways in which even gay men actively compete for position in the masculine hierarchy and obscures the role of economic forces in shaping these identities. Furthermore, this discourse legitimates a cultural understanding of gayness that is conservative and only slightly more inclusive than the dogmatic beliefs of the conservative right. Although these men do challenge the traditional understanding of masculinity as antithetical to homosexuality, they still reinscribe their attempts at traditional masculinity as the only acceptable option.

If we return to Pat Buchanan's (2003) statement that the role of gay characters in reality television is to facilitate the "breaking down of taboos" (p. 26) we find a conservative leader bemoaning the potential power that these images may have over audiences. Here, we can assume that he is discussing the breakdown of taboos among a heterosexual audience, who may still view homosexuality as deviant. These straight-acting gay men, such as Stevestr, fear the ways in which these same heterosexual viewers will come to understand all gay men as "silly fags" who overconsume. Although it is unlikely that people who still consider homosexuality taboo will watch *Queer Eye*, it is quite likely that Buchanan is right about one thing. The purpose of these shows is about media power, but the power he should be concerned about is the power of the capitalist system to reshape gender norms, for better or worse. Pat Buchanan, the popular media, academic critics, and the members of StraightActing.com all fail to consider the ways this show is working to change the definition of hegemonic masculinity. This could be especially problematic for the StraightActing.com members who seem to idealize a heterosexual masculinity that is being changed by capitalism and who will be left fighting for an obsolete masculinity that continues to define their own identities as subordinate.

CONCLUSION

In *Queer Eye*, it appears that heteronormative masculinity is indeed being challenged, but in a way that reidealizes American manhood as one that is predicated on effete style and taste and mandates a visually upper-class identity as a key component of hegemonic masculinity. This reidealized masculinity potentially serves to reposition White, urban, heterosexual masculinity as normative and dominant. It is a masculinity that attempts to replace the idealized gay male image in the media with one that is improved, if only for its heterosexuality and sexual desirability to women. Hart (2004) argues that *Queer Eye* is the most positive representation of gay men on television to date; however, his haste to declare the show positive obscures the ways in which *Queer Eye* represents a particular place for homosexuality and its assumed access to style. The men of *Queer Eye* are likable, knowledgeable, humorous, and accurately represent a fraction of gay male gender identity. They also represent a potentially dangerous capitulation to a market-driven masculinity that depends on high levels of consumption.

It appears that the gay men who hated the show and even those who enjoyed the show, but were opposed to these characterizations of gay men, supported traditional masculinity. These men regarded straight masculinity as unproblematic, and instead of considering the role of the market in manufacturing a particular masculinity, they homophobically lashed out at the feminization of all gay men in the media. These men did not read *Queer Eye* as a positive representation because of the fab five's apparent failure to embody traditional masculinity, and these men extrapolated their concerns about these gender performances to concerns about all gay identities. The discourses of StraightActing.com remind us of the ongoing assimilationist and liberationist tensions in gay communities. Although some radical gay activists claim that assimilationists seek the acceptance of some homosexuals by making them seem normal, or "regular," as TomMichigan said, this normality is simply the emulation of heteromasculine behavior. Although the existence of straight-acting gay men certainly challenges the heterosexual male assumption of masculinity, these gay men, ironically, valorized traditional hetero-masculinity as a necessary component of all male identities. However, in this instance, their rejection of *Queer Eye*'s consumer masculinity is an active rejection of the market forces that conspire to change the look and feel of contemporary hegemonic masculinity. The men of StraightActing.com simultaneously reject the evolving consumer masculinity and support a conservative gender ideology that denies gay men the male privilege that their online community attempts to reclaim.

This analysis demonstrates how these straight-acting men read *Queer Eye* far less positively than Hart (2004) did and questions the notion that any unified gay audience can be assumed for any programming, even the most seemingly gay friendly. Furthermore, as these gay men resist both the construction of straight masculinity as consumer masculinity because, ironically, it was too gay, they simultaneously reject what they see as limited representation of gay men for the lack of traditionally masculine performances for the potential influence that they fear will warp heterosexual audiences. Thus, these men seem to be situated squarely between an emerging masculinity that is based in feminine consumption and a traditional masculinity that is based in homophobia and misogyny. The challenge, then, is to develop a sound critique of these competing forms of masculinity and create space for alternative masculinities while challenging capitalism's need to create gendered identities that are based in consumption.

NOTES

1. From this point, I will use straight-acting gay men without quotations in deference to the labels that many of these men have chosen for themselves. I understand that not all members of this community label themselves straight acting, but recognize that the concept of straight acting is the unifying factor for this particular community, whether it is desire to be or desire for these performances.

2. I have attempted to present these postings in their original form, including emphasis, spelling and grammatical errors, and slang.

REFERENCES

Alexander, S. M. (2003). Stylish hard bodies: Branded masculinity in *Men's Health* magazine. *Sociological Perspectives, 46*, 535–554.

Bordo, S. (1999). *The male body.* New York: Farrar, Straus, and Giroux.

Brookey, R.A.(1996). A community like Philadelphia. *Western Journal of Communication, 60*, 40–57.

Buchanan, P. (2003). Pushing the limits of reality TV. *Human Events, 59*, 26–27.

Butler, J. (1993). Imitation and gender insubordination. In H. Abelove, M. A. Barale, & D. M. Halperin (Eds.), *The lesbian and gay studies reader* (pp. 307–320). New York: Routledge.

Cloud, D. L. (1998). The rhetoric of "family values": Scapegoating, utopia and the privatization of social responsibility. *Western Journal of Communication, 62*, 387–410.

Connell, R. W. (1987). *Gender and power: Society, the person and sexual politics.* Palo Alto, CA: Stanford University Press. Connell, R. W. (1992). A very straight gay: Masculinity, homosexual experience, and the dynamics of gender. *American Sociological Review, 57*(6), 735–751.

Donaldson, M. (1993). What is hegemonic masculinity? *Theory and Society, 22*(5), 643–657.

du Fresne, K. (2004, March 10). Straight path back to manhood. *Nelson Mail*, p. 15.

Ehrenreich, B. (1983). *The hearts of men: American dreams and the flight from commitment.* Garden City, NY: Doubleday.

Fejes, F. (2000). Making a gay masculinity. *Critical Studies in Media Communication, 17*(1), 113–116.

Finn, B. A. (2004, March 25). Metrosexualizing our identity. *Harvard Crimson.* Available from http://www.thecrimson.com

Hart, K. P. R. (2000). Representing gay men on American television. *Journal of Men's Studies, 9,* 59–82.

Hart, K. P. R. (2004). We're here, we're queer—and we're better than you: The representational superiority of gay men to heterosexuals on *Queer Eye for the Straight Guy. Journal of Men's Studies, 12,* 241–253.

Holt, D. B., & Thompson, C. J. (2003). Man-of-action heroes: The pursuit of heroic masculinity in everyday consumption. *Journal of Consumer Research, 31*(2), 425–440.

Kimmel, M.S.(2003). Masculinity as homophobia: Fear, shame, and silence in the construction of gender identity. In T. E. Ore (Ed.), *The social construction of difference and inequality* (pp. 119–135). Boston: McGraw-Hill.

Lowry, B. (2003). Queer eye exposure a worry for some gays. *Los Angeles Times*, p. C6.

Mackinnon, K. (1997). *Uneasy pleasures: The male as erotic object.* London: Cygnus Arts.

Nardi, P. (2000). Anything for sis, Mary: An introduction to gay masculinities. In P. Nardi (Ed.), *Gay masculinities* (pp. 1–11). London: Sage.

St. John, W. (2003, June 22). Metrosexuals come out. *New York Times*, p. 9(1).

Trujillo, N. (1991). Hegemonic masculinity on the mound: Media representations of Nolan Ryan and American sports culture. *Critical Studies in Mass Communication, 8,* 290–308.

Jay Clarkson is an assistant professor of electronic media at Indiana State University.

AUTHOR'S NOTE: *This article is dedicated to Leah R. Vande Berg.*

17 "Where Do You Want to Go Today?"

Cybernetic Tourism, the Internet, and Transnationality

By Lisa Nakamura

There is no race. There is no gender. There is no age. There are no infirmities. There are only minds. Utopia? No. The Internet.

—"Anthem,"
produced for MCI by Messner Vetere
Berger McNamee Schemetterer, 1997

The television commercial "Anthem" claims that on the Internet, there are no infirmities, no gender, no age—"only minds." This pure, democratic, cerebral form of communication is touted as a Utopia, a pure no-place where human interaction can occur, as the voice-over says, "uninfluenced by the rest of it." Yet can the "rest of it" be written out as easily as the word *race* is crossed out on the chalkboard by the hand of an Indian girl in this commercial?

It is "the rest of it," the specter of racial and ethnic difference and its visual and textual representation in print and television advertisements that appeared in 1997 for Compaq, IBM, and Origin that I will address in this chapter. The ads I will discuss all sell networking and communications technologies that depict racial difference, the "rest of it," as a visual marker. The spectacles of race in these advertising images are designed to stabilize contemporary anxieties that networking technology and access to cyberspace may break down ethnic and racial differences. These advertisements that promote the glories of cyberspace cast the viewer in the position of the tourist, and sketch out a future in which difference is either elided or put in its proper place.

I'd like to cite a striking example: the MCI advertisement sells not only MCI Internet services but also a particular kind of *content:* the idea that getting online and becoming part of a global network will liberate the user from the body with its inconvenient and limiting attributes such as race, gender, disability, and age. In a sense, it is positing a postcorporeal subjectivity, an afterimage of the body and of identity. Though "Anthem" illustrates this bracketing off of difference—racial, gendered, aged, and so on—particularly well, it is easy to find plenty of others from other technological discourses that reveal a similar sensibility, though perhaps not in as overt a way. This commercial is, however, unusually above board in its claims that telecommunications change the nature of identity.

The ironies in "Anthem" exist on several levels. For one, the advertisement positions MCI's commodity—"the largest Internet network in the world"—as a solution to social problems. This ad claims to produce a radical form of democracy that refers to and extends an "American" model of social equality and equal access. This patriotic anthem, however, is a paradoxical one: the visual images of diversity (old, young, black, white, deaf, etc.) are displayed and celebrated as spectacles of difference that the narrative simultaneously attempts to erase by claiming that MCI's product will reduce the different bodies that we see to "just minds."

The ad gestures toward a democracy founded upon disembodiment and uncontaminated by physical difference, but it must also showcase a dizzying parade of difference in order to make its point. Diversity is displayed as the sign of that which the product will eradicate. Its erasure and elision can only be understood in terms of its presence; like the word *race* on the chalkboard, it can only be crossed out if it is written or displayed. This ad writes race and poses it as both a beautiful spectacle and a vexing question. Its narrative describes a "postethnic America," to use David Hollinger's phrase, where these categories will be made not to count. The supposedly liberal and progressive tone of this ad camouflages its depiction of race as something to be eliminated, or made "not to count," through technology. If computers and networks can help us to communicate without "the rest of it," that residue of difference with its power to disturb, disrupt, and challenge, then we can all exist in a world "without boundaries."

A television commercial by AT&T that aired during the 1996 Olympics asks the viewer to "imagine a world without limits—AT&T believes communication can make it happen." Like "Anthem," this narrative posits a connection between networking and a democratic ethos in which differences will be elided. In addition, it resorts to a similar visual

strategy—it depicts a black man in track shorts leaping over the Grand Canyon.

Like many of the ads by high-tech and communications companies that aired during the Olympics, this one has an "international" or multicultural flavor that seemed to celebrate national and ethnic identities. This world without limits is represented by vivid and often sublime images of displayed ethnic and racial difference in order to bracket them off as exotic and irremediably "other." Images of this other as primitive, anachronistic, and picturesque decorate the landscape of these ads.

Microsoft's recent television and print media campaign markets access to personal computing and Internet connectivity by describing these activities as a form of travel. Travel and tourism, like networking technology, are commodities which define the privileged industrialized "first world" subject, and they situate him in the position of the one who looks, the one who has access, the one who communicates. Microsoft's omnipresent slogan "Where do you want to go today?" rhetorically places this consumer in the position of the user with unlimited choice; access to Microsoft's technology and networks promises the consumer a "world without limits" where he can possess an idealized mobility. Microsoft's promise to transport the user to new (cyber)spaces where desire can be fulfilled is enticing in its very vagueness, offering a seemingly open-ended invitation to travel and new experiences. A sort of technologically enabled transnationality is evoked here, but it is one that directly addresses the "first world" user, whose position on the network will allow him to metaphorically go wherever he likes.

This dream or fantasy of ideal travel common to networking advertisements constructs a destination that can look like an African safari, a trip to the Amazonian rain forest, or a camel caravan in the Egyptian desert. The iconography of the travelogue or tourist attraction in these ads places the viewer in the position of the tourist who, in Dean

FIGURE 4.1. Mesa (Compaq)

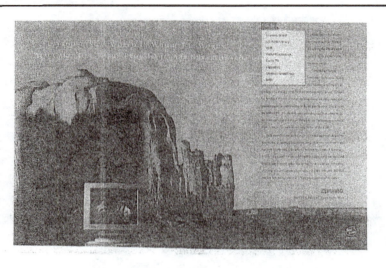

MacCannell's words, "simply collects experiences of difference (different people, different places)" and "emerges as a miniature clone of the old Western philosophical subject, thinking itself unified, central, in control, etc., mastering Otherness and profiting from it" (xv). Networking ads that promise the viewer control and mastery over technology and communications discursively and visually link this power to a vision of the other which, in contrast to the mobile and networked tourist/user, isn't going anywhere. The continued presence of stable signifiers of otherness in telecommunications advertising guarantees the Western subject that his position, wherever he may choose to go today, remains privileged.

An ad from Compaq (see fig. 4.1) that appeared in the *Chronicle of Higher Education* reads, "Introducing a world where the words 'you can't get there from here' are never heard." It depicts a sandstone mesa with the inset image of a monitor from which two schoolchildren gaze curiously at the sight. The ad is selling "Compaq networked multimedia. With it, the classroom is no longer a destination, it's a starting point." Like the Microsoft

and AT&T slogans, this one links networks with privileged forms of travel, and reinforces the metaphor by visually depicting sights that viewers associate with tourism. The networked classroom is envisioned as a glass window from which users can consume the sights of travel as if they were tourists.

Another ad from the Compaq series shows the same children admiring the rain forest from their places inside the networked classroom, signified by the frame of the monitor (see fig. 4.2). The tiny box on the upper righthand side of the image evokes the distinctive menu bar of a Windows product, and frames the whole ad for its viewer as a window onto an "other" world.

The sublime beauty of the mesa and the lush pastoral images of the rain forest are nostalgically quoted here in order to assuage an anxiety about the environmental effects of cybertechnology. In a world where sandstone mesas and rain forests are becoming increasingly rare, partly as a result of industrialization, these ads position networking as a benign, "green" type of product that will preserve the beauty of nature, at least as an image on the screen. As John Macgregor Wise puts it, this is

FIGURE 4.2. Rain Forest (Compaq)

part of the modernist discourse that envisioned electricity as "transcendent, pure and clean," unlike mechanical technology (n.p.). The same structures of metaphor that allow this ad to dub the experience of using networked communications "travel" also enables it to equate an image of a rain forest with Nature—with a capital N. The enraptured American schoolchildren, with their backpacks and French braids, are framed as user-travelers. With the assistance of Compaq, they have found their way to a world that seems to be without limits, one in which the images of Nature are as good as or better than the reality.

The virtually real rain forest and mesa participate in a postcyberspace paradox of representation—the locution *virtual reality* suggests that the line or limit between the authentic sight/site and its simulation has become blurred. This discourse has become familiar, and was anticipated by Jean Baudrillard

before the advent of the Internet. Familiar as it is, the Internet and its representations in media such as advertising have refigured the discourse in different contours. The ads that I discuss attempt to stabilize the slippery relationship between the virtual and the real by insisting upon the monolithic visual differences between "first" and "third world" landscapes and people.

This virtual field trip frames nature as a tourist sight and figures Compaq as the educational tour guide. In this post-Internet culture of simulation in which we live, it is increasingly necessary for stable, iconic images of nature and the other to be evoked in the world of technology advertising. These images guarantee and gesture toward the unthreatened and unproblematic existence of a destination for travel, a place whose natural beauties and exotic natives will somehow remain intact and attractive. If technology will indeed make everyone, everything,

FIGURE 4.3. Arab and Camel (IBM)

and every place the same, as "Anthem" claims in its ambivalent way, then where is there left to go? What is there left to see? What is the use of being asked where you want to go today if every place is just like here? Difference, in the form of exotic places or exotic people, must be demonstrated iconographically in order to shore up the Western user's identity as herself. As Caren Kaplan writes, "[C]reated out of increasing leisure time in industrialized nations and driven by a need to ascertain identity and location in a world that undermines the certainty of those categories, the tourist acts as an agent of modernity" (58). The tourist's need to reorient herself is made all the more pressing by the radically destabilizing effects of cyberspace, which blows older notions of "identity" and "location" out of the water. And as Caplan goes on to note, the links among modernity, travel, and colonialism are strong and of long standing.[1]

The idyllic image of an Arab on his camel, with the pyramids picturesquely squatting in the background, belongs in a coffee table book (see fig. 4.3). The timeless quality of this image of an exotic other untouched by modernity is disrupted by the cartoon dialogue text, which reads, "What

do you say we head back and download the results of the equestrian finals?" This dissonant use of contemporary, vernacular, American technoslang is supposed to be read comically; the man is meant to look unlike anyone who would speak these words.

This gap between the exotic otherness of the image and the familiarity of the American rhetoric can be read as more than an attempt at humor, however. IBM, whose slogan "Solution for a small planet" is contained in an icon button in the lower left-hand side of the image, is literally putting these incongruous words into the other's mouth, thus demonstrating the hegemonic power of its "high speed information network" to make the planet smaller by causing everyone to speak the *same* language—computerspeak. The Arab man's position as the exotic other must be emphasized and foregrounded in order for this strategy to work, for the image's appeal rests upon its evocation of the exotic. The rider's classical antique "look and feel" atop his Old Testament camel guarantee that his access to a high-speed network will not rob us, the tourists/viewers, of the spectacle of his difference. In the phantasmatic world of Internet advertising, he can download all the results he likes, so long as his visual appeal to us as viewers reassures us that we are still in the position of the tourist, the Western subject, whose privilege it is to enjoy him in all his anachronistic glory.

These ads claim a world without boundaries for us, the consumers and target audience, and by so doing they show us exactly where and what these boundaries are, and that is ethnic and racial. Rather than being effaced, these dividing lines are evoked repeatedly. In addition, the ads sanitize and idealize their depictions of the other and otherness by deleting all references that might threaten their status as timeless icons. In the camel image, the sky is an untroubled blue, the pyramids have fresh, clean, sharp outlines, and there are no signs whatsoever of pollution, roadkill, litter, or airborne warning and control systems.

Including these "real life" images in the advertisement would disrupt the picture it presents us of an other whose "unspoiled" qualities are so highly valued by tourists. Indeed, as Trinh Minh-ha notes, even very sophisticated tourists are quick to reject experiences that challenge their received notions of authentic otherness. Minh-ha writes, "The Third World representative the modern sophisticated public ideally seeks is the *unspoiled* African, Asian, or Native American, who remains more preoccupied with his/her image as the *real* native—the *truly different*—than with the issues of hegemony, feminism, and social change" (88). Great pains are taken in this ad to make the camel rider appear real, truly different from us, and "authentic" in order to build an idealized other whose unspoiled nature shores up the tourist's sense that he is indeed seeing the "real" thing. In the post-Internet world of simulation, "real" things are fixed and preserved in images such as these in order to anchor the Western viewing subject's sense of himself as a privileged and mobile viewer.

Since the conflicts of Mogadishu, Sarajevo, and Zaire (all images contained elsewhere in the magazines from which these ads came), ethnic difference in the world of Internet advertising is visually "cleansed" of its divisive, problematic, tragic connotations. The ads function as corrective texts for readers deluged with images of racial conflicts and bloodshed both at home and abroad. These advertisements put the world right; their claims for better living (and better boundaries) through technology are graphically acted out in idealized images of others who miraculously speak like "us" but still look like "them."

The Indian man pictured in an IBM print advertisement that appeared in January 1996, whose iconic Indian elephant gazes sidelong at the viewer as he affectionately curls his trunk around his owner's neck, has much in common with his Egyptian counterpart in the previous ad. (The ad's text tells us that his name is Sikander, making him somewhat less generic than his counterpart, but not much. Where is the last name?) The thematics of this series produced for IBM play upon the depiction of ethnic, racial, and linguistic differences, usually all at the same time, in order to highlight the hegemonic power of IBM's technology. IBM's television ads (there were several produced and aired in this same series in 1997) were memorable because they were all subtitled vignettes with Italian nuns, Japanese surgeons, and Norwegian skiers engaged in their quaint and distinctively ethnic pursuits, but united in their use of IBM networking machines. The sounds of foreign languages being spoken in television ads had their own ability to shock and attract attention, all to the same end—the one thing that was spoken in English, albeit heavily accented English, was "IBM."

Thus, the transnational language, the one designed to end all barriers between speakers, the speech that everyone can pronounce and that cannot be translated or incorporated into another tongue, turns out not to be Esperanto, but rather IBM-speak, the language of American corporate technology. The foreignness of the other is exploited here to remind the viewer who may fear that IBM-speak will make the world smaller in undesirable ways (for example, that they might compete for our jobs, move into our neighborhoods, go to our schools) that the other is still picturesque. This classically orientalized other, such as the camel rider and Sikander, is marked as sufficiently different from us, the projected viewers, in order to encourage us to retain our positions as privileged tourists and users.

Sikander's cartoon bubble, emblazoned across his face and his elephant's, asks, "How come I keep trashing my hardware every 9 months?!" This sentence can be read as a rhetorical example of what postcolonial theorist and novelist Salman Rushdie has termed "globalizing Coca-Colonization." Again, the language of technology, with its hacker-dude vernacular, is figured here as the transnational tongue, miraculously emerging from every mouth. Possible fears that the exoticness and heterogeneity of the other will be siphoned off or eradicated by his use of homogeneous technospeak are eased by the visual impact of the elephant, whose trunk frames Sikander's face.

Elephants, rain forests, and unspoiled mesas are all endangered markers of cultural difference that represent specific stereotyped ways of being other to Western eyes. If we did not know that Sikander was a "real" Indian (as opposed to an Indo-American, Indo-Canadian, or Indo-Anglian) the presence of his elephant as well as the text's reference to Nirvana, proves to us that he is through the power of familiar images. We are meant to assume that even after Sikander's hardware problems are solved by IBM's consultants, "who consider where you are as well are where you're headed," he will still look as picturesque, as "Indian" as he did pre-IBM.

Two other ads, part of the same series produced by IBM, feature more ambiguously ethnic figures. The first of these depicts a Latina girl who is asking her teacher, Mrs. Alvarez, how to "telnet" to a remote server. She wears a straw hat, which makes reference to the American Southwest. Though she is only eight or ten years old, her speech has already acquired the distinctive sounds of technospeak—for example, she uses *telnet* as a verb. The man in the second advertisement, an antique-looking fellow with old-fashioned glasses, a dark tunic, dark skin, and an untidy beard proclaims that "you're hosed when a virus sneaks into your hard drive." He, too, speaks the transnational vernacular—the diction of Wayne and Garth from *Wayne's World* has "sneaked into *his* hard drive" like a rhetorical virus. These images, like the preceding ones, enact a sort of cultural ventriloquism that demonstrates the hegemonic power of American technospeak. The identifiably ethnic faces that utter these words, with their distinctive props and costumes attest, however, to the importance of this otherness as a marker of a difference the ads strive to preserve.

Wired magazine, like *Time, Smithsonian,* the *New Yorker,* and the *Chronicle of Higher Education* directs its advertising chiefly toward upper-middle-class white readers. In addition, it is read mainly by men, has an unabashedly libertarian bias, and its stance toward technology is generally Utopian. Unlike the other ads discussed here, the one for Origin that appeared in *Wired* directly and overtly poses ethnicity and cultural difference as part of a political and commercial dilemma that its product, Origin networks, can solve (see fig. 4.4). The text reads,

> We believe that wiring machines is the job, but connecting people the art. Which means besides skills you also need wisdom and understanding. An understanding of how people think and communicate. And the wisdom to respect the knowledge and cultures of others. Because only then can you create systems and standards they can work with. And

FIGURE 4.4. Black Boy and White Boy (Origin)

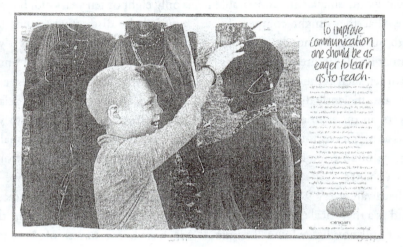

common goals which all involved are willing to achieve.

The image of an African boy, surrounded by his tribe, performing the *Star Trek* "Vulcan mind-meld" gesture with a redhaired and extremely pale boy, centrally situates the white child, whose arm is visible in an unbroken line, as the figure who is supposedly as willing to learn as he is to teach.

The text implies, however, that the purpose of the white boy's encounter with an African boy and his tribe is for him to learn just enough about them to create the "systems and standards that THEY can work with." The producer of marketable knowledge, the setter of networking and software-language standards, is still defined here as the Western subject. This image, which could have come out of *National Geographic* any time in the last hundred years, participates in the familiar iconography of colonialism and its contemporary cousin, tourism. And in keeping with this association, it depicts the African as unspoiled and authentic. Its appeal to travel across national and geographical borders as a means of understanding

the other, "the art of connecting people," is defined as a commodity that this ad and others produced by networking companies sell *along with* their fiber optics and consulting services.

The notion of the computer-enabled "global village" envisioned by Marshall McLuhan (93) also participates in this rhetoric which links exotic travel and tourism with technology. The Origin image comments on the nature of the global village by making it quite clear to the viewer that despite technology's claims to radically and instantly level cultural and racial differences (or in a more extreme statement, such as that made by MCI's "Anthem," to literally cross them out) there will always be villages full of "real" Africans, looking just as they always have.

It is part of the business of advertising to depict Utopias: ideal depictions of being that correctively reenvision the world and prescribe a solution to its ills in the form of a commodity of some sort. And like tourist pamphlets, they often propose that their products will produce, in Dean MacCannell's phrase, a "utopia of difference," such as has been pictured in many Benetton and Coca-Cola advertising campaigns.

Coca-Cola's slogan from the seventies and eighties, "I'd like to teach the world to sing," both predates and prefigures these ads by IBM, Compaq, Origin, and MCI. The ads picture people who are black, white, young, old, and so on holding hands and forming a veritable Rainbow Coalition of human diversity. These singers are united by their shared song and—more importantly—their consumption of Coke. The viewer, who it was hoped would infer that the beverage was the direct cause of these diverse people overcoming their ethnic and racial differences, was given the same message that many Internet-related advertisements give us today. The message is that cybertechnology, like Coke, will magically strip users down to "just minds," all singing the same corporate anthem.

And what of the "rest of it," the raced and ethnic body that cyberspace's "Anthem" claims to leave behind? It seems that the fantasy terrain of advertising is loath to leave out this marked body because it represents the exotic other that both attracts us with its beauty and picturesqueness and reassures us of our own identities as *not other*. The "rest of it" is visually quoted in these images and then pointedly marginalized and established *as other*. The iconography of these advertising images demonstrates that the corporate image factory *needs* images of the other in order to depict its product: a technological Utopia of difference. It is not, however, a utopia *for* the other or one that includes it in any meaningful or progressive way. Rather, it proposes an ideal world of virtual social and cultural reality based on specific methods of "othering," a project that I would call the globalizing Coca-Colonization of cyberspace and the media complex within which it is embedded.

NOTES

1. Kaplan writes that in order to address these connections, we must "consider the specifically Euro-American histories of imperialist nostalgia in the construction of modernist exile, constructions that require the conflation of exile, expatriation, and tourism in the representational practices of cultural production"(35).

The Personals

By David Harrison

I had been consistently perceived as male for at least nine months, after a year and a half on hormones, and hadn't had any surgery yet, when I decided it was time to check out sex with my new body and place my first personal ad. I'd been a lesbian for fifteen years before my transition. Now I was coming out of a long-term relationship and finding myself looking at men. It was during my four-and-a-half-year relationship with none other than the lovely Kate Bornstein, who years earlier had undergone her own gender change, that I transitioned. Kate made it safe for me to face my gender issues which had been chasing me for so long. It was the relationship I had wanted all my life and now, almost as a cruel joke, that too was changing. I was starting to be attracted to men.

Kate saw it coming long before I did. She said: "I have a feeling that if you decide to go through with a gender change, you'll want to be with men and not want to be with me." It was one of her biggest fears, and of course I hotly denied the possibility. But gender changes have their own agendas. Although it took me a long time to actually admit it (because it was such a painful realization), I found myself not attracted to her in the way I used to be. I was not able to give her what she needed because I was so self-involved. And her attraction for me had shifted also. The chemistry had literally changed. "Is it the hormones?" people ask. In my opinion they likely play a large role, but more in facilitating the blossoming of the seed that was there in the first place. I'd had a male homoerotic sensibility as a small child. My first sexual fantasies, at age five, were going to bed at night as Paul and George of the Beatles and taking turns fucking each other.

Anyhow, so here I was, shell-shocked coming out of my relationship (not to mention dealing with my own transition), and really needing to explore sex with men. I was horny as hell and after some encouragement from a couple of friends, I made my first foray into the world of the Personals. I started out by answering other people's ads and it was with one of these encounters that I had my first experience as a transsexual man being with a man. It remains one of my best experiences because we had a great verbal rapport, shared interests, and mutual respect, as well as fun in the sack. We still keep in touch.

When I first started out being sexual as David, I had decided that I didn't want my anatomy getting in the way of me feeling pleasure (although I knew I wanted to get top surgery done). I wanted to be sexual and still feel I could be a man—perhaps stretch the definition of what a man is, in other people's minds—instead of conforming my mind and body to fit someone else's idea. So while I still had breasts, I wore a T-shirt during sex, so I didn't experience dysphoria by being visually reminded of their presence. Different men dealt with me in different ways depending on how limited or open their own conception of gender was.

But before meeting any of them I first had to screen messages left on the voice mail. Let's get real—at the beginning I talked to almost everyone because I really wanted to get laid. And I wasn't as picky as I am now. I was an adolescent—it was time to experiment! Despite seeing hundreds of male clients while working as a professional dominatrix over a span of two years, my experience with men as partners up to that point had been somewhat limited: never having a boyfriend in my life, having had sex with three men (once with each) before I came out as a lesbian at nineteen. How would it be different now? And what kinds of men would be interested in me?

At that time I couldn't conceive that a gay man would want to be with me because of what is and isn't between my legs. Some of that was confirmed initially. I placed my ads in the "Men seeking Men," "Bi," "Trans," and "Other" sections, and I never got a response from "Men seeking Men." For the most part, female-to-male transsexuals are still unknown to mainstream culture. When most people hear or use the word "transsexual" it is understood to mean male-to-female. And there is certainly no pornography (that I've seen) about us. After being approached about being part of a slick "out-there" show on sex by one of the cable networks, and asked if I would possibly model nude, that show was dropped. I asked the researcher (who was quite hip and initially enthusiastic) to tell me the truth. She said that the two producers were a couple of straight guys who couldn't see how they could make an FTM transsexual be sexy. Sexy to them. While

MTF transsexuals are fetishized in pornography (as part of someone else's fantasy, not their own) FTMs have been invisible. And so it follows that most guys answering my ads would be uninformed.

Bruce left only his name and number on my personals voice mail. I called him back.

"Your ad sounded tantalizing."

"Umm hmm." …

"So … how long ago did you begin your sex change?"

"I started hormones a year and a half ago."

"Hmmm … I don't mean to be disrespectful—but what does your body look like?"

"I have what *resembles* female anatomy, but otherwise I look like a man."

"But with your clothes off?" …

"Are you mostly interested in men, or women, or both?"

"I'm heterosexual," he says.

"Well, I doubt that you'd find me attractive, then."

"I'm attracted to masculine-looking women."

"I'm not a woman. People tell me I look like a gay man. … Have you been with transsexuals before?"

"Yeah, once. It was a really *interesting* experience, I'll never forget it."

"Male-to-female, or female-to-male?"

"Uhhh … male-to-female. I played with her cock. … What kinds of things do you like to do in bed?"

"It depends on who I'm with."

"Maybe we can get together." …

"Look—I did not place this ad to be an exotic experience for someone else. Besides, the kind of men I'm attracted to are mostly gay men or gay-identified bisexuals—do you understand?"

"Yes. Maybe we can get together?"

"I don't think so. It wouldn't work."

Sometimes the sex has been great and I've had a lot of fun. The times it hasn't clicked have mostly been with men who described themselves as bisexual, but essentially led straight lives or had straight lifestyles. It usually worked up to a point, and then they lost their erections. After having a whole string of those, I asked one guy. "Is it the chemistry or my body, or what?" thinking, because this was happening with such frequency, that I must be a lousy lay. He said it was partly chemistry, but also guys sometimes lose erections in new and unfamiliar situations. I guess I'd qualify for that. Then he said to me: "You responded like a woman when I was fucking you." And I wish I'd said to him: "Have you ever fucked a man? Do you know how a man responds?"

I'm not typical of most transsexual men, in that I enjoy being fucked in my vagina with a penis. The whole point of my gender transition was to free myself up. If something feels good to me, I'm not going to stop doing it because it doesn't fit someone else's notion of what a man is. And as much as I can show bravado about the whole thing, sometimes I feel very shy—that first of all, I was a boy born with a vagina, and second, that I actually enjoy using it. Although I'd like my genitals to be different, for right now I can deal with what I have.

A guy named Carl left a message saying he'd like to talk.

"I'm looking for a new experience."

"Are you attracted to men?"

"No. I'm straight."

"You should know then, that even though I still have the plumbing I was born with, I'd look like any other guy to you."

"But you have female genitals, right?"

"Sort of … my clitoris has grown a lot. It's about two inches long when erect. It looks like a very small penis."

He wanted to come over and meet me anyway. As he walked in and sat down, he barely looked me in the eye.

"Aren't you supposed to like women?"

"My gender identity, which is who I feel I am inside, is a different issue than sexual orientation, which is who I'm attracted to."

He was already overloaded and this tipped him over the edge.

"You know, a lot of guys have a hard time with this. It brings up a lot—like thinking that if they're turned on to me, maybe they're gay."

His eyes flashed with recognition and he laughed nervously. As I showed him out through my narrow hallway, he walked past making sure that no part of him touched me.

It's a common expectation of men I meet through the ads that I look like a masculine woman or a butch dyke. I have explained again and again, ad nauseum, that I have sideburns, a goatee, a hairy belly—hair all over. That if they saw me on the street they would think I was like any other guy. Is that emphasis enough? But many are still surprised when they meet me. Another assumption is that now that I'm a "man" I should want to be with women and that I would automatically want to assume the "male-dominant" role in sex—in other words, acting out the traditional "hetero" dynamic.

I got a message from a crossdresser named Annabelle, who said:

"It sounds like we'd be perfect for each other."

"What are you interested in?"

"Everything."

"What specifically do you like?"

"Role-reversal."

"I can't imagine what that would be for me."

"Well, you know … I'm looking for someone to escort me. Someone to 'augment' my femininity."

"I don't think we're compatible."

Then I talked to Steve—or Sandra.
"Have you been with guys before?" I ask.
"No."
"Are you attracted to guys?"
"No."
"Then why did you call me?"
"I have this fantasy. Me dressed as Sandra going out with you. You're dressed as a man but really a woman."
"This is not about dressing up, for me."
"Oh, I understand."
"No. You really don't."

I really try to be forgiving because I know most people just don't have the information. I can't blame them for their ignorance—but sometimes I get so angry. I burn out from constantly having to explain myself. Fortunately some guys just innately "get it" and those are the ones with whom I end up having a great time.

I've always felt an inherent power imbalance in hetero relationships. It's unavoidable because of the culture's implicit (and explicit) expectations of gender roles and behavior. It feels quite alien to the way I'm wired. Which is probably why I have always been queer no matter what gender I am. Aside from all I have yet to understand about my own desire, I do know that a relationship starting out with an equal power balance has always been important to me. That can be a safe springboard into exploring erotic power-exchange in a more conscious way.

What I've learned through doing the Personals has been crucial in forming my new identity. By putting myself out there, I got to find out how I want to be related to and also what is unacceptable. That aside—I *love* sex and that's *really* why I do it! Most of the men I've met, and/or with whom I've had sex, have been very personable. Some guys, even though I am a totally new phenomenon to them, have treated

me with great respect and made the adjustment very well. These are usually guys whose main interest is men. It's with them that I've had the hottest sex. I would guess this is because in being being conceived as gay out in the world, one is confronted by society's views of homosexuals as "less than men" and "like women." And this can lead to questioning one's own gender in a way that most heterosexual men never have to. So, having had to find a place in the world as a man on one's own terms, very often it is less of a leap on a visceral level for these men to experience me as just another type of man.

As much as others have had assumptions about me, I have also had to challenge my own preconceptions about men—particularly having been raised as female. I assumed that all gay men were "size queens" and that none would want to be with me because I have a pussy and a tiny dick. I'm discovering that there are plenty of fags out there to whom that's not important. For many, it's about masculinity in all its possible expressions, a dick being only one aspect of that. I also had this idea that a gay man (or any man for that matter) would automatically have a more positive body image and comfort with their sexuality than me, because they have the right "equipment." I was wrong. If anything, it's shown me that I'm not doing too badly at all, and that most people have something about their body they're not quite satisfied with and would like to change.

My sexuality has shifted enormously since my transition. At first when I started having sex with people I met through the ads, old "programming" would creep in. I was raised to be a nice girl. I would have been called a slut if I were working the sex ads as a woman, the way I've been doing. But as a gay man, being told you're a slut is a compliment! There were times (early on) when I played with guys I wasn't really attracted to or didn't even like that much. After they'd leave I'd think, I can't believe I did that. It was partly horniness and partly not knowing my boundaries yet. Nowadays I am more confident that I'm desirable. Every transsexual I know wonders at some time—usually when they're in the first year or two of transition—if they are ever going to have a lover again, and if anyone is going to be attracted to them. I went through that—and sometimes I still do.

So how is sex different now? I actually feel like I'm in my body, which helps. I enjoy sex as recreation more than I did before and I'm able to distinguish between sex and romance whereas in my former incarnation, the lines frequently blurred. Definitely hormones. Since I began my second adolescence I've evolved into being a lot less dick-focused and more into the whole person—which is, after all, how I want to be related to.

Recently I have taken to posting ads online and have been (for the most part) getting better responses:

> *Hi David: I'm a 39 yo Gay man living in SF. I'm 5'9", 190 lbs, bear-type. I have bright blue eyes and brown fur (including a full beard, which I wear short). I'm sexually adventurous, although more top than not, and male identified (e.g., I don't care what's between your legs, as long as you are a man inside). I had many friends in the TS/TV community in Chicago, and have been looking for friends (as well as playmates)*

> *since I moved to SF 2 yrs ago. I'm HIV negative, and plan to stay that way. My interests include music, both playing and lissening, motorcycles, photography, art in general and roller coasters. I don't smoke or drink. I have been told I have a healthy amount of boy left in me.*
>
> *Please drop me a line—I'd love to get to know you and I look forward to hearing from you.*
>
> —*Greg*

When I first started doing the Personals, I was telling a friend about it and reading her my ads. She asked:

"So, do you have gay sex with these guys?"
"What do you mean by gay sex?"
"You know, fucking in the ass."

So … if two women are fucking each other in the ass, are they having gay sex, or are they just fucking each other in the ass? What about when a woman is fucking a man in the ass? And what is it when a dyke and a fag have sex with each other? Or, when a man is fucking a man in the vagina? Is that heterosexual? As my friend James said to me after we had played for the first time: "Sex is not about body parts. It's about the erotic energy that happens between two people."

Lost in the Gap
Between the Discourses and Practices of White Masculinity

By Jason Zingsheim

19

Weaving through time and space, this auto-ethnographic essay uses performative writing to represent and interrogate everyday performances of masculinity and whiteness. I argue for—and illustrate the opportunities in—utilizing autoethnography to investigate how socially dominant subject positions are recreated through individual acts of identity negotiation. Arising out of ethnographic fieldwork in Dublin, Ireland, and interspersed with historical moments preceding and enabling these contemporary performances of self, I suggest autoethnography is uniquely suited to explore the gaps between the discourses and practices of white masculinity. Furthermore, when paired with the representational strategy of performative writing, autoethnography illuminates the micro-practices of white masculinity and suggests tactics for performing resistance. Specifically, whiteness and masculinity are made visible in cemeteries and offices as they enable dominant performances of identity through themes of control, entitlement, mobility, and independence. Yet repeatedly, in gay bars and churchyards, ruptures threaten the coherence of both the journey and performances of identity. Drifting through the streets of Seattle and Dublin, these ecstatic fissures reveal the relational nature of identity, point to the vulnerability of whiteness and masculinity, and demonstrate the power and obstacles of autoethnography as a research practice.

FALLING INTO THE GAP

Sitting at the bar, I stare at my beer, trying to figure out what's going on. The froth dissipates as it, too, tries to get away from me, no longer interested in my company. It is then that the realization hits with startling force.

It is important to get this starting point right. This is not the only starting point, there are many. This particular one is not the beginning of this story despite its location on the page. More accurately, we might call this the bottom of this story—the moment I was thrown, the moment I lost myself. In order to get to the top, however, one must have a clear understanding of the bottom.

The bottom: Apparently I can't have a conversation, a problem vexing me for days. My anxiety over this issue has been increasing rapidly over the last few hours, since not speaking to anyone poses a problem when conducting ethnography. What is worse, the realization that hits as the foam dissipates is that I'm not even good enough for someone to hit on. All night I've been the lone single guy in this Irish gay bar: no judgmental friends to navigate or impress, easy to cruise, nonverbally available, the easiest piece of ass to hit on in the whole joint. Yet not a single attempt. I'm roughly the same age (late twenties) as most of the guys in this place, and while not in possession of celebrity-level looks, I dare say I am at least decent looking. But if that were true, if I was remotely, marginally attractive, then certainly by now someone would have said something. At the very least, someone would have made eye contact. I clearly do not belong in gay bars. I don't know how to do this, how to talk to people. People have no desire to talk to me. I don't know what the hell I'm doing. For a person like me (one who is tied to, and often by, subjectivities of whiteness and masculinity), this isn't supposed to happen.

A man enters and walks up to the bar alone. He orders a pint and sits down one stool away.

This could be it. I just need to give it a shot. I pull myself together to genuinely start a simple conversation; at this point I don't even care what it is about, just a conversation. I ask him how he is doing, "Hey, how's it going?" I slightly raise my eyebrows, open my eyes a little more and make a slight smile (careful not to look or sound too eager, just being friendly, but not too friendly). It feels natural and genuine. I'm cautiously hopeful.

He slowly turns his head toward me. "Hmph," he grunts, and then turns back to his beer.

It is an interesting experience, to simultaneously bottom out and blow up. It is infuriating and disorienting; infuriating in its ability to disorient, and disorienting by the degree to which it infuriates. And it was all set off by a grunt. Not even a word—no dismissive "fine"—just a grunt. I grab my bag and flee. I'm upset, frustrated, humiliated, angry, and not quite sure what other emotional responses I'm feeling. But what I do understand quite clearly is that I am not in control of any of these emotions.

It is this emotional mess that becomes the starting point for this analysis. In short, this was a moment where I lost myself. Familiar ways of performing my self were stymied as the discourses of whiteness and masculinity that produce me did not prepare or equip me for this experience. I've lost many things in my life. I have lost keys and money, hair and time, patience and virginity, just to name a few. Some of these items have been recovered, others are gone for good. But the experience of losing myself, of losing my sense of self, is particularly troubling because when the thing you lose is your self, you simultaneously experience a sense of loss and a sense of being lost. For me, this feeling of both loss and lost evoked dread and rage, disorientation and infuriation. I was overwhelmingly angry, but I trust Lorde (1984) that "anger is loaded with information and energy" (p. 127).

I turn to autoethnography in order to process this anger, seeking to utilize its energy and better understand its information. Moving among various contexts, this autoethnographic chapter uses performative writing to weave through time and space in order to represent and interrogate everyday performances of masculinity and whiteness. In this essay, I argue for—and illustrate the opportunities in—utilizing autoethnography to investigate how socially dominant subject positions are recreated through individual acts of identity negotiation. Arising out of ethnographic fieldwork in Dublin, Ireland, and interspersed with historical moments that preceded and enabled these contemporary performances of self, I suggest autoethnographic analysis is uniquely suited to explore the gaps between the discourses and practices of whiteness and masculinity. Specifically, when paired with the evocative and affective power of performative writing (Pelias, 1999, 2005; Pollock, 1998), autoethnography illuminates the micro-practices of white masculinity, reveals how this cultural identity also harms white male subjects, and suggests tactics for performing resistance. In short, this chapter contributes to our understanding of autoethnography as a creative research practice, demonstrates the power of performative writing to represent the complexity of identity, and extends scholarship on identity negotiation in relation to performances of whiteness and masculinity. The remainder of this introduction articulates autoethnography as a research practice for understanding identity generally, and then highlights the utility of performative writing for interrogating white masculinity specifically.

Autoethnography & Identity

The task of understanding identity, or more accurately, the role of identities in shaping the social world (and vice versa), is additionally complicated by the malleable character of both identities and discourse. Still, conducting a complex analysis of the dynamic nature of identity can be achieved "through a critical interrogation of those sites and practices of articulation (and re-articulation), suturing and unraveling, signification (and re-signification), and other forms of symbolic contestations made manifest through communicative practices" (Mendoza, Halualani, & Drzewiecka, 2002, p. 317). How identities are constituted, and the meanings of those identities "is never individual, but a shifting set of relations that we move in and out of, often without reflection" (Carrillo Rowe, 2005, p. 16).

Yet to fully understand these nuanced constitutive processes and their meanings requires precisely that—an extended time of reflection (Gauntlett,

2007). Consequently, I turn to autoethnography as a "broad orientation towards scholarship" (Gingrich-Philbrook, 2005, p. 298) that draws the researcher's attention to the shifting confluences and contestations between self, culture, and the research process (Adams & Holman Jones, 2008; Anderson, 2006; Berry & Warren, 2009; Ellis, 2004; Ellis & Bochner, 2000; Saukko, 2003). While autoethnography may take many forms (see Ellis & Bochner, 2000), a distinguishing characteristic is its hyper-reflexivity wherein the author, as both subject and object, is simultaneously intensely personal and radically cultural. Autoethnography becomes a research practice that "centers agency and holds complexity" (Simpson, 2006, p. 71) and is "vulnerable" (Rodriguez, 2009, p. 485) but not "immune to critique" (Berry & Warren, 2009, p. 600), one that discovers the intricacies of the social world through the intimacies of personal experience. This approach to research capitalizes on the researcher and writing as invaluable sites of knowledge production (Conquergood, 1991; Gingrich-Philbrook, 2005; Richardson, 2000), specifically recognizing the value of embodied knowledge (Lindlof & Taylor, 2002; Saukko, 2003). Autoethnography is a research practice "that privileges the exploration of a self *in response to questions that can only be answered that way*, through the textual construction of, and thoughtful reflection about, the *lived experience of that self*" (Goodall, 2000, p. 191).

Performative Writing & White Masculinity

To carry out such an inquiry requires a form conducive to representing the overlapping, blending, bleeding, fluctuating subject/object that is the autoethnographic self. Performative writing offers just such a form. As a "creative analytic practice" (Richardson, 2000) that "features lived experience, telling, iconic moments that call forth the complexities of human life" (Pelias, 2005, p.

418), performative writing "constitutes that which it describes" (Berry & Warren, 2009, p. 603). Admittedly, performative writing requests more from the reader (Alexander & Warren, 2002), as this representational strategy casts the reader as a co-producer of "an uncertain, provisional, normative practice" (Pollock, 1998, p. 95) and induces an emotional engagement. Pollock (1998) characterizes performative writing as evocative, obliging readers to respond "in a visceral as well as cognitive mode" (Corey, 2002, p. 356). For readers accustomed to a linear, rational, distant, and disembodied authorial voice, this method of writing can be confusing. To such readers, I submit Hekman's (1997) caution that "coherent theories in an incoherent world … are either silly, uninteresting, or oppressive" (p. 353). Performative writing strives to maintain the incoherence as we theorize identity, to keep the "complexities of human experience intact, to place the ache back in scholars' abstractions" (Pelias, 2005, p. 418).

As this is an inquiry into a self that is created in and through whiteness and masculinity, the evocative and visceral power of performative writing when paired with autoethnography is particularly important for two reasons. The first is its ability to delve into the affective and emotional components of identity. Based on Butler (1990; 1993; 1999; 2004), I approach identity as performative, that is to say, as an effect produced "through a stylized repetition of acts" (1990, p. 270) rather than *a priori* fact. While most immediately concerned with gender identity, Butler's work has been extended to the performativity of race (1993; see also Warren, 2001a). In other words, our racialized and gendered identities are socially constructed through the repetition of often taken-for-granted cultural practices. While not always invoking the language of performativity, much work on masculinity and in whiteness studies has focused on identifying the often invisible cultural practices that (re)create

masculine and/or white subject positions as the centered norm with unearned advantages, privileges, and social superiority (Zingsheim, 2008a, 2008b; Clarkson, 2005; Connell, 1987, 1995; Dyer, 1997; Frankenberg, 1993; Katz, 2003; Kincheloe, Steinberg, Rodriguez, & Chennault, 1998; McIntosh, 1995; Mumby, 1998; Nakayama & Martin, 1999; Roediger, 1998; Trujillo, 1991). Segrest (2002) notes that whiteness, and I suggest to a large extent masculinity, is (re)created through the cultural practice of what she terms the "anesthetic aesthetic," where those identified with dominant subject positions are conditioned to look away from suffering, to ignore the pain and vulnerability of others, lest in looking they recognize a common humanity, a belonging, and be compelled to act. Whereas the anesthetic aesthetic of whiteness and masculinity is a turning away from pain, performative writing directly challenges us to feel that pain, to experience the ache, and compels us to respond.

The second benefit of autoethnographic performative writing is the creative and representational capability to communicate intersectionality. Intersectionality draws our attention to the ways systems and performances of identity "mutually construct one another, or … 'articulate' with one another" (Hill Collins, 1998, p. 63). I work to further illuminate how the social and cultural formations of whiteness and masculinity are often (but not always) aligned with one another, creating a confluence of narrow performative resources that functions as a site of identity (re)construction for white men whose intelligibility relies on an array of often unspoken assumptions. Within various contexts, these racial and gendered identities articulate with other subject positions, such as sexuality, religion, nation, and education. As a result, the available performances in each context shift, as do the performative effects of the cultural practices employed. These social discourses, assumptions, reactions, and relations are not so easily categorized into mutually exclusive sections or subheadings. Instead, they weave and overlap, butting up against and blending into one another, alternating between joining forces to marginalize others and divesting themselves to invoke privilege. As a representational strategy and a "creative analytic practice" (Richardson, 2000), performative writing is flexible and agile enough to keep up with the contextually intersecting identities at the heart of this inquiry.

AN AUTOETHNOGRAPHIC EXPLORATION OF THE GAP

In the autoethnographic analysis that follows, I interrogate my anger and the discourses that make these particular everyday cultural performances of white masculine identity possible. Additionally, I explore some of the assumptions that whiteness and masculinity, as dominant cultural discourses, depend on for their (re)creation—particularly their reliance on performances of control, entitlement, mobility, and independence. I enter this analysis through my reactions when those assumptions were denied or precluded, reactions that were immediate, forceful, and shocking—"loaded with information and energy" (Lorde, 1984, p. 127). Reflecting upon these fissures and ruptures, the gaps between how my body has been produced through discourse and where I find myself in everyday performances of self, points to the relational conditions out of which our identities arise. What follows is my ongoing attempt to make sense out of these conditions, to explore how I hail, and am hailed by, whiteness and masculinity in order to reap favors and privileges, to mark my strategic deployment of tropes, assumptions, and absences. As a white male, I walked into this research project expecting to get what I came for, and when that expectation was not met, I imploded. In short, this essay investigates the

power of a stranger's grunt, a simple "Hmph," to disorient and infuriate.

A final word of caution before moving forward: At points in this reading, you too may feel disoriented and infuriated. The episodes that follow are not arranged according to linear structures of space and time, or rational systems of logic. They do present moments where the performative nature of whiteness and masculinity is revealed by focusing on the unspoken assumptions of control, independence, mobility, and entitlement that when met reinscribe dominant discourses and when denied suggest fissures in the foundations of such discourses. Still, despite this unifying logic, the narratives and arguments are not presented in an orderly, coherent fashion.

This means that at times, you too may feel loss, lost, and/or frustrated. I invite you to use these moments as an opportunity to reflect upon the degree to which your own identity is premised upon notions of control, independence, mobility, and entitlement. In this space of reflexivity, "the self that emerges from these shifting perspectives is, then, a possibility rather than a fact" (Pollock, 1998, p. 87). The self that rises is merely one of many possibilities. Rooted in the pragmatics, pedagogy, and politics of hope (Freire, 1992/2006; Fassett & Warren, 2007; Kincheloe & McLaren, 2000, p. 303), such self-reflexivity, and reflexivity on the self, can assist us in creating a world ever more just than the one we currently find ourselves in. So I encourage you to feel lost and to question what your response reveals about your sense of self. Most importantly, what other possibilities do/could/should exist?

Any City in the World

"Any city in the world!" A regular boast made by Tom, Jon and myself. We claimed that we could find our way around any city in the world. The claim was not unfounded. We had traveled together leading teams of people on mission trips to deliver medical supplies to hospitals in Eastern Europe and Asia. Over the eight years that we worked together, we had navigated our way through St. Petersburg, Paris, Beijing, Budapest, Moscow, Hong Kong, Amsterdam, and many other major cities. We often made a game of it. It was the challenge of figuring out the public transportation systems and finding our way around the city, all without speaking the local language.

I did study Russian for a time, but I was never anywhere near fluent. It was a fun luxury, studying another language to fulfill a degree requirement. I never needed to understand the language, and after all, everyone speaks English. Don't they?

Sometimes we would split the mission team up, each of us leading a group, and race back to the hotel from across the city. After all, what good was the claim that we could master a city unless we could do it on our own, independently? The challenge entailed quickly deciphering and navigating the color coded maps of the underground metro systems along the way, deciding which route had the least amount of stops or transfers, all the while controlling the movements of those in our charge. On those trips, weaving my way through underground mazes with unfettered mobility, I don't ever remember feeling lost. I always seemed to know where I was and where I was going.

Taps & Backs

I walk into the smaller side bar at The George, one of the oldest gay bars in Ireland. I move through the long narrow space to where a door leads into the expansive main bar of the pub. I pass by my boyfriend, hoping he'll just see me and I won't interrupt his research. The main bar is almost empty, but there is a group of four white guys in their thirties sitting together at the end of the bar.

I walk over by the bar taps to order a pint. This is a fresh start in a new bar. I follow the methodological suggestion of Taylor and Bogdan (1998, p. 58), playing naïve with the bartender to present myself as an interested outsider, in order to loosen up and relax. I figure it should be easy to talk to a bartender; they talk to people all night long. So when she asks what I want, I respond inquisitively, "How does Smithwicks compare to Carlsburg?"

She pauses briefly and then says, "Smithwicks is a lager and Carlsburg is an ale."

I look blankly at her. Those labels are on the taps. I can see that under Smithwicks it says "lager" and under Carlsburg it says "ale."

She sighs and looks annoyed but continues, "This [touching the Smithwicks tap] is between Guinness and this [touching the Carlsburg tap]." The words end, but her tone implies, "You dumbass." I get the distinct impression that a man my age should know the difference between lagers and ales. So much for relaxing. I just created an impression of myself as an incompetent idiot.

I walk over toward the end of the bar, hoping that the group of men didn't hear that little exchange. I'm pretty sure they did, but at this point in the night, what do I have to lose? I ask if I can have the seat next to them.

The man closest to me says, "Sure," and then turns his back to me to speak with his friends.

This feels strangely familiar. Because the speaker has his back turned to me, it's hard to hear what they are saying. I feel intrusive trying to eavesdrop. Even if I did catch something, to try to insert myself into the middle of their story would be forceful and invasive. Such a violent approach to interaction would not only be counter to the four seasons methodology (González, 2000, 2003), but it would go against my ethics and my personality. Yet I can't help thinking that perhaps, after days of elusive conversations, of not getting the research data I came for, I should force myself into whatever conversation I can find. Maybe in gay bars, or in Ireland, the only way to have a conversation is to force your way in. Maybe I need to be more assertive, more aggressive to get what I want, what I think I deserve, what I've been trained to expect. Maybe the idea of being invited into a space is bullshit. Maybe I should just jump in, verbally reach over his back and place myself in the middle of their discussion. Just play that role, be the arrogant, selfish American tourist. Maybe that's what it takes to do research here, to get the data I need and expect.

Yet even in the midst of this frustration I realize it would be a completely contrived performance. That isn't how I interact with anyone. If all I present these men with is a caricature, what do I expect to get in return? I expected to share stories. I don't mind sharing stories. I think I'm pretty good at listening. If someone would only tell me a story, I could respond with a story. I was expecting to do that. What happened? What did I miss? These are gay bars, so maybe it is more about cruising and sex. But that's why I've been coming alone. I thought it would be easier if it didn't look like I was already in a relationship. I wasn't prepared for the turning of backs. I wasn't prepared to be so inept. I look down at my Smithwicks and watch as the froth dissipates; it too is turning its back on my company. The realization looms, ready to pounce.

Maps

Looking down at the map, I plan our route. "So it looks like if we get off the bus by Grafton, then we can walk down Dame or through the Temple Bar area to Parliament Street, which becomes Capel after the river. Outhouse, the GLBT community center, is supposed to be there."

He watches through the bus window as cars and bikes come within inches of collision. "Whatever, we can just wander around. I'm sure we'll find it."

I fold up the map and place it back in my bag. Not because I agree with him, but because the map is no longer necessary. Its colors and lines are emblazoned on my mind. I know where I am on the map. I know where I'm going on the map. Wandering is no longer an option for me. I have a plan. I am in control.

In general, wandering is something I don't do well; I'm not good at getting lost. It's just not who I am. Wandering challenges my sense of self-control and privileges the movement of the body over the control of the mind, which is to say that it challenges my whiteness (Dyer, 1997, p. 6). I have been trained to master space and to move through it freely, yet always with purpose, direction, and intention.

Unhinged in Seattle

I was raised to be an independent person. Of course the reality isn't that simple, but as the first male child in my family, I was encouraged to take care of myself. Like many others, I was a latchkey kid and would find my way home using the city bus system. In high school, my parents gave me free reign. When it came time for college, I said goodbye to my dad over the phone, hugged my mom, and drove myself from Phoenix to Seattle. I would talk to both of my parents every couple weeks or so by phone. It was usually when they called me. Being white and male, I grew up being told that I could take care of myself, that I did not need to rely on anyone, and that I would be treated as an individual first and foremost (Dyer, 1997, p. 9; McIntosh, 1995). I too "have been hailed as a subject through countless articulations of 'Individuality'" (Carrillo Rowe, 2005, p. 17). My identity has been premised on the notion that "I" constitutes an independent individual, accessorized (perhaps) by belonging to some group or culture, but at the core a solitary figure. I came to enjoy, even cherish, that independence. Despite my illusory perception of autonomy, Butler (2004) claims that we are all dependent upon others: "[W]e come into the world unknowing and dependent, and, to a certain degree, we remain that way" (p. 23). Put differently, there are limits to our autonomy. We are neither wholly independent from others, nor entirely reliant upon them.

My perception of complete independence was shattered by a phone call. "Your dad died today."

I was thrown.

"He had a massive heart attack. The doctor said it happened so fast that he probably didn't feel a thing."

Neither did I as my body went numb.

"You need to come home."

Yeah … home. I'm the oldest, that's what I should do. It seems simple to write it now, years after the fact, but at that moment, who I was and what I was supposed to do wasn't so clear. The loss of my father brought attention to how my sense of self is connected with him and my vulnerability to the loss of that connection (Butler, 2004). With the severing of that tie, I was thrown. I didn't know who I was, or which part of me to be. I couldn't be a student; I couldn't sit through classes. I couldn't be an RA in the dorm; I didn't know how to talk to the guys on my floor. I couldn't be the oldest child, the man of the family, now. As Carrillo Rowe (2005) argues, our identity does not precede these connections; rather, it is an effect of these relations, so that when these relations are altered, threatened, or transformed, so too is our sense of self. The script had been swapped, leaving me uncertain as to how to perform this self, one crafted as independent yet simultaneously dislodged by the denial of dependence through death. In cases of grief and mourning whereupon we lose a connection, how we know ourselves is also lost as the familiar ways of constructing our identity "undergo a transformation the full result of which you cannot know in advance" (Butler, 2004, p. 18). In this moment, I lost control of my sense of self. I was thrust into the gap between discourse and practice. The discourses of whiteness and masculinity, so ingrained in my everyday performances of self, do not acknowledge affective connections, much less provide performative resources for handling their loss. So I wandered. I aimlessly meandered along the canal, over hills, and under bridges. I stood before a rocket ship, I leaned against a statue of Lenin in the rain, and I sat with a large troll made of sand underneath the Aurora Bridge. I wandered around Seattle for two days before finally flying home.

Swimming

On the mission trips, we would use the subway systems all the time. The rule for the team was that if anyone ever got lost or separated from the rest of the group in the subway system, they should stay where they were and wait for us to come find them. That was often my job. Tom and Jon would take the group on to our destination. I would track our way back through the underground system and find the lost person. It happened every year, at least once. If it happened more than once, it was usually the same person. There was no rule for what to do if I was the one who was lost.

After the infuriating and disorienting "Hmph" of a grunt, I spent the next three days wandering around Dublin in a simmering fit of rage. I was still there physically, but mentally I checked out. Raised a white, middle-class Lutheran, it wasn't polite to yell. Anger was to be repressed, experienced in silence. I was distracted and distant, barely talking to anyone. Occasionally the steam escaped, usually in the direction of my boyfriend. Typically this took the form of a homophobic rant directed at the nameless, faceless men in the Irish gay bars who were simply going about their business, but whom in hindsight I framed as selfish for not giving me what I wanted, what I thought I was entitled to. Never mind my own inexperience in gay bars. Ignore the fact that these were my first forays into such spaces alone, without friends or a boyfriend by my side. I was accustomed to moving through unfamiliar spaces with ease. In those moments, lashing out at these absent men, I was unaware that "the real battle with such oppression, for all of us, begins under the skin" (Moraga, 1981, p. 30). I took every chance I could to remove myself from others. I took long walks through the city and suburbs, drowning myself with my iPod. I found no troll under a bridge or statue of Lenin this time, but out of nowhere, the German Embassy popped up in the middle of a residential neighborhood. Its out-of-place nature evoked a strange feeling of kinship, as we both seemed to occupy locations we were not meant to inhabit. We weren't supposed to be there. Had I been in a subway, I would have stayed put and waited to be found. What do you do when you become lost in your own head, your own body, when you lose your sense of self?

I sought solace in isolated independence and languished in the longings I could not, or would not, name (Carrillo Rowe, 2004; Segrest, 2002). I worked to bury the anger, tried to ignore the information it offered about what lurked beneath my skin, and retreated into that "affective void," the "space from which whiteness and maleness have been mobilized throughout their histories" (Segrest, 2002, p. 169). Faced with the specter of being undone by strangers in a bar, I attempted to withdraw into the familiar "anesthetic aesthetic" of whiteness and masculinity (Segrest, 2002). I went numb.

Constructing the Creepy Guy

I only had an hour. Plenty of time, since I only wanted a conversation. After a number of other unsuccessful fieldwork outings, I was stepping back

and reducing the pressure. I didn't need to find a whole study—just a conversation. Using the Four Seasons methodology of ethnography, the subject of the ethnography is supposed to emerge organically from the context (González, 2000). I didn't need to force anything, just let it emerge. So early that evening, before the "Hmph," I leave my boyfriend at The George and walk a few blocks to The Front Lounge. As I enter, I notice there are a number of people spread throughout the space. It is not crowded, but neither is it barren. Groups of three or four men sit around tables here and there. A couple of women sit in a booth by the corner. I pass by them and up the few steps to the main bar. I order a pint as the bartender begins to pour a pint for an older white gentleman standing next to me.

She hands him his beer and takes his money. I guess that he is in his late fifties or early sixties based on the wrinkles around his eyes and his thinning gray hair.

As the bartender turns away from us and towards the register, he turns to me and says, "There's a thing of beauty."

My mind begins to race—what is he referring to? The pint? Could be, but somehow I don't think so. The way he raised his glass and tilted his head, it seemed like he was referring to the bartender. She does fit all of society's conventions of attractiveness. I realize he is waiting for some kind of response. "Sure is," I stammer. I know my hesitancy comes through in my voice, but, I am confused—did I just assist him in objectifying a woman? In a gay bar?

Maybe he did mean the pint. I am in Ireland after all, and the stereotypes would say that beer is revered here. He could have meant the beer. He probably meant the beer.

He moves toward a table in the middle of the room.

She hands me the beer and takes my ten euro note.

But, what if he didn't mean the beer? What if he was referring to the bartender? That was my gut reaction. It made me feel uneasy, like he violated something. I thought women were supposed to be safe from patriarchal sexual attention in gay bars. This isn't to say that gay men are somehow exempt from perpetuating misogyny. Often our sexual subjectivity makes such oppression even more subtle (see Shugart, 2003). Yet I was thrown by the blatant performance of heteronormative sexual privilege between this stranger and myself. I am again disoriented. Unable or unwilling to perform either as co-conspirator in her objectification or protector in her defense, I equivocate and flee.

She hands me my change and I move down the bar and take a seat. I choose not to follow the older man. I choose not to pursue a conversation with him. Perhaps it was because he gave me an uneasy feeling. Perhaps he was simply commenting on the beer and I projected my own appreciation of the bartender's physical attractiveness onto him. Perhaps I was worried that a conversation might give him the wrong idea. Perhaps I am the one who violated something.

Whatever the reason(s), I walked away and sat down at the bar. I felt like I had made a good decision. I felt justified in my choice. I felt like I was the sensitive and socially conscious male who was able to identify hegemonic masculinity when it raised its ugly head. In my overzealous and self-righteous attempt to rout gay male patriarchy, I ignored the ways my dismissal of this older gay man reinscribed an ageist cultural obsession with youth, myths of a miserable life, predatory stereotypes, and a pervasive fear of the future (Goltz, 2007, 2010). By constructing this man as the creepy guy, the exchange functions as a denial of our mutual "belonging" and our longings to be "in contact/community/communion/communalism/communism with others" (Carrillo Rowe, 2005, p. 27). By constructing him as someone to be avoided, I ignored the ways in which we could be, and already were, in community with one another. More troubling is the way this masculinist elision occurs under the guise of a feminist alliance for gender equality.

Amazing Grace

Most of the time, I find it very difficult to get lost. But who really wants to get lost anyway? Working for the church leading mission trips, I knew that all God's children desire being found, being saved, even if they don't know it yet. That is why it was up to us to go teach them. We, as Christians, were supposed to follow in Jesus's footsteps. And in Luke 19:10 (NIV), it clearly states, "For the Son of Man came to seek and to save what was lost." Really, it's not all that difficult. I mean, we didn't have be crucified or anything. Just take some needed medical supplies for the hospitals, some toys for the kids, some toiletries for the staff, and of course some Bibles. Then we would learn a few songs, perhaps even one or two in the language of the locals. We would gather all the patients together, usually kids, and we'd entertain them for a little bit with skits, puppets and a few songs … about Jesus of course. Come on, everyone sing:

"Amazing Grace, how sweet the sound that saved a wretch like me…

I once was lost, but now am found; was blind, but now I see."

It was while leading mission trips, while trying to "save" others, that I honed my skills at navigating foreign places. Throughout these rehearsals, the mantra was reinforced year after year, both physically and spiritually—don't get lost. Now, whenever I travel, that training kicks in; those years of experience come back to inform my current research practices, my current ways of being in the world (González, 2000, p. 627). Now, I always know where I am. I can control my location in and movement through unfamiliar spaces.

This mastery of space and mobility is an integral part of how I was trained to perform myself, how I trained others to perform. There is no gap here; the discourse meets and constructs my body in perfect alignment. Growing up, being lost wasn't a site of potentiality; wandering wasn't supposed to lead to creative insight (Johnson, 1997). To be lost was to be out of control, out of God's grace. To be lost was a threat to one's subjectivity, to one's physical and spiritual sense of self. In short, being lost was to be in danger, for eternity.

Between the Tree and the Gate

I rush to beat the lowering sun. I wish I had more time, but it closes at sundown. That's okay with me; it's not a place I want to be after dark. Mortality is creepy enough in the daylight. Turning onto the grounds, I slow my car down and idle past the parking lot. I have always wondered if I am supposed to park there. Instead, I slowly creep along the drive, past the fountains and trees, the flowers and tributes. I turn off the drive into a small round patch of asphalt near what is called the Peace Garden. It is not a parking lot, per se, but parked along the side of this small cul-de-sac, I am not worried about blocking any other cars. As I step out of the car, I feel the small rock in my pocket. The last time I was here, a year ago exactly, was a few months before the trip to Dublin. I brought my boyfriend with me, and he explained this Jewish custom to me.

Grasping the rock, I make my way over towards the tree. The tree isn't that large, a Palo Verde, located across from a gate that leads to a smaller enclosure. I can never remember exactly where it is, but I know that it is somewhere near this tree and this gate. I step carefully, admiring a bouquet of fresh flowers here and noticing how dilapidated the fake flowers look by comparison. There is something beautiful about the permanency, solidity, and simplicity of a

rock, remembrance that isn't manufactured plastic, yet doesn't wilt with time. I walk past the tree, still looking for it. It can't be this far. I must have passed it. I circle back and look closely at a different row. I'm almost back to the car again. Where is it? Is anyone watching me? It has to be here somewhere. The place is mostly deserted; the few groundskeepers are too focused on the manicured grass to notice another patron wandering the rows looking for a familiar name.

On the third attempt, I find my father's grave. Relieved to no longer be lost among the tombstones, I consciously mark my father's location between the tree and the gate, so I can find it next time. I've navigated my way through major cities around the world, and I get lost in the cemetery. As I prepare to leave, I stoop and place the rock on his tombstone.

The following year, on the seventh anniversary of his death, two years after Dublin, I clutch a small rock and wander lost among the tombstones again. This time, it takes four attempts to find him. If I didn't know any better, I'd say he moves each year to keep me guessing, to frustrate my mobility, to keep me wandering among the graves, and to remind me how fragile and fleeting any sense of control really is.

Becoming the Creepy Guy

At the other end of the bar, three white men in their twenties sit around talking to each other. In-between us, a handful of seats remain empty as couples and groups come up to order their drinks. I look at the three men, looking for some kind of invitation to speak with them. A look in the eye, a smile, a head nod, some kind of acknowledgement.

They see me looking and continue their conversation. If there was any kind of recognition or emotion or response, I missed it. So I move on to the next part of the plan and pull out a book, "A Sexual Life, A Spiritual Life," by Bishop Pat Buckley

(2005), a recent release written by a gay Irish bishop. I brought it along hoping it might provoke or elicit some kind of comment or conversation. So I read a page or two, stop to take a drink and let the cover fall closed so that people can see what I'm reading. No one looks. I repeat the routine. I get a fair amount of reading done, but no one comments during the frequent and long pauses. I repeat the routine, again and again.

A white male couple walks up and asks if the seat next to me is taken.

"No, go right ahead," I reply, trying to sound friendly but not overly anxious or desperate.

"Thanks," the man nearest to me says as he sits and swivels to face his companion. This leaves me facing the back of his shaved head. I'm not an expert on non-verbal communication, but I'm pretty confident this body positioning is not meant to invite further interaction. I don't press or try to continue talking with them. I feel frustrated at being shut out, but I also feel a little relief.

Back to the book and the beer. During the drinking portions of the routine I look around the room trying to make eye contact with people. I watch again for any kind of invitation or indication. The looks are expressionless. They see me, sitting alone, watching. That's all. I am beginning to feel uneasy again. I am watching them. And they see me watching them. And now I'm aware of them seeing me watching them. And yet, I continue to watch. What do they see, aside from my incessant observing? Do I look desperate? Pathetic? Creepy? Shit. I do. I'm the creepy guy now. I can feel it. I've been here too long, watching the same people. A conversation seems like too much to hope for now. Who wants to talk to the creepy guy at the bar? I didn't.

BEAUTY IN THE BREAKDOWN

Two days after my dad died, I flew home to Phoenix. It was Easter weekend, and the funeral wouldn't be until Monday. I pulled myself together enough to play the role of the responsible one. I would represent the family and keep my mom and my dad's mom away from his second wife, who allegedly burned his will. I would comfort my sister, make arrangements with the pastor, and be sure to keep enough beer in the house for my dad's younger brother, my uncle, to nurse his grief. I was in control, until Sunday morning. The day before the funeral, we decided to go to church for Easter services. Standing outside before the service began, I saw an old friend approaching. I remember my body tightening, and I remember saying out loud to no one in particular, "oh shit." I could feel it coming, and I knew I couldn't stop it. As he embraced me, I lost control of my body. I couldn't see through the tears; I couldn't breathe through the sobbing; I couldn't stand on my own. I was thrown beside myself (Butler, 2004). In the rupture of my father's death, in the ecstatic embrace of a friend, I was made starkly aware of my vulnerability, my lack of autonomy, of how my way of being in the world was possible only by virtue of another (p. 19). It is in those moments that Butler suggests we find ourselves to be ecstatic, to be beside ourselves, and then we can better see the ruptures in our connections to others. These ruptures draw attention to those connections, our need for those connections, and our vulnerability to others through those connections.

Yet this politics of relation is at odds with whiteness and masculinity. Both of these dominant discourses rely on the illusion of ultimate independence. White men are "conditioned into oblivion" (McIntosh, 1995, p. 78) about our autonomy as "concentric subjects" (Mumby, 1998, p. 167) who feel entitled to control the world around us because our values and beliefs, indeed our entire subjectivities, are assumed to be homogenous and universal. Carrillo Rowe (2005) suggests "belonging to whiteness," and I would add masculinity, "evokes a sense of entitlement that the world is [my] oyster" (p. 28). As a result, such belongings are accompanied by assumptions of entitlement, mobility, independence, and control. Given this discursive context, it is not surprising that my unspoken expectations included finding people who speak my language in any city in the world and immediately being given the data I was looking for (González, 2000, p. 631). It is also apparent that the discourses of whiteness and masculinity do not operate in isolation, but are bolstered and challenged in complex and context-specific ways as they intersect with other social formations, such as queerness, nationality, Christianity, and education.

Throughout my time in Dublin, I attempted to translate white male privilege into white queer male privilege (Bérubé, 2001). I attempted to reframe each context, every set of circumstances, in ways that would ultimately reassert my control over how my self was constructed. But just like the (white, male, queer?) Wizard, that damned dog pulled back the curtain, revealing yet another creepy white guy walking into gay bars alone for the first time, accompanied only by a false sense of entitlement. Turns out I am not as great and powerful as I thought. I can't control how others perceive me. I can't make them talk to me. Despite my naïve expectations of recognition, I can't control when they hail me as a subject, or what kind of subject, or if they even hail me at all. Sitting at the bar, under the weight of this realization, I lost my sense of control. It was never about having a conversation, not really. It was about controlling my sense of self, which meant controlling the relations that function to constitute that self. For a hegemonic masculinity founded on force and control (Trujillo, 1991), the inevitable failure to constantly control the shifting vectors of relationality that give rise to

the self leads to the perception of losing one's self. This relational nature of identity "often interrupts the self-conscious account of ourselves we might try to provide in ways that challenge the very notion of ourselves as autonomous and in control" (Butler, 2004, p.19). Granted, I never really had control to begin with. But on the barstool, all I could see, all I chose to see, were the backs being turned, the fleeing beer foam, and the grunting. I'd thought I had control, and in losing that perception/illusion/delusion, I lost a primary method of identity construction. My performance of white masculinity faltered as its foundational assumptions wavered. I no longer had access to the familiar ways I had of crafting myself. I lost them through a "Hmph." I became lost in a grunt.

When control is threatened by blank stares, or entitlement is denied with a grunt, the socially conditioned response I enacted was one of violent rage (Katz, 2003). When these two performative strategies for the reiteration of whiteness and masculinity were challenged, I embraced a third strategic performance through individuality as I strove to reassert control over my mobility. Yet independence was itself debunked through the embrace, through the phone call, through the grunt. For it is in these that the illusion of independence, and I, were undone (Butler, 2004). And in this state of liminality, I find myself finally able to wander.

The goal of this autoethnographic analysis is not to suggest a wholesale rejection of masculinity, whiteness, or any of the dominant discourses functioning through this text. Gingrich-Philbrook (1998) laments that despite his reluctance to reproduce masculinity, he must participate in such a process "for much remains at stake: survival, desire, communicative intelligibility" (p. 206). The same can be said for my reluctance to reproduce whiteness. I cannot abolish either dominant discourse, nor fully remove myself from their subjective hailings. Any attempts to abolish them, to deny how one's own identity is hinged to them, rest upon the privileges afforded by whiteness and masculinity (Warren, 2001b; Carrillo Rowe & Malhotra, 2007). To reject the dominant discourses of one's identity construction is to simultaneously reinscribe them.

Instead, the goal is "to find an antidote to the ways that whiteness [and masculinity] numbs me, makes me not see what is right in front of me, takes away my intelligence, divides me from people I care about" (Bérubé, 2001, p. 259). I suggest the antidote is in the symptom, and that by self-reflexively interrogating the information and energy within the anger (Lorde, 1984) that accompanies the numbness, we shall find that there is beauty in the breakdown. Excavating these affective performances of self has exposed the assumptions of mobility, entitlement, independence and control that are instrumental in constructing myself as a white, U.S. American, gay male in these Irish gay bars. Autoethnographic and performative writing are invaluable practices for turning towards the pain, experiencing the ache, scraping at our own skin, and compelling action. The dissipating foam, the heart attack, the silences and lack of responses, these exist as subjective ruptures, as fissures in the processes of identity (re)construction. The emotions they elicit, whether grief or rage, attest to the perpetual lack of control, entitlement, and independence possessed by subjects. The ruptures reveal the instability of cultural discourses built upon these faulty assumptions, and in these moments, we once again experience the loss of our selves. It is a loss that is educational in that it provides a glimpse into the costs of whiteness and masculinity for white men by demonstrating our loss of affect and our blindness to our belongings and reminding us we are all "given over to the other" (Butler, 2004, p. 23). In so doing, these experiences offer the opportunity to reflexively contribute to a politics of relation (Carrillo Rowe, 2005) and pedagogies of hope (Denzin, 2003; Fassett & Warren, 2007),

both of which strive for the renegotiation of unjust power relations. The first step of such a process is to recreate the inequitable discursive resources we currently possess (and that possess us) to be more democratic. Yet to achieve these goals requires the reflexive interrogation of our own performances of cultural identities in everyday life, our own navigation of the dominant and marginalized discourses of identity construction that surround us. I believe this endeavor begins with attempts to trace our way back through the subway systems, to wander the streets, to swim in our heads, and to create theory that allows us to live in new and more just ways.

REFERENCES

Adams, T. E., & Holman Jones, S. (2008). Autoethnography is queer. In N. K. Denzin, Y. S. Lincoln & L. T. Smith (Eds.), *Handbook of critical and indigenous methodologies* (pp. 373–390). Thousand Oaks, CA: Sage.

Alexander, B. K., & Warren, J. T. (2002). The materiality of bodies: Critical reflections on pedagogy, politics, and positionality. *Communication Quarterly, 50*(3 & 4), 328–343.

Anderson, L. (2006). Analytic autoethnography. *Journal of Contemporary Ethnography, 35*(4), 373–395.

Berry, K., & Warren, J. T. (2009). Cultural studies and the politics of representation: Experience↔Subjectivity↔Research. *Cultural Studies/Critical Methodologies, 9*(5), 597–607.

Bérubé, A. (2001). How gay stays white and what kind of white it stays. In B. B. Rasmussen, E. Klinenberg, I. J. Nexica & M. Wray (Eds.), *The making and unmaking of whiteness* (pp. 234–265). Durham, NC: Duke University Press.

Buckley, P. (2005). *A sexual life, a spiritual life.* Dublin: Liffey Press.

Butler, J. (1990). Performative acts and gender constitution: An essay in phenomenology and feminist theory. In S.-E. Case (Ed.), *Performing feminisms: Feminist critical theory and theatre* (pp. 270–282). Baltimore: Johns Hopkins University Press.

Butler, J. (1993). *Bodies that matter: On the discursive limits of "sex."* New York: Routledge.

Butler, J. (1999). *Gender trouble: Feminism and the subversion of identity.* (10th anniversary ed.). New York: Routledge.

Butler, J. (2004). *Undoing gender.* New York: Routledge.

Carrillo Rowe, A. (2005). Be longing: Toward a feminist politics of relation. *NWSA Journal, 17*(2), 15–46.

Carrillo Rowe, A., & Malhotra, S. (2007). (Un)hinging whiteness. In L. M. Cooks & J. S. Simpson (Eds.), *Whiteness, pedagogy, performance: Dis/placing race* (pp. 271–298). Lanham, MD: Rowman & Littlefield.

Clarkson, J. (2005). Contesting masculinity's makeover: *Queer Eye,* consumer masculinity, and 'straight-acting' gays. *Journal of Communication Inquiry, 29*(3), 235–255.

Connell, R. W. (1987). *Gender and power: Society, the person and sexual politics.* Stanford, Calif.: Stanford University Press.

Connell, R. W. (1995). *Masculinities.* Cambridge, UK: Polity Press.

Conquergood, D. (1991). Rethinking ethnography: Towards a critical cultural politics. *Communication Monographs, 58*(2), 179–194.

Corey, F. C. (2002). Alexander. *Communication Quarterly, 50*(3 & 4), 344–358.

Denzin, N. K. (2003). *Performance ethnography: Critical pedagogy and the politics of culture.* Thousand Oaks, CA: Sage.

Dyer, R. (1997). *White.* London: Routledge.

Ellis, C. (2004). *The ethnographic I: A methodological novel about autoethnography.* Walnut Creek, CA: AltaMira Press.

Ellis, C., & Bochner, A. P. (2000). Autoethnography, personal narrative, reflexivity: Researcher as subject. In N. K. Denzin & Y. S. Lincoln (Eds.), *Handbook of qualitative research* (2nd ed., pp. 733–768). Thousand Oaks: Sage.

Fassett, D. L., & Warren, J. T. (2007). *Critical communication pedagogy.* Thousand Oaks: Sage.

Frankenberg, R. (1993). *White women, race matters: The social construction of whiteness.* Minneapolis: University of Minnesota Press.

Freire, P. (2006). *Pedagogy of hope: Reliving pedagogy of the oppressed.* (R. R. Barr, Trans.). New York: Continuum.

Gauntlett, D. (2007). *Creative explorations: New approaches to identities and audiences.* New York, NY: Routledge.

Gingrich-Philbrook, C. (1998). Disciplinary violation as gender violation: The stigmatized masculine voice of performance studies. *Communication Theory, 8*(2), 203–220.

Gingrich-Philbrook, C. (2005). Autoethnography's family values: Easy access to compulsive experiences. *Text & Performance Quarterly, 25*(4), 297–314.

Goltz, D. B. (2007). Laughing at absence: Instinct magazine and the hyper-masculine gay future? *Western Journal of Communication, 71*(2), 93–113.

Goltz, D. B. (2010). *Queer temporalities in gay male representation: Tragedy, normativity, and futurity.* New York, NY: Routledge.

González, M. C. (2000). The four seasons of ethnography: A creation-centered ontology for ethnography. *International Journal of Intercultural Relations, 24*, 623–650.

González, M. C. (2003). An ethics for post-colonial ethnography. In R. P. Clair (Ed.), *Expressions of ethnography* (pp. 77–86). Albany: SUNY Press.

Goodall, H. L. (2000). *Writing the new ethnography.* Walnut Creek: AltaMira Press.

Hekman, S. (1997). Truth and method: Feminist standpoint theory revisited. *Signs, 22*, 341–365.

Hill Collins, P. (1998). It's all in the family: Intersections of gender, race and nation. *Hypatia, 13*, 62–79.

Johnson, C. (1997). Lost in the woods. In F. Barron, A. Montuori & A. Barron (Eds.), *Creators on creating: Awakening and cultivating the imaginative mind* (pp. 59–62). New York: Penguin.

Katz, J. (2003). Advertising and the construction of violent white masculinity: From Eminem to Clinque for men. In G. Dines & J. M. Humez (Eds.), *Gender, race, and class in media: A text-reader* (2nd ed., pp. 349–358). Thousand Oaks: Sage.

Kincheloe, J. L., & McLaren, P. (2000). Rethinking critical theory and qualitative research. In N. K. Denzin & Y. S. Lincoln (Eds.), *Handbook of qualitative research* (2nd ed., pp. 279–314). Thousand Oaks: Sage.

Kincheloe, J. L., Steinberg, S. R., Rodriguez, N. M., & Chennault, R. E. (Eds.). (1998). *White reign: deploying whiteness in America* New York: St. Martin's Press.

Lindlof, T. R., & Taylor, B. C. (2002). *Qualitative communication research methods.* (2nd ed.). Thousand Oaks: Sage.

Lorde, A. (1984). *Sister outsider: Essays and speeches.* Berkeley: The Crossing Press.

McIntosh, P. (1995). White privilege and male privilege: A personal account of coming to see correspondences through work in Women's Studies. In M. L. Andersen & P. H. Collins (Eds.), *Race, Class, and Gender: An Anthology* (2nd ed., pp. 76–87). Belmont: Wadsworth Publishing Company.

Mendoza, S. L., Halualani, R. T., & Drzewiecka, J. A. (2002). Moving the discourse on identities in intercultural communication: Structure, culture and resignifications. *Communication Quarterly, 50*(3 & 4), 312–327.

Moraga, C. (1981). La güera. In C. Moraga & G. E. Anzaldúa (Eds.), *The bridge called my back: Writings by radical women of color* (pp. 27–34). New York: Kitchen Table.

Mumby, D. K. (1998). Organizing men: Power, discourse and the social construction of masculinity(s) in the workplace. *Communication Theory, 8*(2), 164–183.

Nakayama, T. K., & Martin, J. N. (Eds.). (1999). *Whiteness: The communication of social identity.* Thousand Oaks: Sage.

Pelias, R. J. (1999). *Writing performance: Poeticizing the researcher's body.* Carbondale, IL: Southern Illinois University Press.

Pelias, R. J. (2005). Performative writing as scholarship: An apology, an argument, an anecdote. *Cultural Studies↔Critical Methodologies, 5*(4), 415–424.

Pollock, D. (1998). Performative writing. In P. Phelan & J. Lane (Eds.), *The ends of performance* (pp. 73–103). New York: New York University Press.

Richardson, L. (2000). Writing: A method of inquiry. In N. K. Denzin & Y. S. Lincoln (Eds.), *Handbook of qualitative research* (2nd ed., pp. 923–948). Thousand Oaks: Sage.

Rodriguez, D. (2009). The usual suspect: Negotiating white student resistance and teacher authority in a predominantly white classroom. *Cultural Studies↔Critical Methodologies, 9*, 483–508.

Roediger, D. R. (Ed.). (1998). *Black on white: Black writers on what it means to be white.* New York: Schocken Books.

Saukko, P. (2003). *Doing research in cultural studies.* Thousand Oaks: Sage.

Segrest, M. (2002). Of souls and white folks. In M. Segrest (Ed.), *Born to belonging: Writings on spirit and justice* (pp. 157–175). New Brunswick, NY: Rutgers University Press.

Shugart, H. A. (2003). Reinventing privilege: The new (gay) man in contemporary popular media. *Critical Studies in Media Communication, 20*(1), 67–91.

Simpson, J. S. (2006). Reaching for justice: The pedagogical politics of agency, race, and change. *The*

Review of Education, Pedagogy, and Cultural Studies, 28(67–94).

Taylor, S. J., & Bogdan, R. (1998). *Introduction to qualitative research methods: A guidebook and resource.* (3rd ed.). New York: Wiley.

Trujillo, N. (1991). Hegemonic masculinity on the mound: Media representations of Nolan Ryan and American sports culture. *Critical Studies in Mass Communication, 8,* 290–308.

Warren, J. T. (2001a). Doing whiteness: On the performative dimensions of race in the classroom. *Communication Education, 50*(2), 91.

Warren, J. T. (2001b). Performing whiteness differently: Rethinking the abolitionist project. *Educational Theory, 51*(4), 451–466.

Zingsheim, J. (2008a). Resistant privilege and (or?) privileged resistance: Navigating the boxes of embodied identity. *Liminalities: A Journal of Performance Studies, 4*(2), 1–20.

Zingsheim, J. (2008b). Whiteness and white supremacy. In A. Lind & S. Brzuzy (Eds.), *Battleground: Women, gender and sexuality.* Westport, CT: Greenwood Press.

Acknowledgements: The author would like to thank Sarah Amira De la Garza, Marianne LeGreco, and Kristin Davis for their feedback on an earlier draft of this essay. Additionally, the insights of Kimberlee Pérez and Dustin Bradley Goltz have been instrumental in the subsequent development of this chapter.

Part IV
Performing Identity

20

Introducing Performance
A Doing and A Thing Done

By Dustin Bradley Goltz and Jason Zingsheim

T he final section of this reader looks at identity through the frame of performance, and more specifically, identity as a performance. Richard Schechner (2002) defines performance as "restored behavior" or the completion of a particular set of behaviors. Victor Turner (1982) views performance as the carrying through of a patterned set of behaviors to their "proper finale." The notions of "restored" and "patterned" behavior as guiding frames for performance work to highlight performance as both "a doing and a thing done" (Diamond, 2000, p. 66). The doing of performance, the situated and contextualized action of performance, is perhaps the most familiar and commonsense. A teacher walks into the classroom on the first day of class, confidently and silently walks to the front of the classroom, places their books on the front table, and writes her or his name on the board. In this brief example, there are multiple actions involved: the entrance, the walk, the silence, the placement of books, and the writing on the board. These are the "doings" of performance, the "embodied acts, in specific sites, witnessed by others (and/or the watching of self)" (Diamond, 2000, p. 66). More complicated, alongside the "doing" of performance, is "the thing done," "the completed event framed in

time and space and remembered, misremembered, interpreted, and passionately revisited across a pre-existing discursive field" (Diamond, 2000, p. 66). In other words, performance doesn't "just happen," but it *does* something. Each performance is both shaped and dictated by previous performances and discourses, and the "thing done" has discursive implications and potentials that extend beyond the actual moment of doing. Returning to the very mundane example of the instructor who enters the classroom, we have identified a "doing." But how can we discuss the ways in which these seemingly uninteresting actions are both shaped through previous discourses and working to shape discourses—the thing done? Is the entrance of the instructor easy to visualize, based upon the very sparse details offered? Likely so, because it's not unfamiliar. The silent entrance, the confident walk to the front of the room, the claiming of position in the front of the class, and the writing of the name on the board are all familiar performances of instructor (not just this one instructor, but the more generic discourses around THE college professor). This is what many instructors do, yet each time it happens, each time these patterns of behavior are "restored" in specific contexts and classes (though no performance is an exact duplicate of the ones that precede it), the discourses of instructor are upheld, reified, normalized, and familiarized. This performance of instructor, with each repeated performance, class after class, semester after semester, will build an expectation from students that this behavior is the appropriate and correct way to perform college professor.

Now imagine sitting in class on the first day and no one is at the front of the room. The class sits patiently as class time begins, but there is no authoritative figure claiming the front of the room. There is no name marking the class on the board. You are quietly chatting with the person next to you, making small talk, assuming that the professor is lost or late. Then the person you are chatting with says, "let's get started," sits on top of their desk and turns around to the class to welcome them. More clearly, in this example, we see how the doings of this instructor's entrance have a complex relationship to previous discourses of professor, as well as the potential to shift and challenge the ways you will experience the first day of class and professor expectations in the future. This doing has also done something that extends beyond the temporal moment of the act itself.

To think of identity through a performative frame, we will shift from considering identity as someone or something we *are* to contemplating identity as something we *do*. Often, when people first hear performance, they think of staged performances, likened to theater. In the theatrical arena, often performers adopt scripts, learn predetermined movements (blocking), wear costumes (and perhaps masks), and rehearse their roles for the purposes of an expectant audience. In terms of our work with "performing identity," we ask that you might entertain this metaphor of theater for identity in hopes that the metaphoric distinction will slip away, as identity and theater are, perhaps, not as dissimilar as they at first seem.

Judith Butler's (1999/1990) *Gender Trouble* set forth a highly influential argument, rethinking gender as a performance and a performative accomplishment. In short, she argues that gender is not something we are, innately in nature or essential to our being, but rather, gender is something we do. Returning to our earlier discussion, Butler's work sets the foundation for our engagement with performance, theorizing gender as a doing and gender as the result of this doing—a thing done. Her theory of **gender performativity** is rooted in the logic that the body is unstable, lacking meaning within itself, "but becomes meaningful through discourse" (Lloyd, 1999, p. 117). Critics of Butler have tried to simplify her discussion, suggesting that Butler claims gender is merely theatrical, where one can simply choose in any given situation to perform their gender one way or another. This, however, strongly oversimplifies her discussion in several key ways. Butler argues that gender is shaped and naturalized in the body through regulatory practices, and thus is a performance of culture rather than a biological mandate. For example, consider all the ways you perform your gendered identity. Clothing, hairstyle, and accessories might be easy places to mark this, but look more closely at the way your body moves throughout the world. How do you sit? How do you stand, walk, dance, run, or stroll across campus? If, as an exercise, you were asked to adopt the walk, dance, or movements of a different gender identity than your own, would it be easy? Would it feel uncomfortable? Might you even mark the feeling as "unnatural" or "not me"? According to Butler, while there is no biological determinant for the way you walk, dance, run, and sit, your body has been conditioned through repetition by discourses that preceded you to perform gender according to cultural norms—so much that to violate the norms that have been disciplined in your body would feel unnatural, although it is discourse, and not nature, that conditions these performances.

Can you remember at a young age being told to hold your posture a particular way, to sit, walk, or dress in a way that was assigned according to your biological sex? Now that you are older, when someone doesn't perform his or her gender in a way that is culturally normative, do you take notice? Do you stare? Do you comment to friends you are with? Have you witnessed boys who bully other boys for being too feminine, or girls who do the same to other girls who are not feminine enough? How are these performances both a doing (the teasing) and a thing done? Consider other areas of identity as a performance and a performative accomplishment, shaped and constrained by discourses that precede you. How do you perform your race? Your sexuality? Your age? Your national identity? Your economic class? What patterns and behaviors (and ideologies) are restored in these performances? What are the doings, as well as the things done, in each of your examples?

DISCIPLINE, STRUCTURES, AND STRATEGIES OF RESISTANCE

Central to a performative engagement with identity is the concept of **liminality**, which is the marking of an indefinite or ambiguous state between two fixed points (Turner, 2004, p. 79), or a state of being betwixt and between (p. 79). Broader examples of liminality are often grounded in cultural rituals that mark a crossing over from two fixed points. For example, graduation ceremonies, birthdays, weddings, bat mitzvahs, and quinceañeras, are all events where a threshold is crossed, whether from youth to adulthood, single to married, student to graduate, or one age to the next. Liminality is that indefinite place in-between, yet in that uncertainty, there is space ripe with possibility. If

we denaturalize notions of identity and accept that identity is not something we are, but something we do, then identity is always being done. Each second, moment-by-moment, we are restoring multiple identity patterns in our performances of self. With each gesture, each utterance, each movement and interaction, we are doing identities. If we look to each one of those moments, which leads into the next, as a threshold—a liminal space—then identity is not only something we do (and redo), but there is always the possibility for us to do identity differently. In this respect, performative identity places its attention on the moment-by-moment and always present possibility for us to rearticulate, re-envision, and extend the norms of identity. Let's ground this last claim in an example by returning to the instructor scenario we have been working with. Through sitting with the class, rejecting the authoritative position at the top of the room, and casually chatting in a desk prior to class, the norms of THE professor are rearticulated in that moment. No longer is this performance "not what a professor does," but it materializes as a new possibility. The stakes on this example are admittedly low, as violating cultural norms of race, gender, nation, and sexuality can pose much greater risks, both verbal and physical. Still, it demonstrates the radical potential and power of identity to be performed otherwise.

Michael Butterworth (2005) discusses the post-9/11 nationalistic sentiment through the quasi-religious rituals and performances of patriotism at major league baseball games following the attack on the Twin Towers. As an example, "Take Me Out to the Ballgame," traditionally sung by fans during the seventh-inning stretch, was replaced with "God Bless America" as a public performative ritual of U.S. patriotism. In this historical moment, and within these physical contexts, the performance of patriot was enacted through standing, removing one's hat, and displaying proper reverence and bodily comportment. Butterworth points out that the songs, memorials, tributes, and ceremonies performed in ballparks in the years following 9/11 did not alone guarantee public support for the wars in Afghanistan and Iraq, but these rituals—and the uncritical willingness of those performing them—did function to suppress dissent by leaving little room for ball players or fans to perform patriotism in different ways. While performance has the potential to challenge, rescript, and potentialize new ways of being in the world—extending and troubling discourses of intelligibility—the weight of culturally approved performances of identity and institutional discipline work to prevent and limit these potential ruptures. To resist this performance of identity was to construct oneself as not only unpatriotic, but as aligned with the terrorists, given the declaration of President George W. Bush that "you are either with us, or you are with the terrorists" (p. 123). As you can imagine, performances of resistance pose widely varying degrees of risk (from invisibility to physical violence).

For some, performances of resistance are an integral part of their performance of self; located by discourse in opposition to the normative, resistance occurs simply in asserting an identity in the first place. The performance of marginal identities is a constant and never-ending strategic negotiation. Jacqueline Taylor's (2000) "Exemplary Lesbian" performance is a personal narrative piece where Taylor examines the ways she is positioned and performs the "exemplar," first as a preacher's daughter in her childhood and then as one of the few openly gay or lesbian faculty members at a Catholic University. She crafts a narrative of her performance of "lesbian exemplar" through her interactions with faculty and students, many of whom have had little to no known interaction with a gay or lesbian before. Walking a tightrope of institutional, personal, social, and political investments (and risks) she reflects upon the experiences and pressures of being positioned in the role of representative for a marginalized subject position. Her constant navigation and careful balancing act highlights several of the factors that weigh upon minority "exemplars" under constant surveillance, yet also mark how her femininity and education assist her to be (mostly) favorably received. Consider this discussion of exemplar performance when reflecting on Brenda Allen's reading (Chapter Six). How was her performance of identity—with respect to academic, woman, and African American subjectivities—constrained and pressured due to her minority position in her college? How about the presidential campaign of Barrack Obama in 2008? How was he positioned as an exemplar, and what additional or unique pressures weighed upon his performance as an African American male? How did his identity as a father and his heterosexual marriage assist him in navigating these tensions?

As seen in the previous two examples of Butterworth and Taylor, performances of identity are far more complicated than a simplified dichotomy of either resistance or conformity. José Esteban Muñoz theorizes a strategic resistance in the identity performances of queers of color through his conception of **disidentification**. Disidentification is not the outright and direct rejection of dominant and hegemonic systems of normative performance, which is not always possible "if they hope to survive in a hostile public sphere" (1999, p. 5), nor is it passive conformity to socially accepted norms. Rather, Muñoz articulates the strategy of disidentification as a means of survival and resistance, a claiming of agency by queers of color, by "working on and against dominant ideology" (p. 11) from within restrictive cultural systems and identities. Such a strategy, from a sexual and racial minority position, simultaneously works in and against dominant systems to articulate and activate new modes of being, new social relations, and new potentials for self-production. Again, we see that identity is always an ongoing performative negotiation from a particular social location.

BODIES IN SPACE AND TIME

A performance frame draws close attention to factors that shape and enable the doing, as well as the thing done. Most generally, performance looks to the performing body, the discourses that shape and enable the performing body, and the physical, temporal, and historical contexts in which performance take place. Performance theory considers how discourse brings performances into being, as well as the potential for performances to resist, rearticulate, and extend these discourses.

We can further expand performative doings of identity to include broader notions of culture. In his article "Rethinking Ethnography," Dwight Conquergood (1991) labeled the "rise of performance" and argued that culture is a verb and the body provides a way of knowing that is situated and sensuous. There is the *scriptocentric* approach to studying culture, through the study of words and written texts, but culture is enacted in physical space, in situated contexts, and in and through the body. Culture is not something we are, in some static and fixed permanence, but a performance. Culture is something we do and that which is done. Consider a cultural identity of your own, and take a moment to mentally list how specific actions, rituals, and performances work to produce this culture in specific places and times. Reflecting on Murphy's "dialectical gaze" (Chapter Seven), how do specific actions and contexts produce a specific organizational culture? How were religious, academic, and sexual cultures performed in Goltz's "X-Communication" (Chapter Eleven)? Reentering the LDS church after many years, how did the actions of sitting in specific spaces and remembering sacraments, particular dress, and the singing of

hymns trouble his understanding of identity across space and time? How did the action of walking outside and smoking become a resistant performance of identity to reclaim who he understood himself to be at the time the essay was crafted?

Diana Taylor has been a particularly influential theorist with her works *The Archive and the Repertoire* (2003) and "Performance and/as History" (2006). Taylor challenges the traditional ways that history, as a discipline, has relied upon the archive (documents, films, recorded data) to create history, with little interrogation of how this collection of history is both partial and rhetorical. She locates the **repertoire** as an additional way of thinking about history, via oral traditions, embodied practices, dance, song, theater, and physical memory. She seeks to problematize the ways we think of history, both in a western frame of linearity and also in terms of ethnocentric and privileged notions of what *counts* as history. History is not only an archive of texts, it is a repertoire of embodied actions. We *do* history. It is a performance. Consider official histories of historical moments in your life, such as 9/11, Hurricane Katrina, or the death of Michael Jackson. There are the "official" histories crafted and archived around these events that account for one method for thinking of history. Now consider your own embodied experiences with these events: where you were, how you felt, the emotional shift in your world. Outside of official reports, the history lives and is negotiated and performed within each of our bodies in different and complex ways. These histories continue to play out across time, space, and linear sequencing of events and work to shape and impact how identity is performed.

Beyond offering situated and embodied frameworks for complicating fixed notions of identity (cultural identities, gendered identities, national identities, sexualized identities, racial identities), a performance framework provides a generative and resistant body of theories and concepts to challenge the limitations of identity discourses. Performance not only unpacks, contextualizes, embodies, and situates who we are (as what we do) within discursive fields, but opens up spaces to complicate and disrupt who we can be, who we might be, and what we might become. This line of creative identity work can be described through Butler's notion of **fantasy** as a way of challenging the limitations of perceived rational knowledge, extending the inquiry to the margins and limits of discourse. Butler's fantasy "challenge(s) the contingent limits of what will and will not be called reality" (2004, p. 29). It is a creative challenge that "allows us to imagine ourselves and others otherwise," (2004, p. 29) through embodiment and creation. The body becomes a site to challenge the limitations of discourse. The body becomes a site of potential. This approach opens the future and identity up as site of play, of hope, and unexhausted potentials, challenging the restrictions of "what I am" through the never finished "what I do."

PERFORMING IDENTITY: A PREVIEW

The readings in this last section span a broad discussion of how identity is a performative accomplishment, enabled and constrained by a multitude of shifting discourses. Chapter Twenty-One, Frederick Corey's "The Personal: Against The Master Narrative," provides a bridge from the previous unit on representation, as he opens the chapter reflecting on how the gay male, in theatrical and religious representation, is continually constructed as a stigmatized, self-loathing, and suicidal other. Resisting the hegemonic and heteronormative master narrative of gay male doom and misery, Corey looks to the personal narrative as a potential site to disrupt, unfix, and trouble violent homophobic stories of gay male punishment and self-hatred. He argues that personal stories work to challenge

and interrupt the foreclosures of dominant narratives, wherein he becomes an active participant in the performance and representation of gay male identity. While reading this chapter, consider the following questions:

- What factors worked to shape and construct the master narrative that is mapped onto Corey's gay male identity?
- According to Corey, what is the relationship between the personal narrative and the master narrative? What can/might a personal narrative of experience do in relation to master narratives of identity?
- What master narratives work to story your lives? Think of them as actual stories or sequences of events that weigh upon your many identities. How do you navigate them? Rework them?

Bryant Keith Alexander's "Racializing Identity: Performance, Pedagogy, and Regret" presents an "article/script" in autopoetic form to examine, complicate, and assert his performances of race as a Black queer male. Navigating the tensions and obstacles of performing race "in the face of history and in the company of others," Alexander writes his coming to "feel my melanin" through the cumulative consciousness and negotiation of how his body and identity are positioned in relationship to White and Black bodies (p. 266, this volume). Through a number of performative vignettes, Alexander illustrates the intersectional and bleeding borders—such as his academic and gay subjectivities—that complicate and question his performances of race. Through exploring his own situated performances of identity in light of historical racial representations, Alexander problematizes essentializing racial identifications and questions the limitations of racial categorizations of identity. The piece explores what it means to perform race, and interrogates the discursive, historical, and intersectional factors that weigh upon, shape, and dictate these performances.

- What does it mean to perform race? How does Alexander suggest he performs his race in this chapter? How are these performances shaped and constrained?
- In what spaces, contexts, or interactions do you most feel your racial identity?
- What identities or memberships of yours do you perform in opposition or ongoing tension with one another? How do these tensions get magnified and negotiated in different contexts?

"Growing Pains: Colliding Subjectivities on a Pedagogical Learning Curve" by Kimberlee Pérez offers a personal examination of her experience performing identity as a light-skinned bi-racial queer Chicana within the classroom. As an instructor teaching units on the performances of race and gender, Pérez recounts her own "growing pains" through the narration of a student who is resistant to the cultural examination of white male privilege. Her internal struggle to live within her own body and her competing subjectivities, a struggle complicated through intersecting dimensions of whiteness, queerness, and Chicana identity, are storied through her conflicted sites of belonging. Her story moves between her Mexican father and her white male student, as collisions of privilege, "authenticity," subjectivity, and power disrupt and dislodge identity discourses and examine the ways we are both isolated and undone by one another.

- What obstacles does Pérez face in navigating a biracial identity? How does our language system work to compartmentalize her experience?
- Trace and discuss how performances of race, gender, and instructor/student collide in Pérez's narrative. Where do you see these performances of identity colliding? Working in tandem? What other subjectivities do you see at work?

- Thinking back to Corey, what master narratives weigh upon Pérez's identity? How does she perform her own race, and how does it shift within differing contexts?

Nadine Naber's "Resisting the Shore" builds upon Pérez's discussion of bifurcated ethnic and racial experiences in the U.S. by describing the experience of an Arab American female growing up in the 1970s and 80s. Negative mediated representations of Arab identity are mapped onto her body, her family, and her experiences, producing shame, a longing to fit in, and performances of disguising and degrading her ancestry and culture. In the context of her home, in a complex relationship with her mother, Naber navigates additional identity struggles, as mainstream U.S. cultural norms of gender and sexual performance collide with her mother's own cultural bias toward "the Americans." Her account constructs a narrative of how she negotiates multiple performances (shame, silence, disguise, politicism) in her construction and embodiment of critical bi-cultural consciousness, slowly rejecting the shame and self-hatred she internalized for being an Arab American woman. Simultaneously, her performance carves out a space between American and Arab identity to rescript and rearticulate her own performances within rigid Arab/American and virgin/whore binary constructions.

- In reflecting on Naber's childhood experiences, how can we discuss her friends as embodying and performing hegemonic ethnic identity? In reflection, where and how have you found yourself enacting similar performances? Where? How? Why?
- In your own performances of identity, what binaries or conflicting identifications do you navigate?

- How might we talk about the crafting of a critical consciousness as an identity? How might this be performed and embodied?

In Eli Clare's "Stolen Bodies, Reclaimed Bodies: Disability and Queerness," Clare recentralizes the lived experiences of the body and embodied identity in the politics of disability and queerness. Investigating his same-sex desire and physical disability, both of which collide and inform his use of the term "queer," Clare asks us to not lose sight of the physical, performing body at the center of experience. Speaking against the potential for bodies to simply become "storage sites" for oppression, he calls for us to think about bodies as merely the effect of ableist representations, false images, and stereotypes. Moving from discourses of ableism and oppression, Clare reclaims the lived body, the experiences of the body, at the center of ableist, homophobic, transphobic, and racist violence. Moving beyond the "stolen bodies" of oppressive discourse, Clare calls for the reclamation of the body, hoping to "grow to a place where I can fill my skin to its very edges" (p. 286, this volume). His narrative essay calls for us to understand identity as the living in and through the body.

- What are the influences and forces that would remove the politics of disability from the body and bodily experience? Why does Clare take issue with this approach?
- How does the notion or label of "queer" work in multiple ways in Clare's essay? How does placing the more traditional use of the term alongside more recent academic theorizing work to complicate its use?
- How does a performative frame work alongside and through Clare's placement of the body at the center of political identity struggle and embodied oppression?

Playing with the meanings and narratives that are mapped onto and resisted within differing bodies, Laknath Jayasinghe looks to Australian goth/punk/rock icon Nick Cave's gender parody in "Nick Cave, Dance Performance and the Production and Consumption of Masculinity." Analyzing the "queer kinaesthesia," or the gendered performative effects of Cave's movements, Jayasinghe argues that Cave's performances work to challenge naturalized discourses of, and fixed linkages between, male sex, masculinity and heterosexuality. Located in the context of Australia's OZ rock culture, with situated gendered norms and understandings, Cave's bodily movements enact a parody of hyper-masculine rock star personas, coupled with homoerotic kisses and pirouettes. His onstage persona, specifically the physicality he crafts and performs, works to disrupt and mock the "phallic power of musicians in a 'real rock band'" (p. 296, this volume). Cave's gender and sexual play potentializes a straight form of queer performance and queer pleasure. This embodied playfulness, sometimes occurring while wearing a diaper (called a "nappy" in Australia), disrupts gendered and sexual binaries through hyperbolic pelvic thrusts, ambiguity, and homoerotic/hyper-masculine juxtapositions.

- What are the distinctions between queer performance and queer identity (as queerness, in recent theorizing, is a rejection of rigid identity categorization)?
- What is the value or potential of Cave's parodic movements, according to Jayasinghe? What can or might these ambiguous performances of gender, sex, and sexuality do? Look at his "Nick the Stripper" video on YouTube.com as a reference.
- What contemporary artists do you see physically playing with naturalized discourses and/or gender, sex, and sexuality performances?

José Esteban Muñoz theorizes Kevin McCarty's The Chameleon Club photo work as a site of queer potentiality in "Impossible Spaces." Extending beyond the queer possibilities of Nick Cave's bodily performances, Muñoz asks us to think about the powers, possibilities, and potentials of space to not only shape identity, but to anticipate and gesture to identities and relations not yet actual, but lingering just beyond the intelligible. To put this another way, he is interested in identities not yet in existence, identities and relations that are cast outside of discourse. The anticipation of the photo essay, in Muñoz's conception, offers us the chance to glimpse outside of the limiting identities and relations of current discourse to imagine ourselves and others beyond the actuality of the here and now. He conceptualizes the photo essay as a depiction of "utopian rehearsal rooms," where the amateur aesthetic of the performances draws our attention to an unfinishedness and allows us to linger in a liminal space of potential. Muñoz reflects on his own experiences in mosh pits and punk clubs and how these spaces provided possibilities for enacting, performing, and rethinking identity. Beyond the present, and the present limitations of identity in the here and now, these nostalgic photos mark the past as a productive site to envision and remap potential futures.

- As you look through the photo essay, what physical spaces, in your experience, have provided you with the possibility and potential to experiment with who you are and who you might be in relationship to others?
- What historical moments of events opened a space for us to do future differently, if even for a moment? After 9/11, do you remember a sense that our relationship to one another and the world could have, might have, been very different than it turned out to be?

- How do specific physical spaces contain and foreclose potential performances of identity and relations? School? Work? What parallels can you draw between Muñoz's discussion of utopian space and Sandoval's dissonant globalizations?

The final chapter of the text, D. Soyini Madison's "Crazy Patriotism and Angry (Post) Black Women," returns us to multiple discussions within the book, examining the construction of U.S. American national identity through racialized and gendered systems. Madison enlists the concept of *crazy patriotism* to mark the ways the angry black female stereotype has been mapped onto Michelle Obama in an effort to construct her as irrational and unpatriotic. She looks at the controversial *New Yorker* cartoon of Michelle Obama, revisiting Audre Lorde's "Uses of Anger" essay to complicate and differentiate the anger assigned to her through the workings of crazy patriots. Contemplating the notion of "post-black," Madison explores the complexity of Michelle Obama's performance of identities, her multiple and intersecting subjectivities that both mobilize and shape her performance of blackness. A current and complex reflection on Michelle Obama's reception, navigation, and identity, contemplating the shifting and interwoven discourses of racial identity in the U.S., Madison's brief essay works to suture together many of the threads that move through this anthology.

- What are the dangers and violences of crazy patriotism, according to Madison? How does this concept work in opposition to the potentials sketched out by Muñoz and Sandoval?
- Beyond class and beauty, what other identity factors worked to complicate and exceed the angry black woman stereotype? How was heterosexuality a factor in this negotiation?

- What does, according to Madison, a post-black identity look like? What are the limitations of this conception? What would a post-patriot movement look like?

REFERENCES

Butler, J. (1999). *Gender trouble: Feminism and the subversion of identity* (10th anniversary ed.). New York: Routledge.

Butler, J. (2004). *Undoing gender.* New York: Routledge.

Butterworth, M. L. (2005). Ritual in the "church of baseball": Suppressing the discourse of democracy after 9/11. *Communication and Critical/Cultural Studies, 2,* 107–129.

Conquergood, D. (1991). Rethinking ethnography: Towards a critical cultural politics. *Communication Monographs, 58*(2), 179–194.

Diamond, E. (2000). Performance and cultural politics. In L. Goodman and J. de Gay (Eds.) *The Routledge Reader in Politics and Performance.* New York, NY: Routledge. 66–69.

Lloyd, M. (1999). The body. In F. Ashe, A. Finlayson, M. Lloyd, I. Mackenzie, J. Martin, & S. O'Neill (Eds.), *Contemporary social and political theory* (pp. 111–130). Buckingham: Open University Press.

Muñoz, J. E. (1999). *Disidentifications: Queers of color and the performance of politics.* Minneapolis: University of Minnesota Press.

Schechner, R. (2006). *Performance studies: An introduction* (2nd ed.). New York: Routledge.

Taylor, D. (2003). *The archive and the repertoire: Performing cultural memory in the Americas.* Durham, NC: Duke University Press.

Taylor, D. (2006). Performance and/as history. *The Drama Review, 50*(1), 67–86.

Taylor, J. (2000). On being an exemplary lesbian: My life as a role model. *Text & Performance Quarterly, 20,* 58–73.

Turner, V. (2004). Liminality and communitas. In H. Bial (Ed.), *The Performance Studies Reader* (pp. 79–87). New York: Routledge.

Turner, V. (1982). *From ritual to theatre: The human seriousness of play.* New York: PAJ Publications.

ADDITIONAL SUGGESTED READINGS

Alexander, B. K. (2006). *Performing black masculinity: Race, culture and queer identity.* Lanham, MD: AltaMira Press.

Calafell, B. M. (2007). *Latina/o communication studies: Theorizing performance.* New York, NY: Peter Lang.

Fox, R. (2010). Tales of a fighting bobcat: An auto-archaeology of gay identity formation and maintenance. *Text & Performance Quarterly, 30,* 122–142.

Gilbert, J. R. (2004). *Performing marginality: Humor, gender, and cultural critique.* Detroit: Wayne State University Press.

Gingrich-Philbrook, C. (1998). Disciplinary violation as gender violation: The stigmatized masculine voice of performance studies. *Communication Theory, 8,* 203–220.

Lindemann, K. (2008). "I can't be standing up out there": Communicative performances of (dis)ability in wheelchair rugby. *Text & Performance Quarterly, 28,* 98–115.

Miller, L. C., Taylor, J., & Carver, M. H. (2003). *Voices made flesh: Performing women's autobiography.* Madison, WI: University of Wisconsin Press.

Muñoz, J. E. (2000). Feeling brown: Ethnicity and affect in Ricardo Bracho's 'The Sweetest Hangover (and Other STDs)'. *Theatre Journal, 52,* 67–79.

Park-Fuller, L. M. (2000). Performing absence: The staged personal narrative as testimony. *Text & Performance Quarterly, 20*(1), 20–42.

Pelias, R. J. (1999). *Writing performance: Poeticizing the researcher's body.* Carbondale, IL: Southern Illinois University Press.

Román, D. (1998). *Acts of intervention: Performance, gay culture, and AIDS.* Bloomington: Indiana University Press.

Sandahl, C. (2003). Queering the crip or cripping the queer: Intersections of queer and crip identities in solo autobiographical performance. *GLQ: A Journal of Lesbian and Gay Studies, 9,* 25–56.

Spry, T. (2001). From goldilocks to dreadlocks: Hair-raising tales of racializing bodies. In L. C. Miller & R. J. Pelias (Eds.), *The green window: Proceedings from the Giant City conference on performative writing* (pp. 52–65). Carbondale, IL: Southern Illinois University.

Stern, C., & Henderson, B. (1993). *Performance: Texts and contexts.* White Plains, NY: Longman Publishing Group.

Turner, V. (1990). Are there universals in performance in myth, ritual, and drama? In R. Schechner & W. Appel (Eds.), *By means of performance: Intercultural studies of theatre and ritual* (pp. 8–18). New York: Cambridge University Press.

Zingsheim, J. (2008). Resistant privilege and (or?) privileged resistance: Navigating the boxes of embodied identity. *Liminalities: A Journal of Performance Studies, 4*(2).

The Personal
Against the Master Narrative

By Frederick C. Corey

21

Klein, a nervous young man whose overcoat in winter hung down far below his knees, felt shame …

"Archways," by Joyce Carol Oates

The theater is a remarkable space. The curtain rises. The lights shift. The action unfolds. The drama reflects or resists, explains or confounds, romances or torments what it means to live and breathe. I have long loved the theater. As a child, I sat stunned between my parents as Maureen Stapleton opened the screen door and called out for her little Sheba. I knew and loved knowing Sheba was gone, even before I knew Sheba was a dog. I also loved hearing about the theater, about my mother's first visit to the theater, a story she will tell with minimal provocation, and sometimes with no provocation at all, "The great Ethel Barrymore in *The Corn Is Green*, now *there's* a play." By high school, I took to the theater like a diva to the spotlight. I skipped algebra class to make props for *The Miracle Worker*, and I secured my first role, the delivery boy in *And Miss Reardon Drinks a Little*. Yet for all of my love of the theater, I sensed that the drama, as a literary genre, was not quite right. Something was amiss. The drama never told *my* story.

To an extent, an extent for which I make little apology, my fascination with the theater was a search for identity. I used the theater as I explored the question any teen might ask—Who am I? Am I Brick, in constant battle with the father figure? Is the essence of my life as unnamable as the terror driving *Suddenly Last Summer?* Will I go the way of Martha in *The Children's Hour?* When I played the role of Eugene in *Look Homeward, Angel,* I twisted the text and found a passion for the character by calling upon the deeply rooted secret of my life: I was a little fag in the making. I used drama to search for the man I wanted to become, but my efforts were futile. I found only sickness and silence. If my story was in drama, it was buried deep within the stage of modernity.

During my first week in college, a door opened. In a course titled *Fundamentals of Interpretive Reading,* the professor, Elbert R. Bowen, discussed at some length the characteristics of prose fiction. Another professor, William R. Haushalter, was holding auditions for a performance of "Archways," a short story by Joyce Carol Oates. I was cast as the protagonist and immersed myself in the writings of Oates, a writer new to me, as Oates was none too popular in the expensive suburbs of Detroit. What I admired most about Oates was her ability to get not at what people say but at what people think, and I took an orgasmic delight in her ability to turn time through the turn of a phrase. The narrative, I discovered, is a literary form ideal for lives governed by silence. I was able to read into my character, Klein, a nervous young man; and I understood the essence of his character: shame.

I, too, was ashamed. I was ashamed of my secrets, my desires, my sexuality. And I was a virgin. How could I be ashamed of myself when I was not yet who I was? The now famous 1989 *Report of the Secretary's Task Force on Youth Suicide,* conducted by the U. S. Department of Health and Human Services (Gibson; see also, Sedgwick), may well contain the answer. Gay and lesbian youth, confronted with a hostile and condemning environment, are two to three times more likely than other youth to commit suicide. Was I, like Oates' Klein, a case study in the potentiality of suicide? Klein escaped his self-destruction because, for a fleeting moment, "He had been loved. He had been worthy of love" (Oates 184). But I was not Klein. He was normal (read: heterosexual), and I was homosexual, a word replete with the medicalization of desire. My homosexuality and, therefore, my identity (or lack thereof), were snared within the master narrative, the ongoing ideology passed from generation through generation by way of the stories we tell.

I have woven my way toward the central argument in this essay, that the personal narrative is one way of disturbing the master narrative, and through the performative dimensions of the personal narrative, the individual is able to disrupt—and, dare I say *rewrite*—the master narrative. In *The Postmodern Condition,* a treatise on scientific knowledge as a type of discourse, Lyotard argues that "the grand narrative has lost its credibility" and that *the petit recits*—little narratives—are "the quintessential form of imaginative invention" (37; 60). Here, I borrow and extend Lyotard's argument to claim that the personal narrative constitutes a little narrative which transcends self-indulgence when placed against the backdrop of the master narrative. The heteronormative narrative is public, historical, documented, and hegemonic. The master narrative is an artillery of moral truth, and the personal narrative defixes that truth. The master narrative is a cultural discourse, replete with epistemic implications, and the personal narrative is a mode of "reverse discourse" (Foucault, "Subject"). The personal narrative swings between the public and private, between what is said and what is thought, between the individual and society, between the regulations of language and the regulations of the body, of anality. The master narrative informs the queer's identity, but through the personal narrative, the queer is able to "tell about personal, lived experience in a way that assists in the construction of identity, reinforces or challenges private and public belief systems and values, and either resists or reinforces the dominant cultural practices of the community in which the narrative event occurs" (Stern and Henderson 35). Each queer has a little story, but in the spirit of postmodernism, a little difference becomes a lot of discourse.

The master narrative which governs the social meaning of same-sex desire is composed of multiple and complex texts, but it is possible to trace the essence of the plot throughout the history of Western civilization. The Hellenic Era is (in)famous for the love between men and boys, for the lust of the *Symposium* and *The Phaedrus,* for the antics of Socrates and the lyrics of Sappho, yet the claim of glorious liberty in desire for the Greeks is cursory. The Greeks were a moralistic people, and the relationship between pleasure and pedagogy was an intricate one in which the teacher was to "practice the strictest austerities" (Foucault, *Pleasure* 245). A man may have sexual relations with a boy, but ultimately, the boy was to grow out of this pedagogy and establish the orderliness of marriage and home. In contemporary discourse, the love within Hellenic pedagogy is cast as immoral and pagan, while the tender, romantic love between Achilles and Patroclus is all but ignored. The master narrative conjures images of grown men seducing boys and all but ignores the sublime image of Achilles over the body of his dead lover.

If the Hellenic Era offers a series of complications and paradoxes, the Christian Era offers remarkable clarity. Same-sex desire is a sin. Despite some recent efforts to argue the church conducted and even sanctioned same-sex marriages (e.g., Boswell, *Same-Sex Union*), the general rhetoric of the Middle Ages reflects the narrative of Sodom in Genesis 19 (see Boswell, *Christianity;* Katz, *Almanac,* and McNeill). Sodomites were a wicked people. God sent angels to investigate the problems, but the Sodomites raped the angels, and in the end, the Sodomites were destroyed. This saga has informed the master narrative of the wicked character of homosexuality, and even today the narrative permeates our discourse. Sodomy laws recollect the master narrative through the ideograph of Sodom: gay men are evil and must be destroyed, and women—lesbians, in this instance—must pay for the sins of men. That the immorality of the Sodomites is unrelated to their same-sex practices, that rape and pillage are not values of gay and lesbian communities, or that the Sodomites were not gay in the manner we construct *gay* today, are irrelevant distractions to the master narrative. The master narrative is a dominant cultural discourse that serves to keep gay men and lesbians as sinners, outside the realm of morality.

One might think that science, for all its attention to deduction and falsifiability, would have questioned the fallacies of the master narrative, would have eschewed the Idols of the Theater, to borrow Francis Bacon's rhetoric, would have reframed the questions posed by the Christian tale. Quite by contrast, science, specifically medical science, has resisted its own purpose and lent veracity to a master narrative grounded in Christianity. Medicine has added to the narrative the vocabulary of perversion, inversion, homosexuality, deviant, variant, unnatural, and psychiatric illness (Bullough; Foucault, *History of Sexuality,* Katz, *History*). In the context of desire-as-sin, science has promoted cures such as castration, vasectomy, LSD, shock therapy, and, as late as 1951, lobotomy (Katz, *History* 129). In *Gay American History,* Katz documents 36 medical cases of scientific oppression. The accounts are horrific. In spite of the fact that the accounts are written from the physicians' point of view, the field notes provide portraits of the patients as living, breathing human beings who appear not to be sick at all. That is, not sick *before* becoming subject to science. Take, for example, the case of castration performed by Dr. Charles Hughes (Katz, *History* 153–155). Dr. Hughes describes his patient as "a gentleman of ordinary moral, intellectual and physical parts" (153) who was tired of the dietary treatment of Graham Crackers, a then-popular scientific treatment of homosexuality. Dr. Graham invented the cracker made of unbolted wheat to help men preserve their precious semen, which was to be preserved for procreative sex. The patient wanted surgery to end his desire for same-sex "hand pressing, kissing, and embracing" (154). The physician performed two operations, the first an excision of the dorsales penis nerve, and the second an entire excision of the testes. In the end, the physician notes, this twenty-eight-year-old bookkeeper "lost his erotic inclinations towards his own sex but showed a social inclination towards asexualized ladies" (155).

The personal narratives, *the petit recits,* of the gay bookkeeper and his lesbian friends have escaped the master narrative of scientific discourse. Their experiences, however empirical, do not constitute science and are not "medical." Yet the absence of their stories has contributed to the collective destabilization and discreditation of the master narrative, of scientific knowledge, and though every effort may be made to salvage science as a way of knowing, we are left to ask not only what good science served the bookkeeper, but what good science has served any gay man or lesbian. Science, like Christianity, has effectively ignored lesbians and defined the gay man's body as a house of evil. The gay man's body is inscribed with disease—syphilis, gonorrhea, herpes, hepatitis, HIV—and he has brought the disease upon himself by virtue of his sexuality. The discourse is corrigible, the narrative hegemonic, the identity destructive. The gay man belongs, as reflected in the Library of Congress catalog scheme, in the company of sex crimes, incest, pedophilia, rape, raping children, child pornography—(insert *homosexuality* here)—sadomasochism, prostitution, and child prostitution.

"We need a story," writes Holly Hughes, and toward that narrative, Hughes has woven a series of little stories about how it feels to be a lesbian, and not any lesbian, but how it feels to be Holly Hughes (Introduction 9). Whether one agrees or disagrees with Hughes' specific body politic is not the issue here; what is at issue is the use of the personal narrative as a form of reverse discourse. Hughes uses the personal narrative as a speech act. Her story disturbs the master narrative's ideology of the word *lesbian,* and through her art, Hughes probes issues of transitivity. "What," asks Judith Butler, "does it mean for a word not only to name, but also in some sense to perform and, in particular, to perform what it names?" (197). Hughes' performative explication of what it means to be lesbian provokes controversy among lesbians (see Hughes, "Case"), probes questions of authority, and "explodes our constructions, and performances, of gender and sexual identity" (Miller 46).

The personal narrative has no capabilities the drama could not achieve, given the skill of a fine playwright. My aim is not to start a competition of genre, to say one genre is "better" than another, or to limit the personal narrative to an act that occurs on the stage in front of an audience. My aim is comparison. What are some of the differences between the staged narrative and narrative shared in conversation or the drama? The staged narrative has an economy of distribution the conversational narrative does not realize. The theater is a community space in which we gather to sit, listen, learn, experience, and identify. Like the drama, the staged narrative becomes a point of reference for subsequent discourse, an impetus for conversations about the ideas presented by the narrator. We can talk about a performance whether we saw the performance together or not.

And the drama? The narrative may have some differences in point of view, structure and form, or presentation, but as a narrator can move into a dramatic mode, a playwright is able to deploy a narrative mode. The differences between drama and narrative are not, then, linked exclusively to aesthetics. Politics plays a significant role. High school teachers can enable their students to tell their stories far more easily than they can mount a production of *Angels in America.* The narrative, in particular the personal narrative, expresses what appears to be a grounded truth based in experience. Literary theorists in academic circles will be quick to support the veracity of drama, but in popular discourse, the personal narrative is seen as being "true." In this vein, the personal narrative has made wide appearance in the Presidential political campaigns of 1992 and 1996. Personal narratives—stories about Arkansas, Kansas, or an elderly woman who needs her Medicare—have been used as evidence to support larger claims of character or appropriate social policy. Media pundits have lamented the loss of "political rhetoric" which calls upon grand and noble themes. The pundits fail to recognize the rhetorical power of the little narratives. Contemporary audiences are postmodern: The grand narratives have lost their credibility. The little narratives sell the truth.

I have sold my own truth, however narrated that truth may be. I have performed my story in both written and staged forms, and I have challenged the master narrative of my desires. Do I disturb the Greek narrative of pedagogy, the Christian narrative of sin, or the medical narrative of disease? I am not the one to answer these questions, but I am able to say with confidence that I will not, like Martha, shoot myself when a student exposes my desires. I reveal my own secrets. Through the personal narrative, I participate in the construction of my own identity, my own shame.

WORKS CITED

Boswell, John. *Christianity, Social Tolerance, and Homosexuality.* Chicago: U of Chicago P, 1980.

—. *Same-Sex Unions in Premodern Europe.* New York: Villard, 1994.

Bullough, Vern L. "Homosexuality and the Medical Model." *Journal of Homosexuality* 1 (1974): 99–110.

Butler, Judith. "Burning Acts." *Performativity and Performance.* Ed. Andrew Parker and Eve Kosofsky Sedgwick. New-York: Routledge, 1995. 197–227.

Foucault, Michel. *An Introduction.* Trans. Robert Hurley. Vol. 1 of *The History of Sexuality.* New York: Random 1978.

—. "The Subject and Power." *Critical Inquiry* 8 (1982): 777–795.

—. *The Use of Pleasure.* Trans. Robert Hurley. Vol. 2 of *The History of Sexuality.* New York: Random, 1985.

Gibson, Paul. "Gay Male and Lesbian Youth Suicide." *Report of the Secretary's Task Force on Youth Suicide.* Vol. 3. U.S. Department of Health and Human Services. Washington: GPO, 1989. 110–142.

Hughes, Holly. "A Case Concerning Hughes." *The Drama Review* 33.4 (1989): 10–17.

—. Introduction. *Clit Notes—A Sapphic Sampler.* New York: Grove, 1996.1–22.

Katz, Jonathon. *Gay American History.* New York: Harper & Row, 1976.

—. *Gay/Lesbian Almanac.* New York: Harper, 1983.

Lyotard, Jean-Francois. *The Postmodern Condition: A Report on Knowledge.* Trans. Geoff Bennington and Brian Massumi. Minneapolis: U of Minnesota P, 1984.

McNeill, John J. *The Church and the Homosexual.* 4th ed. Boston: Beacon, 1993.

Miller, Lynn C. "'Polymorphous Perversity' in Women's Performance Art The Case of Holly Hughes." *Text and Performance Quarterly* 15 (1995): 44–58.

Oates, Joyce Carol. "Archways." *Upon the Sweeping Flood.* New York: Vanguard, 1966. 166–185.

Sedgwick, Eve Kosofsky. "Queer and Now." *Tendencies.* New York: Routledge, 1994. 1–20.

Stern, Carol Simpson, and Bruce Henderson. *Performance: Texts and Contexts.* New York: Longman, 1993.

Frederick C. Corey is Dean of the University College at Arizona State University. He received his bachelor's degree from Central Michigan University, where he was a student of Filbert R. Bowen and William R. Haushalter. He received his master's degree from Southern Illinois University, Carbondale and his Ph.D. from the University of Arizona. His dissertation was a study of Martha Graham's use of classical tragedy in modern dance. Corey is the author of numerous essays and editor of HIV Education: Performing Personal Narratives.

Racializing Identity
Performance, Pedagogy, and Regret

By Bryant Keith Alexander

This performative article/script serves as an extended functional definition and a practical exploration of the notion of "racializing identity." Through a series of individually labeled autopoetic movements, the performative article/script creates a typology that compares and analyzes the foci of each form, facilitating the definition and exposing the socially constructed intersection between race and Black queer identity. The performative article/script begins to question the limitations of race as a specified method of categorizing bodies and more specifically questions the conceptualization of "performing race" as a sign of racial authenticity.

Keywords: *racialization; performative writing; performing race; Black gay identity; Black performance studies*

FEELING MY MELANIN

At the age of 25, I began to feel my melanin; it is rather late, I know, but I have also come to understand that it is not about a physical development but a psychological development—a coming into oneself. One day, I actually felt my melanin, but this was not like my White friends who nurse self-inflicted sunburns. It was not something on the surface but reached deep beyond the third degree—burning in that deep place within my soul, that place where I came to an understanding of myself and how I fit and didn't fit within the academic circles in which I walked. Maybe it was Miles's (1988) process of racialization, "any process or situation wherein the idea of 'race' is introduced to define and give meaning to some particular population, its characterizations and actions" (p. 246). That moment, when I came to understand self as other, not other as pathology but other as belonging to a different racial and cultural tradition—a different psychological condition in which my very presence did not mark difference but where my thoughts dictated my character. And where the articulation of my Black experience was not interpreted as some sympathetic revelry, a

Bryant Keith Alexander, "Racializing Identity: Performance, Pedagogy, and Regret," *Cultural Studies ↔ Critical Methodologies*, vol. 4, no. 1, pp. 12-27. Copyright © 2004 by Sage Publications. Reprinted with permission.

personal affront, or even an attack on Whiteness but a coming into my own voice.

The first day that I began to feel my melanin, I felt it as a nervous sensation at the bottom of my stomach when I heard a Black woman described as a bitch by a White friend. He thought I should understand—because Black men often call their women bitches, right?

A year later (because this is a process you know), it turned into a rumbling in my stomach when a White colleague complained to me about Black students. He asked me "why do they act that way," because of course I should know—and worse yet, as Caliban I should provide information to Prospero so he can rule (Karamcheti, 1995, p. 142).

Two years later, it became a pressure in my chest, moving upward to my head when I patiently and very judiciously listened to another White friend's characterization of a Black male as being "full of rage" and how "everything with him is racial"—and how I was different.

By age 30, it was an itch in my throat when I was asked to support a White teacher against an "angry young Black man" who simply complained about a grade. At 33, it bypassed my mouth and entered my head like a throbbing embolism of pain when I was applauded for being a "good Black man."

At 34, it rushed through my ears like fire when as part of a research project, young Black men told me of their pain in the predominately White university and doubtfully asked if I had experienced the same.[1] They asked doubtfully because I was so respected by my White colleagues, doubtfully because I got along, doubtfully because in some ways I could pass (not racially but in that performatively academic way), and without doubt they thought that I was the house nigger, who had learned the language and the tools of the master and no longer performed a racial resistance.

It was then that melanin enflamed—calling me to task for my silence. It called me to attention. It called me to attend to that which I acknowledged as a racial distinction and a felt reality but not a cultural obligation. It called me to name and to claim a racialized identity and a racialized voice—one in which my Black presence served as a filter to my knowledge, a barometer of thoughts, and tempered my interactions with those who would

> have me to ACT or not ACT—Black.
> As if Black is equated with being militant and antisocial;
> as if Black equals anti-White;
> as if Black is being the oppressed and the oppressor.
> Or those folks who would wish me to engage in *race talk* in hushed tones—
> the sanitized talk of academia for their ease.
> When in fact, the scathing edges of their articulate tongues have often left me silenced and bleeding; as if that is not a performance of race or culture.

So, I've been questioning this conceptualization of "performing race" and the "notion of racializing"— as a collective description of the social mandates and expectations of race, as the performance or signification of tribal affiliation. Knowing that I am a member of many tribes that are often at war with each other—Black, academic, gay—to name a few, I am interested in Manthia Diawara's (1993) notion in which he reconstructed the project of Black studies as Black performance studies. He explained that Black performance studies

> would mean study of ways in which black people, through communicative action, created and continue to create themselves within the American experience. Such an approach would contain several interrelated notions, among them that

"performance" involves an individual or group of people interpreting an *existing* tradition reinventing themselves—in front of an audience, or public; and that black agency in the U.S. involves the redefinition of the tools of Americanness. Thus, the notion of "study" expands not only to include an appreciation of the importance of performative action historically but to include a performative aspect itself, a reenaction of a text or a style or a culturally specific response in a different medium. (Diawara, 1993, p. 265)

So, given the tattered and torn history of African Americans in this country, to perform Blackness is in essence to perform an aspect of Americanness or a result of being Americanized—twisting and turning the script, applying it to the Black experience.

Now, I find myself in front of an audience (readers) interested in the promises and pitfalls of performing race. I find myself presenting myself in a voice that is uniquely mine. The form allows for a "materializing possibility in and through a kind of writing that is distinctly performative: writing that recognizes its delays and displacements while proceeding as writing toward engaged, embodied, material ends" (Pollock, 1998, p. 96). It is helping me engage a critical reflexivity and to fuse the multiple aspects of myself into "a figural anthropology of the self" (Lionnet, 1989, p. 99).

I am thinking that the performance of race is not exclusively biological or cultural but, as Hatcher and Troyna (1993) would support, that "race does not work in isolation: it is interfused with other ideologies and social processes" (p. 123). Or, as Tyagi (1996) would suggest, the confluence of "geography, culture and language" works in a tensive creation of racial identity leading to a performance that stands at the borders of social design (p. 43).

Giroux and McLaren (1994) would echo that these intersections play with borders of identity, borders of culture, borders of representation, and borders of power and politics. These borders are real, imagined, constructed, and sedimented within the lived experiences of those who are affected by them, those who are racialized. They are borders marked by difference.

Now, I find myself in front of an audience (readers) interested in the promises and pitfalls of performing race—and as a Black gay performer teacher scholar, the bleeding borders and influences on my identity complicate the issue. Yet I use the presence of my Black male body in contradistinction to the historically perceived and socially constructed Black male body, the articulation of my personal lived experience filtered through my process of sense making, and engage Black cultural traditions of signifyin' and performance—as expressive forms with and without the intention both to perform race and to study the notion of performing race and Black performance in what hooks (1995) called a "struggle for liberation" (p. 211). Diawara (1993) would suggest that "such a performance is both political and theoretical: it refers to and draws on existing traditions; represents the actor as occupying a different position in society; and interpellates the audience's responses to emerging images of Black people" (p. 265). And following Warner's (1993) notion of queer theory as "resistance to regimes of the normal," I accept the spirit of my venture as queer (p. xxvi). This references both the political move that challenges notions of "normalcy" in academic discourse as well as a positionality of divine in-betweenness.

Yet we still use race as categories of performance, and skin becomes the referential signifier, what Appiah (1996) called "criterial beliefs—that define the concept [of race]"—things like skin, point of origin, and the categorical designation of the parents (p. 34).

So, now I find myself interested in the performance attributed to skin.

I AM INTERESTED IN SKIN

(I am interested in "SKIN" on Black bodies.) Skin, that mutable, but consistently present body encasement. Skin that "external limiting layer, especially when forming a tough but flexible cover."

Skin color, what some might suggest is an environmental adaptive trait—based on region and point of origin.

Skin as a visible introduction of otherness or familiarity—which establishes expectations of intelligence, of allegiance, of athleticism, of behavior, of motivation, of virility, of fertility, of sexuality—performance-based expectations of race—as in buying a good work horse. "Show me your teeth." "Show me your papers." "Show me what you are made of." "Show me what you got!"

I am fixated on the cultural politics of skin and color—not as in tanning, or baking, or frying in the sun for aesthetic purposes. BUT, skin as in the freck, freck, freckling color of skin, skin as in race? skin as in a box checked,

skin as in claiming membership in an ethnic community, and claiming that tattered and torn history that tempers your tongue, articulates your vision and sometimes even dictates your body in time and place. I am interested in the politics of dark skin and light skin—a performance of preference, a hierarchy of value, even within the Black community—an extrapolation and

interpretation of an *existing, of an existing, of an existing* tradition that values White beauty—and has some Black folk fading their skin, putting color in their eyes, straightening their nose, their teeth, their hair, their disposition—a racial performance of social acceptability. I am interested in Skin—seeing it, marking it, sharing it, claiming it, trading it,

I am interested in the performative expectations and delimiting implications of skin.

BLACK AND WHITE MAKE BROWN

Do you remember the Glad sandwich bag commercials from a couple of years ago? The ones with the zip-lock top—one side was blue and the other was yellow, and when pressed together they made green. Do you remember those commercials? The logic behind the commercial was that when sealed, when joined, when united, the two colors blended into one.

Sometime ago, I received pictures of a Black man and a White woman—my younger brother, Daniel, and Michelle his wife—posing for a picture, a documentation of their commitment to each other, a relational image captured in time. In the shadows of their images, there was a moment when I could have sworn that ancestors were gathered to remember, when White female bodies were burned at stakes for doing the unspeakable and Black male bodies swung from ropes for doing the unthinkable, and in those shadows, White bodies shrouded in sheets and sirens through the night would sound to signal this union—a ritual performance of race enacted historically. Her White sacred femininity would have been lethal to his Black maleness and to her own survival. But this was the year 2001—and my own interracial unions are also pictured in the background, implicating and complicating my reading of this text.[2]

The next pictures were laughing images of two children, twins, a boy and a girl, Nicholas and Nicole—light brown babies with mischievous smiles on their faces and sparkles in their eyes—the product of this Black–White union.

> Laughing at history.
> Defying time.
> Heralding a new day.

I guess Black and White make (light) brown. But unlike the zip-lock bags that can be separated, retaining their individual colored identities, with the appropriate expected performance of race, these children represent a union that cannot be separated; they have been forever sealed.

> And in that picture
> Black and White hands
> nurtured, held, breathed,
> gave each other some skin
> in ways only love can create.[3]

These children are not this or that; they are both and something more. They represent a union in time and space. Their presence in the world helps to close a gap—but also still signals an ocean of controversy in a world in which one drop still signals race or a different box checked—but they are little racialized bridges of hope and desire. Their Black features are tempered by their White influence, and their pale skin is seasoned with color. They will negotiate a performance of in-betweenness—knowing that some will herald their beauty and others will demonize them as a contamination—a fly in the buttermilk or a blemish on a dark canvas. Their performance of race will be mediated. I look at their picture and I hasten to ask:

GIVE ME SOME SKIN

"Give me some skin": a throwback phrase from the early 1970s.

"And make it slow and easy." I am reminded of "the dap," the Black cultural tradition, an intricately executed handshake in which brothers greeted each other, a cultural performance of manly contact.

To say "give me some skin" was a request for intimacy that far surpassed the simple sharing of a choreographed dance of the hands. It was a move toward connecting, grafting skin in that slow and easy way, a slow sliding of palms across each other, like lifelines crossing, pasts and futures slowly moving across each other, sharing time and space.

"To give skin" is an acknowledgment that skins are shared, not like a coat, belt, or purse but like histories are shared, like traditions are shared, like pains are shared, like dreams and memories are shared.

"Giving skin" is a moment of sharing, like lovers who share skins, intimacy so close that they seemingly embody the same skin; to share the scope of your skin, not just hands or lips but the full-stocking encasement of tender, vibrant, breathing tissue; to have tissue breathing on tissue in extended rhythmic communion; the soft underbelly and those spaces reserved for self and only intimate others; those performances of race and culture that signify membership or departure.

To say "give me some skin" is to ask—for this moment in time and space—connect with me, understand my pain, feel me, touch me in that way that validates my presence and uplifts my soul.

"Yo brother man, give me some skin and make it slow and easy." "Yo sister friend, share some skin with me and make it slow and easy." So slow that I can savor the moment. So slow that I can feel my melanin—"Brother, can you spare a dime?"

Give me some skin. So that I don't feel so all alone.

I extend my open palm to you in cultural communion,

the lines of our past and the lines of our futures will

cross each other slowly bleeding our histories.

So make it slow and easy—like a slow burn, but not one that hurts,

but the felt sensation of oooohhhh yeahhhhhh.

CONTACT AND DESIRE

My office mate, a Mexican patriot, reached over to shake my hand one day, a sign of friendship and acknowledgment between what he describes as "Black man and a Brown man sharing an office together!" But when I reached to shake his hand, our approach was different—me with the "straightforward" approach and him with a arched racialized and culturalized performative expectation. And in that awkward moment of negotiation, he said, "Ah man! What's that man? You better watch out—you're turning White!" And he grabbed my hand, conforming it to his desire. He laughed and walked away. And I thought about performative expectations of race and culture and the bleeding of borders and identities.

Now, I find myself in front of an audience (readers) interested in the promises and pitfalls of performing race—and as a Black gay performer teacher scholar, the bleeding borders of my hyphenated identity complicate the issue. And I find that I have always been in front of an audience trying to perform race, trying to perform culture, trying to perform gender, trying to perform academic, and having those performances deemed unacceptable. They have been unacceptable until someone has grabbed my hand and conformed it to their desire—yet I have my own imperatives, my own desires, and my own regrets.

JE REGRETTE

(*sung*) If I never feel you in my arms again. If I never feel your tender kiss again. If I never hear I love you now and then. Will I never make love to you once again. Please understand if love ends. Then I promise you, I promise you that, that I shall never breathe again. (Babyface, 1993)

Toni Braxton's song, "Breathe Again" was a number 1 hit that topped the charts for weeks. The song, which speaks of a desperate desire to hold on to a love(r), ends with a pledge: "I shall never breathe again."

As a child, I used to play breathing games. You know what I mean. I used to have contests with my brothers as to who could hold his breath longest. I would take the biggest breath that I could—making that gasping guttural sound as if it would expand my lungs bigger. I remember that my abdomen would push out, and I would look like one of Sally Struther's kids on television, like little Domiano. The initial moments felt great—as if I could sustain for days. But then I would feel this pressure in my chest and a strain in my stomach. Then I would feel this pressure pushing up my throat, and from behind my teeth a rush of air would flow forward. I always lost. My brothers were bigger and more athletic, and I was the fragile one. I couldn't compete. But I am not sure what the gains would have been anyway—in not breathing.

I remember that whenever I wanted something really bad, I would also hold my breath in anticipation, as if the energy it took to breathe would somehow disturb the possibility of it happening.

Later, people started using the phrase, "Don't hold your breath," as if to say, "It will never happen." "It" being whatever you wanted to happen.

(*sung*) And I can't stop thinkin' about. About the way things used to be. And I can't stop thinkin' about. About the love that you made to me. And I can't get you out of my head. How in the world will I begin. To let you walk right out my life and blow my heart away. (Babyface, 1993)

She is in a second class of mine this quarter. She is a beautiful, intelligent, articulate, Black Afrocentric sista. Me, a relatively attractive, young, articulate, Black gay brotha docta. The class is Performance Theory and Method. Most of her talk centers on the critique of Black cultural performance. The other sistas in the class critique Black men, Black politics, the Black community, and their positions within and against them all. They do this in some ways because I have created a space for them to do so. They do this as an assertion of their Black womanist presence in my class. And even though I usually applaud their critique (intentionally or not), I often feel silently victimized by it—because in spite of my academic accomplishment, my Black gay identity seems to lessen me in their eyes. Not just these students, but like so many Black women who say things like "What a waste of a good Black man."

(*sung*) And I can't stop carin' about. About the apple of my eye. I can't stop doin without. Without the center of my life. And I can't get you outta my head. I know I can't pretend. That I won't die if you decide you won't see me again. (Babyface, 1993)

In class—as a response to arguments about the relationship between teen violence and teen pregnancy with television as a cultural barometer or catalyst—she announces to the class that she is pregnant. Her friends congratulate and support her. I too offer my congratulations, tempered with a kind of ennui that is reflected in her eyes as she looks at me across the room.

Another Single Black Mother

After class, I hug her and ask her if she's alright.

She says, "Yes." But with tears in her eyes she also says, "You were supposed to marry me." We both laugh uncomfortably.

She, I assume, out of embarrassment and me out of regret.

If I were not gay, I would imagine marrying a Black woman such as she—and in the blink of an eye and in the shadows of night, I still do.

"If I were not gay." And like a child, I am holding my breath hoping that she doesn't say it.

She says, "You were supposed to marry me," and when she does, before the laughter, there is a sweet sincerity that stirs something deep within me, breaking my resistance. She says, "But after your performance the other day I realized that wasn't going to happen." The week before I did a public performance, titled "Gender Markings," in the coffeehouse in the student union. In the performance, I identified myself as a gay man.

Another Single Black Mother

(*sung*) And I can't stop carin' about. About the apple of my eye. I can't stop doin without. Without the center of my life. And I can't get you outta my head. I know I can't pretend. That I won't die if you decide you won't see me again. (Babyface, 1993)

She says, "You were suppose to marry me." And I think

Maybe it's not embarrassment.

Maybe it's regret.

Maybe it's an indictment.

Maybe in her kind-hearted and gentle way she is calling me out—as a traitor, or someone who is not fulfilling a destiny in which she is implicated. Someone who is not performing manly—someone who is not performing Black man. She says, "You were supposed to marry me," and I think about my desire for children. I think about little brown babies with my eyes and my partner's smile. I think about the consequences of desire—pregnancy and impossibility. But of course she didn't want to marry me.

Maybe she wanted to marry what I represent: "a relatively attractive, young, articulate, Black ___ brotha docta"

drop the gay.

She enters my office and she expresses her regrets and I listen. I listen in some strange mixture of teacherly support, brotherly guilt, and a Black Gay Man's regret.

I suspect she is talking to me in some strange mixture of teacherly wisdom, brotherly acknowledgment, and father confessor.

Je Regrette

I listen as she regrets:

She regrets getting pregnant, but she says, "Life is precious."

She regrets being a single parent, but she says, "Children are a gift."

She regrets being a statistic: ANOTHER SINGLE BLACK MOTHER, but she celebrates the single Black mother(s) in her life.

And for a moment I breathe again. For a moment I take a hesitant breath and I wanted to say, "Will you marry me?"

For a moment I wanted to fall to my knees, but not in one of those romantic-film-imaged-one-kneed proposals. I wanted to fall to both knees like in an act of contrition and say:

"Oh my sista I am heartedly sorry for having offended thee, and I detest of all my sins because of thy mispunishment, but most of all because I offend thee my sister, who is good and deserving of all my love. I firmly resolve with the help of thy grace to sin no more and to avoid the near occasion of sin. Will you accept me for the flawed, frail creature that I am?"[4]

(*sung*) And I can't stop thinkin' about. About the way my life would be. No I can't stop thinking about. How could your love be leavin' me. And I can't get you outta my mind. God knows how hard I tried. And if you walk right out my life God knows I'd surely die. (Babyface, 1993)

I wanted to say that, but I don't.

I haven't offended her.

My action should not be that of contrition.

My Black male presence does not dictate her destiny

just as the union of my parents did not dictate my gender identity.

I am her brother and not her lover.

She is my student, not my confessor.

Her presence and predicament is like a
reflecting and refracting mirror of our
culture,
And while I see the images of my
biological sisters—
OTHER   SINGLE   BLACK
MOTHERS—
my responsibility in this moment is to
care for my
student/sista/friend—to offer her the
kind of support
that comes when your people say, "I
will love you no matter what."
Pregnant or gay.

On graduation day. A separate Black graduation
day, I am on the stage being honored as a Black
faculty member. The theme of the event is, "If we
stand tall, it is because we stand on the backs of
those who came before us." Each graduate receives
a certificate and a sash—but not just a sash. It is
made out of kentee cloth, a link to the mother land,
a celebration of culture. To the sound of cheering
family and the rhythmic beats of African drums, the
sash is draped over their shoulders. I am preparing
each kentee sash, handing them to the senior brotha
docta who is regaling the new graduates. It is a ritual
ceremony, a crossing over.

(*sung*) Here she comes: And I can't stop
doin without. Without the rhythm of my
heart. No I can't stop doin without. For
I would surely fall apart. And I can't get
you outta my mind. Cause I know I can't
deny it. And I would die if you decide
you won't see me again. (Babyface, 1993)

She who said, "You were supposed to marry me."
She is beaming either from the joy of the moment
or that glow that pregnant women are supposed to
have. But it doesn't matter why she is beaming.

In that moment when her sash is being
placed,
in that moment when the senior
brotha is reaching over her head
and symbolically embracing her,
in that moment when his lips touch
her cheek,
I see her almost for the first time. She
is not my student anymore.
She is a young Black woman/mother
with a degree moving forward to birth the
future. I call her name and she turns.
Our eyes meet and she says,
"It's only right that you should be
here, now."
She is not a delimiting statistic but an
empowering possibility.
This was not a wedding but a symbolic
birth.
Unlike Toni Braxton she is not holding her breath.
She is replenishing, renewing, and
rejoicing.

(*sung*) If I never feel you in my arms again.
If I never feel your tender kiss again. If I
never hear I love you now and then. Will I
never make love to you once again. Please
understand if love ends. Then I promise
you, I promise you that. (Babyface, 1993)

As a child, I used to play breathing games. You
know what I mean. I remember that whenever I
was afraid that people would say something that
would embarrass me, I would hold my breath, as
if it would prevent them from saying it. Comments
on my single status or my gay identity had me
gasping for air. I held my breath for nearly 20 years.
But they always said it with a kind of suspicion and

disdain—disdain for my desire or a regret for some lost possibility.

The dilemma of the Black gay man lies not in racial identification but culturally specific performative criteria of masculinity and the competing ways in which that notion is perpetuated, rejected, and reconfigured. Contemporary gay men of color are constantly pushing the borders of a narrowly defined horizon of what it means to be Black, what it means to be gay, and what it means to be a man.

BLACK/MAN/GAY: A MOVE TOWARD SELF-DEFINITION

I have often struggled with these three words, Black/Man/Gay.

Words that are nouns—a person.

Words that are verbs—a behavior.

Words that are adjectives—a description.

Which comes first?

Does my position as Black precede my sex and gender?

Does that obligate me to a certain allegiance that dictates my being, my politics, my associations?

Does being a man suggest that I am bound to a code of ethics and behaviors that link me with all other men, restricting me and denying me a free expression of my individual self?

Does being gay negate my positionality as a Black man—with that tattered and torn history—the strength, the pride, the honor?

Does being gay subvert a historical and biological legacy of Black male survival?

I have played with the ordering of my identity:

Black Gay Man—signals my hierarchical allegiance to my Black heritage.

Gay Black Man—signals my sexual identity which precedes and subverts the sometimes pathologized hyper-heterosexual images of Black men, marking my difference.

Man Black Gay—the least of the efforts which places design over desire and collectivizes me with all other men, who are ultimately unequal except in some biblical reading or in a skewed democratic ideal. I am moving toward the construction of Black/Man/Gay to say I am first and always Black—it is my history and heritage marked and written in this dark flesh. It is the first thing noticed and remembered. My Blackness has been predetermined by my divinely pure Black parents with echoes from the dark continent of Africa.

My Blackness was germinated from a Black seed, planted and nurtured in a Black womb and harvested in Black love.

I am a Man second, by genetics—a moment in time, a twist of fate, the balance of heat. As a Black/Man I bare a truth and a legacy, a stigma and a notable presence. I am remembered, reviled, and revered. (*sung*) "I am what I am." My body signals a history, a societal dilemma, and a border crossing of the past, present, and the future.

I am Gay third, but not least—for this positionality signals a way of being that modifies and enhances, encodes and decodes, constructs and deconstructs the potential and possibilities both of the being Black and being a Man. It is a positionality of divine betweenness.

It too signals a history, a societal dilemma, and a border crossing, both in time and space—but one fully engaged as the choice to follow an internal impulse, not clearly dictated like my Black body or my male body, but the divine and dividing impulse to charter one's own destiny.

My identity is mediated by the Diaspora of my people, the design of my body and the object of my desire.

I embrace myself as a Black/Man/Gay and celebrate the problematic and glorious intersection of that positionality.

Toni Braxton's song "Breathe Again" was a number 1 hit that topped the charts for weeks. The song, which speaks of a desperate desire to hold on to a love(r), ends with a pledge: "I shall never breathe again"—and though I loved the song, my earlier breathing lessons taught me that breathing sustains life, exhaling voices desire, and we should live our lives without regrets.

RACE-ING PERFORMANCE—A CONCLUSION

Lately, I've been feeling my melanin not just as pigmentation that marks my body, or the felt tone and texture of Black skin, but the resonant traces of history and the politics of race. I feel the messages written between each racially imbued cellulose-filled fiber of my being. It is something that I feel, that I speak, and I call anyone to task who speaks of it in ways that are problematic or communally pathological or those who find my racialized voice—like so many other Black men—as self-serving, indelicate, or demonizing, as if their voices are not always inflicted or imbued with issues of race, class, and the politics of propriety.

In preparing this presentation, I accessed my computer file in a folder called "Bryant's Skin," and I thought about what that means—Bryant's Black skin—it marks my history and my heritage. It is the first thing noticed and remembered. It signals a racial and cultural tradition, a connection to a community in which shared histories signal common bonds of oppression and survival. Steele (1990), in his book *The Content of Our Character*, said that although

> blackness [is] an invasive form of collective identity that cut[s] so deeply into one's individual space that is seemed also to be an individual identity. It came as something of a disappoint to realize that the two could not be the same, that being "black" in no way spared me the necessity of being myself. (p. 167)

Here, I also echo Wilkins (1996) in the introduction to *Color Conscious: The Political Morality of Race*.

> [I reject a] fluid notion of racial identity by rejecting two common conceptions of the self … that there is an "authentic nugget of selfhood" just waiting to be dug out (invoked by those who see race as a part of that authentic self), and the corresponding view that "I can simply make up any self I choose" (invoked by those who believe that we must be free to reject all forms of ascriptive identity). Instead, … "we make ourselves up" but only from a "tool kit made available by our culture and society." (p. 7)

In running a spell check of this program, my computer rejected the word *nigger* and offered the word *Niger*—as in that great nourishing river that flows through the Black continent of Africa—the computer gave me a choice.

> I paused in my indecision, knowing that was not my intent—
> > but a part of my portent—to signal a history and point of origin. And in that pivotal life moment,
> > like all those moments in which we have to decide how we are going to carry ourselves in the world,
> > and what social, racial, and gendered labels and stereotypes of ourselves that we are going to consume,
> > that we are going to learn, engage, and perform.
> I chose not to add this word into the collective memory of my computer.

In running a spell check of this program, my computer rejected the word *racializing* and offered the word *radicalizing*—the act of making extreme changes in existing views, habits, conditions, or institutions—the computer gave me a choice.

> I paused in my indecision, knowing that was not my intent—but a part of my portent—to engage an act of self-definition.
> I pause, as we all pause when we check ourselves, when we check the quality of our thoughts and the clarity of our expressions.
> I thought about what I meant when I used the word *racializing*—separate from the basic idea of labeling and categorizing.
> It refers to the active process of coming into and understanding of one's own race and embodying a performance that bespeaks that critical process?

It refers to the critical process of examining the social construction of race, the accompanying expected performances and the sanctioning of unexpected performance.

It is like Davis's (1993) critique that "race has become, uh, an increasingly obsolete way of constructing community because it is based on unchangeable immutable biological facts in a pseudo-scientific way" (p. 30).

It is Diawara's notion of Black performance studies made as an individualized project of self-examination—confirming membership without conforming to performative mandates; "interpreting an existing tradition—reinventing [the self]—in front of an audience, or public" (p. 265); claiming membership without engaging in essentializing performances of representation. Performing race is ultimately performing self in the face of history and in the company of others—and negotiating the problems and pitfalls of claiming and maintaining membership.

NOTES

1. My dissertation was an instructional (auto) ethnography that explored the notion of "performing culture" and specifically how Black male teachers and Black male students negotiate culture in a predominantly White university (Alexander, 1998).

2. In this passage, I make allusions to the work of Tami Spry. At the time of this construction, Dr. Spry and I were involved in an ongoing process of "collaborative performances." We created separate performance pieces with intersplicing themes and momentary allusions to the other's performative text.

1. This is a reference to Spry.
2. This is a modification of the Catholic prayer the "act of contrition."

REFERENCES

Alexander, B. K. (1998). *Performing culture in the classroom: An instructional (auto) ethnography*. Unpublished doctoral dissertation, Southern Illinois University, Carbondale.

Appiah, K. A. (1996). Race, culture, identity: Misunderstood connections. In K. A. Appiah & A. Gutman, *Color conscious: The political morality of race* (pp. 30–105). Princeton, NJ: Princeton University Press.

Babyface. (1993). Breathe again [Recorded by T. Braxton]. On *Toni Braxton* [CD]. Atlanta, GA: LaFace Records.

Davis, A. (1993). Rope. In A. D. Smith (Ed.), *Fires in the mirror* (pp. 27–33). New York: Anchor.

Diawara, M. (1993). Black studies, cultural studies: Performative acts. In C. McCarthy & W. Crichlow (Eds.), *Race, identity and representation in education* (pp. 262–267). New York: Routledge.

Giroux, H. A., & McLaren, P. (Eds.). (1994). *Between borders: Pedagogy and the politics of cultural studies*. New York: Routledge.

Hatcher, R., & Troyna, B. (1993). Racialization and children. In C. McCarthy & W. Crichlow (Eds.), *Race, identity and representation in education* (pp. 109–125). New York: Routledge.

hooks, b. (1995). Performance practice as a site of opposition. In C. Ugwu (Ed.), *Let's get it on: The politics of Black performance* (pp. 210–221). Seattle, WA: Bay Press.

Karamcheti, I. (1995). Caliban in the classroom. In J. Gallop (Ed.), *Pedagogy: The question of impersonation* (pp. 138–146). Bloomington: Indiana University Press.

Lionnet, F. (1989). *Autobiographical voices: Race, gender, self-portraiture*. Ithaca, NY: Cornell University Press.

Miles, R. (1988). Racialization. In E. Cashmore (Ed.), *Dictionary of race and ethnic relations* (2nd ed., pp. 246–247). London: Routledge.

Pollock, D. (1998). Performing writing. In P. Phelan & J. Lane (Eds.), *The ends of performance* (pp. 73–103). New York: New York University Press.

Steele, S. (1990). *The content of our character: A new vision of race in America*. New York: St. Martin's.

Tyagi, S. (1996). Writing in search of a home: Geography, culture, and language in the creation of racial identity. In B. Thompson & S. Tyagi (Eds.), *Names we call home: Autobiography on racial identity* (pp. 42–45). New York: Routledge.

Warner, M. (1993). *Fear of a queer planet: Queer politics and social theory*. Minneapolis: University of Minnesota Press.

Wilkins, D. B. (1996). Introduction: The content of race. In K. A. Appiah & A. Gutman, *Color conscious: The political morality of race* (pp. 3–29). Princeton, NJ: Princeton University Press.

Bryant Keith Alexander is a professor of performance and pedagogical studies in the Department of Communication Studies at California State University, Los Angeles. His articles have been published in Text and Performance Quarterly, Theatre Topics, *and* The Speech Communication Teacher. *A series of his essays related to performance, pedagogy, culture, and family were published in* The Future of Performance Studies; Communication, Race and Family *and the upcoming volumes* Black Queer Studies *and* Communicating Ethnic & Cultural Identity. *His short autobiographical essay, "Standing at the Crossroads," was published in* Callaloo *and appears in* The Beacon Best of 2000: Great Writings by Women and Men of All Colors and Cultures *(edited by Edwidge Danticat).*

23

Growing Pains
Colliding Subjectivities on a Pedagogical Learning Curve

By Kimberlee Pérez

This essay is a series of telling, reflecting, and retelling. My story is about how bodies move through time and space with one another. This is a story about what happens when bodies collide with one another through discourses. Discourses infuse us with meanings that in turn shape our communication. How does your body move through the world? What meanings do you attach to your skin color and hair style, your economic-social class, your gender, your relational and intimate desires? What are your histories and how do they move through your body? How does your history—yours and your ancestors'—shape your story, your potential, and choices that you make? Reflect for a moment on how the meanings of your body intersect with how others see you? Are there gaps? Or is it seamless? How do you move through the world? These are questions I often think and write about, talk with my friends about, and raise in my classes. I am interested in the materiality—the movement, the meanings, and the performances of bodies.

One of the reasons bodies interest me so much is because of the ambiguities of my own body. Foucault (1978) explains that cultures generate multiple discourses of meaning around bodies and shape us as subjects. For example, different cultures understand sexuality and gender in specific ways. What it means to be heterosexual, or a man or woman, matters deeply to people both consciously and unconsciously. These fixed categories of meaning, in turn, he explains, shape the contours of our bodies—how they move through the world and what meanings are attached to them. When we reflect upon this, which the pace and rules of our culture do not encourage, there is a fairly narrow margin of what it means to do our gender and (hetero)sexed bodies appropriately. Laws, social codes, and interpersonal interactions discipline us into correct performances, or we face the consequences of an outlaw. Butler uses the theory of performativity to explain the force of gender and sexual norms. She explains that each generation in a culture cites back to previous generations to reinforce the meanings of how gender is done—what doings constitute a woman or man. The enforcement of these norms in categories of gender and sexuality leave us with personal expression but a dualistic system of meaning. Each individual act, then, is both specific to itself and is located in a whole history of doings and meanings. For example, my own body moves through the world as unambiguously female. While the way I express my femininity is in some ways not normative—as a white-looking woman, I wear my hair in dreadlocks and I have a large tattoo on my upper left arm—I have never been mistaken for anything but a woman. Because I perform my gender in an unmistakable way, I am also drawn into meanings of heterosexuality. When I move through the world I am read as a straight woman who performs gender appropriately, even though outside of the mainstream. These powerful discourses that shape subjectivity and meaning are pervasive in many different ways.

In addition to gender and sexuality, Western discourses also shape subjects into racialized categories of meaning. In the United States in particular, like gender and sexuality, race has also primarily been defined through a binary system of white and Black. White subjects, who are also gendered male, heterosexual, middle-to-upper-classed, and able, have long benefited from the privileges associated with those meanings. Segrest (2002) reflects upon the historical and contemporary meanings and experiences of that privilege to argue that the privilege is grounded in philosophical ideas of humans as isolated and competitive individuals. Through detailing Western philosophies, slavery, and contemporary experiences, she reveals the relational disconnect, and therefore individual harm, that our privilege results in and urges action. However much damage privilege might ultimately inflict on an individual, it necessarily affords advantages, and white subjects are defined against what they are not, namely people of color, lower-classed, queer and differently-abled. Discourses that race people non-white, queer, lower-classed, and differently-abled circulate and reinforce meanings through media (de Lauretis, 1987) and historical and contemporary lived experience (Gordon, 1997). This binary system of meaning is attached to bodies and is generally read through the visible register of the body (Alcoff, 2006). In the case of my own body, not only does this mean that my body reads as female and heterosexual, it also means that at six feet tall with light skin and blue eyes, I am also read as white. The intersections of all these visual markers, these markers of privilege, clash with *my* understanding of *myself*. The signifiers of privilege that mark some bodies can mask and complicate other histories, experiences, and identity. Some bodies only make sense through communication and performance. My body is one of those bodies. Though I look white and straight, I am Mexican-American and lesbian. I am a queer Chicana.

These questions, framings, and identities matter to how I begin to tell the story about a series of events that happened between me, as a first-year teacher, and my first-year student in a performance studies classroom. How one begins any story matters. What context do you need? What events matter? Who's doing the telling, to whom, and for what reason? Our narratives are ordered, and they are relational (Langellier & Peterson, 2004). This means that how and when we tell about "what happened," as a communicative act, it *does something* for the speaker and the listener. Storytelling requires both of us, and depends on a shared system of meanings (Langellier, 1999). I assume that we share understandings of how race, class, gender, and sexuality operate in the United States, and I depend on my above framing to produce and reinforce our understanding of how my narrative unfolds.

My story is one of those "theories of the flesh" that comes from my experience and my body as a site of knowledge (Langellier, 1999, p. 136). Cherríe Moraga explains that "a theory in the flesh means one where the physical realities of our lives—our skin color, the land or concrete we grew up on, our sexual longings—all fuse to create a politic born out of necessity" (1983, p. 25). The necessity of my story comes out of, and includes, the legacies of colonization and internalized racism. People who have moved through and beyond lands that were once their own come to find themselves negotiating hybrid and ambivalent post-colonial identities (Bhabha, 1994). Histories of colonization, the forced control of one country over another and the imposition of one culture over another, have multigenerational implications. For example, the colonization of the Mexican people by the United States was a conflict that we might read in mainstream history books as "ending" in 1865 with the signing of the Treaty of Hidalgo-Guadalupe, which assigned a large portion of then Mexico to what is now known as the Southwestern United States. The implications of this transaction for Mexicans living in that area included an overnight change in nationality and racism against the people who were now "American." The identities of these people that emerged—neither fully U.S. yet no longer Mexican—resulted in a hybrid identity (Anzaldúa, 1989; Pérez, 1999). Whether recent immigrants from Mexico, those with long-standing ties to the land, or second-generation families like my father, many Mexican-Americans continue to hold onto the identities of both cultures.

With all this in mind, you can see that there is an intention that underscores my motivation to tell the story. The practice of sharing with another constitutes "a performative struggle for agency rather than the expressive act of a pre-existing, autonomous, fixed, unified or stable self" (Langellier, 1999, p. 129). I want to tell *this* story *to you* and how I tell it reflects back on the experience of the past from the perspective of the present. In other words, I've told this story before, and though the events of the story all did indeed happen, how I tell the story now might be different than how I have told it in the past. We might attribute this to the evolution of life. As my perspectives shift, the meaning of the story changes how I understand it, and this ultimately affects my telling. For example, and here I risk getting ahead of myself, when I first narrated the events to my mentor, I was deeply hurt

and angry. I wanted her to be angry, though I was afraid she might not be, and our communication reflected that intention. However, when I involved my father, there was a very different tone, and there were things I deliberately left out of the story. As you'll see, when he became part of the story, it changed our relationship in ways I never could have imagined. Your own agreement to listen to this story will likely shape how you see me.

Similarly, to whom I tell the story, and how that story is received, matters. Langellier (1999) insists that "without performativity, however, personal narrative risks being a performance practice without a theory of power to interrogate what subject positions are culturally available, what texts and narrative forms and practices are privileged, and what discursive contexts prevail in interpreting the experience" (Langellier, 1999, p. 135). When I construct myself in a story, I am calling upon my and your experience as well as our cultural belongings (De la Garza, 2004). While I want you to see, feel, and reflect upon my individual experience, it exists in a whole host of cultural and discursive meanings. While it is a story about me, it is also a story about us, our pasts, and the meanings we generate together.

My dad calls them growing pains. I don't care what he calls them; I just want the pain to go away. I count on him to make it happen. You see, I reached a full 6 feet by the time I was 12, and I went through a lot of growing pains. They come on suddenly, and mostly at night. There's no telling when they will happen or what brings them on. I'm sure there must be some technical, medical term for this type of pain, some fancy word for adolescent growth spurts. We just call them growing pains. I remember them in my legs the most. Just lying there, it suddenly feels like wooden planks being rammed up my calves and my shins, all the way to my hips. The pain comes so fast, there is no time to cry out, and I have long since learned to take pain quietly. When he is there and I can't take it anymore, I cry out for him.

"Growing pains? Hold on sis, I'm coming," he responds, and the voice that often scares me now soothes me.

I ease into the pain, knowing that he is on his way with the Icy Hot.

He picks me up and lays me down on an old towel and begins a ritual that eases the pain. He rubs the Icy Hot into my legs, and the planks give way to fire as the minty cream makes its way into my muscles and the heady scent reaches my nostrils, making me dizzy.

As he rubs my calves, I look up at his dark brown eyes. I pick at the flecks of white paint in his thick, black curly hair that he can never seem to wash out, and he laughs. I connect the dots of paint on his brown arms that smell of turpentine, the scent of a working-class effort to erase his work as a painter. In the summer, I stay outdoors as long as I can, in my own effort to darken my light skin to match his.

When he gets home, after I've made sure he's in a good mood, I hold my arm out next to his to compare. "Look dad, I'm getting darker."

He laughs, tells me that I will never be as dark as him.

This is where my story begins. Like many of us, my story begins at home and as a child, a being dependent on others for recognition and for survival. Growing up, I didn't know that I was a postcolonial subject; I knew myself as a Mexican because my dad is Mexican and there weren't any other Mexicans in Saginaw, Michigan. At least not any we knew. Growing up, I didn't know about how subjects were made or Mexican and Mexican American history. I certainly wasn't aware of how the history of my Mexican grandparents' migration and assimilation would turn into internalized hatred, leading to the refusal of my family to even talk about the name (Pérez) and the skin (my father is brown and my mother is white) that made us different from the other students I went to school with (a German-Lutheran town) and the families in my neighborhood (white, Black, Korean). Most of my family did not have access to institutions of higher education—we didn't have stories and histories of going to college, learning about theories, and contemplating identity. No one insisted that my brothers and I go to college—our ideas were that we worked out of high school and ultimately, only two of four children even made it that far. With a firm belief in the power of theory (Butler, 2004), I turn it back on my past to make sense of it, and to tell a different story than the silences and the (lack of) stories I inherited.

Emma Pérez (1999) describes the movement of Mexicans within the United States, through land they previously occupied as home. At the site of the current U.S./Mexico border in the Southwest, dominant U.S. rhetoric names and produces the marked bodies of Mexicans and Mexican Americans as immigrants, and largely illegal immigrants, regardless of their citizenship status (Carrillo Rowe, 2004). The ability to identify particular bodies as immigrant functions to maintain narrow constructions of citizenship and belonging; in this way, citizenship becomes connected to whiteness and brown bodies are maintained as other (Carrillo Rowe, 2004). Fixed as other, even assimilated Mexican Americans are considered different. Racialized bodies marked as brown (regardless of achievements in business, education, and government) are always considered skeptically, connected with other nations and migration, and never fully achieve the full benefits and recognition that come with citizenship.

Re-configuring naming practices, Pérez (1999) theorizes the movement of Mexicans and Mexican Americans in the United States not as immigrants, but as a diasporic population—as groups of people that move from their home country to another country because of economic reasons, governmental or military conflict, geographical disaster, and other motivations. A diasporic identity results when those with ties to their country/culture of origin are coupled with an inability to be fully absorbed into a host country. While immigration can imply voluntary or involuntary movement of peoples, the diasporic configuration foregrounds the colonial and illegal histories of land between the United States and Mexico (Pérez, 1999). This understanding leads us to more complicated understandings of diasporic movements and particular lived experiences.

The diasporic movements of Mexican Americans are economically and politically motivated. Many stay in the Southwest, and others migrate to different areas of the United States. My own family, who crossed borders about a hundred years ago, moved from Texas to Michigan for work in the auto industry. Dennis Valdes (2000) distinguishes between the experiences of Mexicans in the Southwest and those living in the Midwest. Although this demographic is rapidly changing, historically there were small populations of Mexicans and Mexican American communities in the Midwest. Valdes (2000) describes a high degree of pressure exerted onto Mexican Americans in the Midwest to assimilate into white culture, which resulted in categorizations of good assimilationist Mexicans and bad Mexicans who wished to hold onto their culture. Characterizations of "good" and "bad" were imposed by dominant white cultural discourse onto Mexican Americans. Pérez (1999) describes moves to assimilate as a strategy of survival on the part of diasporic communities. Rather than a population which conforms to expectations, this particular framing recognizes the agency of Mexican Americans as simultaneously acted upon and acting against under conditions beyond their control. Like many other Mexican American families, my own family's survival tactics began with the practice of speaking Spanish inside the home and English outside. This practice continued through my father's generation, who was the first to

be born inside the United States. He was the first to abandon the home language (Spanish) during adulthood due to the cultural collisions and tensions during his childhood, which left him with an ambivalence and dis-identification with his cultural heritage that he would pass on to his children.

Ambivalence is a common experience among Mexican Americans (Anzaldúa, 1999; Martinez, 2000). The constant negotiation between one's own knowledge of self and the dominant cultural expectations generates a multi-faceted subject position that is experienced psychically with material consequences (Anzaldúa, 1999; Lugones, 2003). Contradicting cultural norms construct who and what is considered desirable. While my parents love each other and have been married for over forty years, desire is never absent its context and cultural norms. In the United States, white femininity is an extension of white male subjectivity (Gordon, 1997). When I think about the love that connects my parents, I cannot imagine it outside of the discursive privileges of whiteness that might have attracted my father to my mother, given my knowledge of his own ambivalence concerning his cultural identity. Ultimately, given the collision of cross-racial and cross-cultural desire, my parents produced four children who all pass as white.

Moraga (1983) describes her experience as the white-passing daughter of a Mexican mother and Anglo father. Passing as white affords a particular mobility at the same time as it generates the cultural costs of distance from one's own multicultural heritage. Passing as white comes with dominant expectations of performances of whiteness that the white body signifies (Warren, 2003). The light skinned passing Chicana moves with white expectations placed upon her body. If she refuses those expectations and brings forth a bi-cultural and bi-racial identity through language, if she "refuse(s) the split" as Moraga (1983, p. 34) describes, there can be consequences. In my own movement through white culture, and particularly as I have come through the university system—a system that was unfamiliar and unanticipated—I have come to claim a Chicana identity that is marked in language. This has produced a closer connection to a bi-cultural heritage as well as to other meaningful and deep emotional and political connections with people of color; at the same time, as it has situated me in particular ways inside the institution as a teacher and as a student. While both student and teacher, as a graduate student, become precarious positions to negotiate, it is the location and subjectification as teacher that I pay attention to here.

The classroom is a site that generates its own particular culture (Alexander, et al., 2005). As a liminal space, we enter differently from when we exit, as we engage with unfamiliar systems of knowledge, people, and histories. Bryant K. Alexander (2005) describes the classroom as "a nexus of desire and disdain for those who enter with competing intentions and lived experience" that "mediate the flow of knowledge" (p. 42). In some classrooms, we engage in conversations that highlight our differences and create tensions among us. Some of us hear voices of experiences that make us uncomfortable, rendering visible our privilege or disadvantages in ways that are often unmarked in other spaces. Calling attention to identity politics in a classroom is also dependent on the geographical location of the university system as well as the discipline we are studying.

Human geographer and cultural historian Doreen Massey (1995) describes the dynamic relationship between identities and the places they play out on. More than merely background or context, spaces hold histories, and as social actors that attach meaning to spaces, the ongoing history of space mutually informs the production of the identities that are attached to them (Massey, 1995). Raka Shome (2003) insists that as communication scholars, we must critically examine the site of space as more than context but as an active component of production. Beyond possessing identities consisting of race, class, gender, sexuality, nation and ability that travel with us as we move through sites, Shome (2003) argues that space plays an active role in the very way we understand ourselves to be. Applying this notion of space to the site of the classroom, we can then understand the institution to produce us as teachers and as students as actively as our historical and cultural identities produce us as the beings we understand ourselves to be. While a student and teacher are recognizable across university systems in this country and have established identifiable practices and norms, the site of each university produces a particular culture of students specific to the land and relational histories that make up that institution (Johnson, 2003; Torres, 2003). It is an ongoing and productive relationship that changes over time, rather than one that is static and unchanging (Shome, 2003).

Growing up in Michigan, I learned little, if any, of Mexican history in school, even though I had some understanding of my name as different than the primarily German names surrounding me. Throughout grade school and high school, my classmates often cruelly called attention to the differences in our names. However, when I moved to Los Angeles after high school, the conversation changed drastically. As I learned of Mexican American and Mexican history, I shifted from being the minority to the majority (through the visual register of my skin). I simultaneously learned of my Mexican and Anglo heritage and swiftly found myself feeling the in-between-ness of what it means to be bi-racial, to be ambiguous in this country. When I moved again from Los Angeles to Maine for graduate school, I had not yet studied the intersections of space, identity, and history that would send me reeling once again.

Some twenty years later, the mere mention of grow-
ing pains sends shivers down my spine. As a graduate
student, I have new growing pains, and I still look to
my dad to make them go away. In the final semester of
my MA program in Maine, I look forward to begin-
ning my PhD program in Arizona, while teaching
my second semester of Performance of Literature. I
start the semester out strong, performing from the first
day, asking students to think about how we perform
our race and our gender. We sit in a circle in our too
small classroom on the fourth floor of Dunn Hall,
right down the hall from my office in the department
where I don't fit in, in the state that's never felt right,
but always felt familiar. Dunn 417, the room with
lots of equipment but not much room, the space too
small for performance and movement, too small for
my big plans. The old radiators run too hot and the
windows are too loose, producing that too hot and too
cold feeling.

For those who adhere to the theorizing of
Paolo Freire, the classroom holds the potential for
liberatory and transformative practices (Torres,
2003). This is the particular pedagogical practice
under which I learned the most as a student and
which I adopt as a teacher in my own classrooms.
It is a practice that begins with the premise that
students and teachers co-constitute the learning
environment and equip everyone in the site with
the tools to resist the restrictive formations of the
state. Rather than a hierarchical model that infuses
the teacher with a particular authority aimed at
producing citizen-subjects, this model rests on the
agency of students and teacher to produce active
subjects (Torres, 2003). Cultivated under a military
state, the pedagogy of the oppressed does not seam-
lessly translate into U.S. cultural classroom models,
where practices of not recognizing students' agency
or interest in resistance are the norm (Torres, 2003).
However, limitations aside, Freire's model remains
meaningfully adapted and guides my own peda-

gogical practices. I find it particularly applicable in
the performance classroom.

On a cold Friday afternoon in January, we watch
Anna Deveare Smith's Twilight LA, where she performs
narratives from the Rodney King riots. I use it to frame
the class, as a performance and a politic I want us to
interrogate. Many of them don't even remember that
it happened; they were too young and too far away.
But they react as they should: angry, sad, struggling.
New students to me, I keep a close watch on their
bodies, trying to read how far to push. If I push too
far, I'll lose them, and I care too much to lose them. I
see him getting uncomfortable, and as discomfort shifts
to anger, I invite him to speak. A tall white student,
taller than me, he established on day one his white
pride and fraternity affiliation. I had secretly hoped he
would have dropped the class, but he didn't.

"You don't know what it's like for a white man to
have a black man or a Hispanic man put a gun in
your face on a regular basis," is where he begins. He
tells us that Maine is different than the South, in a
place where whites are the minority and we just don't
get it.

The intensity, already high, increases exponentially
as comments fly through the room. As several of his
classmates turn on him, voices defiant, righteous,
angry, I struggle with whether to step in and protect
him or let it continue and pray they do not see my
insides squirming.

I shut things down when I feel their exhaustion,
confusion, and pain. I don't know whether I have let it
go too far or not far enough, and I ask them to breathe
and to write for five minutes, to be mindful of each
other, and send them to their weekends. Looking for
an ear on a Friday afternoon in an empty Dunn Hall
leaves me to sit in my own discomfort and wonder
about theirs, how this will play out for the remainder
of the semester.

In the performance classroom "embodiment
is a way of knowing" (Johnson, 2003, p. 230).
This means that the classroom is an active site

of knowledge, wherein there is no gap between theory and practice—it is recognized as inextricable (Conquergood, 2002). There are radical potentials in the performance classroom for ways of knowing that meaningfully change our lives. This has been my experience as a student and as a teacher, and I hold firmly to the belief that this is possible through performance theory and practice. Inside of all the liberatory possibilities of a performance methodology and performance (and all other) classrooms, there lies the reality of intra- and extra-institutional constraints of differently positioned bodies coming together (Alexander, 2005; Johnson, 2003; Torres, 2003). The institutional power assigned to teachers does not usurp the authority of whiteness (Alexander, 2005; Torres, 2003). For the teacher of color, there is the very real negation of white students who enact their privilege on the sites of their teachers with differential racialized and gendered consequences (Alexander, 2005; Torres, 2003). These sometimes result in discursive violences that are experienced as embodied. While my own body does not signify as racially other or Mexican American, my last name and my pedagogical practice do mark me as different, something I found out early on, in what I expect will be a long pedagogical learning curve.

Winter gives way to spring, and through the semester he has kept silent. He performs well, through textual choices designed to provoke reactions: prose with fight and rape scenes, poetry about pot. I limit my comments to the politics of his choices, never restraining him.

The final assignment shifts their authority into authorship as they produce and perform their own personal identity narratives. Their first drafts come across my desk for feedback and his catches my eye with his handwritten note: "CREDIT ONLY, NO FEEDBACK, WILL BE WRITING SOMETHING DIFFERENT FOR FINAL NARRATIVE."

The ink pricks the back of my neck, and my heart races as I read the narrative directed at me. After

several moments caught in the liminal space of confusion, I walk it down to my mentor's office and demand the student's immediate withdrawal from my class. It's not that easy, and as I become interpolated into this institutional nightmare on the fourth floor of Dunn, I eventually find my way home.

A force of habit in times of crisis, I call my dad.

"What's wrong?" says the one person who sees through my voice, listens through every wall I put up.

"My student called me a spic," my deadpan tone filled with the tension of the years of struggle between the two of us.

"What?" His anger snaps to attention, and I am somehow comforted by his rage. I offer up the short version, and as he goes on a rampage, I sink into him over the phone like he is rubbing my calves, rubbing in the Icy Hot and taking away the pain. I barely hear his threats of violence against this student, what he's going to do to him and what my department better do, because it somehow doesn't matter anymore.

He makes me promise not to cry in front of them, tells me to call him if I must cry.

Over the phone I see his shoulder, his dark brown shoulder where I lean my white face, his shirt catching the tears that fall from blue eyes. I'll never be as dark as him, but he is me and I am him. Across the years and the country, my dad is still part of my growing pains.

In seeking to re-theorize the limitations of Western modes of subjectification, Butler (2004) brings our attention to the very conditions of our humanity and what would be possible within a reconfiguration. She argues that when certain bodies are not recognized as human, we can't see each other, and as a result, we cannot grieve each other (Butler, 2004). While occupying such a privileged position in the academy renders me intelligible and visible under certain discursive systems, I am simultaneously marked as other in the moments that I bring my racialized and sexualized identities into being through language. In this moment, language produces me in as much as it fails me. In the context of the classroom, I have institutional authority that intersects with subjectivities that experience more power and more privilege than me. Butler (2004, p. 19) states, "Let's face it. We're undone by each other. And if we're not, we're missing something." The experience of moving through the world with internalized racism and homophobia, of a conditioned consciousness of non-belonging in particular contexts, sometimes offers me insights into my experiences (I look to the past to see where it has informed my communication, my identity, my choices) and sometimes functions as a barrier that separates me from others. It becomes a barrier in the moments it becomes unbearable, when words and silences function as violence.

With multiple subjectivities holding real consequences, there is a very real need for further complicating our understanding of the non-unitary self (Anzaldùa, 1999; Butler, 2004; Lugones, 2003). We need to theorize new points of connection, kinship and possibilities that recognize multiple ways of knowing, moving, and being in the world (Butler, 2004). When we are not "undone by each other," we slip into ambivalence. These are the gaps that have yet to be theorized. In the experiences of my subjectification, there are limitations; to borrow from Martinez (2003), they are the cool theoretical gaps in my burning flesh. Can we reconfigure theories of subjectification that start from the premise of belonging (Segrest, 2002)? Does speaking through narrative give us a glimpse in to how to begin to transform ourselves? What becomes possible when we are willing to engage, are willing to listen?

The ordeal with the student continues to the end of the semester, and the student doesn't get dismissed. I am reminded of why I want to teach and walk him through writing a narrative about his crisis of white male identity that he performs in a kilt from behind a podium. In the tension where his white male privilege clashes against my location as queer Chicana wrapped

up in the institution, no one wins. It's not that kind of battle.

It's been six months since the end of that semester. I saw the student once in town and quickly walked the other way. My dad and I talk from time to time, say I love you and give updates on the good things. For a brief moment, we were undone by each other in an ecstatic experience. Whether it was a moment of transformation is yet to be known. As I try to make sense of what happened then and how it informs the teacher I continue to become, see each moment in every other, I try to live in gratitude for lessons learned, try to be grateful for my growing pains.

REFERENCES

Alcoff, L. M. (2006). *Visible identities: Race, gender, and the self.* New York, NY: Oxford University Press.

Alexander, B. K., Anderson, G. L., Gallegos, B. P. (2005). Introduction. In Alexander, B. K., Anderson, G. L., Gallegos, B. P. (Eds.) *Performance theories in education: Power, pedagogy, and the politics of identity* (pp. 1–11). Mahwah, NJ: L. Erlbaum Associates.

Alexander, B. K., (2005). Critically analyzing pedagogical interactions as performance. In Alexander, B. K., Anderson, G. L., Gallegos, B. P. (Eds.) *Performance theories in education: Power, pedagogy, and the politics of identity* (pp. 41–62). Mahwah, NJ: L. Erlbaum Associates.

Anzaldúa, G. (1999). *Borderlands: The new mestiza.* [La Frontera]. (2nd ed.) San Francisco: Aunt Lute Books.

Bhabha, H. K. (1997). *The location of culture.* London: Routledge.

Butler, J. (1990). *Gender trouble: Feminism and the subversion of identity.* New York: Routledge.

Butler, J. (2004). *Undoing gender.* New York: Routledge.

Carrillo Rowe, A. (2004). "Whose America? The politics of rhetoric and space in the formation of U.S. nationalism." *Radical History Review, 89,* 115–134.

Conquergood, D. (2002). Performance studies: Interventions and radical research. *The Drama Review, 46,* 145–153.

De la Garza, A. (2004). *Maria speaks: Journeys into the mysteries of the mother in my life as a Chicana.* Peter Lang.

De Lauretis, T. (1987). *Technologies of gender: Essays on theory, film and fiction.* Bloomington, IN: Indiana University.

Foucault, M. (1978). *The history of sexuality, Volume 1: An introduction.* New York: Vintage Books.

Gordon, L. R. (1997). *Her majesty's other children: Sketches of racism from a neocolonial age.* New York: Rowman & Littlefield.

Johnson, E. P. (2003). *Appropriating blackness: Performance and the politics of authenticity.* Durham, NC: Duke University.

Langellier, K. M. (1999). Personal narrative, performance, performativity: Two or three things I know for sure. *Text and Performance Quarterly, 19,* 125–144.

Langellier, K. M. & Peterson, E. E. (2004). *Storytelling in daily life: Performing narrative.* Temple.

Lugones, M. (2003). *Pilgrimages/peregrinajes: Theorizing coalition against multiple oppressions.* Lanham, MD: Rowman & Littlefield.

Martinez, J. M. (2000). *Phenomenology of Chicana experience and identity: Communication and transformation in praxis.* Lanham, MD: Rowman & Littlefield.

Massey, D. (1995). Places and their pasts. *History workshop journal, 39,* 182–192.

Moraga, C. (1983). La güera. In Moraga, C. and Anzaldúa, G. *This bridge called my back: Writings by radical women of color.* New York: Kitchen Table, Women of Color Press.

O'Neill, J. (1989). *The communicative body: Studies in communicative philosophy, politics, and sociology.* Evanston: Northwestern University.

Pérez, E. (1999). *The decolonial imaginary: Writing Chicanas into history.* Bloomington: Indiana University.

Segrest, M. (2002) *Born to belonging: Writings on spirit and justice.* New Brunswick, NJ: Rutgers.

Shome, R. (2003). Space matters: The power and practice of space. *Communication Theory, 13,* 39–56.

Torres, E. (2003). *Chicana without apology: The new Chicana cultural studies.* New York: Routledge.

Valdes, D. (2000). *Voices of a new Chicana history.* East Lansing, MI: Michigan State University.

Warren, J. T. (2003). *Performing purity: whiteness, pedagogy and the reconstitution of power.* New York: Peter Lang.

Resisting the Shore

By Nadine Naber

24

My parents immigrated to the United States from Jordan in the mid-1960s for the American dream. My family climbed the economic ladder by running our own business, by believing in capitalism, and by believing that anyone could become president, even an Arab. Climbing the economic ladder meant moving out of our urban, working-class multicultural neighborhood to a so-called enlightened California suburb that believed in "democracy" and "equal rights."

I entered grammar school in the '70s during the U.S.–Arab oil wars. While my parents happily upheld the U.S. census's classification of Arab-Americans as white, my best friend's parents greeted me by imitating my parents' accent (laughing) when I entered their home.

At school, some students called me towel head and camel jockey. They asked me questions like, "So, does your dad own a 7-Eleven or an oil well? Do you have camels in your backyard? Does your dad beat your mom?" During my sophomore year of high school, my friends and I made a music video. We created a skit to the song "Killing an Arab," by a band called The Cure.

We filmed the video at my parents' house since it offered us an "authentic" Arab setting. Each of my friends played undercover U.S. policemen and FBI agents while I played "the Arab." My friends wore "American" clothes, like jeans, plaid shirts, and black leather jackets, while I wore a gallabeya and kuffiyai according to a commonly portrayed stereotype of an Arab or Muslim.

For the opening scene of the music video, I (the Arab) sat under a palm tree sipping Arabic coffee from a small brass coffee cup while smoking fake hashish from an argilah (Arabic water pipe). My white American girl friends (the undercover cops) sat behind popular open-face American magazines like *Rolling Stone, Newsweek,* and *Cosmopolitan* and disguised themselves before the kill. The music played and the chase began, around the backyard and through the house. The American cops chased the Arab (me) up the stairs and eventually threw me over the balcony to my death. The scene ended with the Arab (me) lying face-up on the ground, dead, and the white American cops raising their arms in victory. Together, my friends (and I) joined in laughter as we watched and re-watched the video with larger groups of peers throughout the years,

I remember Killing an Arab (me). I remember turning down the volume of the Arabic music that I love so deeply on our car stereo when my mother dropped me off at school so that none of the other kids would hear it. I remember the isolation. But where was the anger and where was the pain? Was the pressure to become "American" so powerful that the price of denying my history, language, and culture was worth it?

Maybe I practiced silence because I was occupied fighting on the front lines of a different war at home, with my mother, and my culture; or the culture that my parents' generation manufactured after immigrating to the U.S., in the name of protecting us. Perhaps, as a young warrior, I was not yet prepared for multiple battles.

Sometimes, the cultural war would begin on the couch. Mama would be watching TV, holding the remote control, and flipping through the stations. Station after station, a similar picture of an Anglo-American man and woman embracing each other in some sort of sexual way would appear Mama would make comments like, "Sleep-Slept, Sleep-Slept ... that is Amerika!" She would say things like, "el sex il hum, zay shurub al mal (sex, for "them" [the Americans], is as easy as drinking water). At home "Al Amerikan" (the American) was always referred to negatively. It was the trash culture, and anything associated with it was degenerate, morally bankrupt and not worth investing in, while "Al Arab," (the Arab) was always referred to positively, with references to Arab family values, and hospitality, and the ways that "'banatna' ma bitlaau fil lail ['our' daughters don't go out at night]." In our home, it was black and white, good and bad Al Arab versus Al Amerikan, as if there were a boundary, or a box created around everything associated with being Arab. The assumption was that if you do "these things" you will be in the circle, and if you don't, then you are out. And "these things" only applied to daughters. And so it was that controlling my

sexuality became the means toward maintaining our Arabness, and my virginity became the shield that would protect Mama from losing me to the "Amerikan."

That was when my resistance began. I committed myself to dismantling the Arab/American virgin/whore split and crafting my sexuality on my terms. I simply wouldn't tell Mama about my life outside the boundaries of our home. Silence became my resistance. Without speaking, without revealing, I relied on myself for answers to who and what I was going to be.

But freedom always has a price. Mama's pain permeated my sleeping and waking existence. The same person controlling me (Mama), was raising me, holding me, and loving me, while Baba worked at his store from 4 A.M. till evening. So my defiance meant betrayal, guiltpainlove (it's one word), and yearning for her acceptance. "You're crazy, wild, too free!" she would say. "No boundaries and no control! Unbrushed hair, messy-clothed girl, put on a dress! Patch up those clothes! Embarrassing your brothers on the streets with your jeans. Take those earrings out of your holes. What man will ever want to marry you?" While rebellion provided my strength, it also brought my psychological isolation from Mama and my so-called enlightened California suburb that didn't understand me, or the ongoing cultural wars within our immigrant family home.

In college, I finally grasped the connection between my personal isolation and U.S.–Arab political relations. I finally understood the link between U.S. government policies that kill and displace hundreds of thousands of Arab people and Killing an Arab/me/falling off the balcony to my death. At last, memories of childhood, coupled with scenes of the Gulf War's fire and bombs on my TV screen, inspired my transformation.

I adopted the struggle against all forms of oppression. I began working with my Arab and

Arab-American sisters who are combating Arab and Arab-American women's isolation in the United States while increasing the visibility of Arab women writers, activists, and artists among U.S. feminist movements. We're building bridges with our feminist sisters and challenging racism within our communities.

Today I turn up the volume of my Arabic music that I love so deeply. I dance to the beat of Um Kulthoum, who united Arab people, made history just as history made her, and sang, "Demands are not met by wishes; the world can only be taken by struggle," Today, I swim the waves of white, black, olive, green and borders diasporas stones and guns. Earringed, short-haired, turbaned, veiled sisters, we're surviving the oceans and redesigning the shores of Arab/American virgin/whore.

Stolen Bodies, Reclaimed Bodies

Disability and Queerness

By Eli Clare

25

I want to write about the body, not as a metaphor, symbol, or representation, but simply as the body. To write about my body, our bodies, in all their messy, complicated realities. I want words shaped by my slurring tongue, shaky hands, almost steady breath; words shaped by the fact that I am a walkie—someone for whom a flight of stairs without an accompanying elevator poses no problem—and by the reality that many of the people I encounter in my daily life assume I am "mentally retarded." Words shaped by how my body—and I certainly mean to include the mind as part of the body—moves through the world.

Sometimes we who are activists and thinkers forget about our bodies, ignore our bodies, or reframe our bodies to fit our theories and political strategies. For several decades now, activists in a variety of social change movements, ranging from black civil rights to women's liberation, from disability rights to queer liberation, have said repeatedly that the problems faced by any marginalized group of people lie, not in their bodies, but in the oppression they face. But in defining the external, collective, material nature of social injustice as separate from the body, we have sometimes ended up sidelining the profound relationships that connect our bodies with who we are and how we experience oppression.

Disentangling the body from the problems of social injustice has served the disability rights movement well. The dominant paradigms of disability—the medical, charity, supercrip, and moral models—all turn disability into problems faced by individual people, locate those problems in our bodies, and define those bodies as wrong. The medical model insists on disability as a disease or condition that is curable and/or treatable. The charity model declares disability to be a tragedy, a misfortune, that must be tempered or erased by generous giving. The supercrip model frames disability as a challenge to overcome and disabled people as super-heroes just for living our daily lives. The moral model transforms disability into a sign of moral weakness.

Of course, these differing models intersect and overlap. Take, for instance, Jerry Lewis and his Labor Day telethon. He raises money by playing to pity and promising to find a cure. This money does not fund wheelchairs, ramps, or lift bars, nor lawyers to file disability discrimination lawsuits, but research for a cure, for a repair of bodies seen as broken, for an end to disability. Lewis is strategically playing the cards of the medical model and the charity model. Or think about Christopher Reeve as he speaks out about the need to find a cure for spinal cord injuries and insists on his ability to overcome quadriplegia, going so far as to air a Super Bowl ad where, through computer-generated imagery, he is shown actually getting up out of his wheelchair and walking across a stage. Reeve creates himself as a supercrip, the superhero now playing himself offscreen, and is at the same time enmeshed in the medical model. Or consider mothers with hereditary disabilities, who face significant disapproval for their decisions to have children and immense pressure to undergo various medical tests and to consider abortion if their fetuses appear to be disabled. They are caught in a vise-grip between the moral model and medical model. Whatever the permutations, these models unambiguously define disability and disabled bodies as wrong and bad.

In resistance to this, the disability rights movement has created a new model of disability, one that places emphasis on how the world treats disabled people: Disability, not defined by our bodies, but rather by the material and social conditions of ableism; not by the need to use a wheelchair, but rather by the stairs that have no accompanying ramp or elevator. Disability activists fiercely declare that it's not our bodies that need curing. Rather, it is ableism—disability oppression, as reflected in high unemployment rates, lack of access, gawking, substandard education, being forced to live in nursing homes and back rooms, being seen as childlike and asexual—that needs changing.

Locating the problems of social injustice in the world, rather than in our bodies, has been key to naming oppression. It has been powerful for marginalized peoples, including disabled people, to say. "Leave our bodies alone. Stop justifying and explaining your oppressive crap by measuring, comparing, judging, blaming, creating theories about our bodies." But at the same time, we must not forget that our bodies are still part of the equation, that paired with the external forces of oppression are the incredibly internal, body-centered experiences of who we are and how we live with oppression. To write about the body means paying attention to these experiences.

Let me begin with my body, my disabled queer body. I use the word *queer* in both of its meanings: in its general sense, as odd, quirky, not belonging; and in its specific sense, as referring to lesbian, gay, bisexual, and transgender identity. In my life, these two meanings have often merged into one. *Queer* is not a taunt to me, but an apt descriptive word.

My first experience of queerness centered not on sexuality or gender, but on disability. Early on, I understood my body to be irrevocably different from those of my neighbors, playmates, siblings. Shaky; off-balance; speech hard to understand; a body that moved slow, wrists cocked at odd angles, muscles knotted with tremors. But really I am telling a kind of lie, a half-truth. "Irrevocably different" would have meant one thing. Instead, I heard: "wrong, broken, in need of repair, unacceptably queer" every day, as my classmates called out *cripple, retard, monkey;* as people I met gawked at me; as strangers on the street asked, "What's your defect?"; as my own parents grew impatient with my slow, clumsy ways. Irrevocably different would have been easy, compared to wrong and broken. I knew my body was the problem. I stored the taunting, the gawking, the shame in my bones; they became the marrow. This was my first experience of queerness.

Only later came gender and sexuality. Again I found my body to be irrevocably different. At nine, ten, eleven, my deepest sense of self was as neither boy nor girl. I knew this as I flew my kite in the hay fields and sheep pastures. I knew this as I dug fence postholes and hauled firewood with my father. I just knew this. Tomboy, genderqueer, transgender—it wasn't a stage I grew out of. My body never learned to walk in high heels; to feel strong and comfortable, even sexy, in a skirt. I never stopped feeling at home in my work boots and flannel shirts, never lost my penchant for a broad stance and direct gaze, my gender expression shaped by the loggers and fishermen I grew up among. I heard nothing about transgender and transsexual people; it seemed that folks who lived outside the gender binary—or in a complex relationship to it—didn't exist in my world. More accurately, I was the only one.

When I was twelve, I met my first dykes. I developed a sweet childhood crush and wished they would come live with me in my river valley. By the time their visit ended and they had left rural Oregon, I knew I was somehow like them. Sexually queer—it wasn't a stage I grew out of. I heard my father fall tight and silent when he talked about homosexuals. I heard rumors about the county sheriff running faggots out of town. I heard my classmates call me *lezzie* before I even knew what that word meant. All the words and all the silence settled into my body, the experience of oppression undeniably coming to live there. My irrevocably different body.

But it isn't only oppression that lives in my body, our bodies. The many experiences of who we are, of our identities, also live there. I know so clearly that my queerness, my disability, reside in my body—in the ways that I move, dress, cut my hair; in who I am attracted to and who's attracted to me; in my tremors, my slurred speech, my heavy-heeled gait; in the visceral sense of muscle sliding over muscle as I lie with my lover; in the familiarity of tension following tremor, traveling from shoulder to fingertip. Identity, of course, can live in many places all at once—in the communities we make home, the food we eat, the music we play and dance to, the work we do, the people we feel wild and passionate about, the languages we speak, the clothes we

wear. But so much of who *I* am is carried in my irrevocably different body.

Irrevocable difference could be a cause for celebration, but in this world it isn't. The price we pay for variation from the norm that's defined and upheld by white supremacy, patriarchy, and capitalism is incredibly high. And in my life, that price has been body centered. I came to believe that my body was utterly wrong. Sometimes I wanted to cut off my right arm so it wouldn't shake. My shame was that plain, that bleak. Of course, this is one of the profound ways in which oppression works—to mire us in body hatred. Homophobia is all about defining queer bodies as wrong, perverse, immoral. Transphobia, about defining trans bodies as unnatural, monstrous, or the product of delusion. Ableism, about defining disabled bodies as broken and tragic. Class warfare, about defining the bodies of workers as expendable. Racism, about defining the bodies of people of color as primitive, exotic, or worthless. Sexism, about defining female bodies as pliable objects. These messages sink beneath our skin.

There are so many ways oppression and social injustice can mark a body, steal a body, feed lies and poison to a body. I think of the kid tracked into "special education" because of his speech impediment, which is actually a common sign of sexual abuse. I think of the autoimmune diseases, the cancers, the various kinds of chemical sensitivities that flag what it means to live in a world full of toxins. I think of the folks who live with work-related disabilities because of exploitative, dangerous work conditions. I think of the people who live downwind of nuclear fallout, the people who die for lack of access to health care, the rape survivors who struggle with post-traumatic stress disorder. The list goes on and on.

The stolen bodies, the bodies taken for good, rise up around me. Rebecca Wight, a lesbian, shot and killed as she hiked the Appalachian Trail with her lover. James Byrd Jr., an African American, dragged to death behind a pickup driven by white men. Tyra Hunter, a transgendered person living as a woman, left to bleed to death on the streets of D.C. because the EMT crew discovered she had a penis and stopped their work. Tracy Latimer, a twelve-year-old girl with severe cerebral palsy, killed by her father, who said he did it only to end her unbearable suffering. Bodies stolen for good. Other bodies live on—numb, abandoned, full of self-hate, trauma, grief, aftershock. The pernicious stereotypes, lies, and false images can haunt a body, stealing it away as surely as bullets do.

But just as the body can be stolen, it can also be reclaimed. The bodies irrevocably taken from us, we can memorialize in quilts, granite walls, and candlelight vigils. We can remember and mourn them, use their deaths to strengthen our will. And as for the lies and false images: we need to name them, transform them, create something entirely new in their place. Something that comes close and finally true to the bone, entering our bodies as liberation, as joy, as fury, as a will to refigure the world.

The work of refiguring the world is often framed as the work of changing the material, external conditions of our oppression. But just as certainly, our bodies—or, more accurately, what we believe about our bodies—need to change so that they don't become storage sites, traps, for the very oppression we want to eradicate. For me, this work is about shattering the belief that my body is wrong. It began when I found communities committed to both pride and resistance. It was there that I could begin to embrace irrevocable difference—come to know the grace in my shaky hands, the rhythm of tremor and tension in my muscles, the joy in my transgendered butch body, sun on my back, a lover's hand on my belly.

The goal isn't to make irrevocable difference disappear. Certainly, my body is no less different, no less queer, than it was during the years I wanted to cut off my right arm, to be nondisabled—or, failing that, to pass. Every time I walk down a street and someone stares, trying to figure out my body, to make sense of my shaky hands and slow speech, or to determine whether I'm a man or a woman—and if a woman, surely a dyke—I know nothing has changed. What has changed is how I perceive my irrevocable difference, how I frame it, what context I place it into.

I am still in the middle of this work. I think of my lover cradling my right hand, saying, "Your tremors feel so good"; saying, "I can't get enough of your shaky touch"; saying, "I love your CP." Shame and disbelief overwhelm me until I stop and really listen to the words. Another layer begins to shatter. I think of a demonstration I attended several years ago with a whole crowd of disabled people. Being a gimp was the norm. We blockaded a building, shut it down, pressured a politician into supporting important legislation. At the end of the day, I went to sleep adoring irrevocable difference. I think of a book of portraits of lesbian, gay, bisexual, and transgendered writers. I look again at my friend Kenny, leaning on his cane, smiling into the camera. If he can be so beautiful standing on that tree-lined walkway, maybe I can be too. I want to grow to a place where I can fill my skin to its very edges. For any of us to do this work, we need all the allies, lovers, community, and friends we can gather, all the rabble-rousing and legislation, all the vibrant culture and articulate theory we can bring into being.

In the end, I am asking that we pay attention to our bodies—our stolen bodies and our reclaimed bodies. To the wisdom that tells us the causes of the injustice we face lie outside our bodies, and also to the profound relationships our bodies have to that injustice, to the ways our identities are inextricably linked to our bodies. We need to do this because there are disability activists so busy defining disability as an external social condition that they neglect the daily realities of our bodies: the reality of living with chronic pain; the reality of needing personal attendants to help us pee and shit (and of being at once grateful for those PAs and deeply regretting our lack of privacy); the reality of disliking the very adaptive equipment that makes our day-to-day lives possible. We need to do this because there are disability thinkers who can talk all day about the body as metaphor and symbol but never mention flesh and blood, bone and tendon— never even acknowledge their own bodies. We need to do this because without our bodies, without the lived bodily experience of identity and oppression, we won't truly be able to refigure the world, turning it to a place where, to quote the poet Mary Oliver:

… each life [is] a flower, as common as a field daisy, and as singular.

and each name a comfortable music in the mouth, tending, as all music does, toward silence,

and each body a lion of courage, and something precious to the earth.[1]

Eli Clare is a poet, essayist, and activist living in Michigan. He is the author of Exile and Pride: Disability, Queerness, and Liberation *(1999).*

NOTES

1. Mary Oliver, *New and Selected Poems* (Boston: Beacon, 1992), 10.

26

Nick Cave, Dance Performance, and the Production and Consumption of Masculinity

By Laknath Jayasinghe

N ick Cave repeatedly dances in rock stage performances. From gigs with The Boys Next Door in Melbourne, at St Kilda's seedy Banana's Disco in 1979 and the George Hotel's Crystal Ballroom in 1980, to those dances with The Birthday Party at Manchester's Hacienda and London's Lyceum in 1983, Cave performs repertoires that, at the time, were unusual by any measure of mainstream Australian rock perfor- mance. Although his dances are usually episodic, often fleeting and largely informal, Cave frequently performed twists, turns and thrusts, in addition to sophisticated movements and pirouettes. The latter, at least, appear to be composed and executed with remarkable sensitivity and pose. These dance reper- toires were part of a broader corpus of resistive rock music performance in Melbourne's burgeoning and splintered post-punk and alternative rock music milieu. This chapter focuses on Cave's involvement in this rock movement, in particular on some of his dance performances in what later became known, by both academics and commentators alike, as the 'Crystal Ballroom scene', as well as some of his dances performed with The Birthday Party at two gigs at Manchester's Hacienda nightclub.[1]

Rock music critics, such as Vikki Riley,[2] have only mentioned in passing Cave's relationship with dance, most probably because Cave never claimed to be a serious stage dancer, nor is he a trained dancer. In examining Cave's moving body in some of these performances, I argue that Cave's dance routines create potentially deep and visceral tensions for some audiences that can be liberating in terms of gender formation and practice. It must be stressed that throughout this essay, Cave's performative intention—though often important

Laknath Jayasinghe, "Nick Cave, Dance Performance and the Production and Consumption of Masculinity," *Cultural Seeds: Essays on the Work of Nick Cave*, ed. Karen Welberry and Tanya Dalziell, pp. 65-80. Copyright © 2009 by Ashgate Publishing Ltd. Reprinted with permission.

to this analysis—is not always the matter of concern; inevitably there is slippage at times between Cave's performative outlook in these dances and how the dances may be read by audiences.

Cave's dances, moreover, provoke certain questions: is there a specific politics of masculinity attached to his dances? What do these dances suggest about the changing relations between masculinity and rock music culture, and how do audiences understand them? This chapter moves toward answering these questions by focusing on recorded footage of Cave's performances with one of the seminal Australian post-punk bands, The Birthday Party, and considering how notions of the 'choreographed' dimension of gender and sexuality can be used to analyse the ways in which notions of masculinity are produced, sustained and critiqued through Cave's rock music performances. First, I analyse Cave's dance movements on the promotional video clip for the 1981 release 'Nick the Stripper', a clip which former Birthday Party drummer, Phill Calvert, suggests contains representative traces of Cave's dance repertoire in the Crystal Ballroom scene.[3] Next, I examine filmed footage of some of Cave's dances from mid-1982, and again in early 1983, performed with The Birthday Party at Manchester's Hacienda nightclub. In the final section it's argued that some of Cave's performances may be queerly, pleasurably read by audiences. The analysis, overall, is contextualised by the broader politics of masculinity in Australian rock music and English mainstream music culture.

These recorded images of Cave's dances convey a sense of the various discourses of masculinity that choreograph Cave's body in live performance. In doing so they articulate some of the more potent images of the performing male body in Antipodean rock culture. Admittedly, cultural critics such as Paul McDonald have pointed to the limitations of using recorded material to theorise about the performing body, arguing that while such a focus is quite feasible, it does possibly produce a restricted reading of the performance.[4] Yet the point argued, and for which evidence is provided, is that there are certain movements in Cave's repertoire that are *representative* of some of his live dance repertoires in the scene. In this way, we understand both the live performance stage and the medium of video—when analysed as viewing contexts—as spaces adjunct to the social regulation of the norms of masculinity, in particular, the norms of rock music masculinity.

GENDER AND CHOREOGRAPHY IN ROCK MUSIC PERFORMANCE

In his groundbreaking essay, 'Queer Kinesthesia: Performativity on the Dance Floor', dance studies theorist, Jonathan Bollen, develops an original framework for thinking about how the cultural politics surrounding masculinity and queer sexualities are understood through dance performance.[5] Bollen alerts readers to how a 'different mode of dance-floor practice' is often 'premised on a different nexus of movement and pleasure'.[6] One of his central vectors of analysis is the *choreographed* aspect of gender performance and I modify Bollen's insight to help explain how stage performances such as Cave's enact, rehearse, reiterate or conversely rework norms of rock music masculinity.

Bollen's essay examines the 'queer kinaesthesia' in social dance practices at gay and lesbian dance parties in Sydney during the mid-1990s. Queer kinaesthesia serves as an effective analytic tool to examine dance as a 'coalescence of moves and [their] gendered effects'.[7] Queer, according to him, takes on a polymorphous configuration by refusing to signal a clear gendered and sexual position. The dancers Bollen interviewed complicate—or queer—the common view that everyday genders, feminine and masculine identities for example, can be easily mapped sexually. This is the crux of what gender studies theorists, such as Judith Butler, call the sex-gender linkage. In her theorisation, Butler argues that the production of a 'natural' and authentic understanding of the sexed, gendered and heterosexual subject is made possible through the 'regularized and constrained repetition of [gender] norms'.[8]

But this coupling of gender to sexuality is blurred by Bollen's partygoers through their queer dance practices. He insists that at events such as the Sydney Gay and Lesbian Mardi Gras, the dance floor practices he researched do not so much 'materialize' the morphology of gendered bodies as 'choreograph' their kinesthetic capacities' of sexuality,

> and this 'choreography' demands an analysis—a reality-registering apparatus—that cannot so much 'see' kinesthetic habituation as 'feel' it. For kinesthesia cannot be read off the surface of the body in terms of matter, shape, or form. It must be read as movement, in the ongoingness of movement, and in how that movement feels.[9]

Queer dancers at the Mardi Gras attempt to deregulate the cultural constraints that pattern everyday gender behaviour: the social compulsion that 'this' gender will lead to 'that' sexuality. So on the dance floor, the often culturally-determined and socially-sanctioned binaries of masculine/feminine, gay/straight and hetero/homosexual are left open, queered, to be (mis)interpreted by audiences of the dances. Bollen gives an account of dances in gay and lesbian spaces, though 'queer' need not be confined to this narrow purview. Queer can account 'for the expression of all aspects of non-straight cultural production and reception;'[10] therefore, it works against the cultural modes that reproduce

the more repressive aspects of heterosexuality. This has important implications for this analysis as it accepts that heterosexual men such as Cave may participate on stage in the breaking down of the bounds of 'normal' masculine behaviours in rock music culture.

Further, Bollen's frame of queer kinesthesia sees movement predominantly located within a regulated heterosexually-oriented system of gender behaviour, registering 'what matters about a body in terms of the body's experience of moving, its capacity for action, its choreographic repertoire'.[11] This 'choreographic' element of bodily movement forms the kernel for analysing dance practice in this discussion. It emphasises that gendered choreography in dance performance is relational; it is cognisant of other moving bodies in any given space and the cultural meanings of gender circumscribed by these bodies.

The recognition of Cave's performances as gendered choreography must be understood within the frame of a particular genre of Australian pub rock, Oz rock, which dominated the domestic popular music landscape throughout the 1970s and 1980s. The mainstream Australian pub rock culture of the 1970s and early 1980s was often choreographed by traces of Johnny O'Keefe's 'tonic of wildness', a phrase used by historian Raymond Evans to describe how in 1950s and 1960s Australia, O'Keefe's brand of rock 'n' roll performance incited audiences to go 'berserk'.[12] In the Oz rock culture of the 1970s and 1980s, the aggressive wild child rock standard was recycled in images of the drugs, alcohol and sexual overindulgences of commercially-oriented rock musicians such as Rose Tattoo's Gary 'Angry' Anderson, Cold Chisel's Jimmy Barnes, INXS's Michael Hutchence and Marc Hunter from Dragon.[13] It was also exemplified by the rock music sounds linked to entrepreneur, Michael Gudinski, and his label, Mushroom, and similar rock sounds heard at inner-city venues in Melbourne (such as

Martini's in the suburb of Carlton) or the city's outer-suburban pub rock circuit (for example, at venues such as the Village Green in Glen Waverley).[14]

Importantly, the image of the Oz rock pub carried a 'gendered sense of place',[15] and some argue that it functioned mainly as a site of working-class masculine retreat from 'the dominant ideology of family and suburbia'.[16] Moreover, it spoke to working-class concerns that developed as large-scale deregulation of the Australian macroeconomy began during the 1980s. Insecurities emerged as domestic industry and capital and working-class labour were exposed to the potential shocks of the global economy. Tara Brabazon outlines the cultural anxieties along which Oz rock was experienced by its (mainly working-class) fans in her detailed analysis of Australian popular music of the 1970s and 1980s, writing that 'the spaces between the notes' of Oz rock required the 'national narratives of a hostile landscape to access … ideologies of masculinity, work, class and alcohol'.[17] Ideologically, then, Oz rock was politically conservative in its cultural-nationalist function, making it vital to late-1970s and early-1980s Australian popular culture.

It was the desire to escape this prevailing music scene and its attendant value system that drove the development of punk and alternative rock in Australia.[18] Gillian Upton, in her history of St Kilda's George Hotel, suggests that for many in the Crystal Ballroom set, the 'larger enemy' was the 'moribund culture outside' the Ballroom's walls.[19] Chris McAuliffe, researching the Melbourne punk scene of the 1970s and 1980s, argues that the scene was focused on the creation of a new lifestyle more than it was on any form of organised politics.[20] The rail against the 'enemy', therefore, was levelled at both the perceived constraints of the middle class (from which many participants came) and what was felt by many to be the crass, commercial and nationalist Oz rock pub culture scene, a rock culture

that in many respects was additionally encoded as 'relentlessly macho' and homophobic.[21]

If aggressive and hostile masculinities defined the mainstream pub rock circuit in Melbourne, then anti-normative codes of masculinity signalled to some extent the subculture of punk and alternative rock. The Crystal Ballroom scene was no exception.[22] Male performers in the scene, including Cave and others such as Simon Bonney from Crime and the City Solution, incorporated transgressive masculinities and sexualities into their performances, thus flagging the subculture as an 'unmanly' site for rock performance, at least in comparison to the spaces and attitudes of Oz pub rock.

CAVE, GENDER AND DANCE: AUSTRALIA

Cave's choreographic repertoire in the promotional music video for The Birthday Party release 'Nick the Stripper' reveals many of the manoeuvres that he performed in his onstage dances at the Crystal Ballroom and elsewhere. Phill Calvert, the band's drummer at the time, affirms this with his interpretation of Cave's dance in the clip: Calvert overwhelmingly sees Cave's dance as the parodic spectacle of the staged rock persona.[23] Mick Harvey, guitarist for The Birthday Party, says that the song itself is about the perverted form of the singer, its parody 'is in the great tradition of rock and roll's self aggrandisement'.[24] This parodying aspect of the traditional rock spectacle was a common feature of The Birthday Party's performance repertoire.[25]

The clip, directed by Paul Goldman (who has since become a long-time collaborator with Cave), begins with the band performing inside a circus tent, with a medium shot of the shirtless but trousered Cave jitterbugging shortly before the first verse of the song. Throughout the first verse he ducks and weaves his body in front of the camera.

As it concludes, Cave performs a half-pirouette. He has the grace and poise of a danseuse. Immediately following this manoeuvre, there is a fractured edit that signals the shifting location of the action. The narrative moves out of the tent and into a landscape of sheer depravity, a space described by one of Cave's biographers, Ian Johnston, as an 'atmosphere for a carnival of the obscene and the absurd'.[26] In this 'depraved' setting, Cave is clothed only in a nappy. Here, Cave does not so much dance as wastedly stumble through the debauched crowd.

At the launch of the third verse, Cave performs a manoeuvre that closely resembles the sashaying and semi-flamenco style of Crime and the City Solution's Simon Bonney. It is a style that, at some level, according to Birthday Party guitarist, Rowland Howard, made an impact on Cave's approach to performances at the time. Importantly, it demonstrated that being on stage was, in part, a theatrical performance and it also showed Cave that a 'gig could be an event', that there could be a broader purpose attached to playing.[27] Later in the sequence, Cave deftly pirouettes through the wild videoscape and just before the clip concludes he jitterbugs again, this time within the context of a homoerotic exchange with Howard. The two men move apart only after embracing and kissing each other on the lips.

In Mark Williams's review of the clip's DVD release, Cave's dancing style is described as 'prancing about',[20] a remark that dismisses the performative aspect of Cave's gestures. Contrary to Williams's analysis, I read Cave's dancing body in the clip's narrative as an attempt to counter what performance studies theorist José Esteban Muñoz calls 'the stream of a crushing heteronormative tide'.[29] There is a certain pleasure derived by viewing Cave performing against Australian rock music masculinities.

The wasted and almost defiant form of Cave's anti-normative masculinity is apparent in the many close-ups of Cave's cock-sure body: thin, oblique and non-muscular. This is not to suggest that Cave's body is decidedly 'unmasculine' but rather that it's transformed by a preening narcissism in the clip. Goldman's direction ensures that the viewer's gaze is firmly held on Cave's body. It is a gaze that moves against the traditional representation of the male body in Australian rock music culture, and in Australian media culture more broadly;[30] in the latter, the camera historically has constructed a viewing position that focuses on the actions performed by the rock performer's body, rather than explicitly directing the viewer's gaze toward the male body itself, in order to objectify it.

Further, the only area of Cave's body that is clothed-over in the 'obscene' and 'absurd' landscape is the very area of the body where gender is traditionally determined. There are no apparent signs of gendered clothing on Cave's body as he dances through the hellish landscape. Rather, the nappy leads to a reading of Cave's body as ambiguously gendered; or, at the very least, as a refusal to publicly signal normative masculine identity. As such, the nappy creates what could be called an 'eroticised surface' on Cave's dancing body,[31] one that constitutes, in the words of Eve Sedgwick, 'the open mesh of possibilities, gaps, overlaps, dissonances and resonances, lapses and excesses of meaning when the constituent elements of anyone's gender, or anyone's sexuality aren't made (or *can't be made*) to signify monolithically'.[32] The nappy queers Cave's dancing body. It works as a site which disrupts the idea that a particular sexed body—male or female—leads to a particular gender configuration (masculine or feminine respectively) and that this, inevitably, orients to a specific sexuality, usually assumed to be heterosexual. Coupled with Cave's dancing body, a slight and fragile masculine build, the nappy prompts the viewer to find alternative erotic possibilities of both Cave's unexposed *and* exposed body. Through his dance in the 'Nick the Stripper' clip, Cave's body resists the social norms and cultural regulations that largely policed the boundaries of the thoroughly masculine and heterosexually-oriented Australian pub rock music industry.[33]

Cave's queered embodiment in the clip is further amplified by the jitterbug that he performs while circling Howard. Cave's queer dance around Howard was part of a repertoire routinely performed between the two artists, often to draw attention to both the absurdity of the hypermasculine heterosexuality that existed within broader Australian rock culture and the sublimated 'gay schtick' written into the onstage gender dynamic between, say, the Rolling Stone's Mick Jagger and Keith Richards in the 1960s and 1970s.[34] Cave's jitterbug with Howard, furnished with a kiss, simultaneously—and ironically—emphasises and critiques the classic homoerotic aspect of rock performances that Oz rock sought to deny.

Ensconced within the parody, however, there also seems to be a genuine show of affection between Cave and Howard that queers the idea of normative *homosexual* sexuality as well. Cave's kiss demonstrates that it is not only two homosexual men, but also two ostensibly heterosexual men, who can incorporate the common signs of queer masculinities into their everyday behaviour.

When viewed within and through the prism of Oz rock culture's strident heterosexuality and, relatedly, through its subtle homophobia, the kiss functions as an element of gender and sexual transgression.[35] Yet this particular homoerotic kiss is not merely a performance strategy whose purpose is 'shock value'. In his later performances with the Bad Seeds, Cave often kissed guitarist Blixa Bargeld on the lips, a measure of the mutual respect and admiration between these two friends. In this sense, Cave's kiss works at the level of the everyday. Nevertheless, to contemporary viewers of the clip, as well as to those who viewed it upon its initial release, such an act between the two rock musicians largely renders Australian versions of male heterosexuality strange. A kiss between Cave and Howard queers the hegemony of a more stridently masculinised Australian rock mainstream.

As an artist and performer, then, Cave maintained a structured and knowing approach to dance performance. In his often-rapturous gestures his dance is simultaneously critique *and* performance. The performative outlook of both The Boys Next Door and The Birthday Party at one level was born from, as Cave biographer Robert Brokenmouth puts it, a lack of respect 'whatsoever for the sexually aggressive oz-rocker'.[36] At every possible musical and performance opportunity in Australia, Cave and his fellow band members were keen to assault the sensibilities of 'audiences intent on beer, chords, beer, chicks, and beer'.[37] But in the early 1980s, particularly after The Birthday Party's relocation from Melbourne to London, Cave invested his dances with a harder edge, and his choreographic repertoire was frequently sewn together by a series of spectacular phallic thrusts that punctuated his onstage performances.

CAVE, GENDER AND DANCE: ENGLAND

In England, Cave's dancing functions to question not so much the stifling hegemony of Oz rock masculinities as what was perceived by many as the debauched state of English rock and popular music culture in the early 1980s, encapsulated by the fey and effete styles of British 'new wave' pop acts such as Duran Duran and Adam and the Ants. Moreover, Cave's dances arguably reference the experience of the band's 'crushing revelation of disillusionment' upon first arriving in London. Looking on from middle-class Melbourne, members of The Birthday Party had imagined London to possess a 'romantic nocturnal lifestyle of performance'; once the band arrived in England, the London they had envisaged was no more than an 'intellectual fantasy'.[38] Frustrated with what they saw as the apathy of local audiences, they issued a challenge to sycophantic English fans who completely misunderstood the band's critical, parodic and intellectual edge.[39] Cave's performative response was to incorporate into his dance an aggressive choreography in order to 'excite people and confuse their normal way of thinking'.[40] It was a parodically hypermasculine style that directly challenged audiences to respond with an equal intensity. So, in his performance of 'A Dead Song' at Manchester's Hacienda in July 1982, Cave falls on his back, centre stage, and proceeds to thrust his pelvis upwards, rhythmically, sexually. At the same gig, in the performance of 'Junkyard', there is a heightening both in the frequency and in the exaggeration of Cave's spasmodic pelvic thrusts. In early 1983, again at a gig at the Hacienda, he performs similar moves, as well as slower hip grinds.[41]

These dance moves are regulated within the context of the frequently violent and often dissonant performances that later characterised many Birthday Party gigs. Quoting rock journalist, Clinton Walker, to describe Cave's performances in the early 1980s, performance theorist Susan Broadhurst writes that '[d]anger and glamour were crucial to Cave's image ... It was quite apparent to everyone that going to see the "Birthday Party in their heyday" was "like sitting in a bad corner waiting for an accident to happen"'.[42] One fan paints the sense of excitement and unease that characterised the performance of this 'half-man, half-unearthly creature' in England later that year: 'Nick dashes across the stage, throwing his body into another contorted primitive dance ... [he is] a mass of guttural growling, screaming and howling, reaching from the depths of his twisted, exhausted skinny body'.[43] The most (seemingly) subdued

member of The Birthday Party, Mick Harvey, recounts that a 'Birthday Party gig comprised a very volatile mixture of people, the subsequent potential for physical conditions to occur was very high. I think I got tense before we went on [stage] because I never knew what was going to happen, or whether someone was going to get seriously hurt'.[44]

Cave's dance style with The Birthday Party can be understood more deeply in terms of an experimental performative arm of marginal performance that Broadhurst provisionally assembles under the heading of 'liminal performance'.[45] The concept of liminal performance relies heavily on the purchase of Victor Turner's anthropological term 'limen', a concept speaking of a certain hybridised and marginal space. Audiences who experience liminal performances witness the possibility of 'potential forms, structures, conjectures and desires'.[46] Acts that are liminal emphasise artistic performance usually, but not always, of the body: 'a certain sense of excitement is generated ... a feeling almost of awe somewhat akin to discomfort is created'.[47] Cave's performances with The Birthday Party clearly fall into this performative mode by virtue of his gender dissonant choreography of thrusts, grinds and twists, which at times was undoubtedly shocking, provocative and stimulating. Simultaneously, as evidenced by Brokenmouth's transcripts of interviews with fans, they also induced a sense of disquiet, unease and tension, as well as pleasure, within audiences.[48]

AMBIGUITY AND PLEASURE IN CAVE'S ROCK PERFORMANCES

The broad politics of masculinity in Cave's work—his confronting and disturbingly 'erotic' body in the 'Nick the Stripper' clip, the homoeroticism that was written into some of his dance manoeuvres, and his pelvic thrusts and hip grind—point towards the possibility for more progressive gender relations in rock culture. Broadhurst argues that in Cave's work the political

> takes the form of a self-conscious, self-contradictory, self-undermining statement, almost giving the effect of saying something while at the same time putting inverted commas around what is being said. The effect is to 'highlight' or 'subvert' and the mode is therefore a 'knowing' or even 'ironic' one.[49]

Cave's pelvic thrusts, for example, work as a sexually parodic performance of the phallic power of musicians in a 'real rock band',[50] in much the same way as Cave's queerly choreographed dance with Howard works to critique the classic male-bonding 'schtick' of mainstream Oz rock performers. But in this 'self-contradictory' method of performance, there is a paradox. As Broadhurst writes, one of the main features of Cave's performances seems to be his partial commitment to 'duplicity', an upholding of the very structures of masculinity that he seeks to disrupt. In short, Cave cannot escape the mainstream rock masculinity he seeks to overturn.[51] That said, the more progressive qualities of Cave's work can override the more duplicitous qualities of this mode of performance critique.[52] In another context, but with a shared interest, Stan Hawkins shows how the themes of 'polysemy' and 'ambiguity' in the stage performances by 'the artist known as' Prince in the 1980s helped open up the strategy of self-parody through bodily movement, hence exposing the plasticity of gender.[53] Relatedly, Bollen uncovers the 'girly poofter' and 'cool dyke' dance styles that afforded queer dancers at the Sydney Gay and Lesbian Mardi Gras parties in the 1990s the pleasurable indulgence to 'escape from the everyday regulation of gender'.[54] Similar to these varying perspectives from different musical subcultures I argue that 'ambiguity' and 'pleasure' are centralising themes around which ideas of masculinity in Cave's dance performances can be arranged.

The reading of Cave's gendered choreographies as ambiguous is established mainly through his queer gender construction. At gigs with The Birthday Party at the Crystal Ballroom and elsewhere in Melbourne, the performative markers of marginalised genders and sexualities are realised through the grand gestures of effeminacy; later, especially once the band moves to London, Cave's gestures are increasingly laced with the traces of parodic hypermasculinity. Cave's authorship of masculinity, in this regard, parallels that of Prince, whose mobile gender position is characterised, according to Hawkins, through a 'phallic parading' which serves to 'spell out his playfulness'.[55] Cave's adoption of the performance markers that signal a highly labile masculine identity reflects the playful and flamboyant understanding of the political that was integral to many punk and alternative rock acts that emerged from Melbourne during the late 1970s, including the scene that developed around the Crystal Ballroom.[56] Cave wilfully, performatively, uses his body to make particular statements about rock music masculinity, and, similar to Prince, he 'inscribes a calculated control of gender ambiguity' in his dance moves.[57]

Ambiguity, in this sense, is achieved by Cave's engagement with particularly powerful forms of queerness that dissolve the binaries of 'masculine' and 'feminine' underpinning mainstream rock cultures.[58] Writing about 'male queering in mainstream pop', Hawkins explains that 'gender-bending spectacles'—of which Cave's onstage pirouettes and balletic manoeuvres form a part—often 'wrangle with rigid inscriptions of fixed male identity' that audiences may bring to certain viewing contexts.[59] Cave's dances were usually performed in a rock scene peripheral to the mainstream rock culture; and in the latter rock cultures, be it the space of

Oz rock, or the English popular music scene of the 1970s and 1980s, the transgression of normative gender tropes would be more keenly felt. Yet it is clear from evidence presented by critics such as Riley that participants within the Crystal Ballroom scene were more willing than those in the broader rock culture to play with the surface markers of gender for critical, perhaps even pleasurable, purposes.[60]

These plays with queerness by Cave heighten for audiences the ambivalence of his sexuality, and they effectively 'highlight a more ambiguous masculinity'.[61] In some of Cave's performance moves, such as his nappy dance in the 'Nick the Stripper' clip, or in his recurring onstage kiss with Howard, audiences locate these ambiguous queerly-read tensions within a masculine identity that oscillates between the poles of fixity and fluidity. Cave's hyperbolic dance style moves from effeminacy to that of parodic hypermasculinity, simultaneously incorporating the seemingly disparate elements of earnestness, parody, gender fixity and queerness.

Through this strategy of destabilisation, gender ambiguity can also be pleasurable. The notion of pleasure is linked to one of the most important ways of thinking about rock music performance, namely audience reception. In the examples already discussed, the queer pleasures for both Cave and audience in the Crystal Ballroom scene are largely 'contra-straight' in that they are not fuelled by queer desire. Instead, these pleasures are fed by what popular culture critic Alexander Doty has called a form of queer participation that can be enjoyed by heterosexuals, 'straight queerness'.[62] The strong pleasures afforded by witnessing the 'erotic surfaces' on Cave's moving body, for example, can activate—or further, affirm—the ostensibly straight male fan's queered sense of masculinity in relation to the harder-edged masculine subject positions associated with artists performing in the broader Australian rock milieu.

Importantly, straight queer masculinity is represented here as a particular nexus of pleasure. Specifically, these are queer pleasures that enable scene participants to 'experience [a] vicarious if temporary empowerment' in their everyday gender negotiations.[63] An awareness or appreciation of, maybe even an affinity with, Cave's performatively queered masculinity holds the potential to engender a sense of pleasurable affinity. Straight queer masculinity, at root, is an alternative from, and a blurring of, the 'terrible simplicity of male heterosexual experience and the crude simplicity of homocentric narratives'.[64] Pleasure for audiences resides in the knowledge that the hegemony of these normative forms of rock masculinity—and their associations with a thuggish, crude and unsophisticated rawness—slowly dissolves, or is at least temporarily disrupted.

Pleasure for the audiences of the performances I have examined is two-fold. First, by audiences 'eroticising' the surface of Cave's non-normative masculine physique, and by understanding the homoeroticism written into some of his dance moves, there is the possibility of challenging the popular images of masculinity that circulate in rock and popular music culture. Pushing off from this point, the idea of straight queerness allows heterosexual participants, such as Cave, other members of The Birthday Party and straight audiences alike, to imagine a more romantic notion of their subculture. It is indeed a notion which Riley, echoing Upton's earlier comment about the scene at the George Hotel's Crystal Ballroom, describes as one where the artist is 'at war with the outside world into which he didn't fit'.[65] Pleasure through Cave's ambiguous performances of straight queerness is intensified for fans at an actual Birthday Party gig in the late 1970s, as well as for audiences viewing Cave's performances on video many years later; as remarked earlier, such viewing contexts are adjuncts to the social regulation of the norms of rock music masculinities. Therefore, pleasure exists for viewers of Cave's dances—then and now—in the ambiguous and precarious space beyond the regulative parameters of rock music's more repressive forms of masculinity.

CONCLUSION

Cave's queer performances recruit dance to question prevailing mainstream Antipodean and English rock masculinities. Cave was highly aware of the 'performative potential'[66] of his body and used it in ways to highlight the absurdities of the more socially regressive aspects of normative rock masculinity, and, in Australia at least, their articulations to the brand of cultural nationalism associated with Oz rock. Viewed through the primary analytic categories of 'ambiguity' and 'pleasure', Cave's dance performances simultaneously thrill and provoke audiences, and they draw upon constructions of gender and sexual identity which are ultimately diffused by the underlying ambivalence of straight queerness.

BIBLIOGRAPHY

Alomes, Stephen, 'An Austerican Culture?—Australian Rock from Johnny O'Keefe to Jimmy Barnes', *Island Magazine,* 30 (1987): 58–61.

Auslander, Philip, *Presence and Resistance: Postmodernism and Cultural Politics in Contemporary American Performance* (Ann Arbor, MI: University of Michigan Press, 1994).

The Birthday Party, *Pleasure Heads Must Burn,* DVD (London: Cherry Red Records, 2003).

Bollen, Jonathan, 'Queer Kinesthesia: Performativity on the Dance Floor', in Jane Desmond (ed.), *Dancing Desires: Choreographing Sexualities On and Off the Stage* (Madison, WI: University of Wisconsin Press, 2001).

Brabazon, Tara, *Tracking the Jack: A Retracing of the Antipodes* (Sydney: University of New South Wales Press, 2000).

Broadhurst, Susan, *Liminal Acts: A Critical Overview of Contemporary Performance and Theory* (London: Cassell, 1999).

Brokenmouth, Robert, *Nick Cave: The Birthday Party and Other Epic Adventures* (Sydney: Omnibus, 1996).

Buchbinder, David, *Performance Anxieties: Re-producing Masculinity* (Sydney: Allen & Unwin, 1998).

Burt, Ramsay, 'Dissolving in Pleasure: The Threat of the Queer Male Dancing Body', in Jane Desmond (ed.), *Dancing Desires: Choreographing Sexualities On and Off the Stage* (Madison, WI: University of Wisconsin Press, 2001).

Butler, Judith, *Bodies That Matter* (New York: Routledge, 1993).

Cox, Peter, *Real Wild Child: Teen Riots to Generation X* (Sydney: Powerhouse, 1994).

Dawson, Ashley, 'Do Doc Martens Have a Special Smell?', in Kevin Dettmar and William Richey (eds), *Reading Rock and Roll: Authenticity, Appropriation, Aesthetics* (New York: Columbia University Press, 1999).

Desmond, Jane (ed.), *Dancing Desires: Choreographing Sexualities On and Off the Stage* (Madison, WI: University of Wisconsin Press, 2001).

Dollimore, Jonathan, *Sexual Dissidence: Augustine to Wilde, Freud to Foucault* (Oxford: Clarendon, 1991).

Doty, Alexander, 'There's Something Queer Here', in Corey K. Creekmur and Alexander Doty (eds), *Out in Culture: Gay, Lesbian, and Queer Essays in Popular Culture* (London: Cassell, 1995).

Dyson, Mandy, 'Renegotiating the Australian Legend: "Khe Sanh" and the Jimmy Barnes Stage Persona', *Limina,* 4 (1998): 59–68.

Evans, Raymond, 'The Tonic of Wildness: Johnny O'Keefe and Me', *Perfect Beat*, 5.1 (2000): 56–66.

Fiske, John, Bob Hodge and Graeme Turner, *Myths of Oz: Reading Australian Popular Culture* (Sydney: Allen & Unwin, 1987).

Franklin, Paul B., 'The Terpsichorean Tramp: "Unmanly" Movement in the Early Films of Charlie Chaplin', in Jane Desmond (ed.), *Dancing Desires: Choreographing Sexualities On and Off the Stage* (Madison, WI: University of Wisconsin Press, 2001).

Hawkins, *Stan, Settling the Pap Scare: Pop Texts and Identity Politics* (Aldershot: Ashgate, 2002).

——, 'On Male Queering in Mainstream Pop', in Sheila Whiteley and Jennifer Rycenga (eds), *Queering the Popular Pitch* (London: Routledge, 2006).

Johnston, Ian, *Bad Seed: The Biography of Nick Cave* (London: Abacus, 1996).

McAuliffe, Chris, 'Guerrillas, Poseurs and Nomads: The Politics of the Avant-Garde in Art and Music', in Xavier Pons (ed.), *Departures: How Australia Re-Invents Itself* (Melbourne: Melbourne University Press, 2002).

McDonald, Paul, 'Feeling and Fun: Romance, Dance and the Performing Male Body in *Take That* Videos', in Sheila Whiteley (ed.), *Sexing the Groove: Popular Music and Gender* (London: Routledge, 1997).

Miles, Cressida, 'Spatial Politics: A Gendered Sense of Place', in Steve Redhead, Derek Wynne and Justin O'Connor (eds), *The Clubcultures Reader: Readings in Popular Cultural Studies* (Oxford: Blackwell, 1997).

Muñoz, José Esteban, 'Gesture, Ephemera, and Queer Feeling: Approaching Kevin Aviance', in Jane Desmond (ed.), *Dancing Desires: Choreographing Sexualities On and Off the Stage* (Madison, WI: University of Wisconsin Press, 2001).

Riley, Vikki, 'Death Rockers of the World Unite! Melbourne 1978–80: Punk Rock or No Punk Rock?',

in Phil Hayward (ed.), *From Pop to Punk to Post-modernism* (Sydney: Alien & Unwin, 1992).

Smith, Paul, 'Eastwood Bound', in Maurice Berger, Brian Wallis and Simon Watson (eds), *Constructing Masculinity* (New York: Routledge, 1995).

The South Bank Shaw, ep. 607: Nick Cave, TV Documentary (UK TV, 2003).

Upton, Gillian, *The George: St Kilda Life and Times* (Melbourne: Venus Bay, 2001).

Walker, Clinton, *Stranded: The Secret History of Australian Independent Music 1977–1991* (Sydney: Pan Macmillan, 1996).

Williams, Mark. 'The Birthday Party—Review of DVD: *Pleasure Heads Must Burn*' [Online], available at http://www.noise-online.com/birthdayparty.html, accessed 26 Oct, 2004.

NOTES

1. Many thanks to David Carter, Graeme Turner and Joanne Tompkins for guiding with much insight and patience my MPhil research at the University of Queensland during 2003–2005. This chapter is written from that research.

2. Vikki Riley, 'Death Rockers of the World Unite! Melbourne 1978–80: Punk Rock or No Punk Rock?', in Phil Hayward (ed.), *From Pop to Punk to Postmodernism* (Sydney, 1992), pp. 113–29.

3. Brokenmouth, *Nick Cave: The Birthday Party and Other Epic Adventures* (Sydney, 1996), p. 72.

4. Paul McDonald, 'Feeling and Fun: Romance, Dance and the Performing Male Body in *Take That Videos*', in Sheila Whiteley (ed.), *Sexing the Groove; Popular Music and Gender* (London, 1997), pp. 277–94.

5. Jonathan Bollen, 'Queer Kinesthesia: Performativity on the Dance Floor', in Jane Desmond (ed.), *Dancing Desires:*

Choreographing Sexualities On and Off the Stage, (Madison, WI, 2001), pp. 285–314.

6. Ibid., p. 312.
7. Ibid., p. 304.
8. Judith Butler, *Bodies That Matter* (New York, 1993), p. 10.
9. Bollen, 'Queer Kinesthesia', p. 309.
10. Alexander Doty, "There's Something Queer Here', in Corey K. Creekmur and Alexander Doty (eds), *Out In Culture: Gay, Lesbian and Queer Essays in Popular Culture* (London, 1995), p. 72.
11. Bollen, 'Queer Kinesthesia', p. 301.
12. Raymond Evans, 'The Tonic of Wildness: Johnny O'Keefe and Me', *Perfect Beat,* 5.1 (2000): 56–66.
13. Stephen Alomes, 'An Austerican Culture? Australian Rock from Johnny O'Keefe to Jimmy Barnes', *Island Magazine,* 30 (1987): 58–61; Mandy Dyson, 'Renegotiating the Australian Legend: "Khe Sanh" and the Jimmy Barnes Stage Persona', *Limina,* 4 (1998): 59–68.
14. Gillian Upton, *The George: St Kilda Life and Times* (Melbourne, 2001), p. 103; Peter Cox, *Real Wild Child: Teen Riots to Generation X* (Sydney, 1994), p. 32.
15. Cressida Miles, 'Spatial Politics: A Gendered Sense of Place', in Steve Redhead, Derek Wynne and Justin O'Connor (eds), *The Clubcultures Reoder: Readings in Popular Cultural Studies* (Oxford, 1997), p. 66.
16. John Fiske, Bob Hodge and Graeme Turner, *Myths of Oz: Reading Australian Popular Culture* (Sydney, 1987), p. 6.
17. Tara Brabazon, *Tracking the Jack: A Retracing of the Antipodes* (Sydney, 2000), pp. 100, 102.
18. Riley, 'Death Rockers of the Word Unite!', p. 118; Clinton Walker, *Stranded: The Secret History of Australian Independent Music 1977–1991* (Sydney, 1996), pp. 15, 52.

19. Upton, *The George,* p. 103.
20. Chris McAuliffe, 'Guerrillas, Poseurs and Nomads: The Politics of the Avant-Garde in Art and Music', in Xavier Pons (ed.), *Departures: How Australia Re-Invents Itself* (Melbourne, 2002), pp. 192–201.
21. Riley, 'Death Rockers of the World Unite!', p. 121.
22. Ibid., pp. 116–21.
23. Brokenmouth, *Nick Cave,* p. 72.
24. *The South Bank Shaw,* ep. 607: Nick Cave, TV Documentary (UK TV, 2003).
25. Brokenmouth, *Nick Cave,* p. 45.
26. Ian Johnston, *Bad Seed: The Biography of Nick Cave* (London, 1996), p. 71.
27. Brokenmouth, *Nick Cave,* p. 32.
28. Mark Williams, 'The Birthday Party—Review of DVD: *Pleasure Heads Must Burn*' [Online], available at http://www.noise-online.com/birthdayparty.html, accessed 26 Oct 2004.
29. José Esteban Muñoz, 'Gesture, Ephemera, and Queer Feeling: Approaching Kevin Aviance', in Jane Desmond (ed.), *Dancing Desires: Choreographing Sexualities On and Off the Stage* (Madison, WI, 2001), p. 433.
30. David Buchbinder, *Performance Anxieties: Re-producing Masculinity* (Sydney, 1998).
31. Ramsay Burt 'Dissolving in Pleasure: The Threat of the Queer Male Dancing Body', in Jane Desmond (ed.), *Dancing Desires: Choreographing Sexualities On and Off the Stage* (Madison, WI, 2001), p. 226.
32. Quoted in Paul B. Franklin, 'The Terpsichorean Tramp: "Unmanly" Movement in the Early Films of Charlie Chaplin', in Jane Desmond (ed.), *Dancing Desires: Choreographing Sexualities On and Off the Stage* (Madison, WI, 2001), pp. 35–72.
33. Riley, 'Death Rockers of the World Unite!', p. 121.
34. Brokenmouth, *Nick Cave,* pp. 91, 118.

35. Jonathan Dollimore, *Sexual Dissidence: Augustine to Wilde, Freud to Foucault* (Oxford, 1991), p. 25.
36. Brokenmouth, *Nick Cave,* p. 59.
37. Ibid.
38. Ibid., p. 80.
39. Ibid., p. 80.
40. Cave, quoted in Brokenmouth, *Nick Cave,* pp. 147, 162.
41. The Birthday Party, *Pleasure Heads Must Burn,* DVD of various rock music video clips and live concert footage (London, 2003).
42. Susan Broadhurst, *Liminal Acts: A Critical Overview of Contemporary Performance and Theory* (London, 1999), p. 153.
43. Brokenmouth, *Nick Cave,* p. 125.
44. Ibid., p. 122.
45. Broadhurst, *Liminal Acts,* p. 1.
46. Ibid., p. 12.
47. Ibid., p. 13.
48. Brokenmouth, *Nick Cave,* pp. 125–7.
49. Broadhurst, *Liminal Acts,* p. 156.
50. Brokenmouth, *Nick Cave,* p. 145.
51. Philip Auslander, *Presence and Resistance: Postmodernism and Cultural Politics in Contemporary American Performance* (Ann Arbor, MI, 1994), p. 31.
52. Broadhurst, *Liminal Acts,* p. 156.
53. Stan Hawkins, *Settling the Pop Score: Pop Texts and Identity Politics* (Aldershot, 2002), pp. 186–8.
54. Bollen, 'Queer Kinesthesia', p. 308.
55. Hawkins, *Settling the Pop Score,* p. 186.
56. McAuliffe, 'Guerrillas, Poseurs and Nomads', p. 192.
57. Ibid.
58. Ashley Dawson, 'Do Doc Martens Have a Special Smell?', in Kevin Dettmar and William Richey (eds), *Reading Rock and Roll: Authenticity, Appropriation, Aesthetics* (New York, 1999), pp. 125–43.
59. Stan Hawkins, 'On Male Queering in Mainstream Pop', in Sheila Whiteley and Jennifer Rycenga (eds), *Queering the Popular Pitch* (London, 2006), p. 282.
60. Riley, 'Death Rockers of the World Unite!', pp. 121–5.
61. Hawkins, 'On Male Queering', p. 282.
62. Doty, 'There's Something Queer Here', pp. 71–90.
63. Ibid., p. 78.
64. Paul Smith, 'Eastwood Bound', in Maurice Berger, Brian Wallis and Simon Watson (eds), *Constructing Masculinity* (New York, 1995), pp. 77–97.
65. Riley, 'Death Rockers of the World Unite!', p. 123.
66. This is a term that Paul Franklin uses to describe the dancing body of Charlie Chaplin in the Tramp's early films. See Franklin, 'The Terpsichorean Tramp', pp. 35–72.

Impossible Spaces

Kevin McCarty's *The Chameleon Club*

By José Esteban Muñoz

ARTIST'S STATEMENT

Located somewhere in the middle of nowhere, surrounded by cow fields and suburban home developments, in between the ruins of downtown Dayton, Ohio, a post-industrial wasteland, and Wright-Patterson Air Force base, sat the Hills and Dales shopping center. In a retail space at the rear of a strip mall, the Chameleon Club opened. One entered what would have been the sales floor and made one's way back through a single doorway to the storeroom, which had been converted into a punk rock club. The only furnishings were a plywood stage at the far end, flanked by a PA. The dry walling was incomplete, leaving cinder blocks exposed. To the right of the stage was a doorway that led to 1470's, the largest gay bar in Dayton. When one paid admission to the Chameleon Club, one could buy drinks at 1470's. The punks passed back and forth, but no one from 1470's came to the Chameleon Club. With their costumes and their lyrics, the kids on the music scene performed their identities at the temporary venue. For the punks, geographic location was not relevant as long as there were a stage, a soundman, and an audience. Behind the bare cinder blocks of the Chameleon Club, one could hear the beat of dance music. The sweating bodies of intoxicated gay men crowded the dance floor, only to be revealed through the artificial fog by streaks of red, blue, and green lights circling above their heads. Here men forgot about the blue-collar oppressive city they called home and imagined a world where they could be free from shame and embarrassment. Neither place was mine. I observed both from the outside. My utopia existed at the doorway on the threshold—in neither space and in both spaces simultaneously.

In the body of work *The Chameleon Club*, I attempt to describe the experience of existing on the edge of identification, the possibility of transformation, and the construction of utopia. The images represent empty stages at music clubs and gay clubs in Los Angeles. Each stage is lit as if a concert were about to happen. The only human presences are the marks of the people who have crossed the stage, and the debris they have left behind. Placing the viewer at eye level and centered on the stage, I want to isolate him or her as much as the stage.

—Kevin McCarty

In his photographic practice Kevin McCarty attempts to image utopia by examining the potential for utopian space. He is interested in depicting the both interconnected and impossible spaces of gay belonging and punk belonging. To this end, his lens, dedicated to the task of seeing what is not quite there, seeks to glimpse a utopian horizon. The visual evidence of McCarty's performance are haunting, technically beautiful pictures of some of queer and punk Los Angeles's empty stages that are most laden with potentiality: La Plaza, the Catch One, Spaceland, the Parlour Club, the Garage, and the Silver Lake Lounge.

To contextualize and introduce McCarty's work, I turn to an early moment in gay and lesbian studies. The anthology *Lavender Culture* contains a report about queer bars in Ohio. In a short piece titled "The Cleveland Bar Scene in the Forties," John Kelsey reports on the fundamental importance of these spaces: "There was, of course, nothing spectacular about Cleveland's gay male bars in the forties, but the point is simply this: they existed. Gay men had places to meet, not only in San Francisco or New York, but in a city easily scoffed at or ignored by sophisticates on either coast."[1] Kelsey's account of the 1940s resonates powerfully next to McCarty's photographs. McCarty's impressions from the 1990s, fifty years after Kelsey's moment, probably still correspond with a point Kelsey makes about bars: "The curious combination of exploitation and liberation helped define the mood in gay bars then as it is now, though perhaps both elements were more extreme in those days."[2] The calculus of exploitation and liberation dogs queer culture. Kelsey talks about seeing a few good female impersonators and also states that "if the professional entertainment was bad, the amateurs were unbelievably awful."[3] He characterizes a typical scene at the Hide-Out Club's Sunday-afternoon amateur performances, in which "male typists in Grandma's cast-off finery would take the stage, forget lyrics, and flee in tears.

And stockroom boys would take absolutely dreadful spills during their ballet-tap routines. One [performer] I much enjoyed was a short, middle-aged man who would sing part of it ["Indian Summer"] in the voice of Nelson Eddy, and part in the voice of Jeanette MacDonald."[4]

The celebration of an aesthetics of amateurism is reminiscent of punk rock's aesthetics. The performance of amateurism, both in punk and in this example of queer performance, signals a refusal of mastery and an insistence on process and becoming. Again, such performances do not disappear but instead leave remains. In the above example, the short squat singer of "Indian Summer" is loved decades after his performance, and that single audience member's testimonial stands as one of the things that remains after the performance. The performance, in its incompleteness, lingers and persists, drawing together a community of interlocutors. Utopian performativity is often fueled by the past. The past, or at least narratives of the past, enable utopian imaginings of another time and place that are not yet here but nonetheless function as a doing for futurity, a conjuring of both future and past to critique presentness. McCarty's work is fueled by a recollection from his biography that he takes to another time and place and uses to capture this ideal potential of utopian performativity. His stages are lit as though a performance were about to emerge from the realm of the potential into the actual. The lure of the work is its performative dimension, which I would describe as a doing as dwelling; that is, I am particularly interested in how the images dwell in potentiality, aestheticizing the moment of potential, transmitting the power of its ideality. Thus the aesthetic fuels the political imagination.

Installed at a gallery, the images of a punk club are hung next to images of a gay bar's stage. The juxtaposition of these images speaks to subjectivities that travel through the swinging door between temporal and spatial coordinates. For those of us whose relationship to popular culture is always marked by aesthetic and sexual antagonism, these stages are our actual utopian rehearsal rooms, where we work on a self that does not conform to the mandates of cultural logics like late capitalism, heteronormativity, or, in some cases, white supremacy.

The source material for McCarty's images is the past, but not a nostalgic past; instead, it is a past that helps us feel a certain structure of feelings, a circuit of queer belonging. When I look at his images, I remember the sexually ambiguous punk clubs of my youth, where horny drunk punk boys rehearsed their identities, aggressively dancing with each other and later lurching out to the parking lot together. For many, the mosh pit wasn't simply a closet; it was a utopian sub-cultural rehearsal space. The past is not static but instead a resource for the project of imagining futurity. McCarty's project, the visualizing of a queer and punk future, seems especially poignant at times like these, when the specter of fascism looms and the politics of despair abound.

Figure 1. Catch One. All images reproduced with permission of photographer

Figure 2. La Plaza

Figure 3. Silverlake Lounge

Figure 4. Spaceland 2002

Figure 5. Spaceland 2003

Figure 6. The Smell

NOTES

1. John Kelsey, "The Cleveland Bar Scene in the Forties," in *Lavender Culture*, ed. Karla Jay and Allen Young (New York: New York University Press, 1994), 146.
2. Ibid.
3. Ibid., 148–49.
4. Ibid., 149.

28 Crazy Patriotism and Angry (Post) Black Women[1]

By D. Soyini Madison

They're going to try and make me into a scary guy. They're even trying to make Michelle into a scary person.

—Barack Obama

The OED describes a "patriot" as "one who loves his or her country and gives it loyal support." Patriotism for some in the United Slates, during the 2008 Presidential Campaign, exemplified something beyond love and loyalty of one's country, but was more akin to a sacred belief, a fundamentalist nationalism, a divine calling that was intensified into an ideology of "us" against "them," the righteous and faithful against the blasphemous and ungodly. This brand of patriotism turns loyalty and love for country into blind *excess* and sinister chauvinism, what I prefer to call *crazy patriotism*. Crazy patriotism is the unhealthy condition—a pathology of limitations—that impairs the ability to both love and critique, to both honor and re-imagine, to both recognize the noble possibilities of this country while interrogating its wrongs, e.g., its history of obstructionism to transnational freedom movements across the globe, its perpetuation of imperious global profit, and its dubious support of torture and clandestine policies of coercion, to name a few. As crazy patriotism's divisive ideology—blind to its own self-serving tautologies—gained momentum, it became the primary weapon waged against the possibility of an Obama presidency, casting Obama as a threat to "American"[2] greatness. But it was Michelle Obama who was the most vociferously attacked in its crazy excess and sanctimony.

Michelle Obama was cast as the darker, contentious, and hidden side of her husband. She was what many feared about Barack Obama—"a symbol of her husband's Otherness."[3]

Crazy patriotism will continue to cast Barack and Michelle as "scary" rather than concede to the truly scary facts and harmful effects of economic injustice, anglocentrism, and racial terror within the borders of the United States of America. The irony is that the real fear lies within the psyche of crazy patriotism itself, because the recognition of such consequential imperfections would threaten

D. Soyini Madison, "Crazy Patriotism and Angry (Post)Black Women," *Communication and Critical/Cultural Studies*, vol. 6, no. 3, pp. 321-326. Copyright © 2009 by National Communication Association. Reprinted with permission by Taylor & Francis Group LLC.

its veracity and unsettle its authority. Beyond being simultaneously impervious to and fearful of questioning "American" superiority and sanctity, crazy patriotism is quintessentially *racialized*. It constructs an "American" national identity that unproblematizes "Americaness" and the thick divergence of what it means to live in, or be a citizen of, the United States. Crazy patriotism dehistoricizes U.S. identity into a white racial identity that is "conterminous with (racial) whiteness."[4] It is constituted by a racial chauvinism where whiteness becomes the (unspoken) default identity for "American" and the "American" patriot, while it ironically labels "unpatriotic" expressions that are critical of U.S. racism. Crazy patriotism has no need to sustain claims of white superiority, because identity is sufficient. White supremacy is de-articulated—all groups are equally good, and no group is "intrinsically better than the other.[10] This *unspoken* whiteness is in opposition to *spoken* blackness. As crazy patriotism attempts to silence articulations of racial difference while sustaining white supremacy, it also proclaims the "American" common good while supporting the structural machinations that foster inequity in the United States it revels in a braggadocio of "American" democracy while condemning as "Un-American" acts of civil disobedience and social dissent.

When Michelle Obama was said to have equaled "America" with being "mean," crazy patriotism regarded this as blasphemous. When she made the comment of being proud of her country for the "first time," she was an angry, unpatriotic ingrate. When she commented that her husband was a black man and therefore vulnerable to risk, she was irrational and obsessed with race. Her 1985 senior thesis, "Princeton-Educated Blacks and The Black Community," provided proof of her affinity to black militancy and racial division. Juan Williams, the black neo-con of Fox News, warned that Michelle Obama was "Stokley Carmichael in a dress" and

would be a liability for her husband. Sean Hannity described her as "bitter" and preaching a gospel of "despair and hopelessness." The contempt grew as a blog in the Daily Kos revealed an image of Michelle Obama being branded and lynched.

Michelle Obama dared to have a racial politics. As a result, crazy patriotism pulled from its bag of black stereotypes the one marked, "angry black women," and it became the proper fit for the mantra "unpatriotic."

It is said that there is a grain of truth that constitutes every stereotype. Perhaps this is why stereotypes are dangerous. Truth is distorted and used against the better interest of those objectified by the stereotype. Anger, relative to country and citizenship, is existentially different as it is embodied within the daily lives of black women than it is for those who embrace patriotism as sacrosanct.

ANGRY BLACK WOMEN

Anger is loaded with information and energy

—Andre Lorde

Audre Lorde once wrote that "My response to racism is anger. I have lived with that anger, ignoring it, feeding upon it, learning to use it before it laid my vision to waste, for most of my life."[6] Lorde goes on to state that "Women of Color in america have grown up within a symphony of anger, at being silenced, at being unchosen, at knowing that when we survive, it is in spite of a world that takes for granted our lack of humanness."...[7] She chooses the term "symphony rather than cacophony because we have had to learn to orchestrate those furies so that they do not tear us apart" Lorde's words are neither an apology nor an antidote for black women's anger, but an affirmation and a hope for "The Uses of Anger."[9]

I want to contrast anger as described by Lorde to the angry-black-woman (ABW) stereotype projected upon Michelle Obama by crazy patriotism and the media, e.g., the (in)famous cartoon of her burning the American flag, *The New Yorker* magazine's controversial parody of her adorning military fatigues, a large afro, toting a machine gun, and Fox News' absurd accusation of "the terrorist fist jab." Drawing from Lorde, the distinction between the ABW stereotype and the "uses of anger" embodied in the experiences of black women from Ida B. Wells to Eartha Kitt,[10] from black women in welfare lines to picket lines, and from black women poets to university professors is a difference of use and function. Anger in this instance is political and purposeful. To disassemble the stereotype and attempt to comprehend the contexts of black women's anger opens the possibility of radically altering assumptions about *belonging* relative to the rewards, consequences, and constructions of citizenship. It also opens the potential for crazy patriotism to cease its consistent demand for contested identities to attend to its narrow agenda by expanding its purview to attend to the agendas of the contested. Michelle Obama was demonized by crazy patriotism as an ABW because it de-complexified her. To stereotype her was both easier and more compatible with normalized notions of gender and blackness than to engage the more complicated genealogy of black rage in the USA.

Is Michelle Obama angry as crazy patriotism would have us believe or has she employed the useful anger described by black feminist writers as diverse as Audrey Lorde, Ida B. Wells, Wahneema Lubiano, Ella Baker, Saidiya Hartman, Anna Julia Cooper, Michele Wallace, Maria Stewart, Pearl Cleage, Cheryl Clark, Claudia Jones, June Jordan, Paula Giddings, Nannie Burroughs, Pauli Murray and so many others? The misrepresentation of black women's anger, torn from its causes and contexts, aims to leave crazy patriotism intact, infallible, and noble. Michelle Obama becomes an easy target. Projecting her as angry and then casting her anger as irrational, rootless, unjustified and, of course, gendered and racialized is the perfect discursive precursor for the characterization of ungrateful and unpatriotic. Her anger rises from a vacuum in this "great country" that has brought her nothing but freedom, fame, and fortune, because to think otherwise is un-thinkable.

POSTBLACK/POSTPATRIOTISM

Skin color is one of the defining facts of American life. If you don't feel compelled to think about it much, chances are you are white.

—Holland Cotter

In an exhibition of emerging black artists entitled *Freestyling*, at the Studio Museum of Harlem in 2001, the curator Thelma Golden "half jokingly" describes the racial identity resonating from the exhibit as "post-black"—meaning that racial identity must be "defined and kept alive," recognizing that race is a "social construction and a reality with an indispensable history" yet it is simultaneously "privy to a range of poststructural cultural discourses."[12] "Postblack"[13] may sound "cool" for some but what it actually describes "is a precarious balancing act."[14] Postblack "offers a path out of the identity corner but keeps identity as a viable content … pushing beyond multiculturalism's territorial constraints, moving freely among identities and affiliations, deciding to be both insiders and outsiders."[15] Postblack has been described as the "third road" or the "third path that black America is walking"[16] If we can envision a postracial country and "if that adjective is ever to be *more than a stupid, unlettered flourish,* (emphasis mine) then look to those, like Michelle Obama, with a sense of security in who they are—those, black or white, who hold *blackness as more than the losing end of racism.*"[17]

Michelle Obama exceeds the unpatriotic, angry black woman imposed by the crazy patriots because she reclaims a discourse of the (bourgeois) "American dream" and the "common good" of the "American" ideal. Her anger becomes necessarily domesticated in her love for *The Brady Bunch* and her Horatio Alger story of perseverance, hard work, and accomplishment. For many, her "American" identity eclipses her racial identity in her expressions of shared values, domesticity, and opportunity. This beautiful couple with their beautiful intelligence, their beautiful way of speaking, their beautiful daughters, and their beautiful life *outclass* the crazy patriots literally and figuratively. Social class and beauty are as much (or more) a factor in the construction of the Obama identity as race. Charges of elitism withstanding, it has been the combination of class and beauty that eventually made their blackness acceptable, even admirable, for many in the U.S. and a source of pride, specifically, for black people. The crazy patriots' stereotype of the angry black woman could not withstand this new representation of blackness emerging on the national stage. A blackness that did not erase race but, instead, beautified it, (re)classed it, intellectualized it, domesticated it (for better or worse) into a new configuration of patriotism and what it means to be an "American." Although the realities of black intelligence, beauty, social class, and exceptionalism are nothing new (at least to black people), the notion of blackness, for many in the USA, was nevertheless destabilized. Michelle Obama embodied a new symbol of (post)black womanhood that was "*more black than* some of us thought, and *less black than* some of us thought."[18] Postblack or postracial is not necessarily the end or aftermath of blackness,

as some surmise, but an added turn and dimension to the trajectory, complexity, and contradictions of race that are both "intensified and diminished in a variety of contexts."[19] If the Obamas represent a postracial or post black identity, it is this same identity that helped enable Michelle Obama to counter crazy patriotisms' condemnation of her as the stereotypical angry black woman. Displacing the crazy patriotism agenda, from a postracial and postblack positionality, can lead to an alternative agenda of *postpatriotism*. I am imagining a *postpatriotism* where the "distribution of wealth" is a democratic principle—an ethics of equity—not a communist threat; where to be "radical" is a praxis of national critique that deconstructs and re-imagines the operations of power and empire, not a deadly extremism to be feared; where the love and loyalty of country is so deep and strong it can engage the problematics of the words "America" and "American" by recognizing that we are the United States *OF* America and not the United States that *IS* America. Embracing the fact that we are but one great country sharing the North American continent with other great countries whose citizens are also Americans and whose histories on this continent are more ancient than our own and as vastly significant.

In drinking through the possibilities of a postpatriotic movement—while under the backdrop of beauty, class, the "American" dream, and postblackness—it is my hope that Michelle Obama, "The First Lady The World's Been Waiting For,"[20] will safeguard a sufficient space for anger.

NOTES

1. I want to thank Joni Omi Jones for helping me remember the "usefulness" and generative force of anger for black women.

2. I place in quotation marks the terms "'America" and "American" as a critical comment against the disco wise of crazy patriotism and to reflect my own dissatisfaction with these terms as imperialistic and insulting to other histories, populations, and nations that occupy the North American continent.

3. This observation is made in the article by Ta-Nehisis Coales, "America Girl," *The Atlantic Monthly,* January/February, 2009.

4. Nicholas De Genova, *Working the Boundaries: Race, Space, and Illegality in Mexico Chicago* (Durham, NC: Duke UP, 2005], 66.

5. De Genova, 68.

6. Audre Lorde, "The Uses of Anger," in *Sister Outsider* (Berkeley, CA: The Crossing Press, 1984), 124.

7. Lorde, 124.

8. Lorde, 124.

9. See Lorde, "The Uses of Anger."

10. I am referring here to Ida B. Wells' biography by Paula Giddings where Giddings writes of Wells' transforming her anger against racism and lynching into the most acclaimed anti-lynching campaign in the United States, as well as to the (in)famous response by Ertha Kitt toward Lady Bird Johnson and her guests at a White House luncheon in the 1900s where Kitt angrily excoriated the attendees for their complicity in U.S. racism.

11. Relative to the agendas of the oppressed, see Lorde, "The Uses of Anger."

12. Sarah Valdez, "Art in America" in *Freestylin—Studio Museum of Harlem* (New York: Arts Publications, 2001), 1–3.

13. I do not include the hyphen in order to avoid the suggestion that postblack is *after* blackness—a historical marker where "blackness" is surpassed and no longer relevant (e.g., postcolonial as opposed to post-colonial). I include it to underscore an existential shift and political re-articulation that is co-temporal with being "black," where blackness does not disappear in this time and space, and where blackness, race, and racism still interpenetrate in this historical moment, but in ways that are both the same and different from the past.

14. Holland Cotter. "Beyond Multiculturalism, Freedom?" *New York Times,* 29 July 2008, 4.

15. Cotter, 4.

16. Coats, 6.

17. Coats, 6.

18. David. A. Hollinger, "Obama, The Instability of Color Liens, And The Promise of A Postethnic Future," *Callaloo* 31/4 (2008): 1033–37, see 1037.

19. Hollinger, 1037.

20. The March 2009 issue of *Vogue* magazine, with Michelle Obama on the cover, states "Michelle Obama: The First Lady The World's Been Waiting For."

D. Soyini Madison is a Professor in the Department of Performance Studies, African American, Studies, and Anthropology at Northwestern University. Madison is now serving as the Interim Director of the Program of African Studies. Her latest book, Acts of Activism: Human Rights As Performance *(available in November from Cambridge UP), focuses on how local rights activists in Ghana, West Africa employ modes of performance as a tactic in the defense of women's rights, public health, and water democracy. Madison's other recent publications include:* Critical Ethnography: Methods, Ethics, and Performance *and* The Sage Handbook of Performance Studies *(co-edited with Judith Hamera). Correspondence to: D. Soyini Madison, Performance Studies, Northwestern University, Evanston, IL 60208, USA. E-mail: dsmadison@northwestern.edu.*

CPSIA information can be obtained
at www.ICGtesting.com
Printed in the USA
LVHW02s2308260718
585057LV00001B/3/P